Leibniz's
Discourse on Metaphysics

Leibniz's
Discourse on Metaphysics
A New Translation and Commentary

CHRISTOPHER JOHNS

EDINBURGH
University Press

Edinburgh University Press is one of the leading university presses in the UK. We publish academic books and journals in our selected subject areas across the humanities and social sciences, combining cutting-edge scholarship with high editorial and production values to produce academic works of lasting importance. For more information visit our website: edinburghuniversitypress.com

Edinburgh University Press Ltd
The Tun – Holyrood Road
12(2f) Jackson's Entry
Edinburgh EH8 8PJ

Typeset in 11/13pt Ehrhardt MT Pro
by Cheshire Typesetting Ltd, Cuddington, Cheshire,
and printed and bound in Great Britain

A CIP record for this book is available from the British Library

ISBN 978 1 4744 5777 4 (hardback)
ISBN 978 1 4744 5780 4 (webready PDF)
ISBN 978 1 4744 5779 8 (epub)

Contents

Contents

Contents

Acknowledgements

Thanks to Stephan Meier-Oeser at the Leibniz-Forschungsstelle Münster for permission to translate Leibniz's *Discourse on Metaphysics* from the Akademie Edition. I would also like to express my appreciation for the Akadamie Edition, as prepared by the Leibniz-Forschungsstelle in Münster, in particular Herma Kliege-Biller for her guidance on the division of articles 30 and 31. Thanks to Rebecca Englehardt at the Gottfried Wilhelm Leibniz Bibliothek for supplying digital prints of Leibniz's manuscripts, and to publisher Vittorio Klostermann for their permission to translate a portion of *Leben und Werk von G. W. Leibniz*.

I thank the following students for their feedback and encouragement at various points of the drafting process: Ziad El Danaf, Philippe Yahchouchi, and Fatima Sadek. Huria Ibrahim for many fruitful discussions about Leibniz. Sara Mrouwe for thorough proofreading, thoughtful suggestions, and for the index. Thanks also to two anonymous reviewers at the preliminary stage.

Thanks to Lama Bashour for formatting and Ameen Hannoun for the illustration in §XVII.

Thanks to Tamara Fakhoury for permission to use her painting of Leibniz for the book cover.

Thanks to my colleagues at the Philosophy Department of the American University of Beirut for their friendship and perseverance during power outages, viruses, explosions, and political and economic collapse. May Lebanon see better days! Special thanks to Karam Wahab for the extra pair of eyes and valuable suggestions on the final proofs. And thanks to the University Library's Document Delivery Service for their speed and diligence.

Acknowledgements

Most of all I thank Lloyd Strickland for his many valuable comments, suggestions, corrections, and for his always-ready support and advice. At Edinburgh University Press I thank Carol McDonald for commissioning the project; Sarah Foyle for patiently awaiting my drafts; Judith Mackenzie for seeing the project through; and especially copy editor Tim Clark for his sharp eye and thoughtful suggestions. Any remaining errors or shortcomings are my sole responsibility.

And thanks to my mother, Marlene Talbott-Green, for giving me room to study and patience to listen.

Preface

The *Discourse on Metaphysics* has long been considered one of Leibniz's most important works, as the first comprehensive presentation of his central philosophical positions, specifically on God, the soul, individual substance, natural laws, perception, expression, truth, knowledge, ideas, free will, sin, grace, and more. Composed in 1686, but unpublished in his lifetime, it first appeared in 1846 and subsequently in twelve editions of the original French, as well as in thirty-seven translations in as many as fifteen languages, including nine in English. Two French commentaries appeared in 1957 and 1959 and an English translation-commentary appeared in 2020. The work remains an important focus of scholarly attention and is frequently taught in university courses on seventeenth-century (Early Modern) philosophy.

This is a translation of and commentary on Leibniz's *Discours de Métaphysique*, based on the edition published in 1999 by the Berlin-Brandenburgischen Akademie der Wissenschaften (Berlin-Brandenburg Academy of Sciences). It makes extensive use of the Academy's 'variant apparatus', which records every deletion, addition, and revision Leibniz made to his first and second drafts. I translate most of the variants, placing them below the main text of the *Discourse*, and present the main text as a final version, which is virtually identical to Leibniz's second draft (the 'fair copy'). The translation thus provides the reader with the means of tracing the development of Leibniz's thought as he wrote and revised the work. I have also closely examined the digital copies of the manuscripts, consulted other English translations and French editions, and added clarificatory notes. I aim to offer a scholarly translation that is at the same time student friendly. In addition to the commentary, this edition includes a chronicle of Leibniz's work and activity during the year prior to having composed the *Discourse* until one year afterward, and includes several letters during that period, previously untranslated in English.

Although the content of the *Discourse* is comprehensive in scope, it consists of a series of sketches of positions that often lack argument and sufficient detail. Thus, the work can be quite challenging not only for students, but for teachers as well. The aim of the commentary, then, is to provide the philosophical context, both Leibnizian and historical, needed to understand the work more fully and to give it the sort of conceptual unity Leibniz likely had intended for it. The unity of the *Discourse* can be said to lie in the theme of perfection, such that each position follows as a theoretical consequence of the initial claim that God is an absolutely perfect being. Thus, for example, that the world God creates must be the best possible world (though not in an *absolute* sense); that God's creatures express lesser and varying degrees of God's perfection; that they are dependent on God for their creation and continuous existence, and yet retain a measure of freedom and causal independence from God and all other beings; that the laws of nature reflect the wisdom of God; and that God's perfection is compatible with his having created creatures capable of sinning and suffering. In a more general sense, the *Discourse* attempts to show how the diverse phenomena of reality comprise a single, coherent, world – as a perfect being must have determined it. The work, thus, amounts to a remarkable, if not remarkably ambitious, specimen of *metaphysics* – that is, an account of the first principles, causes, and ends of reality. The translation and commentary together should provide university-level students and professors (Leibniz specialists or not) with a useful introduction to this most penetrating thinker and to the main philosophical concerns of the seventeenth century.

The commentary stems from lecture notes I developed while teaching undergraduate and graduate courses on Leibniz and Modern philosophy at the American University of Beirut. When I proposed the project in 2018, the only extant commentaries were in French (as noted above). In the meantime, an English translation-commentary was published in 2020 by Oxford University Press. Hopefully, like the two French commentaries published in the 1950s, these English editions will stand as unique and valuable contributions to a better understanding of Leibniz's philosophy.

Introduction to Leibniz's Life and Work

'*A hundred brooks drive his millwheel*'

–Leibniz on himself (AA IV, 3 N.125)

Gottfried Wilhelm Leibniz (1646–1716) was born in Leipzig, Germany, to Friedrich Leubnitz (Leibniz), a professor of moral philosophy, and Catharina Schmuck, the daughter of a professor of law.[1] A voracious reader and precocious student, by the age of twenty-four Leibniz held doctoral degrees in both Philosophy and Law. He was by occupation a legal advisor and reformer, a diplomat, court counsellor, librarian, engineer, and historian. He made valuable contributions to mathematics, logic, theology, physics, politics, medicine, linguistics, geography, geology, and of course, philosophy. He invented a calculating machine, the differential and integral calculus, binary arithmetic, and was the founder of the Berlin Academy of Sciences, which is still in operation today. He resided in the same city (Hannover, Germany) for forty years, but travelled frequently throughout what was then the Holy Roman Empire. Although suspected of being an 'unbeliever' because he did not attend the local church, he remained committed to the Lutheran confession while actively seeking to resolve doctrinal disagreements between Catholics and Protestants. Cheerful in disposition, though at times impatient, he had many friends and acquaintances, including several prominent women with whom he enjoyed close intellectual friendship. He did not marry or have children. He spent most of his time writing: approximately 50,000 items totalling 100,000 pages, including 15,000 letters sent to some 1,000 correspondents, among them some of the most notable philosophers, theologians, mathematicians, and

---

[1] For a comprehensive biography, see *Leibniz: An Intellectual Biography* by Maria Rosa Antognazza (2009).

scientists of his time.[2] Relatively little of this work was published in his lifetime, but much has been published since.

The seventeenth-century political, scientific, and intellectual background

Reading the *Discourse on Metaphysics*, one will notice Leibniz's frequent concern with defending God's goodness against certain controversies or 'impious' views. A partial grasp, at least, of the historical, scientific, and intellectual background that informed Leibniz's concerns in the *Discourse* can explain why he felt these defences to be important. While detailed and extensive accounts of this background may be found elsewhere,[3] the following background conditions should be borne in mind: (1) the Holy Roman Empire, (2) the Protestant Reformation, (3) the Thirty Years' War, (4) the scientific revolution taking place throughout Europe, (5) the intellectual legacy of ancient and Medieval philosophy, and (6) the ways in which these conditions threatened to undermine religious authority. In general, it must be understood that religious life held a much more central and powerful role in Leibniz's time than it does today.

The religious, political, and economic character of Leibniz's seventeenth-century Germany was largely the legacy of the Holy Roman Empire (CE 800–1806), but was more proximally shaped by the periodic social, political, and economic upheavals consequent to the Protestant Reformation (said to have formally begun in 1517). As Voltaire once quipped, the Holy Roman Empire was neither holy, nor Roman, nor an empire. But it was, nevertheless, conceived as the continuation of western Roman Christendom, which had technically ended with the fall of Rome in CE 476. For much of its duration, the Empire consisted of hundreds of semi-autonomous and semi-stable kingdoms, duchies, and feudal estates, encompassing what is now Germany, Austria, Switzerland, Czech Republic, and parts of France and Italy. From 1440 on, the emperor was usually a member of the House of Habsburg. While succession was often a matter of heredity or ecclesiastical appointment, the emperor was formally elected by the leaders (electors) of the major principalities. Social and economic relations were generally characterised by a stratified and hierarchical

---

[2] Gottfried Wilhelm Leibniz Bibliothek: <https://www.gwlb.de/Leibniz/Leibniz-Nachlass>. The task of editing Leibniz's entire body of work was taken up in 1923 by the Berlin Academy of Sciences. Estimates are that it will take another fifty years to complete.

[3] The following is intended only to provide a general outline of the historical context and setting. For much greater scope and detail on the historical setting, see Whaley 2012. On the intellectual setting of the seventeenth century, see Osler 2010.

feudal class system, consisting of peasants, landowning nobility, the clergy, the military, and royalty.[4]

In the sixteenth century, the Protestant Reformation, from complex beginnings, initiated a complex, evolving, and tumultuous series of conflicts, wars, and religious and political realignments.[5] After Luther, Protestantism spread rapidly to regions within and outside the Empire, prompting the Church's 'Counter-Reformation', embodied in the Council of Trent (1545–63). The Council reaffirmed the Church's sacraments (such as transubstantiation) while reforming the abuses of practices such as indulgences. However, the Council also declared that anyone who opposed its decrees was considered 'anathema' and deserved excommunication. Thus, clashes over rights to worship often erupted into war. One such conflict ended in 1555, with the Peace of Augsburg, a treaty which divided the Empire into numerous Catholic and Protestant states and decreed that the ruler of each state held the right to determine the religion of its inhabitants. However, since the agreement did not provide for equal rights for minorities within states, religious and political divisions intensified, leading eventually to the Thirty Years' War (1618–48). Often cited as one of the most destructive wars in history, it left as many as 5 million dead or displaced (roughly 33 per cent of the Empire's population), including deaths from disease and famine, with millions more robbed, pillaged, and disabled.[6] The Peace of Westphalia (1648), which ended the conflict, reduced the emperor's sovereignty and gave equal rights of worship to Catholics and Protestants, although members of the minority sect within each state remained subject to certain restrictions.

[4] Peasants constituted approximately 85 per cent of a population of roughly 12 million in the sixteenth-century Reich, the overwhelming majority of which 'lived in varying forms and degrees of servitude' (Whaley 2012: 129). But the economic resources were fairly diverse, consisting of agriculture, stock rearing, dairy farming, viticulture, textiles, and mining (Whaley 2012: 123–5).

[5] Whaley argues for a more complex understanding of the conditions in which the Reformation developed: 'Particularly significant was the reform movement that originated with Ulrich Zwingli in Zurich, which survived in the longer term, though Lutheranism remained the overwhelmingly predominant Protestant faith in the Reich. Scholars now view the Reformation generally as a complex amalgam of parallel movements: of clerical reformers, of the lower nobility, of the peasantry, of the Free Cities and towns, and of the ruling princes' (Whaley 2012: 63). This claim reflects another of Whaley's: 'What made the impact of the Reformation so intense was the fact that religious matters were so closely linked with social, economic, and political issues. This was hardly surprising in a society in which no distinction was made between religion and life' (2012: 81).

[6] Whaley: 'If these figures are accurate, then the loss of population during the Thirty Years' War was proportionally greater than in World War II' (2012: 633). For details on the impact on the war see Whaley 2012: Ch. 57.

Leibniz was born two years prior to the Peace of Westphalia and, thus, was raised in a region reeling from the war's political, economic, cultural, and emotional shock.[7] While, as a result of the Peace, political entities within the Empire enjoyed greater political and religious autonomy, conflicts occasionally materialised: for example, Louis XIV's annexations of parts of the Holy Roman Empire and the Habsburg's efforts to contain the Ottoman Empire (the Great Turkish War, 1683–99). Otherwise, while religious tensions remained, they did not give rise to all-out war in the central German principalities. Leibniz himself enjoyed a relatively trouble-free and privileged life, and often advocated on behalf of religious and political unity, while indulging in some political strategising.[8] He spent forty years at the Court of Hannover, including his final eighteen as legal counsellor and historian to Duke Georg Ludwig. The Duke was the son of Princess Sophia of the Palatinate, herself the granddaughter of James I, King of England. Her lineage, and the 1701 Act of Settlement which banned Catholics from ascension to the English throne, ensured that, when both Queen Anne and Princess (now Electress) Sophia died in 1714, the latter's Protestant son Georg Ludwig would in that year become King of Great Britain (as George I). Leibniz had been close friends with Sophia and fully expected to join the Court in London, but the new king insisted that Leibniz remain in Hannover to finish writing his ancestral history. Two years later Leibniz died, leaving the history, and much else, unfinished.

Despite the sixteenth and seventeenth centuries' religious and political conflicts, the scientific and intellectual communities on the continent and in England during that time had undergone their own kind of revolution, imposing their own kind of challenge to religious unity and authority. Astronomical observations and speculations by Copernicus (1473–1543), Kepler (1571–1630), and Galileo (1564–1642) culminated in a challenge to the Church's geocentric cosmology and led the Church to place Galileo under house arrest. The Aristotelian physics of 'substantial forms' and 'qualities' that had dominated Scholastic natural philosophy from roughly the thirteenth century began to give way to the quantitative 'mechanical philosophy' of Galileo, Francis Bacon (1561–1626), René Descartes (1596–1650), Pierre Gassendi (1592–1695), and Robert Boyle (1627–91). These 'natural philosophers' fundamentally changed the way nature was conceived of, by forming hypotheses based only on quantitative evidence: the size, shape, and motion of material atoms or corpuscles.

---

[7] Hsia 1994: 736. See also Whaley 2012: 3, and Ch. 58.
[8] See Strickland 2016.

The mechanical philosophy also took a *methodological* turn, as Bacon criticised Aristotle's 'demonstrative' method and emphasised empirical experimentation and induction, while Descartes argued for 'clear and distinct ideas' as the epistemic foundations for natural investigations. As a result, the new physical hypotheses could eliminate the old substantial forms and qualities, as well as 'final causes' (God's purposes), since these, too, could not be known mathematically or empirically.[9] This did not mean, however, that the new physicists eliminated God from physical explanations altogether, nor did they want to. Due to the absolute inertia of matter, something (namely God) had to be responsible for its initial and continuing motion. As we will see, Leibniz's response to these developments was distinctive by seeking to retain elements of both ancient and modern physics, for the sake of both a more rigorous physics as well as a more pious religion.

These developments in the natural sciences were shaped in part by a deep and complex intellectual background, the main components of which can be generally identified as (1) Platonist conceptions of the soul and of eternal truths; (2) Aristotelian conceptions of substance, matter, truth, demonstration, and ethics; (3) Christian-Scholastic philosophy-theology, especially that of Saints Augustine and Aquinas; (4) the Renaissance era's humanism and individualism; and (5) the discovery of other lands and peoples (the Americas and China). The latter discoveries prompted reflection on and scepticism over the supposed universality of moral and religious truths, as it also became increasingly apparent that moral duties could be discovered by reason, independently of Christian revelation. Leibniz himself was deeply influenced by all of this, and by a great many philosophers, jurists, theologians, and natural philosophers. But in the *Discourse* the influences of Plato, Aristotle, Augustine, Neoplatonism, Scholasticism, and most prominently Descartes and Malebranche, are especially apparent (as discussed in the commentary).

Like many figures associated with the seventeenth and eighteenth centuries' Age of Enlightenment, Leibniz believed in the universal validity and efficacy of reason and science, such that, if we reason properly about God and nature, then religious, political, and scientific disputes could all be settled peacefully. In view of the turbulent political and religious background of his time, one can understand why he sought confessional unity and rational piety; it is why, for example, he would construct demonstrations – for the immortality of the soul or the transubstantiation of the host – that could satisfy both Catholics and Protestants; or why he would argue that personal conviction need not entail ecclesiastical

---

[9] The specific details of these developments are given in the commentary.

5

exclusion.[10] While Leibniz frequently asserts seemingly superficial pieties about God's perfection, goodness, justice, grace, wisdom and love, he also has very precise arguments for how these pieties and qualities are exemplified by the laws of reason and nature.

The *Discourse* in the context of Leibniz's life and work

Although Leibniz produced an immense amount of written material, comparatively little of it was published in his lifetime. On the whole, 60 per cent was written in Latin, very little in German, and the rest, including the *Discourse*, in French. A selected survey of his most important published and unpublished works reveals the astonishing breadth and depth of his interests and abilities and helps place the *Discourse* within its broader intellectual context.[11] In 1666, at the age of twenty, he published his habilitation in philosophy, (1) the *Dissertation on Combinatorial Art*, his first attempt to construct a symbolic language of human thought. In 1667, he published his *Juris Doctorat* dissertation, (2) *New Method for Learning and Teaching Jurisprudence*, containing his foundational positions on jurisprudence, ethics, and politics. He continued working on jurisprudence, and theology

---

[10] For an example of Leibniz's reconciliation efforts, see the letter to Landgrave Ernst von Hessen-Rheinfels, October of 1685, composed a few months before the *Discourse*, translated in this volume.

[11] For convenience, the following information for each of the numbered works below is given here, by original title, location in the Academy Edition, and reference to an English translation, if one is available. My sources are AA; Antognazza 2009; Arthur 2014; Brown and Fox 2006; and Müller and Krönert 1969. (1) *Dissertatio de Arte Combinatoria*, AA VI, I N. 8 / LCA; partial trans. in LL. (2) *Nova Methodus Discendae Docendaeque Jurisprudentiae*, AA VI, I N. 10 / LNM; partial trans. in LL; Johns 2013. (3) *Confessio Philosophi*, AA VI, 3, 116–49 / LCP. (4) *Mars Christianissimus*, AA, IV, 2 N. 22 / LPW. (5) *Nova Methodus pro Maximis et Minimis*, October *Acta Eruditorum*, trans. LMM 271–80. (6) *Meditationes de Cognitione, Veritate et Ideis*, AA VI, 4 N. 141 / AG. (7) *Introductio ad Encyclopediam arcanum*, AA VI, 4 N. 126 / LP. (8) *De Synthesi et Analysi universali seu Arte inveniendi et judicandi*, AA VI, 4 N. 129 / LL and LP. (9) 'Positiones', AA VI, 4 N. 418 / translated as 'Suppositions' in LGR. (10) *Discours de Métaphysique*, AA VI, 4 N. 306 (see bibliography for English translations). (11) *Brevis Demonstratio erroris memorabilis Cartesii et aliorum circa legem naturae*, AA VI, 4 N. 369 / LL. (12) *Meditatio nova de natura anguli contactus et osculi horumque usa in practica mathesi*, June *Acta Eruditorum*; see A'Campo-Neuen and Papadopoulos 2019. (13) *De Geometria Recondita et Analysi Indivisibilium atque infinitorum*, LMM 281–2. (14) *Specimen inventorum de admirandis naturae generalis arcanis*, AA VI, 4 N. 312 / LC and LP. AA dates the piece at '1688?' (15) *Examen Religionis Christianae*, AA VI, 4 N. 420. (16) *Generales Inquisitiones de Analysi Notionum et Veritatum*, AA VI, 4 N. 165 / PL; LGI. (17) *Elementa Rationis*, AA VI, 4 N. 162. (18) *De Natura Veritatis, Contingentiae et Indifferentiae atque de Libertate et Praedeterminatione*, AA VI, 4 N. 303 / LP.

and physics as well, and in 1672 relocated to Paris and composed, (3) *A Philosopher's Confession*, his earliest attempt to reconcile God's goodness with sin and free will. He spent four fruitful and stimulating years in Paris in the company of well-known mathematicians, physicists, theologians, and philosophers. In 1673, he demonstrated his calculating machine in London before the Royal Society. In 1676, on his way from Paris to the Court of Hannover (which would remain his main residence), he passed through Amsterdam and conversed with Benedict Spinoza over, among other things, a proof for God's existence (see commentary on §23 of *Discourse*). The years 1678–9 saw Leibniz re-engage in works on theology (*The Catholic Demonstrations*), on plans for a comprehensive encyclopaedia (*The General Science*), and on physics, mathematics, and probability. He also began investigating the possibility of designing windmills for the purpose of pumping water out of the Harz mountain silver mines, a project that would occupy him periodically until 1685.

During those five years spent intermittently in the Harz mountains, Leibniz's written output slowed considerably, although he managed to remain involved in ecclesiastic and political matters. In March of 1683, in Hannover, a meeting on Church reunification took place between Catholic Bishop Cristoval Royas de Spinola and Gerhard Wolter Molanus, Lutheran professor of mathematics and theology. While Leibniz was not directly involved in the meeting, he wrote four brief texts that year on the subject of reunification and engaged in regular correspondence with these two ecclesiasts until 1695.[12] In September of 1683, Leibniz composed – and in the following year published under the pseudonym 'Germanus Gallo-Graecus' – the pamphlet (4) *Most-Christian War-God*, a bitingly satirical attack on Louis XIV's military appropriations of Dutch and German territories nominally belonging to the Holy Roman Empire.[13] In 1684, he published two articles in the scientific journal he had helped to establish, *Acta Eruditorum* ('Acts of the Erudite'): (5) 'New Method for the Maximum and Minimum', his first published work on the differential calculus, and (6) 'Meditations on Knowledge, Truth, and Ideas', a critique of Cartesian epistemology which would later serve as a basis for §24 of the *Discourse*.

The year 1685 brought two significant changes in Leibniz's official work assignments. While he remained court councillor and librarian to the Duke at that time, Ernst August, the Duke finally ran out of patience and funds for Leibniz's unsuccessful mining experiments. In May, the Duke

---

[12] Although the correspondence with Molanus continued until Leibniz's death in 1716.

[13] The Latin pseudonym means, 'a German French-Greek'. The pamphlet was written in Latin and French and translated into German in 1685.

terminated the project and, in August, at Leibniz's suggestion, assigned Leibniz the task of writing a history of the Duke's ancestry (the House of Guelph). Research for this project (and a desire to continue to tinker with wind- and water-powered pumps) kept Leibniz coming back to the Harz region, though throughout 1685 he managed to complete several minor works, including: (7) *Introduction to a Secret Encyclopaedia*, containing definitions and principles intended to found a 'General Science', i.e., 'the science of what is universally thinkable';[14] and (8) *Of Universal Synthesis and Analysis, or of the Art of Discovery and of Judgment*. Parts of these two papers are similar to §24 of the *Discourse*. He also composed, (9) 'Positions', a short piece strongly asserting the authority of the Catholic Church, and several brief papers on logic, language, metaphysics, theology, and even acoustics.[15]

The year of the *Discourse* (1686, Leibniz is thirty-nine) is recognised as his *annus mirabilis* (marvellous year), in which he produced an astonishing number and range of important works. In January or early February, he composed the first draft of the (10) *Discourse on Metaphysics*, and arranged to have its summary sent to the well-known theologian-logician Antoine Arnauld. In March, Arnauld replied, and their now famous two-year correspondence began. Also by March, Leibniz had finished the 'fair copy' of the *Discourse*,[16] perhaps with the intention of publishing it along with the correspondence; but he never did. Between March and June, he published three articles in the *Acta Eruditorum*: (11) *Brief Demonstration of a Notable Error of Descartes and Others Concerning a Law of Nature*, a piece almost identical to §17 of the *Discourse*; (12) an article on the nature of the angles of tangency and osculation; and (13) his second published paper on the calculus, 'On a hidden geometry and analysis of indivisibles and infinites', which contains 'the first public occurrence of the integral sign $\int$ and a proof of the fundamental theorem of calculus' (Swetz 2015). He also completed but did not publish several substantial works closely related to the *Discourse* in content: (14) on natural philosophy: *Specimen of Discoveries of the Admirable Secrets of Nature in General*; (15) on religion: *Examination of the Christian Religion*; (16) a lengthy investigation into logical matters relevant to the *Discourse*: *General Inquisitions on the Analysis of Notions and Truths*; (17) on methods of reasoning applied to metaphysics: *The Elements*

---

[14] Parkinson trans., LP 5.

[15] The paper on acoustics, *Cogitationes novae, quomodo formetur sonus et per aerem propagatur atque in organo auditus exprimatur* [*New thoughts on how sound is formed and propagated through the air and expressed in the auditory organ*] is found in LGD, 16–27.

[16] According to the Akademie editors, AA VI, 4, 1530. The 'fair copy' is designated l² in the Akademie edition and translation. It remains an unedited manuscript, except insofar as changes made to it are shown on the first draft (L¹).

of Reason; and (18) *Necessary and Contingent Truths*. The last provides details on the distinction between these types of truths, on the notion of 'liberty of indifference', and on how Judas is not necessitated to sin, which are points relevant to §13 and §30 of the *Discourse*.

After his *annus mirabilis*, Leibniz remained fairly prolific for the rest of his life; but only a few of his works during that time need be noted here. From 1691 to 1693, he composed, but did not publish, the *Protogaea*, an intensive study of the geological formation and history of the Earth. Some of this study stems from his travels through the Harz region in 1685, during his preliminary investigations into the history of the House of Guelph (LPP xiii). Also in 1693, he published the well-received *Diplomatic Code of the Law of Nations*,[17] which contains a preface outlining a theory of international law, drawing from his early foundations in jurisprudence, along with a nearly 500-page collection of treaties and agreements 'supporting the position of the [Holy Roman] Empire against claims of the French' (LPW 165). In 1695, the *Acta Eruditorum* published one of his most important works: part 1 of his *Specimen of Dynamics* (LGM VI/AG). This article extended his initial criticism in the *Discourse* of Descartes' laws of nature and set out his mature theory of force as constitutive of the essence of bodies, over and above their extended properties. That same year, the *Journal des Savants* published his *New System of Nature and Communication of Substances and of the Union of the Soul and Body*.[18] Autobiographical in form and much shorter, the work contains several similarities to the *Discourse*, and since the latter had not been published, the *New System* stands as the first public presentation of Leibniz's system (AG 138). It includes refined accounts of the nature of substance, criticisms of Cartesian extension and Malebranche's occasionalism, and a proposed solution to the relation between mind and body, which in the *Discourse* is called 'concomitance', but will soon come to be widely known as 'pre-established harmony'.[19] *On Nature Itself*,[20] published in the *Acta Eruditorum* of 1698, also one of his most important papers, contains a number of positions stemming from the *Discourse*, including further development of his dynamics (theory of forces), and one of his first uses of 'monad' as an alternate term for 'substance', thus signalling a change in the conception of substance he had established in the *Discourse* (AG 161).

---

[17] *Codex Juris Gentium*, Dutens IV / LPW.
[18] *Système nouveau de la nature et de la communication des substances, aussi bien que de l'union qu'il y a entre l'âme et le corps* (LGP IV, 477–87 / LNS and AG).
[19] *Éclaircissement du nouveau système . . .* [*Clarification of the new system . . .*], *Journal des Savants*, April 1696 / LNS 51.
[20] LGP IV, 504–16.

Between 1702 and 1705, Leibniz composed, among other works, *The New Essays*, a paragraph-by-paragraph pseudo-dialogue with John Locke's *Essay on Human Understanding*.[21] This huge and fascinating work sets these two great thinkers in comparison on a full-range of philosophical topics. When Locke died in 1704, Leibniz decided not to publish it, and it remained unpublished until 1765, fifty years after Leibniz's death. Also in 1702–3, Leibniz composed a mature statement on his theory of justice, *Meditation on the Common Concept of Justice*,[22] in which he argued for a rationalist rather than voluntarist foundation for moral and political principles. He argues similarly in §2 of the *Discourse*. In 1710, aged sixty-four, Leibniz published the work for which he became most well known as a philosopher, *Theodicy*, which contains his mature conception of God's justice in view of moral and physical evil. The work for which he is most well known today, *Monadology*, written in 1714, was published posthumously in 1720.[23] This work, representing his mature and final metaphysical system, in ninety brief paragraphs, departs from the *Discourse* by outlining a theory of substance, not in terms of the 'complete notion of an individual' but in terms of *monads*, that is, partless immaterial substances, the ultimate constituents of reality, containing only perception and appetition. Finally, his correspondence with Samuel Clarke (cleric, philosopher, and friend of Isaac Newton) debated the reality vs. ideality of space and time, and discussed Leibniz's principle of the 'identity of indiscernibles', which had been first alluded to in §9, line 6, of the *Discourse*. This fruitful and influential correspondence ended upon Leibniz's death, and Clarke published it shortly afterward in 1717.

Despite his prodigious output, Leibniz left a number of major works unfinished: revisions to his published *New Method* on jurisprudence, ongoing for nearly thirty years, remained incomplete; his long-promised and more often postponed history of the Guelph ancestry remained unfinished, much to the frustration of his Hannover dukes; his periodic attempts to negotiate a reunification of the Catholic and Protestant confessions would fail to bear fruit; and his attempt to reconfigure the concept of force in physics would, soon after his death, be superseded by Isaac Newton. He never composed a complete, systematic, and detailed account of his system. It is arguable whether he *had* a complete system. His intellectual curiosity, ability, and practical sensibility drove him to begin many projects, but the depth and diversity of his interests and the demands of his employers prevented him from completing most of them. Nevertheless, he

---

[21] *Nouveaux Essais*, AA VI, 6, 1990 / LRB.

[22] Found in Mollat 1885; translated by Riley in LPW.

[23] LGP VI, 607–23 / LM; AG.

made substantial contributions to just about every field that came within the scope of his interest. His philosophical work formed the basis of academic philosophy in Germany, from Christian Wolff through Kant. A complete assessment of Leibniz's influence will not be possible until all his handwritten work has been thoroughly edited – a task in progress for the past 100 years and not likely to be finished for another fifty.

The provenance of the 'little discourse'

On February 1/11 of 1686, Gottfried Wilhelm Leibniz wrote the following to his close friend, the Landgrave Ernst von Hessen-Rheinfels:[24]

> I have recently (being in a place for some days during which I had nothing to do) made a little discourse on Metaphysics, on which I would be very pleased to have the opinion of Mr Arnauld. For questions on grace, God's concourse with creatures, the nature of miracles, the cause of sin and the origin of evil, the immortality of the soul, on ideas, etc., are touched on there in a manner that seems to provide new openings liable to shed light upon some very great difficulties. I have attached here the summary of articles that it contains, since I have not yet been able to make a clean copy. I therefore entreat Your Serene Highness to send this summary to him and ask him to consider it a bit and to express his opinion. For as he excels equally in Theology and philosophy, in reading and in meditation, I find no one more suitable than him to judge it. And I would strongly wish to have a critic as exact, enlightened, and as reasonable as is Mr Arnauld, being myself the man most inclined in the world to yield to reason. Perhaps Mr Arnauld will find a few things not entirely unworthy of his consideration, especially since he has been rather occupied with examining these matters. If he finds some obscurity, I will explain myself sincerely and openly, and lastly if he finds me worthy of his instruction, I will ensure that he has cause to be not at all dissatisfied with it. I beg Your Serene Highness to attach this [letter] to the summary that I am sending him, and to send both to Mr. Arnauld.

The time and place Leibniz first composed his 'petit discours de Métaphysique' was likely late January or early February 1686, in Zellerfeld, Germany,[25] the administrative base for the Harz mountain silver mine project, where for five years he had intermittently engaged in experiments

---

[24] 'Extract of my letter to My Lord the Landgrave Ernest', 1/11 (Julien/Gregorian calendars) February 1686, translated from AA II, 2 N. 1 (also in AA I, 4 N. 334 and in LAV 2). The extract was written alongside Leibniz's 'summary' of the *Discourse*, as explained below.

[25] AA sets the date of composition to the beginning of 1686. Müller and Krönert (see 'Context I' in this volume) show that Leibniz was in Zellerfeld from the beginning of January.

with windmills and pumps in order to drain the frequently flooded mines. The likely reason he had nothing to do is that a few months earlier his employer in Hannover, the Duke Ernst August, had ordered an end to the mining project, largely due to Leibniz's failure to make much progress; and yet there he remained, or returned, perhaps to tinker with yet another windmill design, to finish up operations or to start work on the Guelph history.[26] In any case, Leibniz was never long with nothing to do. As the letter to his Landgrave indicates, he sought the opinion of Antoine Arnauld, the well-known theologian, logician, and enlightened and able critic, for the purpose of sharpening his own views and, likely, to obtain favourable public approval of them. In addition, as frequently speculated, the Protestant Leibniz may have hoped to advance his ongoing confessional reconciliation efforts by gaining approval for his views from a prominent Catholic, such as Arnauld. Whatever his intent, Leibniz's letter, along with the 'summaries' of each of the *Discourse*'s thirty-seven articles, eventually reached Arnauld, who, on March 13, responded with 'fright' and 'shock' over the summary of §13, adding 'I do not see what the utility could be of a work that to all appearances will be rejected by everyone' (LAV 13). Arnauld went on to advise Leibniz to give up his alarming theological views and to care for his salvation by converting to Catholicism – clearly, not the response Leibniz had hoped for. Nevertheless, this exchange would mark the beginning of an extremely fruitful (at least for Leibniz and us) two-year correspondence. By March of 1686, Leibniz had managed to produce a clean 'fair copy' of the *Discourse*, based on the rough, original draft composed in February. Perhaps he had the intention of sending a clean version of the full *Discourse* to Arnauld, or of publishing it along with the correspondence (LAV xvii). But Arnauld never saw a full version of the *Discourse*; nor did Leibniz publish it or the correspondence.[27]

Sometime after Leibniz's death in 1716, the summaries and the 'fair copy' – but not the original draft – were found among Leibniz's vast collection of papers. Based on these two texts, the first edition of what has come to be called the *Discours de Métaphysique* was printed, along with the correspondence, in 1846 by C. L. Grotefend. In 1857, an edition of the *Discourse* by Foucher de Careil appeared, and in 1880, C. J. Gerhardt included the *Discours de Métaphysique* (without the summaries) in his

---

[26] See Müller and Krönert 1969: 74–80, translated in this volume. Also, Antognazza 2009: 212, 227–30; 239–40. For details on the mining project see Wakefield 2010.

[27] Now known as the *Leibniz-Arnauld Correspondence*, first published by Grotefend in 1846; translated by Mason (LAM 1967) and most recently by Stephen Voss (LAV 2016). For more on the Leibniz-Arnauld correspondence and its relation to the *Discourse*, see Sleigh 1990.

seven-volume collection of Leibniz's philosophical works.[28] The main text of these and several subsequent editions and translations was based on Leibniz's 'fair copy', not on the original manuscript. Nearly thirty years after Gerhardt, Henri Lestienne discovered, hidden among the Leibniz archives in Hannover, the original manuscript, which had been originally catalogued by Bodemann under the title *Traité sur les perfections de Dieu [Treatise on the perfections of God]*. This draft was, and is, very difficult to decipher, as it contains numerous deletions and additions of words, phrases, paragraphs, and sections. It also includes the original article summaries. Lestienne's 1907 edition would be the first to record these variations (variants) and thus to produce a 'definitive' edition of the *Discours de Métaphysique*. His edition features the fair copy as the main text, with the summaries placed at the head of each article, and the variants on the original draft placed below the main text and indicating the order in which Leibniz made them. Thus, the reader could trace Leibniz's revisions from first to last, the last being the fair copy.

While Lestienne's became the definitive edition at that time, not all subsequent editions and translations have followed it. Since Grotefend's, at least twelve French editions of the *Discours* have been published, thirty-seven translations in as many as fifteen languages, first in Russian in 1890, and since 1902 in at least seven English translations. The Montgomery (1902) translation is based on Gerhardt, while the most widely available translations – Loemker (1956) and Ariew and Garber (1989) – utilise both the Gerhardt and Lestienne editions, but not much of Lestienne's variant record. Lucas and Grint (1953) basically reproduce Lestienne's edition and variants, while Martin and Brown's translation (1988) is based on Lestienne's main text (thus on the 'fair copy') and includes some of the variants. The present edition is based on the Akademie Edition and its variant-apparatus, with some important differences, as explained below.

Guide to the Akademie Edition, its variant-apparatus, and the present translation

The Deutsche Akademie der Wissenschaften (German Academy of Sciences, or 'Akademie'), the institution in charge since 1923 of editing and publishing critical editions of Leibniz's entire body of work, published its edition of the *Discours* in 1999.[29] Like Lestienne's, the Akademie

---

[28] LGP IV, 427–63, without title. The summaries are printed in Vol. II, along with the correspondence with Arnauld.

[29] Leibniz's complete works, *Sämtliche Schriften und Briefe*, are now overseen by the Berlin-Brandenburgischen Akademie der Wissenschaften and the Akademie der

Edition is based on all available handwritten drafts and it records the variants Leibniz made on each, in the order that he made them. However, the Akademie's 'variant-apparatus' provides the most complete, detailed, precise, and easiest to follow variant record of any edition, and its editors are unsurpassed in their ability to discern the order of Leibniz's revisions and to decipher an otherwise illegible word buried beneath layers of scribbles. The Akademie Edition is now the definitive edition of the *Discourse on Metaphysics*.

Leibniz's first draft of the *Discourse* consists of thirty-seven articles, written on twenty-four pages (sized 21 x 33 cm), peppered with hundreds of deletions and revisions. He typically wrote on the left half of the page, leaving the right for additions, such as the original article summaries.[30] The main text of the Akademie Edition is based on – is a reconstruction of – this first draft (designated L^1), while the variants on that text, on the 'fair copy' (designated l^2), and on the summaries (L^2) are recorded below the main text. The variants are marked by line numbers, key words, and other signals that indicate precisely where in the main text (and thus on the first draft and fair copy) the variant occurred. The great advantage of the Akademie's variant-apparatus is that it presents a clean version of Leibniz's first draft (his 'Konzept', as they put it) without any distracting symbols, while placing a *complete* record of the variants below the text. The interested reader may then check the variants and trace the development of Leibniz's thought, from the first variant to the last – the last being the main text. In sum, the main text of the Akademie Edition (AA) is a reconstruction of the first handwritten draft, its 'final variant' so to speak, after all of Leibniz's preceding variants have been recorded below the main text. The variant section also records the variants made on the other drafts. Here is a summary of the Akademie's draft designations, which this translation uses as well, along with digital samples of the original drafts:

L^1 = Leibniz's first draft, the heavily revised autograph of the full *Discourse* (LH I 3,1 Bl. 1–12),[31] written in February of 1686 and discovered by Lestienne in 1907. The AA version is in VI, 4 N. 306.

Wissenschaften in Göttingen, while the editing and publication of the series of *philosophical* works and correspondence is under the care of the Leibniz-Forschungsstelle in Münster. The Akademie's *Discours de Métaphysique* is found in Series VI, Band 4 Number 306, pp. 1529–88 and is accessible online.

[30] Lloyd Strickland observes that Leibniz must have added the summaries after he completed the draft, since they are placed within brackets on the right side of the page (Strickland 2020: 56).

[31] LH and LBr (below) refer respectively to 'Leibniz-Handschriften' and 'Leibniz-Briefwechsel', Leibniz's handwritings and letters, which are housed at the Niedersächsische Landesbibliothek in Hannover, Germany.

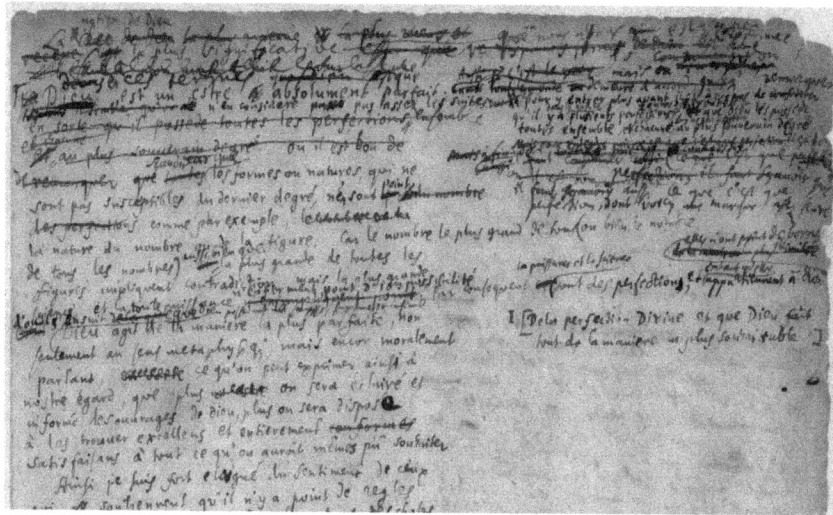

Page 1 of L¹

L² = Leibniz's fair copy of the 'summary of articles' (LBr 16 Bl. 46–7; AA II, 2 N. 2), that is, the headings of each of the thirty-seven articles based on the summaries written in L¹. This four-page summary was the only part of the *Discourse* that Arnauld ever saw. The right side of its pages contains the 'extract' of Leibniz's letter to the Landgrave (translated above), with a few edits in Leibniz's hand. In the Akademie Edition, and in almost every edition and translation, including this one, the summaries appear at the top of each article; although it is not certain that Leibniz intended to include them there.

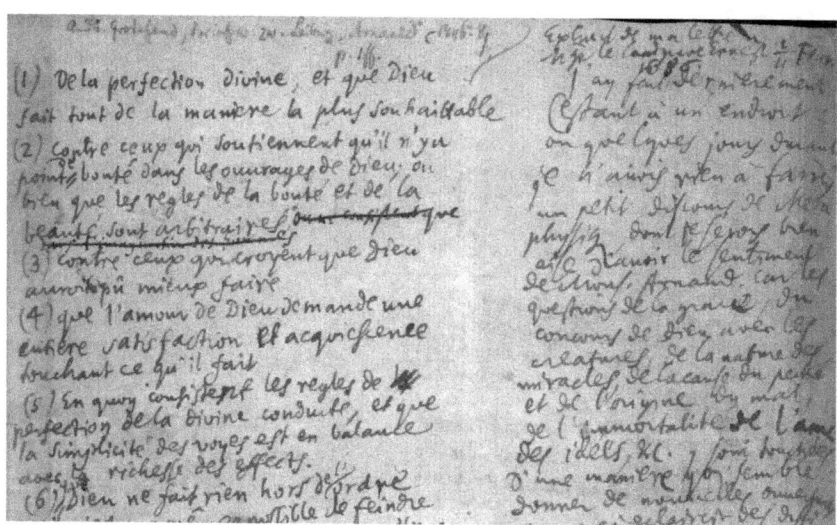

Page 1 of L², the summary

l^2 = The fair copy of the main text of the *Discourse* (LH IV, III, 7 Bl. 1–18), based on L^1, drafted in March of 1686. This thirty-five-page manuscript is essentially a finished version of L^1. Articles 1 and 2 are written in Leibniz's hand, while the rest are written by a scribe, although nearly every page contains corrections in Leibniz's hand. Most translations are based on l^2 and L^2, presumably because l^2 appears to be most finished. Notably, it does not contain any summaries, though it has become customary for translators to add them straight from L^2.

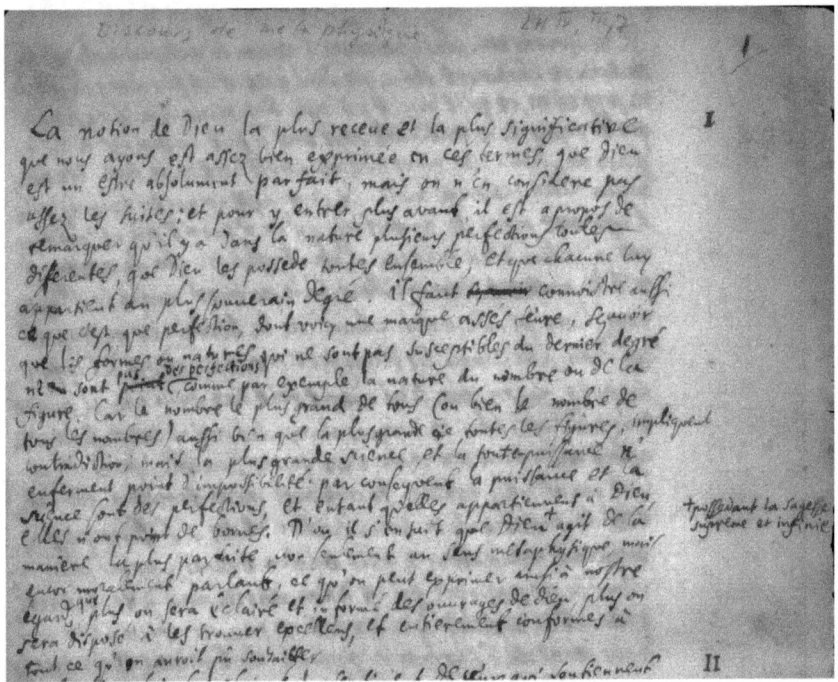

Page 1 of l^2

The following two drafts were determined by the Akademie to be unreliable, and thus are not much referred to in the variant record and translation:

l^1 = the fair copy of articles 5–7, drawn from L^1.
l^3 = the fair copy of articles 1–17, drawn from l^2.

The present translation makes extensive use of the Akademie's variant-apparatus, with, however, the following differences: I record most, but not all, of the Akademie's variants, that is, those I consider having philosophical or semantic significance, or that indicate Leibniz's thought process, and some that mark only a minor correction.

16

Secondly, like the Akademie, I present the main text as the last variant; however, my presentation is different, since the variants *from* L^2 and l^2 are built into the main text (and marked), so that the reader does not need to find the variant in a footnote. The variants *on* L^1 are indicated in the main text and placed in a footnote below, should the reader wish to learn more about them. In addition, to ensure that the locations of the variants are correct, I have double-checked the Akademie's variant record against digital copies of Leibniz's original manuscripts (the three drafts identified above). In sum, the main text can be read straight through as Leibniz's final intended version of the *Discourse*, l^2 (although, as noted, l^2 does not include the summary headings). And, by studying the variant record, the reader can trace the development of Leibniz's thought, from first intention to final.

The clearest way to understand the difference between the Akademie Edition, my translation, and other translations, is to compare some examples. Here is the first sentence of the *Discourse* (not including the summary), as it appears in the *main text* of the Akademie Edition:

> La notion de Dieu la plus significative que nous ayons est assez bien exprimée en ces termes, que Dieu est un estre absolument parfait;

This is not, however, the first sentence that Leibniz wrote. As can be seen in the sample of L^1, the draft is quite a mess; but the Akademie's variant record shows that Leibniz began the *Discourse* with (in translation) 'It is necessary in my opinion to keep it assured that'. He then went on to revise that phrase several times before arriving at the above sentence. The order of revisions is difficult to determine, for the untrained eye, but is evident from the placement and strike outs. The Akademie's variant record also indicates that between 'Dieu' and 'la', the words 'la plus receue et' were included in the fair copy (l^2), a fact which is unmarked on l^2 itself, as can be seen on the sample above. Thus, the variant record allows you to trace the development of the first sentence, from its first attempt in L^1 to its final version in l^2. Now, here is my version of that sentence as it appears in the main text of my translation:

> The <most accepted and>[2] most significant notion of God that we have is expressed rather well in these terms, that God is an absolutely perfect being;

Footnote 2, below the main text, indicates that the phrase between brackets was included in the fair copy, l^2. Thus, in my version the fair copy is built into the sentence; it is not necessary to go to the footnote in order to read the final version of the text. The footnote also records, following the Akademie, Leibniz's revisions in L^1 leading up to the final version of that sentence. Thus, if you wish to study that development, you still can.

Some passages are even more complicated, but the procedure is the same (see 'How to track. . .' below). In sum, the main text of my translation can be read straight through as Leibniz's final version of the *Discourse*.

It is clarifying to see how other translations have handled this first sentence. Here is the translation from RP (2020), which also bases its translation on the Akademie Edition:

> The most significant notion of God that we have is well enough stated in these terms, that God is an absolutely perfect being;

While this translation closely follows the Akademie's main text, and the text is clear of marks, it does not indicate the variant that ended up in the fair copy, l^2. Nor does it indicate the several revisions that led up to it. Now, here is the translation from LG (1953), which is based on the Lestienne edition:

> ᵃ*The notion of God which is the most widely received and the most significant that we have is well enough expressed in these terms, that† God is an absolutely perfect being,

This is close to my version, word-wise. But the variant record does not clearly or accurately indicate how the sentence ended up that way. The words between * and † are supposed to indicate additions Leibniz made to the first draft, L^1, but it is uncertain what was added. The small letter 'a' indicates a footnote which says 'this sentence was repeatedly corrected by Leibniz'. That is correct; but then it cites 'God is an absolutely perfect being', which, according to the Akademie, is not the first sentence. Additional variants are then listed, but the relationship between them and the signals in the main text is unclear. Nor does the text indicate that 'the most widely received' is included in l^2.

Finally, the AG (1989) translation, based on the Gerhardt edition, which is based on only the fair copy, l^2, has the following:

> The most widely accepted and meaningful notion we have of God is expressed well enough in these words, that God is an absolutely perfect being;

Minor differences in word choice aside, this version is clear of apparatus but does not indicate any variant. There is no mistake here; it just doesn't tell you how the sentence got that way.

In sum, translations based on the Akademie's main text, even if they show some variants, mainly amount to a translation of Leibniz's first draft (L^1). Admittedly, the difference between (1) the Akademie's main text (their reconstruction of L^1) and (2) the fair copy, l^2, is not major. If Leibniz struck something from L^1, it almost always did not make it into l^2. Still, it is useful to be able to follow these changes. Translations based only on the fair copy (l^2), while providing a main text relatively free of apparatus, do not include many of the variants to L^1 that would otherwise contribute to a more comprehensive understanding of the work. And when translations do provide important variants, they often do not sufficiently indicate how the main text was reconstructed. This translation endeavours to record and present the variations comprehensively, accurately, and clearly, while retaining readability. I treat the summaries (L^2) similarly, by inserting their revisions into the main text and marking deletions below.

How to track the variants in the translation

The above examples already provide some indication of how to study the main text along with the variants. Below are four examples showing more clearly how to do this in my translation. They also show how the reader can use the variants to dig deeper into Leibniz's thought. Note that all variants are signalled in the main text by angle < > brackets and a footnote number either inside or outside the brackets.

Example 1 shows how Leibniz struck out some words from the first draft, L^1. Here in article 13, lines 14–16, the main text of the translation reads:

> But it seems by this <7> that the difference between contingent and necessary truths will be destroyed,

Footnote 7 says: 'Struck from L^1: that all events will become necessary by a fate'.

This means that at this precise point in L^1, indicated by the brackets, Leibniz had written, but then struck, 'all events will become necessary by a fate'. Thus, he intended L^1 to be read as it is in the main text (excepting, of course, the bracket and number). No further changes were made to this passage. (Note that almost always there is no punctuation closing a variant.) The reader may then speculate on why Leibniz removed this phrase. The most important variants will be discussed in the commentary.

Example 2 shows how Leibniz struck something from a later draft (L^2 or l^2) that he had retained in the first draft (L^1). Article 12, lines 4–7 read:

> I believe that anyone who will meditate on the nature of substance, which I have explained above, will find <2> that the whole nature of body does not consist solely in extension,

Footnote 2 says 'In L^1 but struck from l^2: either that bodies are not substances, in metaphysical rigour, (which was in effect the opinion of the Platonists) or'.

Thus, at this point in L[1], indicated by the < > brackets, Leibniz had the phrase 'either that bodies are not substances, in metaphysical rigour, (which was in effect the opinion of the Platonists) or'. But he *struck* it from l[2], thus striking it from the final draft. Now, the interesting question is why he struck it. We should note that this is but one example in the *Discourse* of Leibniz's hesitation to say that bodies are not substances, likely because he did not wish openly to oppose the prevailing view at the time (namely Descartes') that bodies *are* substantial. More likely is that he was undecided at this time over whether bodies by themselves were true substances, in some sense, even though he insists throughout the *Discourse* that Cartesian 'extension' could not explain the nature (substantiality) of bodies. This example shows that close attention to the variants can be extremely informative. For detail on this point, see the commentary.

Occasionally, however, where Leibniz heavily worked over the text, the variants are much more complicated. Such variants are indicated by numbers and letters within parentheses, from first variant to next-to-last, including variants embedded within variants. The Akademie determined the order in which Leibniz made them. Here is an example of how I handle these more complicated variants:

Example 3. The translation of article 8, lines 28–30 is:

Thus <[12]> <the quality of King which belongs to Alexander the Great, abstracting it from the subject, is not sufficiently determined to an individual,>[13]

Starting with footnote 12:

In L[1] Leibniz initially had, but struck: (1) the circular figure of the ring of (a) Gyges | (b) Polycrates | does not contain all of what the notion of this individual ring comprehends; whereas God (aa) knowing (bb) seeing the individual notion of this ring

and following the order of the numbers and letters, we can reconstruct Leibniz's thought this way:

Thus the circular figure of the ring of ~~Gyges~~ Polycrates does not contain all of what the notion of this individual ring includes; whereas God ~~knowing~~ seeing the individual notion of this ring

Thus, Leibniz first wrote 'the ring of Gyges', and 'God knowing' before changing the former to 'Polycrates' and the latter to 'God seeing'. But then the whole passage was struck. And then, as footnote 13 will indicate, Leibniz added 'the quality of king which belongs to Alexander. . .'. We know he added this passage after he struck the previous, because he wrote it above the passage he struck, as the manuscript itself shows.

Now, this record allows us to do some interesting interpretive work. What might these changes mean? While it may seem trivial to change 'Gyges' to 'Polycrates', we can guess that Leibniz may have wanted an example taken from actual history rather than from myth (the ring of Gyges story, from Book II of Plato's *Republic*, is thought to be mythical, whereas the story of Polycrates is thought to be historical). But more importantly, the fact that Leibniz subsequently changed the example from a ring to that of Alexander indicates that Leibniz did not think that the *notion* of a ring was appropriate for illustrating the notion of an individual substance; and the likely reason is that material things like rings do not have souls and thus cannot properly be substantial individuals (this is explained in the commentary). We can also speculate that Leibniz thought it better to indicate that God 'sees' individual notions, suggesting that God recognises them, rather than 'knows' them, as if he had designed them himself (arguably, God does not *design* individual notions; he sees, understands, and *chooses* them, based on their fittingness). In fact, as additional footnotes show, Leibniz changes 'knowing' to 'seeing' twice. Indications like these contribute to our evolving understanding of the author, the text, and its context.

Finally, *Example 4* shows how to handle a single passage with five footnotes. The last sentence of article 30 says:

> But it is not always sufficient to overcome <34> the inclinations of man, for otherwise he would not strive for anything,[35] and this is reserved solely for the absolutely efficacious grace which is always victorious <36> <37> <whether it be by itself, or by the congruity of the circumstances.>[38]

Footnote 34 says that 'the will of' was struck from L^1. Footnote 35 gives the French for the preceding line ('car autrement il ne tiendroit plus a rien'), because it may be questionable whether 'strive' is a fair translation of 'tenir'. Footnote 36 indicates that at this point in L^1 Leibniz initially wrote: 'Finally, creatures are obliged to God by the graces that he gives to them'. He then wrote 'but they have not', and then struck that and wrote 'and have no right'; then he inserted 'neither over those that he gives to them, nor', before writing 'over those that he does not give to them, otherwise this would not be grace'. But then he struck out *all* of it. Footnote 37 discusses a complex break-off that divides article 30 from 31. Footnote 38 indicates that the phrase in brackets was added in 1^2. It was not in the first draft. The significance of these changes is discussed in the commentary. But the footnotes may be ignored, if the reader simply wants to read the text as Leibniz's final intention.

Why another English translation?

Unlike Ancient Greek or Latin, seventeenth-century French does not pose many difficulties for the English translator. Much of the vocabulary and syntax are very similar to English, and the cultural context of French is more familiar and recent. Moreover, translating philosophy is much easier than translating a novel or a poem, where one typically must contend with a great deal of semantic nuance and contextual differences. Even though Leibniz employs philosophical terminology that may be obscure to many, his use of terms is consistent, his vocabulary otherwise plain, and his syntax fairly standard, despite the occasional lengthy sentence.

As a result, most English translations of the *Discourse*, of which we currently have nine, are just fine; and without disregarding their particular merits and interesting differences, they do not differ *significantly*. So, why do we need another? As already indicated, this translation has several distinctive features: it contains the most complete and accurate variant record, and the main text is presented as a final version, rather than as a version of the first draft. It also includes two passages that do not appear in some translations: a long and interesting passage in §14 that Leibniz struck out; and in §20 a passage from Plato's *Phaedo* that was omitted in spite of Leibniz's explicit instructions in the first draft to include it.[32] I include two versions of that passage, both of which Leibniz had translated from the original Greek, one into French and the other into Latin. I also include, which other translations do as well, though not as much, notes on persons, technical terms, historical and philosophical references, explanations of my rendering of a certain word or passage, clarifications of difficult passages, and explications of textual matters. The notes are discussed in detail in the commentary if need be. Some readers may feel that the numerous footnotes and apparatuses distract from attention to the main text; however, I suggest that these features in their aggregate contribute to a richer understanding of it.

Translators typically attempt to strike a balance or compromise between *faithfulness* to the text and *good prose*; in other words, to render the original in the most exact yet readable translated form. This task can be difficult, since faithfulness can spoil readability, and vice versa. Naturally, I have tried to render Leibniz's French as literally as possible, while adjusting for the idiosyncrasies of French and good English prose; but again, the difficulty is not great. Some terms require special attention to their meaning within their seventeenth-century context. In cases where I differ significantly from other translations (e.g., by translating *notion* as

---

[32] LG and MB include these passages. AG and WF do not. RP includes the Plato passage.

22

'notion' rather than as 'concept'), or where my rendering might be questionable, I explain in a footnote.

One peculiarity of the *Discourse*, at least for a philosophical text, is that each article is written in a continuous stream, without paragraph breaks, sometimes without a clear sentence break, and without signalling a change in topic. I think it is important to maintain this stream-like quality, because it closely reflects not only the rapid pace of Leibniz's thought but also his intention to present a sketch of his positions – which is what the *Discourse* is – rather than a finished treatise. It is as if Leibniz had said to himself, 'It's cold, I have nothing to do at the moment, maybe I'll sketch out some metaphysical thoughts, send a summary of them to Arnauld and see what he thinks.' To preserve these qualities, I do not break the articles into paragraphs, as do other translations. I also tend to replace his commas with semi-colons, to reflect English standards and to maintain sense, while maintaining his flow. I preserve his capitalisations, even though they do not seem to have much significance, and silently correct non-standard spellings, which were few. In sum, I aim to preserve Leibniz's style and sense as much as possible.

Why a commentary?

As indicated in the Preface, although the *Discourse* is one of the most widely read and taught works in the history of philosophy, its brevity, complexity, and seventeenth-century setting make it difficult to understand, for students and scholars alike. As an undergraduate reading it for the first time, I found it full of obscure, dull, and antiquated ideas. As a philosophy professor (specialising in Leibniz), I find some of my students asking whether Leibniz was out of his mind. He races through a multitude of provocative, important, and seemingly bizarre claims, all without providing much reasoning for them; or he provides elaborate if not fantastical solutions to problems few of us even know are problems. It took several professors of mine to show me how to read philosophy, Leibniz in particular, and to see how a brief and cryptic statement could implicitly contain a whole world of fascinating ideas and good reasons for holding them. A commentary on the *Discourse*, then, can help unpack its rich, intricate, and fascinating depth.

Leibniz scholar Benson Mates once wrote that studies in the history of philosophy typically have two methodological aims. One is 'to discover and set forth, as accurately, objectively, and completely as possible, the philosophical views of various historical figures'. To achieve this aim one must, in short, 'remain very close to the text', that is, without reading any claims *into* it that the philosopher does not make. The second aim is to use a philosopher's argument to solve 'a philosophical problem in which one is interested'.[33] My aim for this commentary is primarily the first: to clarify and reveal the meaning of Leibniz's text through close reading and analysis. Once that aim has been met, it is my hope that the reader will be in a better position to take up the second aim. Once you understand, say, Leibniz's positions on free will, perfection, sin, or moral rightness, you will be in a better position to think about those philosophical problems and work them out for yourself.

I take 'close reading' to consist of several steps, though not all are necessary: first, the clarification of important terms and a restatement of a passage in plain language; then, if needed, a restatement or reconstruction of the author's argument, especially if the argument is complex or its premises or conclusion are not explicit. Second, close reading can involve understanding the argument in its immediate context, and, more broadly, in the context of the author's other works. Thus, where needed, I will track the argument as it develops throughout the *Discourse* and, where helpful, appeal to relevant explanations from Leibniz's works written before and after the *Discourse*, although I try to stay close to the time period of the *Discourse*. Third, close reading may require reference to figures and arguments in the history of philosophy, as well as to the secondary (scholarly) literature on Leibniz. I provide these references as needed, but the secondary literature is so huge that I must limit references to those that clarify rather than heavily engage in contemporary debates. Hopefully, the commentary will make the mountain of secondary literature easier to ascend. Finally, close reading can involve anticipating possible problems or misunderstandings and constructing illustrative examples.

For example, in article 8 Leibniz suddenly introduces 'the complete notion of an individual substance'. Most readers will have no idea what this means nor why they should care. And yet, the question of 'substance' ('primary being') is arguably the single most important question in the history of philosophy and crucial for understanding the core of Leibniz's thought, from beginning to end. He provides *some* indication of why he needs this notion (to distinguish the actions of creatures from God's actions). But understanding how the complete notion performs its philosophical work requires clarification of a number of technical terms, some background in the history of philosophy, and some background in Leibniz's prior work on the 'principle of individuation'. A similar approach is taken to articles 10, 12, 17, and 18, which focus on Leibniz's criticisms of Descartes' laws of matter and motion. These sections will be unintelligible without some explanation of Descartes' laws, their background, as well as some background in Aristotelian natural philosophy. Of course, the

---

[33] Mates 1986: 83–4, quoted in Sleigh 1990: 2.

background cannot be exhaustive, but I try to provide what is sufficient for the reader to gain a working sense of Leibniz's claims in the *Discourse* and what motivates them.

The work of close reading inevitably verges on interpretation. My own background, convictions, and proclivities will determine the arguments and contexts I take to be relevant for understanding the work. While I try faithfully to represent Leibniz's positions, occasionally I may offer an interpretation that diverges somewhat from the 'standard interpretation' (if there is one). But when I do, I show that the interpretation is well-grounded in the text and context of the *Discourse*. For example, I argue that Leibniz's principle of individuation in the *Discourse* is ultimately the creature's unique degree of perfection, which is not a standard view. Other times, I make a connection that may seem a stretch; for example, I bring in some contemporary linguistic theory to clarify Leibniz's claims for 'innate ideas' in §26 and §27. But again, the reader should find the explanation well-grounded in Leibniz's text. Generally, I avoid criticism, while remaining critical. On free will, for example, I argue that Leibniz's persistent attempts to preserve it fall short – however, I try to make what I think is his best case for it. In no case, however, do I claim to present Leibniz's definitive position on any subject. To do so would lack sufficient consideration of the secondary literature. My overall methodological aim is to apply the 'principle of charity', which means to make the best case on the author's behalf. Then, and only then, should the commentor or reader turn to serious critical reflection. In several places Leibniz defends his position against possible objections – usually those of Descartes and Malebranche. The principles of close reading and charity require representing their arguments faithfully, as well.

The *Discourse on Metaphysics* provides a sketch of a metaphysics for the 'best possible world' that Leibniz will defend more extensively twenty years later in his famous *Theodicy*. Is a metaphysics of perfection compatible with a seemingly imperfect world? Are God's power and goodness compatible with human sin, suffering, and free will? How can the seemingly soulless mechanism of nature exhibit God's wisdom? Finding unity among a multiplicity of seemingly incompatible notions was Leibniz's distinguishing philosophical mark. Hopefully, the *Discourse* will place the reader in a better position to think substantially about these important questions.

Summary of symbols used in the translation, footnotes, and commentary

- L^1 = The heavily revised first draft of the *Discourse*.
- L^2 = The fair copy of the thirty-seven article summaries of the *Discourse*.
- l^2 = The fair copy of the *Discourse*.
- The numbers on the left margin of the translation refer to each line of the translation, starting with the first line of the article summary, and they are used as reference points in the commentary. For example, 'ln 45' refers to line 45 of the article under discussion. 'lns 47–51' refers to lines 47–51. These numbers have no relation to the margin numbers in the Akademie Edition.
- All footnotes are inserted by the translator. Footnote numbers in the main text, placed inside or next to angle < > brackets, indicate a variant occurrence that is explained or translated below the main text. Footnote numbers not enclosed in angle brackets but placed immediately next to a word (for example, knowledge[2]) pertain, not to a variant, but only to the word or phrase immediately before the number.
- Unless clearly indicated, any words in the footnotes occurring *after a draft number and a colon* are my translations of Leibniz's variants. The exceptions to this are numbers such as '(1)' and letters such as 'aa' which the Akademie uses to track the order.
- Words between bars | . . . | indicate a variant embedded within another variant, as can be found in *Example 3*, above.
- Words or phrases inside square [ ] brackets are used only by the translator for purposes of clarifying the text by supplying a missing but likely intended word. They are also used in the variant footnotes to distinguish the translator's words from Leibniz's.
- All parentheses (. . .) and the words they contain in the main text and variants, but not in the commentary, are Leibniz's.
- Words omitted either by the Akademie or the translator are indicated by ellipses.
- Non-French words in the main text, usually Latin, are translated in a footnote.
- In the translation's footnotes, words within quotation marks usually contain untranslated words from Leibniz's original French or Latin, in order to signal an interesting or debatable translation of those words.
- Words or phrases that Leibniz had underlined for emphasis (which the Akademie indicates with expanded characters), usually phrases in Latin, are *italicised* in the translation.

The reader is encouraged to make close study of the variants and their relation to the main text – to study their implications, to speculate on their motives, and to venture deeply into the mind of a great philosopher. While some variants will seem unimportant, most are important. But I recommend *first* reading the main text of the *Discourse* straight through without interruption. Then read it again along with the footnotes and variants. Then read the commentary. Then read the main text again.

Topical summary of the *Discourse on Metaphysics*, by article

Lucas and Grint (LG vii–xii) usefully divide the thematic content of the *Discourse* accordingly:

On God: I–VII
Substances: VIII–XVI
Force and Final Causes: XVII–XXII
The Human Understanding: XXIII–XXIX
The Human Will: XXX–XXXI
Piety and Religion: XXXII–XXXVII

For brief descriptions of each article, see the Table of Contents. The descriptions mostly follow Leibniz's summary headings but more accurately reflect the content of the commentary.

A natural and indispensable follow-up to the *Discourse on Metaphysics* is Leibniz's correspondence with Arnauld, which focuses intensively on the problems of substance and free will. The full correspondence is available in translation by H. T. Mason (LAM 1967), and a new and expanded edition, including the original French, is provided by Stephen Voss (LAV 2016). For indispensable commentary on the correspondence, including important details on the *Discourse*, see Robert Sleigh's *Leibniz & Arnauld: A Commentary on their Correspondence* (1990). For a recent and relatively brief synopsis of the *Discourse*, see Strickland 2020. For additional references on the *Discourse*, see the bibliography. *Any questions, problems, confusions, mistakes, corrections, or comments may be gladly referred to the translator-commentator.*

Translation of the Discourse on Metaphysics[1]

I. On the Divine perfection, and that God does everything in the most desirable way.

The <most accepted and>[2] most significant notion of God that we have
5 is expressed rather well in these terms, that God is an absolutely perfect
being; <[3]> but the consequences of this are not sufficiently considered.
And so to enter the matter further, it is appropriate to remark that there are
in nature several completely different perfections, that God possesses them
all together, and that each one belongs to him in the most supreme[4] degree.
10 One must also know[5] what a perfection is, for which there is a rather certain
mark, namely, that the forms or natures that are not capable of a highest
degree <are not perfections>;[6] as for example, the nature of number or
of figure. For, the greatest number of all (or, the number of all numbers)

---

[1] Leibniz did not title the work on any of his manuscripts.
[2] Added in l². In L¹ Leibniz repeatedly revised this first sentence in the following order,
beginning with (1) and leading up to the sentence as it appears in l² above: (1) It is necessary in my opinion to keep it as assured that (2) The idea of God (a) the most ancient
and the most accepted (b) the most accepted and most significant is that (3) The most
significant idea that we can form of God is that
[3] In L¹ the following passages were attempted, then struck: (1) such that he possesses all
the perfections together and each one in the most supreme degree. Where it is good to
remark that (2) One must consider also what a perfection is, for (3) Also one must consider what is a perfection where it is good (4) But to understand better what a perfection
is, it is good (5) But finally (a) to try (b) to know better what a perfection is, one must
know that [. . .] (6) It is what everyone remains agreed on although it seems that one
[4] 'souverain'
[5] In l² 'connoistre' was struck and replaced by 'scavoir'
[6] Added in l², replacing 'n'en sont point'

as well as the greatest of all figures, imply contradiction. But the great-
15 est knowledge, and omnipotence, imply no impossibility. Consequently,
power[7] and knowledge[8] are perfections, and <[9]> in as much as they belong
to God, they have no limits. Whence it follows that God, possessing
supreme and infinite wisdom, acts in the most perfect manner, not only
in the metaphysical sense, but also morally speaking; thus, what can be
20 expressed in regard to ourselves, the more we are enlightened and informed
about God's works, the more we will be disposed to find them excellent and
<in complete conformity with all that one could have desired>.[10]

II. Against those who maintain <[1]> that there is no goodness in God's
works, or that the rules of goodness and beauty are arbitrary <[2]>.

Thus I am far removed from the sentiment of those who maintain that
5 there are no rules of goodness and perfection in the nature of things or in
the ideas God has of them, and that the works of God are good only for the
formal reason that God made them. For if that were so, God, knowing
that he is the author of them, would have no reason to regard them after
<having made them>[3] and find them good, as Holy Scripture attests –
10 which appears to use this anthropology[4] only to make us understand <[5]>
that their excellence is recognised by regarding them in themselves, even
as one makes no reflection on this completely empty <[6]> denomination,
which relates them to their cause.[7] Thus it is all the more true that by

---

[7] 'puissance'
[8] 'science'
[9] Struck from L[1]: and belong to God in the most unlimited manner
[10] As in l[2]. L[1] had: entirely satisfying to everything that one could even desire.
[1] Struck from L[1]: that the beauty or goodness of things depend only on the opinion of
men,
[2] Not in L[1], but struck from L[2]: or consist only in men's imagination
[3] In L[1] Leibniz had struck out this phrase, and it does not appear in l[2]. I include it to
clarify his meaning in this passage.
[4] The term can be used to refer to expressions in Holy Scripture that attribute human
actions and affections to God (*Dictionnaire de L'Académie française 4e édition* (1762)).
[5] Struck from L[1]: that there was some goodness in them.
[6] This word is in L[1] but struck from l[2]: exterior
[7] Lines 7–13 are difficult and other editions try to make sense of what the text does not. I
take Leibniz's meaning to be this: If things are good only for the reason that God made
them, then, since God knows they are good, he does not have to 'see' that they are good
in order to find them good ('And God saw that the light was good', Genesis 1:4). This
expression in Scripture, however, reflects a human way of saying that the goodness (or
excellence) of things is contained in the nature of the things themselves; and this is so
even as we make no reference to their dependence on having been made by God. That is,

consideration of the works one can discover the worker; these works must
15 therefore bear his character in them. I confess that the contrary sentiment seems to me extremely dangerous, and closely approaches that of
some <[8]> <recent Innovators>[9] whose opinion is that the beauty of the
universe and the goodness that we attribute to the works of God are only
the chimeras of men, who conceive of God in their [own] manner.[10] Also,
20 in saying that things are good, not by any rule of goodness but only by the
will of God, one destroys, it seems to me, without realising it, all the <[11]>
love of God and all his glory. For why praise him for what he has done, if
he would be equally praiseworthy for doing just the contrary? Where then
will his justice and wisdom be, if there remains only a certain despotic
25 power, if <the will takes the place of reason>,[12] and if, according to the
definition of tyrants, whatever pleases the most powerful is for that reason
just?[13] Besides, it seems that all willing supposes <some reason for the
will>[14] or that this reason is naturally prior[15] to the will. This is why I still
find the expression of <certain other philosophers>[16] entirely strange,
30 <who say>[17] that the eternal truths of Metaphysics <and>[18] Geometry
(and also by consequence the rules of goodness, justice, and perfection) are
only the effects of the will of God, whereas it seems to me, rather, that they
are the consequences of his understanding, which <[19]> does not depend on
his will any more than does his essence.[20]

---

even though God makes excellent things, 'God-made' is not the quality that makes the
things excellent. For Descartes' opposing view, see 'Author's Replies to the Sixth Set of
Objections' (CSM II, §8, 293–4 / AT VII, 435). For further discussion, see commentary.

[8] Struck from L[1]: Spinozists, who conceive that (a) goodness, harmony

[9] Added in L[1].

[10] See Spinoza's *Ethics* 1, Appendix, pp. 109–15.

[11] Struck from L[1]: the worship and all

[12] In L[1] Leibniz had *ubi stat pro ratione voluntas*, but replaced it with an equivalent expression in French. The Latin comes from Juvenal's *Satires*, 6.223 and is frequently cited by
Leibniz.

[13] According to Plato's Thrasymachus, *Republic*, Bk I (338c).

[14] L[1] and l[2] both had '*aliquam rationem volendi*' but Leibniz struck it from l[2] and replaced it
with the equivalent in French.

[15] L[1] had 'prior' which in l[2] was struck and replaced with 'anterior'. Leibniz may have
considered that 'prior' ('prieure') *can* mean 'superior', whereas *he* means that reason
informs the will's act of willing *before* it acts, or better, logically prior to an act of the will.
But 'anterior' sounds a bit awkward in English.

[16] In l[2]. In L[1] Leibniz had struck: Mr Descartes

[17] Added in l[2].

[18] In l[2]. L[1] had: or

[19] Omitted in l[2]: assuredly

[20] Compare with Descartes' letter to Mersenne (27 May 1630): 'In God, will, understanding, and creating are all the same thing without one being prior to the other even

III. Against those who believe that God could have done better.

I can no more approve the opinion of certain <¹> moderns who boldly
maintain that what God does is not of the highest perfection and that he
5 could have acted much better.² For it seems to me that the consequences of
this sentiment are entirely contrary to the glory of God. *Uti minus malum
habet rationem boni, ita minus bonum habet rationem mali.*³ And to act with
less perfection than one could have is to act imperfectly. To show that an
architect could have done better is to find fault with his work. This goes
10 against Holy Scripture, where it assures us of the goodness of God's works.
For if [their opinion] were sufficient, as imperfections descend to infinity,
in whatever manner God had made his work, it would always have been
good in comparison to the less perfect; but a work is hardly praiseworthy
when it is done only in this way. I also believe that one will find a multitude⁴
15 of passages from divine Scripture and the Holy Fathers⁵ favouring my
opinion, but one will find hardly any of them among these moderns, whose
opinions, I believe, are unknown from all antiquity, and are only based on
insufficient knowledge of the general harmony of the universe, and of the
hidden reasons for God's conduct, which makes us judge rashly that many
20 things could have been rendered better. Besides, these moderns insist on
certain unstable subtleties. For they imagine that nothing is so perfect that
it cannot be more perfect, which is an error. <⁶> They also believe by this
to provide for the freedom of God, as if it would not be the highest freedom
to act in perfection following sovereign reason. For to believe that God acts

conceptually' (CSM III, 25–6 / AT I, 151–3). Also see 'Sixth Replies' (CSM II, §6,
291–2 / AT VII, 431–3).

¹ Struck from L¹: Scholastics, who imagine
² Leibniz is possibly referring to Malebranche's *Treatise on Nature and Grace*, Discourse
I, §14. But see commentary.
³ 'As a lesser evil contains a portion of good, a lesser good contains a portion of evil.' The
source of this phrase is uncertain, but something like it may be found in Aristotle's
Nicomachean Ethics (Bk V, 1131b) in a discussion of a species of justice designated 'the
proportional'. The relation of that discussion to Leibniz's criticism of 'certain moderns'
here is perhaps this: that this widely accepted notion of justice could be used to suggest
that if God acted less than perfectly (with less than absolute goodness) then God could
be thought to act with a portion of evil. Yet, Leibniz would object, God's actions, as
proportional as they may be, cannot be evil in the least.
⁴ 'an infinity'
⁵ Translated from 'SS. Peres' in AA. 'SS' is the plural abbreviation for 'Saints'. Some
typographical variations: L¹ has 'SS peres' and l² has 'S.S. Peres'.
⁶ Struck from L¹: For example, there is an infinity of regular figures, but one is the most
perfect, namely, the circle; if it were necessary to make a triangle, and there were not one
determination of the species of this triangle, God would assuredly make an equilateral
triangle, because absolutely speaking it is the most perfect.

31

25 in some matter without having any reason for his will, besides that it seems this cannot be, is a sentiment little conforming to his glory. For example, suppose God should choose between *A* and *B*, and that he takes *A* without having any reason to prefer it to *B*. I say that this action of God would at least not be praiseworthy, since all praise must be founded in some reason,
30 which is not found here *ex hypothesi.*[7] I hold rather that God does nothing for which he does not merit being glorified.

IV. That to love God demands complete satisfaction and acquiescence regarding what he does <[1]>.

The general knowledge of this great truth, that God always acts in the
5   most perfect and the most desirable manner possible <[2]> is, in my opinion, the foundation of the love we owe to God above all things, since <[3]> the one who loves seeks his satisfaction in the felicity or perfection of the object loved and <[4]> his actions. *Idem velle et idem nolle vera amicitia est.*[5] And I believe that it is difficult to love God well when one is
10 not in the disposition to will what he wills, even if changing his will were in our power. Indeed those who are not satisfied with what God does seem to me to resemble disaffected subjects, <[6]> whose intention is not much different from rebels. I hold then that following these principles for acting in conformity with the love of God, it does not suffice to have
15 patience perforce, but one must be truly satisfied with all that happens to us according to his will. I mean this acquiescence to apply to the past. As for the future, one must not be a *quietist,*[7] nor wait ridiculously with arms crossed for what God will do, according to the sophism that the ancients

---

[7] That is, *from the hypothesis* that God has no reason for his will.

[1] In L[1] but omitted in L[2]: without, for that, requiring us to be quietists

[2] Struck from L[1]: is the foundation of the love of God over all things, and of a true contentment for those who love him and who

[3] Struck from L[1]: to love is nothing other than to be brought to find pleasure

[4] Struck from L[1]: consequently this sovereign goodness, this immutable justice, this profound wisdom, (a) this power without limits (b) which gives laws to this power without limits

[5] 'To will the same and not to will the same is true friendship.' AA ref: Sallust, *The Conspiracy of Catiline*, Ch. 20: 'I am aware, too, that whatever advantages or evils affect you, the same affect me; and to have the same desires and the same aversions, is assuredly a firm bond of friendship' (Perseus online).

[6] Struck from L[1]: of a king or of a republic

[7] Underlined in l[2]. Quietism is a Christian spiritual doctrine. See footnote in commentary.

call λόγον ἄεργον, lazy reason.[8] But we must act according to the *presump-*
20 *tive will of God,*[9] as far as we can judge of it, trying with all our power to
contribute to the general good and particularly to the adornment and
perfection of all that involves us or is near to us and so to speak within our
reach. For if the circumstance perhaps will have shown that God has not
willed at this moment that our good <will>[10] should have its effect, it does
25 not follow from this that he does not want us to do what we have done.
On the contrary, as he is the best of all masters, he only ever asks for the
<right>[11] intention, and it is for him to know the hour and proper place
to make good intentions succeed.

V. What the rules of the perfection of divine conduct consist in, and that the simplicity of the ways is in balance with the richness of the effects.

5 It suffices therefore to have this confidence in God, that he does everything
for the best, and that nothing could harm those who love him. But to know
in detail the reasons that could have moved him to choose this order of the
universe – to allow sins, to dispense his saving graces in a certain manner –
would surpass the power of a finite mind, especially when it has not yet
10 attained enjoyment of the vision of God. However, one can make several
general remarks concerning the course of providence in the government
of things. We can therefore say that <[1]> one who acts perfectly resembles
an excellent geometer, who knows how to find the best constructions for a
problem; a good Architect, who organises his space and the funds allotted
15 for the building in the most advantageous manner, leaving nothing to give
offence or which lacks the beauty of which it is capable; a good paterfamil-
ias, who manages his property in a way that leaves nothing uncultivated or
barren; a skilled engineer who achieves his effect in the least cumbersome
way one could choose; and a learned author, who includes the most realities
20 in the least volume that he can.[2] Now, the most perfect of all beings, and
which occupy the least volume, that is to say, which impede each other the
least, are minds,[3] whose perfections are the virtues. It is why one must not

---

[8] Transliteration of the Greek is 'logon ergon'. See footnote in commentary.
[9] Underlined in l². The notion of 'presumptive will' for Leibniz has roots in his early
jurisprudential writings. See commentary.
[10] In l². In L¹ Leibniz originally had: intention
[11] In L¹ Leibniz originally had 'good' (*bonne*) but replaced it with 'right' (*droite*) meaning
'upright' or 'morally correct'.
[1] Struck from L¹: what contains the most reality in the least volume is most perfect
[2] These examples reflect Malebranche from his *Treatise*. See commentary.
[3] 'espirits'

doubt that the <⁴> felicity of minds is the <⁵> principal aim of God, and that he brings about only as much as <⁶> the general harmony permits.
25 We will say more about this below.[7] Now, what is meant by the simplicity of God's ways belongs properly to the means, as opposed to the variety, richness, or abundance, which belong to the ends or effects. And the one must be in balance with the other, as the expenses destined for a building [are in balance with] the grandeur and beauty that one expects from it. It is
30 true that nothing has a cost for God, much less than for a philosopher who makes hypotheses for the construction of his imaginary world, whereas God has only to make decrees to give birth to a real world; but in matters of wisdom, decrees or hypotheses take the place of expenditure, insofar as they are more independent of each other: because reason wants to avoid
35 multiplicity in hypotheses or principles, <almost>[8] as the simplest system is always preferred in Astronomy.

VI. <That>[1] God does nothing out of order and it is not even possible to contrive events which are not regular.

The Volitions or Actions of God are commonly divided into ordinary or
5 extraordinary. <²> But it is good to consider that God does nothing out of order. Thus what passes for extraordinary is so only in regard to some particular order established among creatures. For relative to the universal order, everything conforms to it. This is so true that not only does nothing happen in the world that is absolutely irregular, but one could not even
10 contrive such a thing. For let us suppose for example that someone makes a number of dots on a paper quite at random, as do those who practise the ridiculous art of Geomancy.[3] I say that it is possible to find a geometric line, the notion of which is constant and uniform according to a certain rule; of a sort that this line passes through all these points, and in the same order
15 that the hand had drawn them. And if someone could trace in one motion a line which would be now straight, now a circle, now some other nature, it [would be] possible to find a notion or rule or equation common to all the points on this line, in virtue of which these very modifications had to occur.

---

⁴ Struck from L¹: greatest perfection of minds
⁵ Struck from L¹: aim of God, as well as nature
⁶ Struck from L¹: the order of
⁷ See §XXXVI.
⁸ Added in l² and l³.
¹ In L².
² Struck from L¹: but this difference holds only in regard to creatures
³ A method of divination that finds meaningful patterns in seemingly random arrangements of objects, lines, or marks.

And there is no face, for example, whose contour does not make part of a
20 Geometric line and cannot be traced all in one stroke by a certain regulated
movement. But when a rule is very complex, what conforms to it passes
for irregular. Thus one can say that in whatever manner God had created
the world, it would always have been regular and in a certain general order.
But God has chosen the one which is the most perfect, that is to say the
25 one which is at the same time the simplest in hypotheses and the richest in
phenomena; as could be a line in Geometry whose construction would be
easy and whose properties and effects would be very admirable and of great
extent. I make use of these comparisons in order to draw some imperfect
resemblance to the divine wisdom, and to say something that can at least
30 elevate our minds to conceive in some fashion what one may not be able
adequately to express. But by this I do not pretend to explain the great
mystery on which the whole universe depends.

VII. That miracles conform to the general order, although they are
counter to subaltern maxims. On what God wills or permits, and on
the general or particular will.

5 Now since nothing can be done which is not in order, we can say that
miracles are just as much in the order as are natural operations, so-called
because they conform to certain subaltern maxims[1] that we call the nature
of things. For we can say that this nature is only a custom of God, <[2]>
from which he can exempt himself in case of a reason stronger than the
10 one which moved him to make use of these maxims. Concerning general
or particular volitions,[3] according to how one takes the matter, we can say
that God does everything following his most general will, which conforms
to the most perfect order that he has chosen; but we can also say that
he has particular volitions, which are exceptions to the aforementioned
15 subaltern maxims; for the most general of God's laws, which regulates the
whole series of the universe, is without exception. We can also say that
God wills everything that is an object of his particular volition. But as far
as the objects of his general will, such as the actions of other creatures,
particularly those which are reasonable[4] and with whom God wishes to

---

[1] Subaltern maxims are simply physical laws. The term 'subaltern maxim' stems from
the genus-species classification system, in which a genus (such as *animal*) contains one
or many 'subalternates' or species (human, horse, dog). So, here the genus is *universal
order*, of which physical laws and miracles are species.

[2] Struck from L[1]: (1) who is always subject (a) to the general order, as (b) to the exemption
which can

[3] A central distinction of Malebranche's *Treatise on Nature and Grace*. See commentary.

[4] That is, rational creatures.

20 concur, one must make a distinction: now if the action is good <⁵> in itself
we can say that God wills it and sometimes commands it, even when it does
not happen; but if it is bad in itself, and becomes good only by accident,
because the series of things, particularly punishment and reparation,⁶ cor-
rects its malignity and repays the evil with interest, such that in the end
25 more perfection is found in the whole series than if all this evil had not happened, then one must say that God permits it and does not will it, although
he concurs with it because of the laws of nature that he has established and
because he knows how to draw a greater good from it.

VIII. In order to distinguish the actions of God and of creatures, we explain in what consists the notion[1] of an individual substance.

It is rather difficult to distinguish the Actions of God from those of crea-
5 tures, <as well as the Actions and passions of these same creatures>.²
For there are some who believe that God does everything,³ and others who
imagine that he acts only to conserve the force he has given to creatures:⁴
the following will show how much of one or the other can be said. Now
since actions and passions properly belong to individual substances
10 (*actiones sunt suppositorum*),⁵ it will be necessary to explain what such a substance is. It is indeed true that when several predicates are attributed to the
same subject, and that this subject is attributed to no other, we call it <⁶>

---

⁵ Struck from L¹: or indifferent

⁶ 'satisfaction'

1 Most of the scholarship on Leibniz uses the term 'concept' instead of 'notion'.

2 The passage was in L¹ but omitted by the copyists in l² and l³.

3 That is, those who subscribe to Malebranche's doctrine of occasionalism. AA note: see
Malebranche, *Search after Truth*, VI, 2, 3. Malebranche accuses the ancients of having
mistakenly assigned causes to forms, minds, bodies, and natural laws, and he insists
'there is only one true cause because there is only one true God; that the nature or power
of each thing is nothing but the will of God; that all natural causes are not true causes but
only occasional causes' (MS 448). On Leibniz's rejection of Malebranche's occasionalism, see §33 commentary.

4 AA: See Descartes, *Principles* II, §§36–44, where Descartes sets out his famous laws of
motion, particularly the law of conservation of motion, which in §§36 and 43 of *Principles*
he identifies with force. Leibniz critiques this law in §17. On divine conservation see §14
and §30 of the commentary.

5 'actions belong to substances'. AA refers to Aquinas' *Summa Theologica*, II–II, q.58, a.2:
'Whether justice is always toward another, . . . And forasmuch as it belongs to justice to
rectify human acts [. . .] this otherness which justice demands must needs be between
beings capable of action. Now actions belong to supposits and wholes and, properly
speaking, not to parts and forms or powers, for we do not say properly that the hand
strikes, but a man with his hand. . .'.

6 Struck from L¹: a certain

an individual substance. But this is not enough, and such an explanation is only nominal. One must therefore consider what it is to be attributed truly
15 to a certain subject. Now, it is established that all true predication has some foundation in the nature of things, and when a proposition is not identical, that is to say, when the predicate is not expressly included in the subject, it is necessary that it be included virtually, and this is what the philosophers call *inesse*[7] <when saying that the predicate *is in* the subject.>[8] Thus it is
20 necessary that the subject term always contain that of the predicate, such that one who perfectly understood[9] the notion of the subject, would also judge that the predicate belongs to it. This being so, we can say that the nature of an individual substance, or of a complete Being, is to have a notion so complete that it is sufficient <[10]> to understand[11] and to deduce
25 from it all the predicates of the subject to which this notion is attributed. On the other hand an accident is a being whose notion does not contain all that can be attributed to the subject to which one attributes this notion. Thus <[12]> <the quality of King which belongs to Alexander the Great, abstracting it from the subject, is not sufficiently determined to an indi-
30 vidual,>[13] and does not contain <the other qualities of the same subject, nor>[14] all of what the notion of this <[15]> Prince includes; on the other hand God, <[16]> seeing the individual notion or haecceity[17] of Alexander, sees in it at the same time the foundation and reason for all the predicates that can truly be said of him, as <[18]> for example that he would vanquish

---

[7] The Latin means 'being in', a term drawn from Scholastic logic, probably originally from Aristotle's *Prior Analytics*, I.1, 24b27: 'That one term should be included in another as in a whole is the same as for the other to be predicated of all of the first' (AB).

[8] Not in L[1] but added by Leibniz in l[2].

[9] 'entendroit'

[10] In L[1] Leibniz added, then struck out: in itself

[11] 'comprendre'

[12] In L[1] Leibniz initially had, but struck: (1) the circular figure of the ring of (a) Gyges | (b) Polycrates | does not contain all of what the notion of this individual ring includes; whereas God (aa) knowing (bb) seeing the individual notion of this ring [AA notes: For the Gyges reference see Plato's *Republic*, 359d–360b. For Polycrates see Herodotus, *Histories*, III, 41–2.]

[13] Added to L[1].

[14] Added to L[1].

[15] Struck from L[1]: individual ring

[16] Struck from L[1]: knowing

[17] A Scholastic term meaning 'thisness' or 'this one' in reference to the property a thing is supposed to have by virtue of which it is a distinct individual.

[18] Struck from L[1]: that it will be swallowed by a fish, and nevertheless returned to its master. [This refers to the ring.]

35 Darius and Porus,[19] <[20]> even to the point of knowing *a priori* (and not by experience) whether he died of a natural death, or by poison – which we can know only through history. Thus, when one well considers the connection of things, we can say that there is from all time in the soul of Alexander vestiges of everything that happened to him, and marks of everything that
40 will happen to him, and even traces of everything that happens in the universe, although it belongs only to God to recognise them all. <[21]>

IX. That each unique[1] substance *expresses*[2] the whole universe in its manner, and that included in its notion are all its events with all their particularities and the whole series of exterior things.

5 Several considerable paradoxes[3] <follow from this>,[4] among others, that it is not <[5]> true that two substances entirely resemble each other while differing *solo numero*,[6] and what St Thomas affirms on this point about angels or intelligences (*quod ibi omne individuum sit species infima*)[7] is true

---

[19] Darius III, king of Persia, d. 330 BCE. Porus, Indian king, d. 315 BCE.

[20] Struck from L[1]: (1) and knows it *a priori* (a) (and not from experience) (b) what we can know only through the actual history

[21] Struck from L[1]: I speak here as if it were assured that this ring is a substance. [This sentence is a vestige of Leibniz's initial attempt to trace the notion of the ring belonging either to Gyges or Polycrates.]

[1] 'singuliere'

[2] Underlined in L[2].

[3] See the commentary for the usage of this term.

[4] Grammar corrected in l[2].

[5] Struck from L[1]: possible

[6] 'Only by number'. Lines 6–7 express a version of Leibniz's so-called 'principle of the identity of indiscernibles'. See commentary.

[7] 'that with them every individual is a lowest species'. A lowest species is an individual member of a species, but which is not a genus for another species. The Latin phrase is often attributed to Aquinas' *Summa Theologiae*, I, q.50, a.4, but it does not appear there or anywhere in Aquinas, although it may be implied there: Since angels are immaterial 'pure intelligences', 'it follows that it is impossible for two angels to be of one species' (<http://www.logicmuseum.com/authors/aquinas/summa/Summa-I-50-53.htm>). That is, having no matter, the only way for angels to differ individually is by their form or species difference. So, each intelligence is its own species, below which there is no further differentiation of angels. Or, perhaps the idea is expressed here: 'Whereas in immaterial things there is no separate determinator [form] and thing determined [matter]; each thing by its own self holds a determinate grade in being; and therefore in them "genus" and "difference" are not derived from different things, but from one and the same' (q. 50, a.2, reply to objection 1). That is, angels are individuated not by matter, nor by their genus (pure intelligence), but by their particular *grade of being*, which makes each its own species. Perhaps closer yet is Aquinas' reference to Ibn-Sînâ in *On Being and Essence*: 'The second difference is that the essences of composed things, because they

38

of all substances, provided that one takes the specific difference, as the
10 Geometers take it regarding their figures.[8] <9> Also that a substance can
begin only by creation, and perish only by annihilation. That a substance
cannot be divided into two, nor can two be made into one, and thus
that the number of substances does not naturally increase or diminish,
although they may often be transformed. Furthermore every substance is
15 like an entire world and like a mirror of God or rather the whole universe,
that each one expresses it in its own way, somewhat as the same city is
diversely represented according to the different situations of the one who
regards it. Thus the universe is in some way multiplied as many times as
there are substances, and the glory of God is even redoubled by as many
20 entirely different representations of his work. We can even say that every
substance bears in some way the character of God's infinite wisdom and
omnipotence, and imitates it as much as it is capable. For it expresses,
although confusedly, all that happens in the universe, past, present, and
future, having some resemblance to an infinite perception or knowledge.
25 And as all other substances express this one in their turn and accommodate
themselves to it, one can say that it extends its power over all the others in
imitation of the omnipotence of the Creator.

X. That the opinion on substantial forms has something solid, <1> but that these forms change nothing in the phenomena, and must not be employed to explain particular effects.

5 It seems that the ancients <2> as well as many diligent people accustomed
to profound meditations, who taught theology and philosophy some

are received into designated matter, are multiplied according to its division. And this is
why it happens that certain things are the same in species and diverse in number. But
since the essence of a simple thing is not received into matter, such a multiplication is
impossible here. And this is why, of necessity, many individuals of a same species are not
found among these substances; rather, as Ibn-Sînâ expressly says, there are among them
as many species as there are individuals' (paragraph 75).

[8] In a letter to Arnauld (14 July 1686), Leibniz says that '"difference in species" must be
taken not following the common usage (on which it would be absurd to say two men
differ in species), but according to the usage of mathematicians, for whom two triangles
or two ellipses that are not similar differ in species' (LAV 85). See commentary.

[9] Struck from L¹: Also if bodies are substances, it is not possible that their nature consist
solely in size, figure, and motion, but that something else is required. [This statement
expresses Leibniz's opposition to Descartes' central claim that bodies are substances by
virtue of their extended qualities (size, figure, motion) – a point Leibniz will criticise in
several places throughout the *Discourse*. See commentary.]

[1] In L¹ but struck from L²: if bodies are substances

[2] Struck from L¹: in distinguishing *being in itself* [*ens per se*] *from Being as accident* [*Ente per accidens*] [. . .] and introducing substantial forms

centuries ago, some of whom are commendable for their saintliness, had some knowledge of what we have just said, and this is what made them introduce and maintain the substantial forms which are so decried today.

10 But they are not so far from the truth, nor so ridiculous as the common lot of our new philosophers imagine. I do agree that the consideration <³> of these forms is useless in the detail of physics and must not be employed in the explanation of particular phenomena. And this is where our Scholastics have failed, and the Physicians⁴ of the past following their example,

15 believing they could correctly account for the properties <⁵> of bodies [by] mentioning the forms and qualities without bothering to examine the manner of operation, as if one wanted to content oneself by saying that a clock has an horodictic quality⁶ originating in its form, without considering in what all this consists. This indeed suffices <⁷> for the one

20 who buys [the clock], provided that he abandon the care of it to another. But <⁸> this failure and misuse of the forms must not make us reject the knowledge of something so necessary in Metaphysics that without it, I maintain, one would be quite unable to know the first principles <⁹> nor to elevate the mind sufficiently to the knowledge of incorporeal natures and

25 the marvels of God. However just as a Geometer has no need to burden the mind with the famous labyrinth of the composition of the continuum,¹⁰ no moral philosopher and still less a jurisconsult¹¹ or politician has any need to trouble over the great difficulties found in the reconciliation of free will and the providence of God, since the Geometer can conclude all

30 his demonstrations, and the politician can terminate all his deliberations, without entering into these discussions, which do not cease to be necessary and important in philosophy and theology. Likewise, a Physicist¹² can provide an account of experiments, at one time using simple experiments

---

3 Struck from L¹: knowledge
4 'Medecins'
5 Struck from L¹: phenomena
6 That is, a clock, 'une horloge', has a time-telling quality.
7 Struck from L¹: perhaps for a lord
8 Struck from L¹: in the end
9 Struck from L¹: principles of things
10 The composition of the continuum has to do with the composition of continuous quantities, for example, whether matter is infinitely divisible, or composed of an infinity of indivisible wholes. Leibniz also conceived of the continuum as involving free will: 'For there are two labyrinths of the human mind: one concerning the composition of the continuum, and the other concerning the nature of freedom, and they arise from the same source, infinity' ('On Freedom', 1689, AG 95). For a full explanation of the subject see the introduction to LC.
11 The term can refer to a lawyer, judge, or legal expert.
12 'Physicien', a specialist in physics, that is, a natural philosopher.

already done, at another by using geometrical and mechanical demonstra-
35 tions, without having need <[13]> of general considerations from another
sphere; and if he employs the <[14]> concourse of God or as well some soul,
or Arche[15] or something else of this nature, he extravagates as much as one
who in an important practical deliberation would prefer to enter into grand
reasonings on the nature of destiny and our liberty; as men indeed make
40 this fault rather often without thinking of it when they burden the mind
with the consideration of fate, and even sometimes are thereby diverted
from some good resolution, or from some necessary care.

XI. That the meditations of Theologians and philosophers who are called Scholastics are not to be despised <entirely>[1].

I know that I advance a great paradox by pretending to rehabilitate in
5 some way the ancient philosophy, and to recall *postliminio*[2] the nearly banished substantial forms <[3]> – but perhaps one will not condemn me easily
when it is known that I have long meditated on the modern philosophy,
that I have given much time to experiments in physics and to demonstrations in Geometry, and that I have long been persuaded by the vanity of
10 these Beings, that I have finally been obliged <[4]> in spite of myself to
take them up again as if by force, after having done my own studies which
made me recognise that our moderns do not give enough justice to St
Thomas, and to the other great men of that time; and there is much more
solidity in the sentiments of the Scholastic Philosophers and Theologians
15 than one imagines; provided that one uses them appropriately and in
their place. I am even persuaded that if some exact and meditative mind

---

[13] Struck from L[1]: (1) of forms and other con (2) of considerations (a) of substantial forms and (aa) if (bb) he employs the ext concourse

[14] Struck from L[1]: extraordinary

[15] Greek for 'principle' or 'origin' often conceived of as an animating, moving, or vital force, or 'the first point from which a thing either is or comes to be or is known' (Aristotle, *Metaphysics*, Bk V, 1013a1). Leibniz criticised a number of figures (e.g. Henry More, Paracelsus) for their appeal to occult qualities and plastic natures as principles of motion and change in mechanical phenomena. For numerous references see Loemker's index entries on 'archeus' and 'hylarchic' (LL). See especially Leibniz's *Specimen Dynamicum* (*Specimen of Dynamics* 1695, LL 441). For references to the 'world soul' see 'Reflections on the Doctrine of a Single Universal Spirit' (1702, LL 555).

[1] Added in L[2].

[2] 'After the threshold', a Latin juridical term used in the context of persons or goods being returned to their rightful place after banishment or war.

[3] Struck from l[2]: (which I do, however, only *on the hypothesis* that one can say that bodies are substances)

[4] Struck from L[1]: by these researches

would take the trouble to clarify and digest their thoughts in the manner of the analytic Geometers, he would find in them a treasure of many very important and wholly demonstrative truths.

XII. That the <¹> notions which consist in extension contain something imaginary and cannot constitute the substance of body.

But in order to take up again the thread of our considerations, I believe
5 that anyone who will meditate on the nature of substance, which I have explained above, will find <²> that the whole nature of body does not consist solely in extension, that is to say, in size, figure, and motion, but that one must necessarily recognise in it something that has some connection to souls and to what one commonly calls substantial form, such that it
10 changes nothing in the phenomena, no more than does the soul of beasts, if they have one. One can even demonstrate that <³> the notion of size, figure, and motion is not so distinct as one imagines, and that it contains something imaginary and relative to our perceptions, as do (although more so) colour, heat, and other similar qualities that one can doubt whether
15 they are truly found in the nature of things outside of us. It is why these sorts of qualities are not known⁴ to constitute any substance. And if there is no other principle of identity in bodies than what we just said, a body would never subsist for more than a moment. However, the souls and substantial forms of other bodies are very different from intelligent souls,
20 which alone know their actions, and which not only do not perish naturally, but even always retain <the foundation for>⁵ the knowledge of what they are; which renders them alone liable to punishment and reward, and makes them citizens of the Republic of the universe, of which God is the Monarch: it also follows that all other creatures must serve them, which we
25 will speak more fully about soon.

---

¹ Struck from L¹: (1) qualities (2) If there is nothing in body other than what consists in extension (3) the qualities of bodies
² In L¹ but struck from l²: either that bodies are not substances, in metaphysical rigour, (which was in effect the opinion of the Platonists) or
³ Several passages struck from L¹: (1) extension is not a clearly and distinctly known notion (2) figure and motion are not [. . .] (3) extension is not a primitive and distinctly known notion
⁴ 'ne sçaurois'
⁵ Added in l².

XIII. As the individual notion of each person contains once and for all everything that will ever happen to him, one sees in it the *a priori* proofs or reasons for the truth of each event, or why one has happened <1> rather than the other. But these truths, although
5 assured, are no less <2> contingent, being founded on the free choice[3] of God or of creatures. <4> <It is true that their>[5] choice always has its reasons <but they>[6] incline without necessitating.

But before going further, one must try to meet a great difficulty, which
10 can arise from the foundations we have set forth above. We have said that the notion of an individual substance contains once and for all everything that could ever happen to it, and that in considering this notion, one can see in it everything that could truly be said of it; as we can see in the nature of a circle all the properties that one can deduce from it. But it seems by
15 this <7> that the difference between contingent and necessary truths will be destroyed, <8> that human freedom will have no place, and that an absolute fate will reign over all our actions as well as over all other events in the world. To which I respond that one must make a distinction between what is certain and what is necessary: everyone agrees that future contin-
20 gents are assured, since God foresees them, but one does not admit that for this they are necessary. But, one will say, if some conclusion can <9> be deduced infallibly from a definition or notion, it will be necessary. Now indeed we maintain that all that must happen to some person is already included virtually in his nature or notion, as properties are in the definition
25 of a circle. Thus the difficulty still remains. To meet it firmly, I say that the connection or consecution is of two sorts: the one is absolutely necessary, the contrary of which implies a contradiction, and this deduction holds among the eternal truths such as those of Geometry; the other is necessary only *ex hypothesi*, and so to speak by accident, but it is contingent in itself,
30 when the contrary does not imply [contradiction]. And this connection is

---

[1] Struck from L[1]: and why it is reasonable
[2] Struck from L[1]: free
[3] 'arbitre'
[4] Struck from L[1]: although one sees in it the basis for judging what is the more reasonable, and consequently assured
[5] Replacing 'whose' in L[2].
[6] Replacing 'which' in L[2].
[7] Struck from L[1]: that all events will become necessary by a fate
[8] Struck from L[1]: (1) that the fate of the Stoics will take the place of freedom (2) and that an absolute fate [Note: AA says that this passage was struck from l[1]; but since l[1] is a fair copy of §§5, 6, and 7 only, 'l[1]' must be a typo.]
[9] Struck from L[1]: demonstrate

founded not on the completely pure ideas and on the simple understanding of God, but rather on his free decrees and on the series of the universe.

[10]We come to an example: since Julius Caesar will become perpetual dictator and master of the Republic and overthrow the liberty <of the Romans>,[11] <[12]> this action is included in his notion, since we suppose that it is the nature of such a perfect notion[13] of a subject to comprehend everything, so that the predicate may be contained[14] in it, *ut possit inesse subjecto*.[15] One could say that it is not in virtue of this notion or idea <[16]> that he must commit this action, <[17]> since it pertains to him only because God knows all. But one will insist that his nature or form answer to this notion, and since God has imposed this personage on him, it is henceforth necessary for him to satisfy it. I could reply to this by citing future contingents, for they do not yet have anything real, except in the understanding and will of God, and since God has given them this form in advance, they must all the same answer to it. But I prefer to resolve difficulties, rather than to justify them by the example of some other similar difficulties. And what I am going to say will serve to shed light on one as well as the other. It is now then that one must apply the distinction of connections; and I say that what happens in conformity with these prior conditions is assured, but it is not necessary, and if someone would do the contrary, he would do nothing impossible in itself, although it be impossible (*ex hypothesi*) that this happen. For if any man were capable of completing the whole *demonstration* by virtue of which he <could prove>[18] this connection of the subject who is <[19]> Caesar and the predicate that is his successful campaign, he would indeed reveal that the future Dictatorship of Caesar has its foundation in his notion or nature, that one sees in it a reason for why he had resolved to cross the Rubicon rather than to stop there, and why he had won instead of lost the day at Pharsalus, and that it was reasonable, and by consequence assured, that this would happen, but not that it is necessary in itself, nor that the contrary implies contradiction.

[10] A paragraph break seems to be indicated on L[1], but there is no break on l[2].
[11] Added in l[2].
[12] In L[1] Leibniz initially used the example of St Peter, before striking it out and changing it to Caesar: Let us suppose St Peter will deny our Lord
[13] The sense of 'perfect' here is 'complete' rather than 'excellent' or 'morally approved'.
[14] 'enfermé'
[15] 'so that it can be in the subject'
[16] Added and struck from L[1]: or (1) form (2) nature
[17] Struck from L[1], in reference to St Peter: that he will sin
[18] Changed in l[2] from 'would prove'.
[19] Approximately here in L[1] Leibniz had: St Peter and the predicate which is the denial, he would reveal that St Peter's renouncement

In almost the same way, it is reasonable and assured that God will always do the best, although what is less perfect implies no [contradiction].[20] For one would find that this *demonstration* <[21]> of this predicate of Caesar is not so absolute as those of numbers or of Geometry, but that it supposes
65 the series of things that God has chosen freely, and which is founded on the first free decree of God, which is always to bring about what is the most perfect; and on the decree that God has made (following the first) with regard to human nature, which is that man will always do (although freely) what would appear the best. Now every truth which is founded on
70 these sorts of decrees is contingent, even though it be certain; for these decrees do not change the possibility of things, and as I have already said, although God always chooses the best assuredly, this does not prevent what is less perfect from being and remaining possible in itself, even though it will not happen, for it is not its impossibility, but its imperfec-
75 tion which makes him reject it. Now nothing is necessary for which the opposite is possible. We shall therefore be in a position to meet these sorts of difficulties, however great they would appear (and indeed they are not less pressing in respect of all the others who have ever treated this matter) – provided that we consider well that all <[22]> contingent proposi-
80 tions have reasons to be thus rather than otherwise, or as well (what is the same thing) that they have *a priori* proofs of their *truth*, which render them certain and which show that the connection of the subject and the predicate of these propositions has its foundation in the Nature of the one and the other; but that they do not have demonstrations of *necessity*,
85 since these reasons are founded only on the principle of contingency, or of the existence of things, that is to say, on what is or appears to be the best among several other equally possible things; whereas necessary truths are founded on the principle of contradiction, and on the possibility or impos-sibility <[23]> of essences themselves without having regard in this to the
90 free will[24] of God or of creatures.

---

[20] This word does not appear in either draft, but it is implied by the grammatical construc-tion. Without it the phrase would read, 'what is less perfect is not implied', which makes little sense here.

[21] Struck from L[1]: of the action of St Peter

[22] Struck from L[1]: truths have reasons for their truth | which renders them certain | *a priori*

[23] Struck from L[1]: provided, I say, that one consider this distinction of things in itself

[24] 'volonté'

XIV. God produces diverse substances according to the different views that he has of the universe. And by the <intervention>[1] of God the nature proper to each substance brings it about that what happens to one corresponds[2] with what happens to all the others, without their
5   acting immediately upon each other.

After having learned to some degree in what the nature of <[3]> substances consists, we must try to explain the dependence they have on each other, and their actions and passions. Now it is first of all quite manifest that
10   created substances depend on God, who conserves them, and who even produces them continually by a kind of emanation, similar to how we produce our thoughts. For God turns, so to speak, on all sides and in all ways the general system of phenomena that he finds good to produce in order to manifest his glory, and regards all the faces of the world in all
15   possible ways; since there is no relation that escapes his omniscience, the result of each view of the universe, as regarded from a certain <place>,[4] is a substance that expresses the universe conforming to this view, if God finds it good to render his thought effective and produce this substance. And as God's view is always true, our perceptions are true as well, but those of
20   our judgments come from us and mislead us. Now, we have said above, and it follows from what we have just said, that each substance is like a world apart, independent of every other thing except God; thus all our phenomena, that is to say, all the things that can ever happen to us, are only consequences of our <[5]> being, and as these phenomena maintain a certain
25   order conforming to our nature or, so to speak, to the world that is in us, this enables us to make observations useful for regulating our conduct and which are justified by the success of future phenomena; and thus we can often judge the future by the past without being mistaken. This suffices to say that these phenomena are true[6] without troubling ourselves
30   with whether they are outside of us and whether others are also aware[7] of

---

[1] In L[1] Leibniz had written 'intervention' above 'mediation' and L[2] retained 'intervention'.

[2] 'répond'

[3] Struck from L[1]: created

[4] In L[1] Leibniz originally had 'point' but struck it and wrote 'place'.

[5] Struck from L[1]: (1) nature (a) and of our will | (since we are free substances) of our will

[6] 'veritable'

[7] 'apperçoivent', from 'apperception', a term which traditionally meant 'to reveal' or 'to realise' but which Leibniz had himself coined meaning an awareness of something in which one knows that one is aware (consciousness of self along with perception). The term is distinguished from mere 'perception' and thus marks an important distinction in his philosophy of mind. See *La 9ᵉ édition (1992–. . .) du Dictionnaire de l'Académie française*, <https://academie.atilf.fr/9/consulter/APERCEPTION?options=motExact>. Also see commentary on §33.

them; however, it is very true that the perceptions or <8> expressions of all substances mutually correspond,[9] such that each one following closely certain reasons or laws that it has observed meets with[10] the other who does the same, as when several people having agreed to meet in some place on
35 a certain prearranged day can do so effectively if they wish. Now although all express the same phenomena, this is not why their expressions should be perfectly similar, but it suffices that they be proportional, as several spectators believe they are seeing the same thing and indeed understand each other,[11] although each one sees and speaks according to the measure of
40 his view. And yet there is only God, (from whom <12> all individuals continually emanate, and who sees the universe not only as they see it, but also entirely differently from all of them)[13] who is the cause of this correspondence of their phenomena, and who makes what is particular to one public to everyone; otherwise there would be no association[14] among them. One
45 could therefore say in some way, and in a good sense, although removed from ordinary usage, that a particular substance never acts on another particular substance, nor suffers from another,[15] if one considers that what happens to each one is a consequence only of <16> its complete idea <or complete notion>[17] alone, since this idea already contains all predicates
50 or events and expresses the whole universe. In fact nothing can happen to us but thoughts and perceptions, and <18> all our future thoughts and perceptions are only consequences, although contingent, of our preceding thoughts and perceptions, such that if I were capable of considering distinctly everything that is happening or appearing to me at this time, I
55 could see there everything that will happen to me or that ever will appear to me; this would not fail and would happen to me all the same, even if everything outside of me were destroyed, provided there remained only God and me. But since we attribute to other things what we perceive[19] in a

---

8 Struck from L[1]: qualities
9 's'entrerepondent'
10 'se rencontre'
11 'entrentendent'
12 Struck from L[1]: all substances
13 The parentheses around this phrase appear only in l[2].
14 'liaison'
15 'nor suffers from another' could also be rendered as 'nor is acted upon by another'. 'To act upon' and 'to be acted upon' are equivalents for Aristotle's 'activity' and 'passivity', which are natural and constant states of substances, as explained in the commentary.
16 Struck from L[1]: (1) its nature (2) its essence
17 Added in l[2].
18 Struck from L[1]: our past perceptions
19 'appercevons'

47

certain manner as causes acting upon us, we must consider the foundation
60 of this judgment, and how much truth it has.

[20]It is established above all that when we desire some <phenomenon>,[21]
and it happens at the right time, and this occurs ordinarily, we say we have
acted and are the cause of it; as when I want, as we say, to move my hand.
65 Also, when it seems to me that by my will something happens to what I
call another substance, and that this would have happened to it thereby (as
I judge by frequent experiences), even when it had not willed this, I say
that this substance is passive,[22] as I admit it of myself when this happens
to me following the will of another substance. Also, when we have willed
70 something that happens, and yet what follows is something we have not
willed, we do not fail to say that we did it, provided we understood how
this follows from it. There are also some phenomena of extension that we
attribute to ourselves more particularly, and whose foundation *a parte rei*[23]
is called our body, and since everything considerable that happens to it,
75 that is to say, [when] all the notable changes in it that would appear to us
are strongly felt, at least ordinarily, we attribute all the passions[24] of this
body to ourselves, and with great reason; for even if we did not notice[25]
them at first, we do not fail to notice[26] well the consequences, as when we
have been transported from one place to another while sleeping. We also
80 attribute the actions of this body to ourselves, as when we run, hit, [or]
fall, and that <[27]> our body, continuing the motion commenced, makes
some effect. But I do not attribute to myself what happens to other bodies,
since I notice that major changes[28] can happen which are not sensible to
me, except if my body is exposed to them in a certain way that I conceive
85 to be proper. Thus one clearly sees that although all bodies in the universe

---

[20] In L[1] Leibniz had struck the following paragraph entirely and it did not appear in any
copy. Much of it seems to have been reworked in §15; but it is worth including here for
its clarification of the way in which we experience and express the modes of substance in
the metaphysical terms of activity and passivity. See commentary.

[21] In L[1], added in place of: perception

[22] 'patit', which can also mean 'is acted upon' or 'suffers'

[23] 'as a part of the thing' meaning a property belonging to a thing not merely conceptually
but as an inseparable part. So, here, extension is a conceptual abstraction of body, but
inseparable from it.

[24] Not strictly speaking *emotions*, but anything that *happens to* the body.

[25] 'apperceu'

[26] 'appercevoir'

[27] Struck from L[1]: this impulsivity [of]

[28] 'changemens'

belong to us in some way, and sympathise with ours, we do not attribute to ourselves what happens to them. For when my body is pushed, I say that I myself have been pushed, but when someone else has been pushed, although I may notice it, and this may give rise to some passion in me,
90 I do not say that I have been pushed, since I measure the place where I am by that of my body. And this language is very reasonable, because it is appropriate for clear expression in ordinary practice. We can say a few words about the mind, that our wills, and our judgments or reasonings are actions, but that our perceptions or sentiments are passions; and about
95 the body we say that the change which happens to it is an action when it is the consequence of a preceding change, but otherwise it is a passion. In general, to give our terms a sense which reconciles Metaphysics with practice, when several substances are affected by the same change (as indeed every change affects them all) we can say that the [substance] that
100 thereby immediately passes to a greater degree of perfection or continues in the same [degree], acts, but the one that becomes thereby immediately more limited, <29> such that its expressions become more confused, is acted upon.

XV. <1> The action of one <2> finite substance on another consists only in <3> the increase of degree of its expression, joined to a decrease in that of the other, inasmuch as God <4> <has formed them in advance so that they>5 accommodate themselves to one another.
5

But without entering into a long discussion, it suffices at present, in order to reconcile the language of Metaphysics with practice, to remark that we attribute to ourselves more, <6> and with reason, the phenomena that we express more perfectly, and we attribute to other substances what each
10 one expresses best. Thus a substance that is of an infinite extension, in as much as it expresses everything, becomes limited by the manner of its

---

29 Struck from L¹: that is to say which has less
1 In L¹ several attempts to begin this article preceded the first line: (1) Substances being limited, in as much as they imperfectly express God and the universe, impede each other and are obliged to accommodate themselves to one another (2) The nature (a) or expression (b) of each substance, or its expression of the universe being limited (3) One conceives that substances act
2 Struck from L¹: created
3 Struck from L¹: the augmentation of perfectio[n]
4 In L¹ but struck from L²: obliges them to
5 Added in L².
6 At this point in L¹, blocks of text were struck and passages added to replace them. The most notable deletions are: (1) the perceptions | or expressions | clearer and more

expression, more or less perfect. It is therefore in this way that one can conceive that substances impede or limit each other, and consequently one can say in this sense that they act on one another, and are obliged,
15 so to speak, to adapt themselves[7] to each other. For it can happen that a change which augments the expression of one, diminishes that of the other. Now the virtue of a particular substance is to express well the glory of God, and it is thereby less limited. And each thing when it exercises its virtue or power, that is to say when it acts, changes for the better, and
20 extends itself, in as much as it acts: when therefore a change happens by which several substances are affected (as indeed every change affects them all), I believe one can say that [the substance] that immediately passes thereby to a greater degree of perfection or to a more perfect expression exercises its power and *acts*, and that which passes to a lesser degree
25 makes known its weakness, and *suffers*.[8] I also hold that every action of a substance that has some perception introduces some *pleasure*,[9] and every passion some *pain*,[10] and *vice versa*.[11] However it can well happen that a present advantage is destroyed by a greater evil in the consequence, from whence it comes that one can sin while acting or exercising [one's] power
30 and finding some pleasure in it.

distinct, (a) and likewise one can in general attribute the clearer and more distinct expressions more to a substance [. . .] (b) the phenomena that we express more perfectly, [. . .] the whole virtue of a substance is to express well the glory of God, and in as much as we pass immediately to a more (2) [. . .] (a) And (aa) in this manner a substance (aaa) that would otherwise be (bbb) considered infinite becomes limited. (bb) following this consideration a substance supposed infinite passes for limited [. . .] one can conceive that they interfere and limit each other since it can happen that a change which augments the expression of one, diminishes that of the other [. . .]

Now the virtue of a substance is to express well the glory of God, and it is thus that it is less limited. Now (aaaaa) all action or passion (bbbbb) all action consists in a variation, and each thing, when it exercises its virtue or power, without being impeded or limited [. . .] that is to say when it acts, has the advantage in changing, in as much as it acts, or changes for the better and expands in as much as it acts. (c) Thus . . . perfection | or . . . the exercise [of] its power, and acts [. . .].

7 's'accommoder'
8 'patit' or 'suffers', or 'is passive' or 'is acted upon'
9 'volupté'
10 'douleur'
11 In L[1] only 'acts' and 'suffers' were underlined, while in l[2] those plus 'pleasure' and 'pain' but not 'vice versa' were underlined. Also in l[2] the sentence ending in 'and vice versa' does not end but continues with 'however' and so on.

XVI. The extraordinary concourse of God is included in what our
essence expresses, for this expression is extended to everything, but it
surpasses the forces of our nature or of our distinct expression
<which>[1] is finite and follows certain subaltern maxims.

It remains at present only to explain how <[2]> it is possible that God should
have at times some influence on men or on other substances by an extraordinary concourse and miracle, since it seems that nothing extraordinary
or supernatural can happen to them, seeing that all their events are only
consequences of their nature. But one must recall what we have said above
in regard to miracles in the universe, which are always in conformity with
the universal law of the general order, although they may be above the
subaltern maxims.[3] And in as much as every person or substance is like a
small world which expresses the large, one can equally say that <[4]> this
extraordinary action of God on this substance does not cease to be miraculous, although it is included in the general order of the universe, in as much
as it is expressed by the essence or individual notion of this substance. It
is why, if we include in our nature everything that it expresses, nothing is
supernatural to it, for it extends to everything, an effect always expressing
its cause, and God being the veritable cause of substances; <[5]> but since
what our nature expresses more perfectly belongs to it in a particular
manner, since its power consists in this, and that it is limited, as I am about
to explain, there are many things which surpass the forces of our nature,
and even [the forces] of all limited natures. Consequently, in order to speak
more clearly, I say that miracles and the extraordinary concourses of God
have this peculiarity, that they cannot be foreseen <[6]> by the reasoning
of any created mind, however enlightened it may be, because the distinct
comprehension of the general order surpasses them all. In contrast,
what one calls natural depends on less general maxims that creatures can

---

[1] Replacing 'la quelle' in L². In their footnote, AA omits 'distinct', though it is clearly
in L².
[2] Struck from L¹: God has influence on man by (a) his grace (b) an extraordinary and
miraculous concourse, since it appears that everything that must happen to him must be
natural, as much as it is a consequence of his substance
[3] See §7. Again, the universal order is the genus, of which physical laws and miracles are
species. As suggested by §7, God can change a physical law in order to cause a miracle.
[4] Struck from L¹: this extraordinary concourse
[5] In this area, struck from L¹: Because we are accustomed to attribute to our nature what
it expresses more particularly.
[6] Struck from L¹: and deduced

30   comprehend <⁷>. In order therefore that the words may be as irreproach-
able as the sense, it would be well to link certain manners of speaking with
certain thoughts, and one could call our essence <⁸> that which comprises
everything that we express, <⁹> and as it expresses our union with God
himself, it has no limits and nothing exceeds it. But that which is limited
35   in us could be called our nature or our power, and in this regard that which
exceeds the nature of all created substances is supernatural.

XVII. Example of a subaltern Maxim or Law of Nature; where it is
shown that God always conserves <regularly>¹ the same force, but not
the same quantity of motion, against the Cartesians and several others.

5   I have already made frequent mention of subaltern maxims, or Laws of
Nature,² and it seems it would be good to give an example of them: Our
new philosophers commonly make use of this famous <³> rule, <⁴> that
God always conserves the same quantity of motion in the world. Indeed
it is highly plausible, and in the past I held it as indubitable. But I have
10   since recognised a fault in it. It is that Mr Descartes and many other able
Mathematicians have believed that quantity of motion, <⁵> that is to say,
the speed multiplied by the size of the moving body, agrees entirely with
motive force; or, to speak <⁶> geometrically, that forces are composed of
proportions of speeds and bodies.⁷ Now it is <⁸> <⁹> reasonable that the
15   same force is always conserved in the universe. <¹⁰> Also, when we attend
carefully to the phenomena, we see very well that perpetual mechanical
motion has no place, because the force of a machine, <which is always
a bit diminished by friction and must soon run out, would restore itself

---

7 Struck from L¹: in order therefore to say nothing of these Maxims (a) which might be
shocking
8 AA has 'or idea' in L¹ and says it was omitted by the copyist in l². But Leibniz may have
intended to leave it out, because in l² he sees that 'ce qui' (that which) is missing and
inserts it without adding 'or idea'.
9 Struck from L¹: but what is limited in us, could
1 Added in L².
2 In §VII and §XVI.
3 Struck from L¹: maxim
4 Struck from L¹: advanced by Mr. Descartes
5 Struck from L¹: is the same thing as force, or [. . .] expresses it perfectly
6 Omitted in l²: more
7 AA note: see Descartes, *Principles* II, §36.
8 In L¹ but not in l² and l³: very
9 Struck from L¹: manifest
10 Struck from L¹: since taking the whole universe nothing resists it

and consequently>[11] would increase on its own, even without any new
20 impulsion from outside. One also observes that the force of a body is
diminished, only in proportion to the force it gives to some contiguous
body <or to its own parts, insofar as they have a separate motion>.[12] Thus
[the Cartesians] believed that what can be said about force can also be said
about quantity of motion. But to show the difference, I *assume* that a body
25 falling from a certain height acquires the force to regain [that height], if its
direction carries it thus, at least if it does not encounter any impediments;
for example, a pendulum would perfectly regain the height from which
it had descended, if the resistance of the air and other small obstacles did
not slightly diminish its acquired force. I also *assume* that as much force
30 is needed to raise a one-pound body A to a height of <[13]> four fathoms,
CD, as to raise a four-pound body B to a height of one fathom, EF.[14] All of
this is in accord with our new philosophers.[15] It is therefore apparent that
body A, having fallen from height CD, has acquired precisely as much
force as body B falling from height EF; for, body (B) having reached F
35 and from there having the force to rise again to E (by the first assumption),
consequently has the force to bring a body of four pounds, that is to say
its own body, to height EF at one fathom; and similarly body (A) having
reached D, and from there having the force to rise to C, has the force to
bring a body of one pound, that is to say its own body, to height CD at
40 four fathoms. Therefore (by the second assumption) the force of these two
bodies is equal. Now let us see whether the quantity of motion is also the
same on both sides: but at this point we will be surprised to find a very

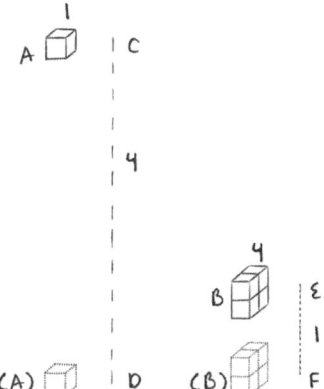

[11] In L[1] and added by Leibniz in l[2].
[12] In L[1] and added by Leibniz in l[2].
[13] Struck from L[1]: 20 feet as to raise a two-pound body to a height of ten feet
[14] The French *toise* roughly equals one fathom, or two metres.
[15] Leibniz draws a diagram like the following in both L[1] and l[2].

great difference. Now, it has been demonstrated by Galileo that the speed acquired by the fall *CD* <is double the speed acquired by the fall *EF*>,[16]
45 even though the height is quadruple. When therefore we multiply body *A*, which is as 1, by its speed, which is as 2, the product or quantity of motion will be as 2; and on the other side we multiply body *B*, which is as 4, by its speed, which is as 1, the product or the quantity of motion will be as 4;[17] thus, the quantity of motion of body (*A*) at point *D* is half the
50 quantity of motion of body (*B*) at point *F*, and yet their <[18]> forces are equal; therefore, there is a great difference between quantity of motion and force, as was needed to be shown. One sees by this how *force* must be estimated by the quantity of the effect that it can produce, for example by the height to which a heavy body of a certain size and kind can be raised,
55 which is very different from the speed that one can give to it. And to give it double the speed it must be given more than double the force. Nothing is simpler than this proof, and <[19]> Mr Descartes fell into error here only <[20]> because <[21]> he trusted his thoughts too much, <even when they were not yet developed enough>.[22] But <[23]> I am amazed that his follow-
60 ers had not noticed this fault since: and I am afraid that little by little they begin to imitate those Peripatetics,[24] whom they mock, and like them only become accustomed to consulting the books of their master, rather than reason and nature.

---

[16] In L^1 but added by Leibniz in l^2.

[17] Leibniz's expressions are a bit awkward in English. I have rendered the French 'qui est comme' literally as 'which is as', though perhaps 'comme' is best rendered here as 'as it were'. The likely reason Leibniz uses this expression in reference to the given quantities is that the units of measure for weight and speed need not be given; because whatever they are, the demonstration works by reference to the given quantities. See the commentary.

[18] Struck from L^1: forces are the same

[19] Struck from L^1: it is without doubt by precipitation | and by his accustomed confidence [. . .] | that Mr Descartes has (a) fallen in (b) here fallen in error (aa) since he (bb) trusting his first thoughts too much (cc) by a confidence (dd) confounding two things so different

[20] Struck from L^1: by his habitual confidence founded on the happy success of (a) his *Meditations* (b) [. . .] and on experiences he had of the penetration of his mind, which rendered him in the end a little too bold and too affirmative

[21] Struck from l^2: in the end

[22] Added by Leibniz in l^2.

[23] Struck from L^1: (1) it is impossible (2) these followers could not fail to notice their fault, if they had custom, as well as the Peripatetics, [. . .]

[24] Followers of Aristotle. Leibniz is accusing Descartes' followers of blindly following authority, in the way that the Moderns would accuse the Scholastics, and the Scholastics would accuse the Peripatetics.

XVIII. The distinction between force and quantity of motion is important, among other reasons, for judging that one must have recourse to metaphysical considerations separate from extension in
5 order to explain <¹> the phenomena of bodies.

This consideration of force distinguished from quantity of motion is rather important, not only in physics and mechanics for finding the true laws of nature and the rules of motion, and even for correcting several errors of practice which have slipped into the writings of some capable
10 Mathematicians, but also in metaphysics for understanding the principles better. For motion, <if one considers only what it comprehends precisely and formally, that is to say, a change of place,>² is not something entirely real, and when several bodies change situation among themselves, it is not possible to determine, by the sole consideration of these changes, to
15 which among them motion or rest must be attributed, as I could show geometrically, if I wished to dwell upon that now. But the force or proximate cause of these changes is something more real, and there is enough ground for attributing it to one body more than to another; also, it is only in this way that one can know to which the motion belongs more. Now,
20 this force is something different from size, figure, and motion, and we can judge thereby that not everything that is conceived in bodies consists <³> uniquely in extension <and in its modifications>⁴, as our moderns are persuaded. Thus we are still obliged to re-establish some beings or forms that they have banished. And it would seem more and more – even though
25 all the particular phenomena of nature can be explained mathematically or mechanically by those who understand them – that nevertheless the general principles of corporeal nature and of mechanics itself are metaphysical rather than Geometric, and belong to certain indivisible forms or natures as causes of the appearances rather than to corporeal mass or extension.
30 This is a reflection capable of reconciling the mechanical philosophy of the moderns with the circumspection of some intelligent and well-intentioned persons, who fear, with some reason, that we are moving too far away from immaterial beings, to the prejudice of <⁵> piety.

---

¹ Struck from L¹: the nature of bodies
² In l², this phrase had been mistakenly placed after 'Mathematicians'.
³ Struck from L¹: in these three notions
⁴ Added in l².
⁵ Struck from L¹: religion

XIX. The utility of final causes in physics.

Since I do not like to judge <1> people in a bad way, I do not accuse <2> our new philosophers <3>, who <pretend>4 to banish final causes from physics, but I am nevertheless obliged to confess <5> that the consequences
5 of this sentiment seem dangerous to me, especially when I join it to the one I have refuted at the beginning of this discourse, which seems bound to remove them altogether, as if God intended not one end or good in acting, or as if the good were not the object of his will.6 <7> I hold, on the
10 contrary, that it is there where one must seek the principle of all existences and of the Laws of nature, because God always intends the best and the most perfect. I am quite willing to admit that we are liable to fool ourselves when we want to determine the ends or councils of God, but this is only when we want to limit them to some particular design, believing that he
15 had only one thing in view, when instead he has regard for everything at the same time; as when we believe that God has made the world only for us, it is a great abuse, although it is very true that he has made everything in its entirety for us, and that there is nothing in the universe that does not concern us, and which is not also accommodated to the regard that he
20 has for us, following the principles set out above. Thus when we see some good effect, or some perfection that occurs or follows from God's works, we can say surely that God has intended it. For he does nothing by chance, and is not like us, sometimes avoiding to do good. This is why, very far from failing in this, as do the extreme politicians who imagine too much
25 sophistication in the designs of Princes, or as do the commentators who seek too much erudition in their author, we could not attribute too many reflections to this infinite wisdom, and there is no subject in which there is less error to fear while we make only affirmations, and provided that one here avoids negative propositions that limit the designs of God. All
30 those who see the admirable structure of animals find themselves drawn to recognise the wisdom of the author of things, and I counsel those who have some sentiment of piety and even some genuine Philosophy, to avoid the

---

1 Struck from L1: the intention of people, judging them only favourably, if I can
2 Struck from L1: and not even suspect someone [. . .] of some bad intention
3 Struck from L1: of impiety
4 In L1 replacing: want [The sense of 'pretend' here is closer to 'claim' rather than to 'imagine'.]
5 Struck from L1: that I do not recognise in it their spirit and their usual prudence. I will admit that it is not for man alone that all is done.
6 See §2. See also Descartes, *Principles* I, §28, and Spinoza, *Ethics* 1, Appendix, 109–15.
7 Omitted in l2: As for myself

phrases of certain would-be freethinkers,[8] who say that we see because it so happens we have eyes, without the eyes having been made in order to see.
35 When one is seriously given over to these sentiments that assign everything to the necessity of matter or to a certain chance (although both must appear ridiculous to those who understand what we have explained above), it is difficult to be able to recognise an intelligent author of nature. For the effect must correspond to its cause, and <it>[9] is even known best by knowledge of
40 the cause; and it is unreasonable to introduce a supreme[10] intelligence as the arranger of things, and then instead of employing his wisdom, to use only the properties of matter to explain the phenomena. As if in order to give an account of a conquest that a great Prince had made, in taking some place of importance, a Historian were to say it is because small particles of gun-
45 powder were set off by the touch of a spark, escaping with a speed capable of pushing a hard and heavy body against the walls of the fortress, while the branches of small particles composing the copper of the cannon were rather well interlaced, in order not to come apart by this speed; instead of making us see how the conqueror's foresight had made him choose the suitable time
50 and means, and how his power surmounted all obstacles.

XX. A <memorable>[1] passage of Socrates in Plato's *Phaedo* against the overly materialistic philosophers.

This reminds me of a beautiful passage of Socrates in Plato's *Phaedo*,
5 which marvellously conforms to my sentiments on this point, and seems to be made expressly against our overly materialistic philosophers. This connection has also given me the urge to translate it, even though it is a bit long. Perhaps this excerpt could give occasion for some of us to share in many other beautiful and solid thoughts which are found in the writings of
10 this <[2]> famous author.

[To be Inserted here from Plato's Phaedo *where Socrates ridicules Anaxagoras, who introduces Mind without using it.][3]*

15 One day, said Socrates, I heard someone read from a book of Anaxagoras, where there were these words, *that an intelligent being* was the cause of

---

[8] 'esprits forts pretendus'
[9] Added to l[2].
[10] 'souveraine'
[1] In L[2], replacing 'remarkable' in L[1].
[2] Struck from L[1]: great man
[3] '*Inseratur locus ex Phaedone Platonis ubi Socrates Anaxagoram irridet, qui Mentem intro-ducit nec ea utitur.*' In L[1] this phrase, written in Leibniz's hand, in Latin and between

all things, and that *it had arranged and adorned them*. This pleased me extremely, for I believed that if the world were the effect of an intelligence, everything would have been made in the most perfect manner
20 that had been possible. That is why I believed that anyone who wished to explain why things come to be, or perish, or subsist, would need to search for what is suitable to the perfection of each thing. Thus a man would only have to consider in himself or in some other thing what would be the best and most perfect. For anyone who knew the most perfect <would easily
25 judge>[4] thereby what would be imperfect, because the science of the one and of the other is the same. Considering all this, I rejoiced to have found a master who could teach the reasons of things: for example whether the earth be round rather than flat, and why it had been better to make it thus rather than otherwise. Moreover, I expect in saying that the earth is
30 or is not in the middle of the universe, he would explain to me why this had been the most suitable. And that he would tell me as much about the sun, the moon, the stars, and their motions. And that finally after having shown what would be suitable to each thing in particular, he would show me what would be the best in general. Full of this hope, I gathered and
35 I skimmed through the books of Anaxagoras with great eagerness, but I found myself very far from my expectation. For I was surprised to see that he made no use of this governing Intelligence that he had put forward, that he would no longer speak of the adornment and perfection of things, and that he would introduce certain <[5]> ethereal matters, hardly

---

brackets, is immediately followed by §XXI. l² simply has a blank space between §XX and §XXI. Leibniz never provided the intended passage, which is approximately 97c–99c in *Phaedo*. However, he had closely paraphrased/translated that passage, likely based on the original Greek, at least twice: in March 1676, in Latin, as part of an abridgement of the whole dialogue (*Platonis Phaedo Contractus*, AA VI, 3 N. 20, 284–97); and then in 1678–80, in French, as the final two paragraphs of *Sentiments de Socrates Opposes aux Nouveaux Stoiciens et Epicureens* (AA VI, 4 N. 263, 1384–88). This text was printed in Gerhardt (VII, 333–6), though not along with the *Discourse*, and is well known in English as 'Two Sects of Naturalists' (AG 281–4). Lestienne places these concluding paragraphs at the end of §XX, reproducing them, with minor differences, from Gerhardt; and LG and MB and translate Lestienne's version. The Akademie Edition also includes the relevant *Phaedo* passage but takes it from the manuscript version of *Sentiments de Socrates*. There is no way to know for certain which version, Latin or French, or either, Leibniz intended to insert; but I think the French version is best. It is longer, more eloquent, and better reflects Leibniz's intention in the *Discourse* to oppose the 'overly materialistic philosophers', as expressed in lines 2 and 6 above. I translate the Akademie's excerpt, but from AA VI, 4 N. 263, because it shows the variants. I also translate Leibniz's Latin version, which follows, because it contains interesting differences.

[4] Struck from manuscript: could easily understand
[5] Struck from manuscript: subtle

40 convincing. In this he had done as someone having said that Socrates does
things with intelligence, and coming by afterward to explain in particular
the causes of his actions, would say that he is seated here because he has
a body composed of bones, skin, and nerves, that the bones are solid, but
that they have gaps or joints, that the nerves can be stretched or relaxed,
45 that it is by this that the body is flexible and finally that I am seated. Or, if
wanting to explain this present discourse, he would have recourse to
the air, to the organs of voice and hearing and similar things, forgetting
however the true causes, namely that the Athenians believed it would be
better to condemn me than to absolve me, and that I believed it better for
50 me to remain seated here than to flee. For by my faith,[6] without this, these
nerves and bones would have been with the Boeotians and Megarians[7]
long ago, if I had not found it more just and more honourable[8] for me to
suffer the penalty that the country wished to impose on me, than to live
elsewhere vagabond and exiled. This is why it is unreasonable to call these
55 bones and nerves and their motions causes. It is true that those who would
say that I could not do all this without bones and nerves would be right.
But the true cause is something else, while this is only a condition without
which the [true] cause could not be a cause. These people who say, for
example, that only the motion of bodies surrounding the earth keeps the
60 earth where it is, forget that the divine power disposes everything in the
most beautiful way, and do not comprehend that <[9]> it is the good and
the beautiful which together form and maintain the world. Up to here,
Socrates, for what follows in Plato on the ideas or forms is not less <[10]>
excellent, but a bit more difficult.
65

[Translation of approximately the same passage from Leibniz's Latin
abridgement of Plato's *Phaedo*:]

Thus as I often meditated on these things, I heard by chance about a Book
70 of Anaxagoras, which taught that the mind arranges everything and is the
cause of everything. With this kind of cause I was greatly delighted, since,
if mind arranges everything, I thought, then each thing is ordered, and
would be ordered in the best way. And so if anyone should inquire into
the generation or perishing of a thing, he need only ask what is the best for

---

[6] The expression that Plato uses here is 'by the dog', a common Greek expression which
     refers to the dog-headed Egyptian god Anubis.
[7] The city-state of Megara was located about 37 km west of Athens, and Boeotia 85 km
     northwest.
[8] 'honneste'
[9] Struck from manuscript: it is only the sovereign beauty which makes that
[10] Struck from manuscript: beautiful

75 each one. But he who knows what is best also understands what is worse, since the one and the other belong to the same science. Thus to particular things is assigned what is best for each, and then to all things, the common good. But when I obtained Anaxagoras' books themselves, my hopes were completely crushed. For he did not go on to use Mind to explain the

80 arrangement of things, but rather invented certain ethereal things, such as air and water; and this would be just as if someone were to say that my mind causes me to do everything, and then in citing the reason I sit here, alleges it is my bones and sinews and manner of sitting; and that the cause of my speech was air and tongue, all the while forgetting the true causes,

85 namely that the Athenians saw it better to condemn me, and I saw it better to sit here. For surely, as I believe, these bones and sinews would already be among the Megarians or Boeotians, as if carried off by the best option, if I had not considered it more just and more honourable to pay the civil penalty, rather than to escape and live in exile. But if someone were to say

90 that my sitting here would not be possible without bones and sinews, he will have spoken rightly; but he must not say that these are causes. When, therefore, I could not find within myself, nor learn from another the causes of things taken from the choice of the best, I embarked, as it were, on a second voyage, another entry point, and turned my mind toward another

95 kind of cause remaining for me; one that, even if it does not explain everything, does not suffer to say anything false. I began without doubt to turn my mind away from the things themselves toward the contemplation of the forms or reasons for them; whatever is not in harmony with them, I boldly declare to be false; and whatever follows from them, is true; the rest

100 I leave in the middle. Now these things will suffice for you to understand the demonstration of the immortality of the Mind.

XXI. If mechanical rules depended solely on Geometry without Metaphysics the phenomena would be entirely different.

Now since God's wisdom has always been recognised in the detail of the
5 mechanical structure of certain particular bodies, it must also be displayed in the general economy of the world and in the constitution of the laws of nature. This is so true that we observe the councils of this wisdom in the laws of motion in general. For if there were in bodies only an extended mass[1] and <if there were>[2] in motion only change of place,[3] and <if>[4]

---

[1] Descartes, *Principles* II, §4.
[2] Added in l[2].
[3] Descartes, *Principles* II, §25.
[4] In l[2], replacing: that

10 everything must and could be deduced from these definitions by geometric necessity alone,[5] it would follow, as I have shown elsewhere, that a smaller body, upon contact with a greater body at rest, would impart <[6]> its speed [to that body] without losing <any of its own; and one would have to admit>[7] many other <[8]> such rules completely contrary to the formation
15 of a system.[9] But the decree of divine wisdom to conserve always the same force and the same direction in sum[10] has provided for this. I even find that several effects of nature can be demonstrated doubly, namely by consideration of the efficient cause; and also separately by consideration of the final cause, by using, for example, the decree of God always to produce his effect
20 in the easiest and most determined ways, as I have shown elsewhere in accounting for the rules of catoptrics and dioptrics, about which I will say more later.[11]

XXII. Reconciliation of the two ways, <of which one goes by final causes and the other by efficient causes>[1], in order to <[2]> satisfy both those who explain nature mechanically and those who have recourse
5 to incorporeal natures.

It is good to make this remark to reconcile those who hope to explain mechanically the formation <[3]> of the first tissue of an animal, and of the whole machine of the parts, with those who account for this same structure by final causes. Both are good, both can be useful not only for admiring the
10 artifice of the great worker, but also for discovering something useful in physics and in medicine. And the authors who follow these different routes should not mistreat each other. For I see that those who set out to explain

---

[5] Descartes, *Principles* II, §64 and IV, §206.
[6] Struck from L¹: all its speed
[7] Added in l², replacing: any of its own; and
[8] Struck from L¹: rules of this nature
[9] Other editions (LL, LG, MB) have cited Leibniz's 'Theory of Abstract Motion' (1671, AA VI, 2 / LL, 139–42) as the place which showed the mistake in this rule. However, AG provides the reference to 'On the Nature of Body and the Laws of Motion', AG 249 (titled in AA VI, 4 N. 362, 'Principia Mechanica Ex Metaphysicis Dependere', 1678–80/81). See §21 of the commentary.
[10] 'Direction in sum' is what we now call conservation of linear momentum, the product of a body's mass and velocity (the latter being a vector quantity).
[11] The work referred to is *Unicum opticae, catoptricae et dioptricae principium*. On this work and the rules of reflection and refraction (catoptrics and dioptrics) see §22 of the commentary.
[1] Added in L².
[2] Struck from L¹: defend
[3] Struck from L¹: of the foetus

the beauty of the divine anatomy, mock others who imagine that a movement of certain fluids that appears fortuitous could have produced such a
15 variety <⁴> of members, and treat these latter persons as rash and profane. And those latter, on the contrary, treat the former as simplistic and superstitious, as resembling those ancients who would take physicists⁵ to be impious when [these physicists] maintained that it is not Jupiter who thunders, but some matter which is found in the clouds.⁶ The best would be to join both
20 considerations; for, if it is permitted to use a base comparison, I recognise and <⁷> praise the skill of a worker not only for showing what plans he had while making the parts of his machine, but also for explaining the instruments he used to make each part, especially when these instruments are simple and ingeniously contrived. And God is a skilful enough artisan to
25 produce a machine a thousand times more ingenious <⁸> than that of our body, while using only some rather simple fluids formed expressly so that only the ordinary laws of nature are needed to sort them out as necessary in the end to produce so admirable an effect: but it is also true that this would not happen <⁹> if God were not the author of nature.
30 However, I find that the way of efficient causes, which is in fact more profound, and in some way more immediate and *a priori*,¹⁰ is, in recompense, rather difficult when it comes to detail; and I believe that our philosophers are most often still very far from it. But the way of final [causes] is easier and not without frequent use for divining the important
35 and useful truths that one would be seeking a long time by the other, more physical, route <¹¹>, of which anatomy can furnish considerable examples. I also maintain that Snell,¹² who is the first discoverer of the rules of refraction, <¹³> would have waited a long time to find them, if he had first wanted to find out how light is formed. But he apparently followed

---

⁴ Struck from L¹: of organs
⁵ 'physiciens'.
⁶ A similar example can be found in Plato's *Apology* (26d), where Socrates is accused of not believing in the state-sanctioned gods, and of being a physicist (a pre-Socratic philosopher), that is, one who says the sun and moon are not gods, but a rock and a mass of earth.
⁷ Struck from L¹: admire equally
⁸ Struck from L¹: if it is possible
⁹ Struck from L¹: or seldom
¹⁰ Leibniz's use of '*a priori*' in reference to efficient causes follows an older (pre-Kantian) use of the term which means reasoning 'from causes to effects', as opposed to reasoning from effects and inferring back to causes, which would be *a posteriori*.
¹¹ Struck from L¹: and which is more *a priori*
¹² Willebrord Snellius, Dutch astronomer and mathematician, 1580–1626.
¹³ Added and struck from L¹: which he had taught publicly in Holland, (although death had prevented him from publishing his work, which we know to have been completed)

40 the method which the ancients used for catoptrics, which is in fact by final [causes]. For, in searching for the <[14]> easiest way to conduct a ray from one given point to another given point by reflection on a given plane, <supposing that this is the intention of nature>,[15] they found the equality of the angles of incidence and of reflection, <as one can see in a little treatise of
45 Heliodor of Larissa, and elsewhere>.[16] This is what Mr Snell, as I believe, and after him (although without knowing anything of him) Mr Fermat,[17] have applied more ingeniously to refraction. For when rays in the same media observe the same proportion of sines, which is also that of the resistances of the media, this is found to be the easiest way, or at least the most
50 determined, for passing from a given point in one medium to a given point in another. And the demonstration of this same theorem that Mr Descartes wished to give by the way of efficient [causes] is far from being as good.[18] At least there is room to <suspect>[19] that he would never have found it that way, if he had not learned anything in Holland of Snell's discovery.

XXIII. To return to immaterial substances, we explain how God acts on the understanding of minds, and whether we always have the idea of what we think.

5 I found it appropriate to insist a bit on these considerations of final causes, <[1]> incorporeal natures, and an intelligent cause in relation[2] to bodies, to make known their use even in physics and mathematics: on one hand to purge the mechanical philosophy of the profanity that has been imputed to it, and on the other hand to elevate the mind of our philosophers from
10 material considerations alone to more noble meditations. Now it will be appropriate to return from bodies to immaterial natures and particularly to minds, and to say something of the means God employs to enlighten them and act on them, where one must not doubt but that there are also certain

---

[14] Struck from L[1]: shortest
[15] Added in L[1] from the margin.
[16] Added in L[1] from the margin. Leibniz is referring to Heliodor von Larissa's *Opticorum libri II* (E. Bartholinus, Paris 1657). According to AA, a later publisher (R. Schoene, Berlin 1897) attributed this work to Heliodor's son or pupil Damianos. See commentary.
[17] Pierre Fermat, French lawyer and mathematician, 1601–65.
[18] See Descartes, *Dioptrique*, §2 (AT VI, 93–105 / '*Optics*', Second Discourse, pp. 75–83). Also see Leibniz's *Unicum opticae . . .* (LU).
[19] In L[1] and l[2] 'doubt' was struck and 'suspect' added.
[1] Struck from L[1]: (1) and efficient causes to make them (2) intelligent causes which can make them
[2] 'rapport'

laws of nature, about which I could speak more fully elsewhere. Now it will
15 suffice to touch on something of ideas, and whether we see all things in God,
and how God is our light.[3] Now, it will be appropriate to remark that the
inadequate use of ideas gives occasion to several errors. For when we reason
about something, we imagine ourselves to have an idea of this thing, and
that is the foundation on which some ancient and new philosophers have
20 built a certain demonstration of God, which <[4]> is very imperfect. For,
they say, it must be that I have an idea of God or of a perfect being, since
I am thinking of it, and one cannot think without an idea; now the idea of
this being contains all perfections, and existence is one [of them], consequently [this being][5] exists. But as we often think of impossible chimeras,
25 for example, of the ultimate degree of speed, of the greatest number, of the
intersection of the conchoid with its base or rule,[6] this reasoning does not
suffice. It is therefore in this sense that one can say that there are true and
false ideas, according to whether the thing that [the idea] is about is possible or not. And it is then that one can boast of having an idea of the thing,
30 when one is assured of its possibility. Thus the argument above proves at
least that God necessarily exists, if he is possible. This is in fact an excellent
privilege of the divine nature, to have need only of its possibility or essence
to exist actually, and it is precisely this that one calls an *Ens a se*.[7]

---

[3] Note from AG: See Malebranche, *Search after Truth*, III, 2, 6.

[4] Added and struck from L[1]: to speak rigorously

[5] 'il'

[6] A conchoid is the shape of a line formed by a circle whose midpoint moves across a base
line. A line is drawn through the diameter of the circle to some fixed point outside the
circle and below the base. As the circle moves along the base, from one side of the fixed
point to the other, the two endpoints of the diameter, maintaining their alignment with
the fixed point, will trace a conchoid above and below the base. No matter how short
the distance from the base line to the fixed point, the extreme ends of the conchoid will
infinitesimally approach, but never intersect, the base line along which the circle moves.
This way of constructing a conchoid, which cannot easily be done using only compass
and ruler, was used by Nicomedes in 200 BCE to trisect an acute angle.

[7] A term of Scholastic philosophy, 'being from itself', or, a being which exists necessarily
from itself, as opposed to existing from another (*ens ab alio*); also an attribute called the
'aseity' of God. For example, '[God] does not have [perfection] from another but from
the formal eminence of his own nature' (Suarez (1597) *Metaphysical Disputations*, 30.1.2,
trans. Penner). See also, 'The Division of Being into Being by Itself and Being from
Another' (*Meta. Disp.* 28.1.6, trans. Doyle).

XXIV. What is clear or obscure knowledge;[1] distinct or confused; adequate, <or inadequate, intuitive>[2] or suppositive; nominal, real, causal, and essential definition.

5 To understand better the nature of ideas, we must touch on something of the varieties of knowledge. <[3]> When I can recognise one thing among others, without being able to say in what its differences[4] or properties consist, the knowledge is *confused*. It is thus that we know sometimes *clearly*, without being in doubt in any way whether a poem or painting is
10 done well or badly, because there is an *I know not what*[5] which satisfies or shocks us. But when I can explain the marks that I have, the knowledge is called *distinct*. And such is the knowledge of an assayer, who discerns the true from the false by means of certain proofs or marks[6] which make up the <[7]> definition of gold. But distinct knowledge has degrees, for ordinarily
15 the notions which enter into the definition would themselves need definition and are known only confusedly. But when everything that enters into a definition or distinct knowledge is known distinctly, down to the primitive notions, I call this *adequate* knowledge. And when my mind comprehends at once and distinctly <[8]> all the primitive ingredients of a notion, it
20 has an *intuitive* knowledge of it, <[9]> which is very rare, most of human knowledge being only confused or merely *suppositive*.[10] It is also good to distinguish nominal and real definitions: I call a definition *nominal* when one can still doubt whether the notion defined is possible, as for example

---

[1] 'connoissance'

[2] As in L[2].

[3] Added then struck from L[1]: When I know the possibility of the thing only from experience, (a) the idea that I have of it is (b) the know (c) because all that exists is possible, the knowledge is confused, | it is thus that we know bodies and their | but when I can prove its possibility *a priori*, this knowledge is distinct

[4] That is, species differences.

[5] '*je ne sçay quoy*'

[6] 'Marks', according to Hobbes, are 'sensible moniments . . . by which our past thoughts may be not only reduced, but also registered every one in its own order', Molesworth, Vol. I, *Elements of Philosophy, Concerning Body*: Part I, Ch. II, Of Names, §1, pp. 13–14.

[7] Struck from L[1]: nominal

[8] Struck from L[1]: all this analysis

[9] Marginal note on L[1] by Leibniz in Latin: NB: A notion is intermediate between intuitive and clear when I have at least a clear cognition of the ingredients of all notions.

[10] Also called 'symbolic'.

if I say <[11]> that an endless screw[12] is a solid line <[13]> whose parts are
25 congruent or can be superimposed on one another;[14] anyone who does not
know <[15]> from elsewhere what an endless screw is could doubt whether
such a line is possible, although in fact this is a reciprocal property <[16]>
of the endless screw; for, other lines whose parts are congruent (which are
only the circumference of the circle and the straight line), are *planar*, that
30 is to say which can be described *in plano*.[17] This shows that every reciprocal
property can serve as a nominal definition; but when the given property
makes known the possibility of the thing, it makes the definition real. And
as long as one has only a nominal definition, one cannot be sure of the
consequences that are drawn from it; for if it conceals some contradiction
35 or impossibility, one could draw opposing conclusions from it. This is
why truths do not depend on names and are not arbitrary, as some new
philosophers have believed.[18] For the rest, there is still considerable difference between <the species of>[19] real definitions, for when the possibility
is proved only by experience, as in the definition <[20]> of quicksilver,[21]
40 which we know the possibility of because we know that such a body is
actually found, which is an extremely heavy fluid and nevertheless rather

[11] Struck from L[1]: that (a) the circle is a plane figure, of which (b) the circle is (c) the Helix
     is
[12] A 'vis sans fin', also called a 'worm screw' or 'Archimedes screw', used, for example, as
     part of the tuning mechanism on a guitar. Leibniz used a large worm screw for the hori-
     zontal windmill he designed for pumping water out of the Harz mountains silver mines.
     See <https://www.gwlb.de/Leibniz/Leibnizarchiv/english/Leibniz_Life/windmill.
     htm>
[13] Added then struck from L[1]: (1) (that is to say what cannot be described on a plane) (2)
     (that is to say which passes through several parallel planes between them)
[14] That is, if you take any part of the line and stack it onto any other part of the line, the
     two lines will be congruent. For a line that spirals, this property may not be immediately
     apparent.
[15] Struck from L[1]: the Helix
[16] Struck from L[1]: of the cycloid [a cycloid is a curve generated by a point on the rim of a
     circle, as the circle is rolled along a straight line.]
[17] In other words, one can easily see that the parts of a plane, a two-dimensional figure,
     such as a straight line or a circle, are congruent; but it is not immediately apparent that
     the parts of a three-dimensional figure, like the endless screw, are congruent.
[18] Leibniz frequently accuses Hobbes of arguing that truth depends on how words are
     defined, rather than on the ideas represented by the words. For Leibniz, ideas have a
     reality independent of the names given to them. See 'Preface to an Edition of Nizolius'
     (1670), LL 128. Also see Hobbes, in Molesworth, Vol. I, *Concerning Body*, Part 1, Ch. II,
     Of Names, §§2–5, pp. 14–17; and Hobbes, *Elements of Law: Natural and Politic* [1640],
     Part I, Ch 5, §§1–7, pp. 17–20.
[19] Added in l[2].
[20] Struck from L[1]: of gold, it is still rather imperfect
[21] mercury

volatile, the definition is merely *real* and nothing more; but when proof of the possibility is made *a priori*, the definition is both <*real* and>[22] *causal*, as when it contains the possible generation of the thing. And when it pushes
45 the analysis to the end, as far as the primitive notions, without supposing anything that needs proof <[23]> *a priori* of its possibility, the definition is perfect or *essential*.

XXV. In what case our knowledge is joined to the contemplation of the idea.

Now it is manifest that we have no idea of a notion when it is impossible.
5 And when the knowledge is only *suppositive*, when we do have the idea, we do not contemplate it, for such a notion is known only in the same manner as occultly impossible notions,[1] and if it is possible, <[2]> it is not by this manner of knowing that one learns [of its possibility]. For example, when I think of a thousand, or of a chiliagon, I often do it without contemplat-
10 ing the idea, as when I say that a thousand is ten times a hundred, without putting myself to the trouble of thinking <[3]> what 10 and 100 are, because I *suppose* I know it and do not believe I have need at present to stop and conceive it. Thus it could well happen, as it happens in fact rather often, that I am mistaken in regard to a notion that I suppose or believe I under-
15 stand, although in truth it is impossible, or at least incompatible with other [notions] to which I have joined it. And whether I am mistaken or not, <[4]> this suppositive manner of conceiving remains the same. It is therefore only when our knowledge is *clear* in confused notions, or when it is *intuitive* in distinct notions that we <[5]> see the whole idea of it. <[6]>

XXVI. We have all ideas in us; and on Plato's reminiscence.

In order to conceive well what an idea is, one must prevent an equivocation, for several others[1] take the idea for the form or difference of our thoughts,

---

[22] Added in l².
[23] Struck from L¹: of its possibility *a priori*
[1] That is, notions containing a hidden impossibility.
[2] Struck from L¹: it is from elsewhere that one must know it
[3] Struck from L¹: of the definition of 10 and of 100
[4] Struck from L¹: that does not do anything to this manner of conceiving
[5] Struck from L¹: contemplate
[6] Struck from L¹: However we actually have in mind all possible ideas and even think of them | at all times | in a confused manner.
[1] AA note: for example, Simon Foucher, see VI, 3 N. 21, 315. [Translated in LL 155, where Leibniz notes that Foucher distinguishes ideas as (a) the quality or form of thought and (b) the immediate object or cause of perception.]

5   and in this manner we have the idea in mind only insofar as we think it,
and every time we think it anew, we have other ideas of the same thing,
although similar to the first. But it seems that some others take the idea
for an immediate object of thought, or for some <²> permanent form that
remains when we do not contemplate it. And in fact <³> our soul always

10 has in it the quality of representing to itself some nature or form whatsoever, when the occasion to think of it presents itself. And I believe that this
quality of our soul, insofar as it expresses some nature, form, or essence,
is properly the idea of the thing, which is in us, and which is always in us,
whether we think of it or not. For our soul expresses God and the universe,

15 and all essences as well as all existences. <⁴> This agrees with <my>⁵ principles, for nothing enters the mind naturally from the outside, and it is a
bad habit <⁶> that we have to think as if our soul receives some messenger
species and as if it had doors and windows.⁷ We have all these forms in the
mind, and even from all time, because the mind always expresses all of its

20 future thoughts, <⁸> and already thinks confusedly about everything that
it will ever think distinctly. And nothing can be learned whose idea we do
not already have in the mind, which [idea] is as the matter from which that
thought is formed. This is what Plato so excellently considered when he
put forward his *reminiscence*,⁹ which is very solid, provided that one takes

25 care to purge it of the error of pre-existence, and that one does not imagine
that earlier the soul must already have known and thought distinctly
what it learns and thinks now. He also confirmed his sentiment by a fine
experiment, introducing a <¹⁰> little boy that he leads imperceptibly to
some very difficult truths of Geometry, touching on incommensurables,

30 without teaching him anything, solely by posing questions in order and

---

² Struck from L¹: subsistent
³ Struck from L¹: one cannot deny that our soul has in it (a) the quality of expressing some
nature that (b) always the quality of us
⁴ Struck from L¹: (1) It is this that one must understand (2) Also we see that (3) This (a)
follows from (b) accords with
⁵ As in l². L¹ has: our
⁶ Struck from L¹: of thought, when we conceive our soul as if it
⁷ Compare with *Monadology* §7: 'Monads have no windows through which anything
could enter them or depart from them. Accidents cannot become detached, or wander
about outside of substances, as the sensible species of the Scholastics once did' (trans.
Strickland). The notion of 'messenger species' comes from the ancient Epicurean,
Lucretius' theory of perception: 'there are what we call images of things stripped off the
surface layers of substances, like membranes – these fly to and fro in air' (Lucretius, *De
Rerum Natura*, Bk IV, lines 39–41, trans. Johnston, p. 138).
⁸ Added then struck from L¹: although confusedly
⁹ Or *recollection*. Emphasis in the text. See Plato's *Phaedo*, 72e–77a.
¹⁰ Struck from L¹: (1) child in his dialogue entitled *Meno*, that he removes

apropos.[11] This shows that our soul knows all this virtually, and only has need of *animadversion*[12] to know the truths, and consequently that it <[13]> has at least the ideas on which these truths depend. One can even say that it already possesses these truths, when one takes them for relations of ideas.

XXVII. <[1]> How our soul can be compared to blank tablets, and how our notions come from the senses.

Aristotle preferred to compare our soul to tablets still blank, where
5 there is space <[2]> for writing,[3] and he maintained that nothing is in our understanding that does not come from the senses.[4] That accords better with popular notions, as in the manner of Aristotle, whereas Plato goes deeper. However, these sorts of Doxologies[5] or practicologies[6] can pass into ordinary usage, much as we see that those who follow Copernicus
10 do not stop saying that the sun rises and sets. I even find that one can often give a good sense to them, according to which they have nothing false, as I have already remarked on what way one can truly say that particular substances act on each other, and in this same sense one can also say that we receive <[7]> knowledge from outside by ministry of the
15 senses, because some external things contain or express more particularly the reasons which determine our soul to certain thoughts. But when it is about the exactitude of metaphysical truths, it is important to recognise

[11] AA note: See *Meno*, 82b–85c.
[12] Or *attention*. Etymologically, a turning of the mind towards something. Underlined in l[2]. The word is also used to mean 'critical thoughts'.
[13] Added then struck from L[1]: knows them already
[1] Struck from L[1]: In what sense our
[2] Struck from L[1]: to write everything
[3] The relevant passage in Aristotle likely is: 'Have we not already disposed of the difficulty about interaction involving a common element, when we said that mind is in a sense potentially whatever is thinkable, though actually it is nothing until it has thought? What it thinks must be in it just as characters may be said to be on a writing-tablet on which as yet nothing actually stands written: this is exactly what happens with mind' (*On the Soul*, Bk III, Ch. 4, 430a1).
[4] This phrase, often rendered in Latin as *nihil est in intellectu quod non sit prius in sensu*, often attributed to Aristotle, and often cited as an axiom among Scholastic philosophers, does not occur in Aristotle, but rather in Aquinas (see *On Truth*, q.2, a.3, arg. 19). Some passages in Aristotle, however, do suggest it. See *On the Soul*, Bk III, Ch. 8, 432a3–8; *Nicomachean Ethics*, Bk VI, Ch. 3; *Posterior Analytics*, Bk I, 81a38–9, but especially Bk II, Ch. 19. Also see Leibniz's take on the Aquinian phrase (LRB II.i.2.111).
[5] In a liturgical context, a hymn sung in praise of God.
[6] Probably refers to a common or traditional way of speaking.
[7] Struck from L[1]: species and knowledge by the senses

the extent <8> and independence of our soul, which goes infinitely
further <9> than the vulgar think, although in ordinary usage of life, one
20 attributes to it only what one apperceives more manifestly, and which
belongs to us in a particular manner, for it serves nothing to go further. It
would be good however to choose proper terms for the one sense and the
other, to avoid equivocation. Thus those <10> expressions which are in
our soul, whether we conceive them or not, can be called *ideas*, but those
25 which we conceive or form can be called *notions, concepts*. But in whichever
way one takes it, it is always false to say that all our notions come from the
senses that we call exterior, for the one that I have of myself and of my
thoughts and consequently of being, substance, action, identity, and of
many others, come from an internal experience.

XXVIII. God alone is the immediate object of our perceptions, which exists outside of us, and he alone is our light.

Now, in the rigour of metaphysical truth, <1> there is no external cause
5 which acts on us, except God alone, and he alone <communicates himself
to us>2 immediately in virtue of our continual dependence. From which it
follows that there is no other external object which <3> touches our soul
and immediately excites our perception. Also we have in our soul the ideas
of all things only in virtue of the continual action of God on us, that is to
10 say because every effect expresses its cause, and thus that the essence of
our soul is a certain expression <or>4 imitation or image of the essence,
thought, and will of God, and of all the ideas that are included in him. One
can therefore say that God alone is our immediate object outside of us, and
that we see all things through him;5 for example when we see the sun and
15 the stars, it is God who has given them to us and who conserves the ideas
of them in us, and who determines us to think of them actually, by his

---

8 Struck from L1: and force of the soul
9 Struck from L1: than what we conceive more distinctly and attribute to ourselves more
particularly in the usage of ordinary life
10 Struck from L1: forms | *conceptus*
1 Struck from L1: (1) nothing acts on us (a) immediately (b) from all external causes but
God alone, and nothing (2) we can say that God is the sole immediate external object of
our thoughts.
2 As in l2. L1 has: communicates with us
3 Struck from L1: touches us immediately, than God alone.
4 As in l2.
5 This important expression 'we see all things through him' comes from Malebranche
(MS, III, 2, 6), who says, however, not 'through' God but 'in' (*en*) God. On L1 Leibniz
originally had '*en*' but changed it to '*par*', which could be rendered 'by God'. However, I
think both 'in' and 'by' are awkward in English, but 'through' best captures the meaning.

ordinary concourse, at the time our senses are disposed in a certain manner, following the laws he has established. God is the sun and the light of souls, *lumen illuminans omnem hominem venientem in hunc mundum.*[6] And it is not
20 only in our time that people are of this sentiment. After Holy Scripture and the Fathers, who have always favoured Plato over Aristotle, I remember having previously remarked that from the time of the Scholastics some had believed that God is the light of the soul, and according to their manner of speaking, *intellectus agens animae rationalis.*[7] The Averroists gave this
25 a bad sense,[8] but some others, among whom is found, I believe, William of St Amour,[9] <[10]>, and several mystical Theologians, have taken it in a manner worthy of God and capable of elevating the soul to the knowledge of its good.

XXIX. Yet we think immediately through our own ideas, and not through those of God.

However, I <[1]> am not of the sentiment of certain able philosophers,[2]
5 who seem to maintain that our very ideas are in God, and not at all in us. In my opinion this comes about because they have still not considered enough what we have just explained concerning substances, nor the entire extent and independence of our soul, which makes it contain everything that happens to it, and that it expresses <[3]> God and <with him>[4] all
10 beings possible and actual, as an effect expresses its cause. Also it is a thing inconceivable that I should think by means of the ideas of another. <[5]>

---

[6] John 1:9: 'The [true] light that lights every man who comes into this world'. Also quoted by Malebranche at the end of *Search after Truth* (MS III, 2, 6).

[7] God is 'the active intellect of the rational soul'. The notion of an 'active' or 'agent' intellect stems from Aristotle's *On the Soul*, Bk III, §5, and in general designates the capacity of the soul to form abstractions by drawing from the 'passive' intellect, which receives images from sensible things. Discussion continues over whether the active intellect is something separable from the body. Also see Aristotle's *Metaphysics*, Bk XII, Ch. 7, on the relation of the active intellect to divine thought.

[8] Leibniz is referring to certain Christian followers of Averroes (Ibn Rushd, 1126–98), 'the great Arabic commentator on Aristotle, who held that the active intellect in each man is part of a single active intellect. The doctrine of a single world-soul was condemned as heresy' [by the Church] (AG 60). See commentary for additional notes and references.

[9] Philosopher, theologian, commentator on Aristotle, d. 1272. AA note: Guillame de St Amour, *Opera omnia*, 1632. Konstanz.

[10] Struck from l²: Doctor of the Sorbonne

[1] Struck from L¹: do not approve

[2] Referring specifically to Malebranche in *Search after Truth* (MS III, 2, 6).

[3] Struck from L¹: the essence of God

[4] Added in l².

[5] Struck from L¹: And an effect must express its cause.

The soul must also be actually affected in a certain manner, when it thinks of something, and it must have in it in advance not only the passive power to be able to be affected thus, which is already wholly determined, but also an
15 active power, in virtue of which it always had in its nature the marks <6> of the future production of this thought, and of the dispositions to produce it in its time. And all this already envelops the idea comprised in this thought.

XXX. How God inclines our soul without necessitating it; that we do not have the right to complain; <1> that we must not ask why Judas sins, since this free action is included in his notion, but only why Judas the sinner is admitted into existence in preference to some other
5 possible persons. On <2> the original imperfection <or limitation>3 before sin, and on the degrees of grace.

Concerning the Action of God on the human will, there are a number of rather difficult considerations that would take too long to pursue here.
10 Nevertheless, <4> here is what can roughly be said. God, in concurring with our actions, ordinarily does no more than to follow the laws <5> that he has established, that is to say he continually conserves and produces our <6> being in such a way that [our] thoughts come to us spontaneously <7> or freely in the order that the notion of our individual substance brings about,
15 in which one could foresee them for all eternity. Moreover, in virtue of the decree he has made that the will should always tend to the apparent good, in expressing or imitating the will of God under certain particular respects, in regard to which this apparent good always has something real, he determines our will to the choice which appears best, without necessitating it nonethe-
20 less. For absolutely speaking, in as much as it is opposed to necessity, [the will] is in [a state of] indifference, and it has the power to do otherwise or even to suspend its action altogether; the one and the other option being and remaining possible. It therefore depends on the soul to take precautions against the surprises of appearances through a firm will <8> to make
25 reflections, and not to act or judge in such encounters until after having

---

6 Struck from L1: or dispositions
1 Struck from L1: (1) if Titius (2) that (a) Titius (b) Judas if he did not sin would not be the one who he is;
2 Struck from L1: the origin of evil comes from the
3 Added in L2.
4 Struck from L1: in order to touch on something of it, we must distinguish indifferent, good, and bad actions.
5 Struck from L1: of nature
6 Struck from L1: nature
7 Struck from L1: and naturally
8 Struck from L1: (1) to suspend (2) to fortify through practice

deliberated well <and>⁹ fully. It is true, however, and it is even assured from all eternity, that a certain soul will not make use of this power on such an occasion. But who could do more?¹⁰ And could [the soul] complain of anything other than itself? For all these complaints after the fact are unjust, if they would have been unjust before the fact. Now this soul, a little before sinning, would it have good grace to complain of God, <¹¹> as if he had determined it to sin?¹² The determinations of God in these matters being <¹³> things that one would not be able to foresee, from where does it know <¹⁴> that it is determined to sin <if not>¹⁵ that it actually sins already? It is only a matter of not willing, <¹⁶> and God could not propose an easier and more just condition; thus any judge, <¹⁷> without seeking the reasons that have disposed a man to have a bad will, stops only to consider how this will is bad. But perhaps it is assured from all eternity that I will sin? Answer for yourself: perhaps not. And without dwelling on what you cannot know and which cannot give you any light, act according to your duty that you do know. But another will say, whence it comes that this man will assuredly commit this sin? The reply is easy, that otherwise it would not be this man. For God sees from all time that there will be a certain <¹⁸> Judas, whose notion or idea that God has of him contains this future free action. Only this question remains, why such a <¹⁹> Judas the traitor, who is possible only in God's idea, exists actually. But to this question there is no reply to expect here below, unless in general one must say that since God has found it good that he should exist, notwithstanding the sin that he foresaw, this evil must be compensated with interest in the universe, <²⁰> that God will derive a greater good from it, and that in sum it will be found that this series of things <²¹> in which the existence of this sinner is included, is the most perfect among all the other possible ways. But always to explain <²²> the admirable

---

9 Added in l².
10 Reading the idiomatic expression 'Mais qui en peut mais?' based on the etymology of *mais* from Latin *magis* meaning 'more'.
11 Struck from L¹: who does not determine it to flee the sin
12 Leibniz ends this sentence with a period; but it seems to be a question.
13 Struck from L¹: insensible
14 Struck from L¹: (1) that God determines it, if not that (2) that one most certainly must (3) that it (a) sin
15 Added in l².
16 Struck from L¹: can one propose something easier in practice
17 A whole line of something illegible is struck from l², not mentioned in AA.
18 Struck from L¹: Titius
19 Struck from L¹: Titius
20 Struck from L¹: and that in sum
21 Struck from L¹: which includes the existence of this Titius
22 Struck from L¹ and l²: in detail

economy of <²³> this choice, this cannot be while we are travellers <²⁴> <in this world>.²⁵ It is enough to know it, without understanding it. And
55 it is here that it is time to recognise the *altitudinem divitiarum*,²⁶ the depth and abyss of the divine wisdom, without seeking a detail that encompasses infinite considerations. One sees clearly however that God is not the cause of evil. For not only after man's loss of innocence did original sin take hold of the soul; but even beforehand there was an original limitation or imper-
60 fection connatural to all creatures, <²⁷> which renders them capable of sin or error.²⁸ Thus there is no more difficulty in regard to the supralapsarians, than with regard to others.²⁹ And it is what in my opinion must reduce <³⁰> to the sentiment of St Augustine and other authors, that the root of evil is in nothingness, that is to say in the privation or limitation of creatures,³¹ which
65 God graciously remedies by the degree of perfection that it pleases him to give. Though this grace of God, whether ordinary or extraordinary, has its degrees and measures, it is always efficacious in itself to produce a certain proportioned effect, and moreover it is always sufficient <³²> not only to secure us from sin, but even to produce salvation, supposing that man joins
70 himself to it <by what is from him>.³³ But it is not always sufficient to overcome <³⁴> the inclinations of man, for otherwise he would not strive

²³ Struck from L¹: this wisdom
²⁴ Struck from L¹: in this valley of miseries [The allusion is likely to Psalms 83:7 (Vulgate) or to 23:4.]
²⁵ In L¹, but likely mistakenly omitted from l².
²⁶ 'depth of riches', Romans 11:33: 'O the depth of the riches and wisdom and knowledge of God! How inscrutable are his judgments and how unsearchable his ways.'
²⁷ Struck from L¹: (1) in particular which (a) has inclined some | (b) inclines them | to sin, and perhaps without special grace from God (aa) they would have all sinned. [But for] the grace of God | all minds would be fallen. [This last sentence was also struck from l².]
²⁸ On sin *as* error see Leibniz's 'Confession of a Philosopher', LCP 135, a translation of AA VI, 3 N.7.
²⁹ 'Supralapsarian' refers to the doctrine that 'before the fall' God decreed which humans would be either saved or damned, in contrast with 'post' or infralapsarianism, which says that God made his decrees after the fall, as a consequence of Adam's free choice to sin. One dispute between the two doctrines would be that the former makes God responsible for everything, including sin, while the latter would limit God's responsibility. Leibniz seems to be saying that either way it was in the nature of humans to sin, due to their original imperfection. See *Theodicy* I §§82–4.
³⁰ Struck from l²: this grace of God
³¹ See Augustine, *The City of God*, XIV, 13: 'That it is a nature, this is because it is made by God; but that it falls away from Him, this is because it is made out of nothing.' See also XII, 1, 6–8. Also *Enchiridion*, 3, 11; 8, 26–7; 22, 81; *Confessions*, Bk V, 10–11; Bk VII, 12.
³² Struck from L¹: (1) for (a) to produce salvation, (b) to keep us from evil, and
³³ In L¹ Leibniz first wrote and dot-underlined 'by his will' and above that wrote 'by what is from him'. In l² only the latter phrase appears.
³⁴ Struck from L¹: the will of

for anything,[35] and this is reserved solely for the absolutely efficacious grace which is always victorious <[36]> <[37]> <whether it be by itself, or by the congruity of the circumstances.>[38]

XXXI. On the motives[1] <[2]> of election, on faith foreseen, on middle knowledge,[3] on the absolute decree <[4]> and that everything is reduced to the reason why God <has chosen and resolved to admit to>[5] existence such a possible person, whose notion contains such a series of graces and free actions. This makes all the difficulties cease in one blow.[6]

Finally, the graces of God are wholly pure graces over which creatures have no claim.[7] <[8]> However, just as it does not suffice to account for

---

[35] 'car autrement il ne tiendroit plus a rien'

[36] Struck from L[1]: (1) Finally, creatures are obliged to God by the graces that he gives to them, (a) but they have not (b) and have no right | neither over those that he gives to them, nor | over those that he does not give to them, otherwise this would not be grace. [These passages seem to reflect Paul, Romans 11:6. 'But if by grace, it is no longer because of works; otherwise grace would no longer be grace.']

[37] At this approximate point near the bottom of L[1], Leibniz continues: 'Finally the graces of God are wholly pure graces over which creatures have no claim.' Under the beginning of that sentence, and above some struck passages, he then draws a thick and meandering line all the way to the top of the page and continues: 'Even so, in order to account for God's choice that he makes in the dispensation of his graces. . .'. These two sentences became the first two sentences of §31, and the heavy line served to divide the page in two, with §30 on one side and §31 on the other. Leibniz does not indicate that §31 has begun; but this is clear in l[2]. The division makes sense, since §30 concludes the discussion on efficacious grace, while §31 turns to the dispensation of grace.

[38] Added in l[2]. On 'congruity', see commentary.

[1] 'motifs' can mean 'grounds' or 'reasons' in French.

[2] Struck from L[1]: (a) for the dispensation of graces and (b) for foresight | of election, on middle knowledge, on the absolute decree

[3] On 'middle knowledge' (la science moyenne), see commentary.

[4] AA ends the sentence at 'decree' and begins a new sentence with 'And'. But L[1] shows no break.

[5] In L[2] replacing from L[1]: has chosen for

[6] The original summary of §31 is found on the page containing §25 and part of §26. The reason Leibniz put it there is that he had completely filled the page containing §30 and §31; the following page was also filled; so rather than inserting a new page to write the summary, he wrote it sideways on an empty spot on the verso side of the folio page, which contained §25, and then drew a line from the summary to §31. Thanks to Herma Kliege-Biller at the Leibniz-Forschungsstelle for figuring this out for me.

[7] In L[1], after Leibniz had decided to end §30 at this point, this became the first sentence of §31.

[8] In L[1] below the previous sentence and near the bottom of the page Leibniz struck the following heavily revised passages, similar in content to §31, since they indicate Leibniz's reluctance to accept God's foresight of faith and works as sufficient reasons

God's choice that he makes in the dispensation of these[9] graces to resort
10 to the absolute or conditional foresight of the future actions of men, we
must also not imagine absolute decrees having no reasonable motive. As for
foreseen faith or good works, it is very true that God has elected only those
whose faith and charity he foresees, *quos se fide donaturum praescivit;*[10] but
the same question returns, why God will give the grace of faith or of good
15 works to some rather than to others. And as for <[11]> this knowledge God
has, which is the foresight, not of faith and good acts, but of their matter
and predisposition, or of what the man would contribute to them from his
side (since it is true that there is diversity on the side of men where there
is diversity on the side of grace, and in fact it is very necessary that a man,
20 <although he needs to be stimulated to the good and converted, act on it
also thereafter)>,[12] it seems to several people that one could say that God,
seeing what the man will do without grace or extraordinary assistance, or
at least what he will have from his side, setting aside grace, could resolve
himself to give grace to those whose natural dispositions would be the best
25 or at least less <[13]> imperfect or less bad. But even if this were so, one can
say that these natural dispositions, in as much as they are good, are still the
effect of grace, although ordinary, God having favoured some more than
others; and since he knows well that the natural advantages he gives will
serve as motives for grace or extraordinary assistance, is it not true, follow-
30 ing this doctrine, that in the end everything reduces entirely to his mercy? I
believe, therefore (since we do not know how much or in what way God has
regard for natural dispositions in the dispensation of grace), that the most
exact and surest thing to say, following our principles, and as I have already

---

for the dispensation of grace: However (a) there is (b) that one | has certain (aa) reasons
very (bb) great reasons of wisdom | (c) as it does not suffice to have recourse to (aa) faith
foreseen | (bb) foresight of faith or of good works | or to (aaa) some | (bbb) others |
similar foundations to account for the choice of God, for it always comes back to the
same question why God gives to one rather than to others the grace of faith or works, one
must not | also | imagine absolute decrees without (aaaa) any reason (bbbb) any reason-
able motive. But one must say (aaaaa) with St Paul (bbbbb) that (ccccc) in conformity
with St Paul | (2) However | (3) But (4) Though

9 L[1] has 'ses' which could mean 'his', 'her' or 'its'. l[2] has 'ces' which means 'these'. I'm
going with the latter.

10 'those he foreknew he would endow with faith'. Romans 8:28–9: 'We know that all
things work for good for those who love God, who are called according to his purpose.
For those he foreknew he also predestined to be conformed to the image of his Son, so
that he might be the firstborn among many brothers.'

11 Struck from L[1]: middle knowledge

12 As in l[2]. L[1] has: (although he needs to be stimulated to the good) act on it also

13 Struck from L[1]: malicious

76

remarked, is that there must be among possible beings <[14]> the person of
35 Peter or John whose notion or idea contains <[15]> all this series of ordinary
and extraordinary graces and all the rest of his events with their circumstances, and that it pleased God to choose him to exist actually, from
among an infinity of other equally possible persons, after which it seems
there is nothing more to ask and that all the difficulties vanish. As for this
40 single and great question why <[16]> it pleased God to choose him among so
many other possible persons, one would have to be very unreasonable not
to be content with the general reasons we have given, the detail of which is
beyond us. Thus instead of resorting to an absolute decree, which, being
without reason is unreasonable, or to reasons which do not manage to
45 resolve the difficulty and have need of other reasons, the best thing will be
to say, in conformity with St Paul, that there are <for this>[17] certain great
reasons of wisdom or of congruity that God has observed, unknown to
mortals and founded on the general order, the goal of which is the greatest
perfection of the universe. This is what the motives[18] for the glory of God
50 and the manifestation of his justice come down to, as well as his mercy
<and generally his perfections;>[19] and finally that immense depth of riches
which had so enraptured the soul of St Paul himself.[20]

XXXII. The utility of these principles in matters of piety and religion.

For the rest it seems that the thoughts that we have just explained, particularly the <great>[1] principle of the perfection and operations of God,
5 and <that of the>[2] notion of substance which contains all its events with
all their circumstances, very far from harming, serve to confirm religion,
to dissipate some very great difficulties, to inflame souls with a divine love,
and to elevate minds to the knowledge of incorporeal substances, much
more than the hypotheses we have seen up to now. For we see <[3]> very
10 clearly that all other substances depend on God, just as thoughts emanate

---

[14] Struck from L[1]: the person of Titius
[15] Struck from L[1]: (1) all (2) all his events, and (3) all (a) his fortune (b) this fortune, and all
the graces
[16] Struck from L[1]: God has chosen
[17] Added in l[2].
[18] Meaning 'grounds' or 'reasons'
[19] Added in l[2].
[20] Romans 11:33, as quoted in §30, ln 55.
[1] Added in l[2].
[2] Added in l[2].
[3] Struck from L[1]: (1) perfectly (2) very clearly (a) how everything depends on God

from our substance; that God is all in all,[4] and <that>[5] he is intimately
united with all creatures, in proportion, nevertheless, to their perfection;
that it is he alone who <[6]> determines them <from the outside>[7] by his
influence, and if to act is to determine immediately, one can say in this
15 sense, in the language of Metaphysics, that God alone operates on me,
and alone can <[8]> do me good or evil, the other substances <[9]> contributing only to the reason for these determinations; because God, having
regard for all, distributes his goodness and obliges them to accommodate
themselves to one another. Hence God alone makes the liaison or com-
20 munication of substances, and it is by him that the phenomena of the one
meet and agree with those of others, and consequently that there is reality
in our perceptions. But in practice one attributes action to <[10]> particular
reasons, in the sense that I have explained above, because it is not necessary always to make mention of the universal cause in the particular case.
25 We also see that every substance has a perfect spontaneity (which becomes
freedom in intelligent substances), that everything that happens to it is a
consequence of its idea or its being, and that nothing determines it except
God alone. And this is why a person whose mind was highly elevated and
whose saintliness is revered had the habit of saying that the soul must often
30 think as if there were only God and itself in the world.[11] Now nothing
makes us comprehend immortality more strongly than this independence
and this extent of the soul, which shelters it absolutely from all exterior
things, since it alone makes its whole world <[12]> and is sufficient with
God; and it is as impossible that it should perish without annihilation, as
35 it is impossible that the world (of which it is a perpetual living expression)

---

[4] AA note: 1 Corinthians 15:28. 'When everything is subjected to him, then the Son
himself will [also] be subjected to the one who subjected everything to him, so that God
may be all in all.'
[5] In l[2] 'how' was struck and 'that' added.
[6] Struck from L[1]: acts alone on them, and
[7] Added in l[2].
[8] Struck from L[1]: render [me] happy or
[9] Struck from L[1]: being only occasional causes for these determinations
[10] Struck from L[1]: occasional causes
[11] Leibniz is referring to St Theresa of Avila (1515–82), a Spanish Carmelite nun, and
particularly to a passage from her *Book of Life* [*Libro de la vida*] (1588), Ch. 13, par. 9:
'for the utmost we have to do at first is to take care of our soul and to remember that in
the entire world there is only God and the soul; and this is a thing which it is very profit-
able to remember'. Leibniz mentions her influence upon him in a letter to André Morell:
'And as for St Theresa you are right to esteem her works. I found in them one day this
fine thought that the Soul must conceive things as if there were only God and it in the
world. This even provides a considerable reflection in philosophy that I have employed
usefully in one of my hypotheses' (10 Dec. 1696, in Grua, *Textes*, p. 103).
[12] Struck from L[1]: and comprehends (a) all things (b) everything

should destroy itself; <13> hence it is not possible that the changes of this extended mass which is called our body should do anything to the soul, nor that the dissipation of this body should destroy what is indivisible.

XXXIII. Explanation of the <commerce>[1] of the soul and the body, which has passed for inexplicable or miraculous; and of the origin of confused perceptions.

5 We also see the <unexpected>[2] clarification of this great mystery of *the union of the soul and the body*, that is to say, how it happens that <3> the passions and actions of the one are accompanied <4> by the actions and passions, or the appropriate phenomena, of the other. For there is no way to conceive that the one should have influence on the other, and it is
10 not reasonable <5> simply to resort to the extraordinary operation of the universal cause in such an ordinary and particular matter. But <6> here is the true reason for it: we have said that everything that happens to the soul and to each substance is a consequence of its notion, therefore the very idea or essence of the soul carries with it that all of its appearances <7>
15 or perceptions must arise (*sponte*)[8] from its own nature, and precisely in such a way that they answer of themselves to what happens in the whole universe, but more particularly and more perfectly to what happens in the body assigned[9] to it, because it is in some way and for some time follow- ing the connection of other bodies to its own that the soul expresses the
20 state of the universe <10>. This also makes known how our body belongs to us without, however, being attached to our essence. And I believe that persons who are able to meditate will judge favourably of our principles for just this, that they can easily see in what consists <the connection that there is between>[11] the soul and the body, which appears inexplicable in
25 any other way. We also see that the perceptions of our senses, even when they are clear, must necessarily contain some confused sentiment, for

---

[13] Struck from L[1]: or that an atom should perish
[1] Replacing 'union' in both L[1] and L[2].
[2] In L[1], but omitted in l[2].
[3] Struck from L[1]: all
[4] Struck from L[1]: by some
[5] Struck from L[1]: to introduce an extraordinary concourse of God for this
[6] Struck from L[1]: the true reason is that each substance expresses the whole universe,
[7] Struck from L[1]: (1) follow, which answer | of themselves | to what happens (2) or perceptions (a) would spring to it, which
[8] Spontaneously, meaning that the source of the perceptions is the soul itself.
[9] 'affecté'
[10] Struck from L[1]: by its essence
[11] Added in l[2]. Struck from L[1] and l[2]: the union of

as all bodies in the universe are in sympathy <^{12}>, our own receives the impression of all the others, and <although our senses correspond with>^{13} everything, it is not possible that our soul should <^{14}> attend to everything
30 in particular; this is why our confused sentiments are the result of a variety of perceptions which is altogether infinite. And it is somewhat like the confused murmur heard by those who approach the seashore, which comes from the accumulation^{15} of the repercussions of innumerable waves. Now if from several perceptions (which do not add up to make one) there is none
35 which rises above the others, and if they make impressions almost equally strong or equally capable of determining the attention of the soul, it can apperceive them only confusedly.

XXXIV. On the difference of Minds from other substances, souls, or substantial forms, and that the immortality one expects implies memory.

5 <^{1}> Supposing that bodies <which make an *unum per se*, as a man does>^{2} are substances and that they have substantial forms, and that beasts have souls, we are obliged to admit that these souls and substantial forms cannot perish entirely, any more <^{3}> than atoms or <the ultimate>^{4} parts of matter, in the sentiment of other philosophers; for no substance perishes,
10 although it may become completely different. They also express the whole universe, although more imperfectly than minds. But the principal difference is that they do not know what they are, nor what they do, and consequently being unable to make reflections, they cannot discover <necessary and universal>^{5} truths. It is also due to a lack of reflection on themselves
15 <^{6}> that they have no moral quality; <^{7}> whence it comes that passing through a thousand transformations, somewhat as we see when a caterpillar changes into a butterfly, it would be the same, for morals or practice,

---

12 Struck from L^1: they must express [. . .] their action
13 As in l^2. L^1 had: as our senses withdraw
14 Struck from L^1: have attention to everything
15 'assemblage'
1 L^1 and l^2 begin with this passage, but it was struck from l^2: There is one thing that I do not undertake to determine, whether bodies are substances (to speak in Metaphysical rigour), or whether they are only true phenomena as is the rainbow, nor consequently whether there are substances, souls, or substantial forms which are not intelligent. But
2 Added in l^2.
3 Struck from L^1: (1) than ours, and that they (2) than atoms (if there are any)
4 Added in l^2.
5 Added in l^2.
6 Struck from L^1: that it does not make a character ['personage']
7 One and a half lines of something illegible is struck from l^2 and not recorded in AA.

as if we said that they perish; and indeed one can say the same physically, as when we say that bodies perish by their corruption. But the intelligent
20 soul, knowing what it is and able to say this ME, which says so much, <⁸> does not merely remain and subsist <⁹> Metaphysically, much more than the others, but it also remains the same morally and makes the same personality.¹⁰ For it is memory, or the knowledge of this *me*, which renders it subject to punishment and reward. Thus the immortality that one expects
25 in morals and religion consists not <¹¹> merely in this perpetual subsistence, common to all substances; for without the memory of what one has been, it would have nothing to desire. Let us suppose that some <¹²> individual all of a sudden should become King of China, but on the condition of forgetting what he has been, as if he had just been born completely anew;
30 does it not amount to the same in practice, or as far as the effects that one can apperceive, as if he were annihilated and a King of China created in his place in the same instant? Which this individual has no reason to desire.

XXXV. The excellence of Minds, and that God considers them preferably to other creatures. That Minds express God rather than the world, but that the other <simple>¹ substances express the world rather than God.²
5

But in order to judge by natural reasons that God will always conserve, not only our substance, <³> but also our person, that is to say the memory and the knowledge of what we are (although the distinct knowledge of it is sometimes suspended in sleep and in fainting), one must join Morals to
10 Metaphysics, that is to say one must not only consider God as the principle and cause of all substances and all Beings, but also as chief of all persons or intelligent substances, and as the absolute Monarch of the most perfect city or Republic, as is the universe, composed of all Minds together, God himself being the most complete⁴ of all Minds, as he is the greatest of all
15 beings. For assuredly Minds are <the most perfect and best express the

---

⁸ Struck from L¹: it always knows
⁹ Struck from L¹: the same
¹⁰ 'personnage'
¹¹ Added then struck from L¹: only
¹² Struck from L¹: miserable
¹ Added in L².
² This sentence, although it appears in the heading of this article on both L¹ and L², may have been intended, according to LG, to appear in the heading of §36, since the same point is made in that article at lines 21–22.
³ Struck from L¹: (as it is manifest by our meditations explained up to here)
⁴ 'accompli'

Divinity>.[5] And the whole nature, end, virtue, and function of substances being only to express God and the universe, as has been sufficiently explained, there is no basis to doubt that substances which express it with knowledge of what they do, and which are capable <[6]> of knowing great
20 truths with regard to God and the universe, express it incomparably better than those natures which are either brute and incapable of knowing the verities,[7] or utterly destitute of sentiment and knowledge; and the difference <between intelligent substances and those which are not>[8] is as great as there is between a mirror and the one who sees. And as God himself is
25 the greatest and wisest of Minds, it is easy to judge that <[9]> Beings with which he can, so to speak, enter into conversation and even into society – communicating to them his sentiments and volitions in a particular manner and in such way that they could know and love their benefactor – must concern[10] him infinitely more than all other things, which can pass only
30 as the instruments of Minds, just as we see that all <[11]> wise persons make infinitely more of the condition <[12]> of a man than of some other thing, however precious it be; and it seems that the greatest satisfaction an otherwise contented soul can have is to see oneself loved <[13]> by others. Although in regard to God there is this difference, that his glory and our
35 worship can add nothing to his <[14]> satisfaction, the recognition of creatures being only a consequence of his sovereign and perfect felicity, very far from <contributing to it or>[15] being in part the cause. However, what is good and reasonable in finite Minds is found eminently in him; and just as we should praise a King who preferred to preserve the life of a man over
40 his most precious and rarest of animals, we must not doubt that the most enlightened and just of all Monarchs would be of the same sentiment. <[16]>

---

   5 Added in l[2], replacing the following in L[1] and struck from l[2]: either the only substances found in the world (in case bodies are only true phenomena) or they are at least the most perfect.
   6 Struck from L[1]: of inventing and [likely meant in the sense of discovering]
   7 For Leibniz, 'verities' can refer simply to 'truths', but also to the highest, most abstract truths, such as those of mathematics, geometry, morals, and theology, what he often calls 'eternal verities'.
   8 Added in l[2].
   9 Struck from L[1]: Substances with which
  10 'toucher'
  11 Struck from L[1]: reasonable
  12 Struck from L[1]: (1) of a person (2) of another person
  13 Struck from L[1]: and esteemed
  14 Struck from L[1]: perfect felicity
  15 Added in l[2].
  16 Struck from L[1]: These great and important truths have been very little known by ancient philosophers; there is only Jesus Christ, who expressed them divinely well

XXXVI. God is the Monarch of the most perfect republic composed of all minds, and the felicity of this City of God is his principal purpose.

Indeed, Minds are the most perfectible substances, and their perfections
5 have this in particular, that they interfere with each other the least,[1] or rather they help each other, for only the most virtuous can be the most perfect friends;[2] from which it manifestly follows that God, who always aims for the greatest perfection in general, will care the most for minds, and will give to them, not only in general, but also to each one in particular,
10 the most perfection that the universal harmony can permit. One can even say that God, in as much as he is a mind, is the originator of existences; otherwise, if he lacked the will to choose the best, there would be no reason for one possible to exist in preference to others. Thus the quality God has of being <[3]> Mind itself[4] precedes all other considerations he can have
15 with regard to creatures; minds alone are made in his image, as if from his kind or as children of the household, since they alone can serve him freely and act with knowledge in imitation of the divine nature. A single mind is worth a whole World, <[5]> since it not only expresses it but also knows it and governs itself in the manner of God. So much so that although it
20 seems that every substance expresses the whole universe, nevertheless other substances express the world rather than God, while Minds express God rather than the world. And this nature, so noble of Minds, bringing them closer to divinity as much as is possible for simple creatures, means that God draws from them infinitely more glory than from all other Beings,
25 or rather, other beings provide only the matter for minds to glorify him. It is why this moral quality of God, which makes him Lord or Monarch of Minds, concerns him personally, so to speak, in a Manner entirely singular. It is in this way that he humanises himself, that he is willing to

---

[1] As mentioned in §5.

[2] 'Complete [perfect] friendship is that of good people, those who are alike in their virtue: they each alike wish good things to each other in so far as they are good, and they are good in themselves' (Aristotle, *Nicomachean Ethics*, Bk VIII, Ch. 3, 1156b5).

[3] Struck from L^1: the Lord or Monarch of Minds | concerns him, so to speak, personally and in a manner entirely singular and

[4] L^1 reads: 'the quality that God has of being Mind itself. . .', while l^2 reads: 'The quality of God, that he has of being Mind itself'. In both drafts there is no article for 'Mind', and 'itself' is translated from 'luy même'. My rendering thus differs from AG, LL, WF, RP, MB, and LG where 'Mind' gets the article, as for example, 'the quality that God has of being a mind himself. . .' (AG) and translating 'luy même' as 'himself', thus rendering 'God himself' rather than 'Mind itself'.

[5] Struck from L^1: and this quality of God

suffer anthropologies, and that he enters into society with us, as a Prince
30 does with his subjects, and this consideration is so dear to him that the
happy <and>[6] flourishing state of his Empire, <[7]> which consists in the
greatest possible felicity <[8]> of [its] inhabitants, becomes the highest of
his laws. For felicity is to <[9]> persons what perfection is to beings. And
if the first principle of existence of the physical world is the decree to give
35 it the most perfection possible, the first <[10]> purpose of the moral world,
or of the City of God, which is the most noble part of the universe, must
be to distribute the most possible felicity throughout. One must not therefore doubt that God has ordered everything such that Minds could not
only live forever, which is unmistakable, but also that they should always
40 conserve their moral quality, so that his City does not lose a single person,
as the World does not lose a single substance. And consequently they will
always know what they are, otherwise they would not be subject to reward
or punishment, which is however the essence of a Republic, but especially
of the most perfect, where nothing can be neglected. Finally, God being at
45 the same time the most just and debonair[11] of Monarchs, and who asks only
for good will, provided it be sincere and serious, his subjects could not wish
for a better condition, and in order to make them perfectly happy, he wants
only that they love him.

XXXVII. Jesus Christ has disclosed to men the mystery and admirable laws of the Kingdom of Heaven and the grandeur of the supreme felicity that God prepares for those who love him.

5 The ancient philosophers knew very little of these important truths. Jesus
Christ alone has expressed them divinely well and in a manner so clear
and familiar that the crudest of minds have understood them; thus his
Gospel has entirely changed the face of human affairs; he has brought us
to know <[1]> the Kingdom of heaven, or this perfect Republic of Minds

---

[6] Added to l[2].

[7] Struck from L[1]: is the supreme of the subaltern laws of his conduct

[8] Struck from L[1]: of his subjects

[9] Struck from L[1]: minds

[10] Struck from L[1]: principle of existence

[11] 'debonnaire'. While it sounds odd in this context to render the French so literally, the seventeenth-century meaning of 'debonnaire' was not that of today's 'stylish' and 'charming'. It could be used appropriately in reference to a gracious and benevolent Monarch, such as the canonised Louis IX. It could also be used in its etymological sense 'of good-birth' or 'good-natured' (see Cayrou 1948).

[1] Added then struck from L[1]: how much God loves us and such care he has for the least of intelligent souls, that he has provided [. . .] for all that concerns us

10   which merits the title of City of God, whose admirable laws he has dis-
     closed to us. He alone has shown how much God loves us, and with what
     <²> exactitude he has provided in everything that concerns us; that having
     care for the sparrows, he will not neglect <³> rational creatures which are
     infinitely more dear to him; that all the hairs of our head are numbered;⁴
15   that heaven and earth will perish before <⁵> the word of God and every-
     thing belonging to the economy of our salvation be changed;⁶ that God has
     more regard for the least of intelligent souls than for the entire Machine
     of the World;⁷ <⁸> that we must not fear those who can <⁹> destroy
     bodies, but cannot harm souls, since God alone can make them happy or
20   unhappy,¹⁰ and that those of the just are in his hand protected from all the
     revolutions <¹¹> of the universe, [since] nothing can act on them but God
     alone;¹² that none of our actions is forgotten; that everything is taken into
     account, including idle words, and even a spoonful of water well used;¹³
     finally that everything must culminate in the greatest well-being <¹⁴> of

---

²   Added then struck from L¹: such care
³   Added then struck from L¹: (1) souls (2) minds
⁴   All biblical refs provided by AA. 'Are not five sparrows sold for two small coins? Yet not
    one of them has escaped the notice of God. Even the hairs of your head have all been
    counted. Do not be afraid. You are worth more than many sparrows' (Luke 12:6–7).
⁵   Struck from L¹: that he change nothing
⁶   'Heaven and earth will pass away, but my words will not pass away' (Mark 13:31).
⁷   'What profit would there be for one to gain the whole world and forfeit his soul
    [psyche]?' (KJV: Matthew 16:26).
⁸   Struck from L¹: (1) that they are all in the (2) that we (3) that the souls have nothing to
    fear but God alone
⁹   Struck from L¹: kill the body
¹⁰ 'And do not be afraid of those who kill the body but cannot kill the soul; rather be afraid
    of the one who can destroy both soul and body in Gehenna' (Matthew 10:28).
¹¹ Struck from L¹: (1) of the World, and finally that nothing (a) will remain (b) will be
    which concerns us
¹² 'But the souls of the just are in the hand of God, and no torment shall touch them'
    (Wisdom 3:1).
¹³ 'I tell you, on the day of judgment people will render an account for every careless word
    they speak' (Matthew 12:36). 'And whoever gives only a cup of cold water to one of these
    little ones to drink because he is a disciple – amen, I say to you, he will surely not lose his
    reward' (Matthew 10:42).
¹⁴ Struck from L¹: for those who love God

25 the good;[15] that the just will be like suns;[16] and that neither our senses nor our mind has ever enjoyed[17] anything approaching the felicity that God prepares for those who love him.[18]

---

[15] 'We know that all things work for good for those who love God, who are called according to his purpose' (Romans 8:28).

[16] 'Then the righteous will shine like the sun in the kingdom of their Father' (Matthew 13:43).

[17] 'gousté'

[18] 'But as it is written: "What eye has not seen, and ear has not heard, and what has not entered the human heart, what God has prepared for those who love him"' (1 Corinthians 2:9).

Commentary on the Discourse on Metaphysics

§1. On the very idea of an absolutely perfect being.

The most important and consequential claim in the *Discourse* is in the opening sentence: 'God is an absolutely perfect being'. Much of the rest of the *Discourse* serves to satisfy this claim, as well as to defend its implications against anticipated objections and misunderstandings. Even if the attribute of perfection is the most widely recognised attribute of God, the primary danger is that the very idea of 'an absolutely perfect being' could turn out to be incoherent. Thus, Leibniz begins the *Discourse* by examining this idea in order to determine whether it is an idea at all, let alone an attribute of God. Examining and clarifying ideas taken for granted has always been one of the main tasks of philosophy and it is certainly Leibniz's. Yet his explanation of what counts as a perfection is not straightforward. To understand it, we need to dig into the deeper layers of his metaphysical and epistemological principles, as well as bring to light the historical background informing them.

We might first wonder why Leibniz begins with the idea of God's *perfection*; after all, other ideas of God are more common, for example, *loving*, *merciful*, and *just*. However, the philosophical-theological tradition informing Leibniz maintains that God is best conceived of as *perfectly* loving, merciful, and just – or simply, as most perfect in every way. This tradition is very much influenced by a certain strain of Platonism, which, however, does not conceive of a *personal* god having such qualities. Instead, *ideas themselves*, or 'the Forms', are the self-sustaining perfections of things: whole, complete, flawless, eternal – standing in stark, yet invisible contrast to our divided, incomplete, defective, and ever-changing world. Worldly objects are then said to be understood through their other-worldly, perfect ideas.

We comprehend the variety of geometrical shapes, for example, through the knowledge of their perfect definitions. Through contemplation of the forms of *knowledge* and *goodness* we can strive to become wise and good, and thereby perfect ourselves, at least to some degree. The forms themselves do not admit of degrees; they are nothing less than complete in their kind – and indeed *completeness*, or *wholeness*, lies at the core meaning of perfection.[1]

This sort of Platonic perfectionism could be readily adapted to Christian perfectionism.[2] The Ideas or Forms of Plato become the ideas of a personal God whose essence consists of perfect knowledge, goodness, love, and justice, and who acts in perfect accord with them.[3] Leibniz was directly influenced by Medieval philosophers such as St Anselm, who famously formulated the idea of God as 'that, than which nothing greater can be conceived'.[4] Anselm's formulation informed Descartes' argument for God's existence in the *Meditations on First Philosophy*, which is based on the idea of God as 'a supremely perfect being'.[5] In §23, we will find Leibniz claiming to have improved upon Descartes' 'extremely imperfect demonstration', for virtually the same reasons that he establishes here in §1 – that this idea of God must be shown to be *possible*.

As an attribute of God, perfection has broad, intuitive appeal. Whether or not you believe in God, you can probably agree that *if* God exists then he[6] must be perfect. Consider the consequences of maintaining that God is less than all-knowing, all-powerful, and all-good. What God says would not be authoritative; something other than God could be more powerful; and lacking confidence in God's complete goodness we might remain uncertain about what our religious and moral duties are. So, a notion of God that includes these attributes (all-knowing, etc.) appears to be sound and agreeable, at least as a start. In this spirit, Leibniz quite reasonably begins the *Discourse* with this 'most accepted' and 'most significant' idea of God.

---

[1] See Aristotle on the senses of 'complete', a term commonly translated as 'perfect' (*Metaphysics*, Bk V, Delta, §16, 1021b12).

[2] The influence of 'Neoplatonism', as a kind of bridge between Platonism and Christianity, largely through St Augustine, runs deep in the *Discourse*, as we will see. An excellent source on Neoplatonism is A. H. Armstrong's *Plotinus*.

[3] A number of passages in the Hebrew and Christian Scriptures imply, either directly or indirectly, that God is perfect: 'The Rock, his work is perfect, and all His ways are just (Deut. 32:4). 'Be perfect, therefore, as your heavenly Father is perfect' (Matthew 5:48).

[4] *Proslogion*, 7.

[5] *Meditation* V, CSM II, p. 45/AT VII, p. 65. The idea of the Christian God as 'perfect' and as 'having all perfections' arguably belongs to Descartes.

[6] I would prefer to use a gender-neutral pronoun or to alternate the masculine and feminine in reference to God, but in a seventeenth-century context in which the masculine pronoun was invariably used, the use of a different pronoun would misrepresent the character of that time.

What Leibniz is most concerned to establish here, however, is whether we even know what we are talking about when we say such things. If we can have any knowledge at all about God, then the ideas we have must at least be *coherent* ideas, such that they can be at least *possible* attributes of God. As a philosopher, Leibniz firmly maintains that our ideas about anything ought to be rationally consistent, including, certainly, our ideas about God. As a philosopher with serious theological commitments, Leibniz is also concerned that misconceptions about God may lead to impiety and atheism. The first thing we must do, then, is to determine clearly what a perfection is. His brief remarks require a lot of unpacking.

Leibniz begins with the established idea that there are 'in nature' (ln 8) different perfections and that God has them all in the highest degree. By 'in nature' he means that each perfection has a nature (or essence) that distinguishes it as a perfection and as different from other perfections. This means we can know what the perfections are *a priori*, that is, by reflecting on the nature of the ideas supposed to be perfections. But how can we do this? Leibniz does not tell us what perfections *are*, except through what they are not: anything not capable of a highest degree is not a perfection. For example, (a) *the greatest number* and (b) *the greatest figure* (size of body) are each incapable of a highest degree, and therefore are not perfections. He does not, however, say why they are not so capable, other than that these ideas 'imply contradictions'. But it is important to understand how Leibniz can say this. Consider this reconstruction of his argument so far, focusing on the idea of (a) the greatest number.

1. If something is not capable of a highest degree, it is not a perfection.
2. The idea of greatest includes that of a highest degree, or, that degree to which no greater degree may be added.
3. The idea of number includes that, for any number, there is another, greater, number.
4. Therefore, the idea of greatest contradicts the idea of number (from premises 2 and 3).
5. Therefore, the idea of number is not capable of a highest degree.
6. Therefore, the idea of the greatest number is not a perfection.

This appears to be a sound argument (it is logically valid and the premises all seem to be acceptable, although you should question them). It shows that the problem with the idea of 'the greatest number' is that it is composed of two ideas that cannot be combined to form any idea whatsoever. That is, the idea of 'greatest' *contradicts* the idea of 'number'. The same holds for (b) 'the greatest figure', since the idea of figure includes that, for any figure, there is another greater (larger) figure.

The role of contradiction in the analysis is worth a closer look, since Leibniz's analysis of ideas, especially of ideas taken for granted, depends on it. To determine whether an idea is a true idea, each term contained within the idea must be defined. If we discover a contradiction among any of the terms, then we know *a priori* (by the analysis of terms) that the idea in question is *impossible* – not really an idea at all. But if we do *not* find a contradiction, then at least we have an idea of a *possible* property or thing.[7]

To understand this method more clearly, consider that the idea of 'the greatest number' is initially misleading because it *seems* to be conceivable. That is, you can easily conceive of each constituent idea, 'greatest' and 'number', such that you might think you have a genuine idea. But when you actually try to conceive of these ideas together, as composing one thing, you cannot, because it is logically impossible (contradictory) for any number to have the property of being the greatest, at least according to the definition of number. Note that the point is not that it is *physically* impossible for a greatest number or largest figure to exist; nor that our finite minds are simply incapable of conceiving of anything infinitely large; rather, the combination of these ideas is *impossible*, because the combination is contradictory in conception. This method of analysis indicates how Leibniz conceives of the nature of ideas and their relation to truth, impossibility, and possibility – notions that will arise crucially in subsequent articles. It also helps us to understand what Leibniz says next.

So far, we understand why (a) and (b) are not perfections – not only are they not capable of a highest degree, they are impossible to conceive. This does not, however, tell us what a perfection *is*; although, from what we have seen, we can derive something of a definition: *some attribute is a perfection just in case it is capable of a highest degree.* Now, Leibniz offers two attributes he says *are* perfections: (c) greatest knowledge and (d) greatest power; or, as they are commonly expressed, *omniscience* and *omnipotence.* Again, these attributes (essential qualities of God) sound promising, since much of mainstream theology and philosophy typically assume them. But we must analyse them; and here Leibniz's account becomes a bit puzzling.

The key question is: what makes (c) and (d) perfections but (a) and (b) not? Leibniz offers two reasons: first, (c) and (d) 'imply no impossibility' (ln 15). This must mean, as we may now infer, that the idea of 'greatest' and that of 'knowledge' do not contradict each other. So, knowledge must be capable of a highest degree; and the same must hold for power or omnipotence. But how are they so capable? Consider Leibniz's second reason for saying these attributes are perfections: insofar as they are in God, they have

---

[7] As we will see in §23, Leibniz applies exactly this sort of analysis to Descartes' proof for God.

no limits. But wait – can something have a highest degree if it has *no limits*? The number series has no limit; that's why it is not a perfection. So, how can knowledge have no limits yet be a perfection? Here is what I mean:

1. Some attribute is a perfection just in case it is capable of a highest degree (def).
2. If some attribute has 'no limits' there can be no highest degree of it (assumption).
3. In God, knowledge and power have no limits (Leibniz).
4. Therefore, knowledge and power cannot have highest degrees (from 1 to 3).
5. Therefore, knowledge and power cannot be perfections (from 1 and 4).

The basic problem is that the ideas of knowledge and power contradict the idea of 'greatest' just as we saw previously in the case of number and figure; thus, they cannot be perfections. Has Leibniz contradicted himself?

The problem is that Leibniz has not told us enough about how he properly conceives of terms such as 'perfection' and 'no limit', such that a perfection *can* have a highest degree and yet be unlimited. We also need to understand that God is not the only being that *has* perfections; that is, God is the only perfect being, but creatures like us can possess perfections in lesser degrees.

To explain all this, we must refer to some ideas that Leibniz set down both before and after having written the *Discourse*, ideas that will likely seem rather obscure and complex.[8] First of all, Leibniz defines a perfection generally as 'a completely positive quality', which means that negative qualities cannot be perfections.[9] Thus, if someone were to say 'the greatest ignorance' is a perfection, Leibniz could reply that ignorance is not a positive quality, since it designates a *lack* or *absence* of knowledge. The point is not that we simply prefer positive qualities to negative ones, but rather that positive qualities are said to have *being*, whereas negative qualities constitute absences of being.[10] This requirement that a perfection be a completely

---

[8] For the following analysis I depend in part on Adams 1994, Mercer 2004, and Strickland 2006.

[9] 'A perfection is what I call every simple quality that is positive and absolute, that is, it expresses without any limits whatever it expresses. But a quality of this sort, since it is simple, is therefore unanalysable or indefinable' (from 'Two Notations for Discussion with Spinoza, I. That a Most Perfect Being Exists' (1676), LL 167 / AA VI, 3. N. 81, 578). Also see 'The Ultimate Origination of Things' (AG 150) and 'On Freedom and Possibility' (AG 19–20).

[10] The key Neoplatonic-Augustinian idea here is that being, which is positive, has reality, whereas negations have no reality. The idea of a negation as an absence of reality will be discussed in relation to sin in §30.

positive quality implies that it must be *capable* of being complete, whole, and *lacking in nothing* of its quality. Second, understanding perfection as capable of completion points to its original Greek meaning, namely *telos*, which means 'goal' or 'end'.[11] Thus, a perfection is a quality capable of a development or progression by degrees *toward* its becoming complete. So, while we have much less than complete knowledge, knowledge remains a fully positive quality in itself because it is *capable* of completion, if not by us. For this reason, it is useful to think of perfections generally as *completable qualities*. Power and knowledge are each perfections because they are capable of completion, of being whole, and lacking in nothing of their quality. This is the sense in which these perfections have 'no limit'. Unlike numbers and figures, which are always capable of a higher degree, knowledge and power are perfections because they have a highest degree.

In this way we can understand how power and knowledge, 'in as much as they belong to God, have no limits' (lns 16–17). God is not lacking in power to be the cause of any possible event or being, nor lacking in knowledge of anything possible to know. So, not only are these qualities perfectible (completable) in theory, they are also *actualised* in God because they are complete in God; and if God did not have these perfections (or indeed, *all* perfections) God would not be a perfect being.

The above provides us with a much clearer way of making the distinction Leibniz wants to make between qualities (or attributes) that are perfections and those that are not. Power and knowledge are completable and whole, while number and figure are not. And yet a sticking point arises where Leibniz refers to God's attributes as 'infinite' (as in line 18, in reference to wisdom). Since 'infinite' often denotes an endless quantity, as in number or figure, it seems we are again hard-pressed to distinguish perfections from non-perfections.

To deal with this complication, we are forced to descend, as we often must, into the rabbit-hole of Leibniz's metaphysics, namely, into his conceptions of *infinity*, *the absolute*, and *continua*.[12] The following passages from his later work, *New Essays*, provide a convenient entry point into the difference between *infinity* and *absolute*:[13]

> It is perfectly correct to say that there is an infinity of things, i.e. that there are always more of them than one can specify. But it is easy to demonstrate that there is no infinite number, nor any infinite line or other infinite quantity, if

---

[11] One of Aristotle's definitions of *telos* (τέλειος) is 'complete' (*Metaphysics*, Bk V, Delta, §16, 1021b12), which in Latin is rendered as *perfectus*.

[12] For the following analysis I depend on Look 2007, Arthur 2013, and Antognazza 2015.

[13] Though written some twenty years later, the *New Essays on Human Understanding* plausibly represents Leibniz's conception of infinity in the *Discourse*.

these are taken to be genuine wholes. [. . .] The true infinite, strictly speaking, is only in the *absolute*, which precedes all composition and is not formed by the addition of parts.[14]

A bit further down Leibniz writes:

It would be a mistake to try to suppose an absolute space which is an infinite whole made up of parts. There is no such thing: it is a notion which implies a contradiction; and these infinite wholes, and their opposites, the infinitesimals, have no place except in geometrical calculations, just like the use of imaginary roots in algebra.[15]

The key to these passages lies in determining which type of infinity can be a genuine whole. First, the number series, often said to be infinite, cannot be a genuine whole, since, as we saw, each number may be followed by one greater. However, conceiving of infinity as a *limit* provides some semblance of a genuine whole. For example, an endlessly repeating fraction, such as 1.99999. . . *approaches* 2, infinitely (endlessly), without ever reaching it. Thus, we say that 2 is the *limit* of 1.9 repeating. In fact, any whole number can be a limit for some approaching infinite series. This is just what infinity is – not 'the greatest number', nor a number at all – but that *quasi-limit* toward which an endless series of numbers converges. In this sense we can speak of an infinite series as a *genuine whole*, but only as a useful fiction to be employed in mathematics and geometry. The only *true* infinite – the idea of something genuinely whole, complete, lacking in nothing – is the absolute.

Before discussing the absolute, we need to understand more fully why 'the greatest figure' cannot qualify as a perfection. It is not only because the idea implies a contradiction, as we saw, but because *continua*, that is, space, matter, and motion, cannot form genuine wholes – or better, genuine *unities*.[16] This point is important for understanding Leibniz's criticisms of Descartes and 'Cartesian mechanics' throughout the *Discourse*, as we will see. Consider a wooden block. It appears to be a complete whole because it has a spatial boundary. However, because it is spatial, it can be divided infinitely (Leibniz denied *atoms*, conceived of as indivisible material wholes). Thus, a block is an endless aggregation of matter, not a genuine whole or unity. Nor could you attain a genuine whole by *adding* blocks, since one more block could always be added. Thus, any way you slice it (or compile it), spatial and material things lack completion and involve infinity in the bad sense, and thus cannot be perfections. That is the nature of

---

[14] LRB II.xvii.1.157.

[15] LRB II.xvii.3.158.

[16] Leibniz explains what he calls 'the composition of the continuum' most notably in his dialogue, 'Pacidius to Philalethes' (1676), AA VI, 3 N. 78, 528–71 / LC 127–221.

the *continuum* of matter and space. What we can say, however, is that any apparently bounded block of matter imposes a *limitation* on the continuum, or that it carves out a subset of matter. That is, every time we take a chip off the infinite block (of time, space, or matter), or add to it, we are not adding or subtracting *parts* of a whole, but rather imposing limits upon an 'absolute' whole. Again, these limits, these objects, are to be understood as useful tools for doing geometry and physics, but not as constituents of a *completable* whole. In this way we can understand why 'the greatest figure' is not only a contradictory idea (since any figure can always be larger) but is also an *incompletable* idea, since an aggregation of figures can never constitute a complete whole. Thus, all continua (whether numbers or bodies) are essentially imperfect.

At this point we are prepared to understand *the absolute* as that which 'precedes all composition'.[17] That is, the absolute does not consist of a collection of parts put together to form a complete whole. Rather, the absolute is the inexhaustible source of all composition – the source of all infinities, of all lines, figures, numbers, and motions – but is not itself composed of them.[18] With this conception of infinity as absolute, we can understand how a complete whole can have 'no limits' – not because it is unendingly divisible or aggregated, but because it is the complete, inexhaustible source of all being. The absolute is being itself, whole and complete – nothing can be added to it nor taken from it.

It should come as no surprise that Leibniz conceives of God as the absolute. God is that complete whole from which all composition is drawn, upon which all limitation (the introduction of forms, the creation of matter, the composition of all continua) depends. This understanding is, finally, contained deep within the very first sentence of the *Discourse*: 'God is an absolutely perfect being'. It also clarifies the sense in which perfections are complete, yet without limits, 'in as much as they belong to God' (lns 16–17). Number and figure are not perfections, because they are infinite in the incomplete sense, while power and knowledge are perfections, because they are completable attributes of God.

Despite this clarification, it may still not be clear how and why *power* and *knowledge* form genuine wholes, thus perfections; for, it might be objected that they are divisible into smaller quantities of power, into discrete knowledge claims, or somehow capable of endless aggregation. Thus, they would not be genuine, completable wholes. Suppose, however, that we conceive of their perfection as *scalar*, that is, as having degrees,

---

[17] As quoted above from LRB II.xvii.1.157.
[18] This sense of absolute has much in common with 'the One' in Plotinus. See Armstrong 1953: 31.

but not divisible or aggregable in the way that material bodies are. Let us instead define them as *capacities,* and as perfections *lacking in nothing of their kind.* Here is what I mean. First, we shall define 'power', as Aristotle and Leibniz do, as 'the capacity to cause change'.[19] This definition has two advantages: it avoids the reduction of power to a single type, by conceiving it more broadly as any capacity for change. These capacities can include physical strength and mechanical force, but also any capacity typically conceived as *mental* – such as reasoning, willing, knowing, and *moral* reasoning. Thus, we can *reason* about what is to be done, *recognise* what is to be done, *will* that it be done, *know how* to execute what is to be done, and perform the action required (with force, if needed) for it to be done. Second, the definition touches on the *teleological* core of perfection, which says that a thing is perfect when it fulfils or completes its nature – or better, when it fulfils what its nature implies. Power (change) implies action, and human action in its perfection implies *purposeful* action. Purposeful action implies reasoning (for example, deliberating over desires, drawing valid conclusions from well-grounded premises). Of course, we humans reason more or less perfectly; but insofar as we exercise our rational powers, we are performing abilities implied by our nature and thus possess a portion of this perfection. Thus, creatures can participate in perfection without *being* perfect. While *we* possess perfections to a much lesser degree, God possesses them without limits – that is, as able to cause any possible change.

A similar account can be given for *knowledge,* which, as already suggested, contributes to power as the capacity for change. Thus, knowledge informs a rational agent about what to do, increasing its capacity for action. (The capacity for action is at the core of Leibniz's account of 'substance', as we will see.) Knowledge also contains a teleological aspect, since the idea of knowledge implies *complete* knowledge – lacking in nothing knowable. Again, we possess only a portion of complete knowledge, which is *perfectible* because it contains an ultimate degree. Power and knowledge are perfections for us, then, because they are ultimately completable in God, who possesses them to the 'most supreme degree' (ln 9).

This leads to Leibniz's concluding point for §1. As a consequence of God's absolute perfection, God acts perfectly in a *metaphysical* sense. This means that God's actions are perfectly executed, since they are the

[19] 'If "power" corresponds to the Latin *potentia*, it is contrasted with "act", and the transition from power into act is "change". That is what Aristotle means by the word "movement", when he says that movement is the act – or perhaps the actualizing – of that which has the power to be. Power in general, then, can be described as the possibility of change' (LRB II.xxi.1.169). See Aristotle, *Physics* III, 201a10, where he defines 'motion' as 'the fulfilment of what is potentially' (LRB note on 169).

consequences of his perfect wisdom and power – but God's actions are also perfect in a *moral* sense, since they are completely good. (While Leibniz has not mentioned it here, he certainly counts *goodness* as among God's perfections.) Leibniz thinks that as our understanding of God increases, the more we will find his actions metaphysically as well as morally *excellent* – and conformable to our highest expectations and aspirations.

No doubt many readers will find these gushing expressions of God's metaphysical and moral excellence somewhat jarring, in view of what appears to many as a world full of imperfection, cruelty, and pointless suffering. Accordingly, the astute reader may wonder, since God is supposed to have *all* of the perfections, whether they are *compatible* with each other. For it might turn out that God's omnipotence is incompatible with the all-goodness he is expected to have. Thus, Leibniz will need to demonstrate the moral limits on the exercise of absolute power, or that moral evil is compatible with perfection. These objections and problems, against which Leibniz defends God, as they reflect the notorious 'problem of evil', should be borne in mind as we proceed through the *Discourse*. The next section forms part of this defence, by defending God's goodness against the 'impiety' of those who say that *goodness itself* is determined by God's will and power.

§2. On the charge that moral goodness is arbitrary.

Who is saying that God's goodness is arbitrary? And what does this even mean? These questions have far-reaching theological, metaphysical, epistemological, and moral consequences, and to understand them, some historical and conceptual background is required.

First, to say of anything that it is 'arbitrary' is to say that it is a matter of judgment (think of an *arbiter*, or a judge). But the term is commonly used to refer to a judgment of poor quality, that is, one based on a whim, or, more to the point, a judgment made without proper reason. For example, judging someone's ability to perform a job based on their skin colour would be an arbitrary judgment, because skin colour is irrelevant to performance. More commonly, judgments about *the common good* based on personal preference or un-reflected desire are considered arbitrary. A judge who handed down sentences because she did not like the way the accused is dressed would be considered an unfair, 'arbitrary' judge. On the other hand, a judge who decided on the basis of appropriate reasons and evidence would of course be considered fair, just, and good.

Leibniz was accustomed to thinking of God as a judge, due to his religious background as well as his law background. As a trained jurisconsult (an expert on the law), he often drew parallels between the terms of jurisprudence and those of theology – referring to the latter as 'a species of jurisprudence'.[1] Thus, to say that God's *goodness* is arbitrary means that God judges or determines anything to be 'good' without God having any reason or proper justification for the judgment. Leibniz thought that this view was not only incoherent, but that it would render God unworthy of respect and worship, or worse, that it made God out to be a tyrant.[2] Even worse is that such a view threatened to render the very idea of goodness incoherent. But to understand these matters rightly requires taking a slight detour into the history of the debate about the relationship between God's will and moral values, which is often discussed in terms of a conflict between *voluntarism* and *rationalism* or *intellectualism*.[3]

The notion that the very idea of 'the good' might be arbitrary, instead of based on a reason independent of the will, is famously depicted by Socrates in Plato's dialogue, the *Euthyphro*. In fact, in a later work, Leibniz ties the 'Euthyphro question' directly to his own concerns about the relationships among justice, piety, and God's will.[4]

> It is agreed that whatever God wills is good and just. But there remains the question whether it is good and just because God wills it or whether God wills it because it is good and just: in other words, whether justice and goodness are arbitrary or whether they belong to the necessary and eternal truths about the nature of things.[5]

This is a question about what *determines* some thing or action to have the quality of goodness, justice, or holiness. In Plato's dialogue, Euthyphro's view seems to be that holiness (or piety) is determined by whatever pleases the gods. On the other hand, Socrates appears to maintain that the reason a thing (or action) pleases the gods is that the thing is holy *in itself*. That is to say that holiness is not arbitrary, but rather it is a quality of actions that holds naturally and independently of the gods' judgment or wish. Similarly for Leibniz, the rules of piety, goodness, justice, perfection, and beauty are not the *effects* of God's will, but rather 'the consequences of his understanding' (ln 33). This means that actions (or things) have a quality in-themselves that God recognises or understands. So, God does not make something good by virtue of his will, but rather *understands* the good that

---

[1] See *New Method for Learning and Teaching Jurisprudence*, in Johns 2013: 150 / AA VI, I Part II, §5, p. 294.

[2] See Leibniz's *Meditation on the Common Concept of Justice* (1702) in LPW, and *On the Principles of Pufendorf* (1703) in LPW.

[3] In contemporary ethics the voluntarist position is often called 'divine command theory'.

[4] Leibniz's *Meditation on the Common Concept of Justice* is well worth reading on this question.

[5] Leibniz, *Meditation on the Common Concept of Justice*, LPW, 45.

something has in–itself. His *power* then makes what is good in–itself a reality. Only if we conceive of God's will as rational and non–arbitrary can we conceive of God as worthy of respect, love, and worship.

It is important, however, to see what motivates the views of the 'voluntarist', as well as to see what dangers both voluntarism and rationalism present from a theological viewpoint. To get a handle on this we need to know something about what are called 'the will' and 'the understanding'. Throughout the Medieval and Modern periods, these were conceived as the two main faculties or powers of the mind, by virtue of which human beings could act and think. (Today we commonly designate these faculties as 'volition' and 'cognition'.) Furthermore, the will is that faculty or power the nature of which is to be drawn toward *the good*; and the understanding is that faculty the nature of which is to be drawn to *the true*. Simply put, the will motivates us to seek the good and the understanding enables us to recognise what is true. Take, for example, 'love is good' and '2 + 2 = 4'. I am drawn to pursue the objects of love and to acknowledge the truths of mathematics. I acknowledge the latter by virtue of my understanding, which has the innate capability to recognise the truth of such a proposition, once its components are understood.

We can also see how these faculties enter into our judgments and actions in ways that are not clearly separable. For example, I see the cherry pie and am drawn to it for its appealing sensual qualities. Thus, a desire for the good I perceive in the pie is created in me. My understanding acknowledges these qualities and the desire I have; but it also *knows* through experience that it is not good to eat every cherry pie I desire. So, my understanding weighs the merits of eating the pie, and the merits of my desire, and thus determines what is best for me to do. As long as I am sufficiently informed, such that my judgment of what is good provides enough incentive to overcome the sensuous desire that urges me to consume the pie, and since my will aims for the *true* good, as reason has determined, I may refrain from eating the pie. It is also quite possible for us to make *mistakes* in judgment, which can result in the will leading me to choose what my better–informed understanding would not. You might want to object that desire is always stronger than judgment, or that judgment is simply the last desire in deliberation. These matters are up for reasoned debate; but to explain human action it will be useful to conceive of the process of deliberation and the act of choice as involving an interplay of these two faculties: will and understanding.

Now, let us transfer these faculties to God, keeping in mind that God exercises them perfectly. Thus, God infallibly knows what is good and true and infallibly acts on it, by virtue of his perfect goodness, reason, and power. What I have explained thus far, however, is characteristic of the *intellectualist* viewpoint: that the will, and the action resulting from it, are determined by the degree to which the understanding recognises the good and true. In contrast, from the *voluntarist* viewpoint God's will is *not* determined by his intellect; rather, the will is unconstrained in its determination of even the very ideas of the good and the true themselves. In other words, God can make the good and the true *anything he wills them to be*. To set limits of any sort on God's will is to undermine God's *omnipotence*, or to subject God's will to human standards of reason that we have no right to impose on God.

For the intellectualist, the voluntarist view entails that *goodness and truth are arbitrary*, because they are not grounded in reason, or at least, not in any reason we can recognise. Accordingly, slaughtering the innocent would be *good* and '2 + 2 = 4' would be *false*, if God willed it so. Now, of course, these results seem preposterous to us. But what makes them so? The voluntarist wants to maintain that God would not will these things because God is *good*, and because God knows *the true*. Sure, but this does not explain what God's goodness consists in, nor what makes a statement true; and it is difficult to understand how the act of *willing itself* provides the explanation; and so God's goodness and omniscience become mysterious. To avoid this result the intellectualist claims that God does not *create* the good and the true by virtue of his will, but rather God *understands* the nature of things – goodness itself and truth itself, which form the rational basis of his will. In this way, God may be affirmed as a rational being.

The voluntarist, however, is ready with additional objections. Not only does the intellectualist undermine God's omnipotence, but God's moral authority is destroyed, since God's will must conform to independent standards that he did not create nor can change. Furthermore, if God's will *is* to be determined by his understanding, then it appears that God does not have *free will*. That is, God cannot act or judge otherwise than according to his rational essence; and if morality requires freedom of the will, as many think it must, then, on the intellectualist view, God cannot be a moral being. Despite these serious objections, the intellectualist is not moved. She responds (as Leibniz does) that God cannot be a moral or free being *unless* God's will and understanding are determined by his intellect – and so the debate rages on. The problem poses a dilemma, since both positions entail troubling consequences.[6]

What is interesting about §2 of the *Discourse* is that Leibniz touches on all of these problems in subtle ways, if all too briefly, while even subtly suggesting a way out of the dilemma. Now, again, who would say that God's

---

[6] A useful and accessible discussion of the debate can be found in Schneewind's 'Voluntarism and the Foundations of Ethics' (1996).

goodness is arbitrary? According to Leibniz, no one really; that is, no one who really understood what they were saying. But his implicit targets are some very respectable philosophers: Descartes, Hobbes, and Spinoza, whose works Leibniz knew very well. For instance, Descartes' reply to an intellectualist critic of his *Meditations* clearly expresses the 'voluntarist' position that Leibniz opposes:

> If anyone attends to the immeasurable greatness of God he will find it manifestly clear that there can be nothing whatsoever which does not depend on him. This applies not just to everything that subsists, but to all order, every law, and every reason for everything's being true or good.[7]

Descartes' most basic assumption is that there is nothing that does not depend on God, including the very criteria for truth and goodness. As he goes on to say:

> If some reason for something's being good had existed prior to his preordination, this would have determined God to prefer those things which it was best to do. But on the contrary, just because he resolved to prefer those things which are now to be done, for this very reason, in the words of Genesis, 'they are very good'; in other words, the reason for their goodness depends on the fact that he exercised his will to make them so.[8]

Here then we can clearly see Descartes' preference for the voluntarist position over that of the intellectualist: God makes good things through willing them to be good, not because they have some pre-existing goodness in them. Descartes then goes on to explain that such truths and laws, including moral (moral entities), mathematical, and metaphysical truths, come to be through the same type of causality through which God creates physical things (namely, *efficient* causality). But while we can understand the cause of these truths, it is admittedly difficult for us to understand how these truths could have been otherwise than they are:

> Again, there is no need to ask how God could have brought it about from eternity that it was not true that twice four make eight, and so on; for I admit that this is unintelligible to us. Yet on the other hand I do understand, quite correctly, that there cannot be any class of entity that does not depend on God; [. . .] Hence we should not suppose that eternal truths 'depend on the human intellect or on other existing things'; they depend on God alone, who, as supreme legislator, has ordained them from eternity.[9]

---

[7] Descartes, 'Author's Replies to the Sixth Set of Objections' (CSM II, §8, 293–4 / AT VII, 435). Descartes' reply stems from his remarks on immutable natures in *Meditation* V.

[8] Ibid.

[9] Ibid.

Clearly, then, Descartes takes, at least here, the voluntarist position that there is no determination of goodness and truth prior to God's willing them to be so. To emphasise the point, God's freedom and omnipotence depends on this: there is no priority of 'rationally determined reason' in the determination of what is good and true. It is only because God willed to create the world that it is good. It is because God 'willed that the three angles of a triangle should necessarily equal two right angles that this is true and cannot be otherwise'.[10] Again, it is hard if not impossible for us to conceive of a triangle whose angles, properly constructed, do not together equal 180 degrees; and yet such a triangle must be possible, since God could have willed it to be so.

In the *Discourse*, Leibniz's first counterpoint appears to directly address Descartes' above reference to Genesis. For Leibniz, when God sees that the light is good, God recognises or acknowledges the inherent goodness of light. The light is good, not because God wishes to create it; rather, God wishes to create it because the light is good in itself – and similarly for all else that God wishes to create. Nor does God create the laws of mathematics and geometry; rather, he *uses* them to create the world in a certain way. Nor does God create the rules of morality; rather, his goodness and reason *employ* them.

But what is the basis for Leibniz's counterpoint? It reflects a fundamental truth of his: *the principle of sufficient reason*.[11] As that principle is employed here, it means that 'all willing supposes some reason for the will' (ln 27). That is, if the will is not to be arbitrary, it requires some steady and true reason for it. Thus, whatever God wills must be informed by his understanding, which knows what is good. But by depending on the understanding rather than the will, Leibniz does not fall into the intellectualist trap of making God's will subject or subordinate to the laws of reason. This is suggested by the last line of the article, in the claim that the truths of the understanding cannot depend on God's will, 'any more than does his essence'. That is, it is not possible for God to will himself into existence (to will his essence), since he would already have to exist in order to will himself to exist – which is absurd. Similarly, it is not possible for the will to create the rules of reason in the understanding, without God already possessing an understanding in order to create them. More specifically, it

---

[10] Descartes, CSM II, §6, 291–2 / AT VII, 431–3.

[11] This is a central principle for Leibniz that he employs in many of his philosophical works, for example, the *Philosopher's Confession* (1672), *Primary Truths* (1689), and *Monadology* (1714). It will be further discussed in §§3, 8, 13, and 30. For a thorough discussion of the principle see the SEP entry: <https://plato.stanford.edu/entries/sufficient-reason>

follows from God's rational nature (part of God's essence) that God cannot create the laws of geometry and mathematics, because these rules constitute his essence by which he reasons. In other words, God would need a rational nature in order to create one. Therefore, God's essence must already be rational and good. Thus, Leibniz supplies an effective response to the dilemma posed by the voluntarist and intellectualist positions: All truths depend on God's essence – which is composed of both reason and goodness. His reason knows what is good; his will inclines him to what is good; and his causal power makes the good a reality.

Leibniz also refers to certain 'innovators'[12] who would say that Leibniz's view is *anthropomorphic*, namely, that the ideas of 'goodness' and 'rationality' are human conceptions that we mistake for divine attributes. The figure Leibniz has in mind is Spinoza, who, in his appendix to the *Ethics*, argues that ideas such as good, evil, order, beauty, and the idea of God as a 'final cause' are merely projections of human desires, needs, and imaginations.[13]

> Men have been so mad as to believe that God is pleased by harmony. Indeed there are philosophers who have persuaded themselves that the motions of the heavens produce a kind of harmony. All of these things show sufficiently that each one has judged things according to the disposition of his brain; or rather has accepted affections of the imagination as things.[14]

Far from having any transcendent value or ground, our most esteemed and transcendent ideas and values are merely the products of how things seem and feel to us, in accord with our relatively narrow range of desire and understanding.

Indirectly responding to Spinoza, Leibniz writes in 1678, 'The appendix [to the *Ethics*] is a mixture of truth and falsehood. Even though it is true that not everything happens for the sake of men, it does not follow that God acts without will or knowledge of the good.'[15] For Leibniz and most of his contemporaries, views such as Spinoza's were characterised as impious at best and atheistic at worst. As Leibniz claims here, these 'innovators' are impious, because they provide no reason to praise God. 'For why praise him for what he has done if he would be equally praiseworthy for doing just the contrary?' (ln 22). That is, we cannot suppose that God's ends are rational and good, if the rules of reason and goodness are arbitrary.

---

[12] A pejorative term for those who seek to establish doctrines independently of established authority.
[13] Spinoza, *Ethics*, Appendix to Part I (pp. 109–14).
[14] Ibid., p. 114.
[15] LL 205 / LGP I, 150.

For similar reasons Leibniz also implicitly has in mind Hobbes, whose nominalism and voluntarism Leibniz attacked in several key works.[16] These attacks reflect Socrates' attack on Thrasymachus in Book I of the *Republic* on the question of justice, which Leibniz draws attention to here: 'if the will takes the place of reason' (ln 25) and justice consists in 'whatever pleases the most powerful' (ln 26) then God would be no different than a tyrant.

For all these reasons, the voluntarist conception of God's will must be mistaken, Leibniz holds, because it fails to show how God can be both good and rational, and thus it undermines any reason we have to find God praiseworthy. What he insists on is that the truths of reason, geometry, and justice are uncreated and eternal, and constitute the very essence of God. We can also find here an implicit solution to the compatibility of the perfections of power and goodness. God's omnipotence is tempered by *goodness*, which is qualified by *reason*. No limitation upon God's power is implied, since the fullest expression of God's power is rational, rather than arbitrary. This does not mean, however, that Leibniz has solved all the problems entailed in this view, for it is not clear, at least, how God's will can be *free* on this account, since it appears that God can do nothing other than will according to the dictates of reason. In the next article, Leibniz will provide an important hint of a solution to this problem. Let us see whether it succeeds.

§3. On those who say that God could have done better.

At this point one might begin to think that Leibniz is most anxious that anyone should have a negative conception of God. But it helps to keep in mind Leibniz's overall motive for writing the *Discourse*, in view of the context of sectarian discord in which it was written. Having been born in 1646, just two years before the end of the Thirty Years' War, one of the most destructive wars in human history, Leibniz's sensibilities were no doubt deeply conditioned by the fallout from this complex religious and political conflict.[1] By engaging with the famous Catholic theologian and logician Antoine Arnauld (1612–94), Leibniz, the Protestant, could promote his persistent and lifelong aim of reconciling the Catholic and Protestant confessions.[2] Much of this effort would involve showing how

---

[16] See *Preface to Nizolius* (1670) in LL 128; 'Meditations on Knowledge, Truth, and Ideas' (1684) in AG 26; *Meditation on the Common Concept of Justice*; and *On the Principles of Pufendorf* (LPW).

[1] See the introduction for more detail and references.

[2] See Jolley 2019: 21, and Antognazza 2009: 256.

certain impious and dangerous theological views are the result of a faulty understanding – as Leibniz showed in the previous article. The immediate targets in this article are certain 'moderns', possibly Nicolas Malebranche (1638–1715), but certainly Arnauld himself, who seems to hold that God could have made things better than he did.[3] Certainly, in the context of the Thirty Years' War, this claim is quite believable. If these moderns are right, then God's perfection would be undermined, since, if God could have done better, he would not be perfect, nor worthy of glory or praise. God's *freedom* would also be undermined, since if God could not have made things better than he did, then God is not free to act *otherwise* than he did. This would undermine God's moral authority as well, since morality is generally said to depend on freedom. Let us see what the arguments are and how Leibniz counters them.

Suppose someone attempts to defend God's perfection, or simply God's goodness, by proposing that God is good in comparison to the infinite degrees of imperfection *below* him. Leibniz has three objections to this: First, it would be 'hardly praiseworthy' (ln 13), since it makes God's goodness relative to imperfection, rather than to a positive quality. Second, this idea of relative perfection conflicts with Sacred Scripture and the Holy Fathers' repeated praise of God's unqualified perfection.[4] But the third objection is much more far-reaching: we fail to acknowledge God's perfection when we fail to recognise 'the general harmony of the universe' and the 'the hidden reasons for God's conduct' (lns 18–19).

Harmony is a central metaphysical concept for Leibniz, stemming from his early writings on jurisprudence, where he defines it as 'diversity

---

[3] AA and AG refer the reader to Malebranche's *Treatise*, Discourse I, §XIV: 'God could, no doubt, make a world more perfect than the one in which we live' (MT 116). This reference suggests that Malebranche is the target of Leibniz's criticism. However, this seems doubtful because Malebranche does not actually maintain this view, since he goes on to qualify it: 'for our world, however imperfect one wishes to imagine it, is based on laws of motion which are so simple and so natural that it is perfectly worthy of the infinite wisdom of its author' (MT 117). In other words, a world whose laws of motion are simple and general better reflects God's wisdom than does a world whose laws must be adjusted to particular conditions, as if God should need to make arid regions wetter and wet regions drier to satisfy our conception of what is best. This would reduce the simplicity of God, as Leibniz would agree, as will be seen in §5. Thus, Leibniz seems far from targeting Malebranche here. The target is more likely Arnauld. Although much later than the *Discourse*, Leibniz argues in *Theodicy* that Arnauld's criticism of Malebranche (that Malebranche's 'general will' fails to recognise God's power to save all souls from damnation, if he so wills it) implies that God could have done better by saving them; and it is simply a contradiction to say that God could have done better. See Arnauld, *Reflexions*, p. 385, cited by Leibniz in *Theodicy* §223.

[4] Both the Hebrew and Christian scriptures contain numerous references to God's perfection (Hebrew *taman* and Greek *teleioi*).

compensated by identity, or the uniformity of different forms'.[5] It is also central to his doctrine of the 'pre-established harmony' of soul and body, although he does not discuss this doctrine directly in the *Discourse* (see §14 and §33). But the core idea is similar to musical harmony. Any single tone contains a multitude of underlying tones that together contribute to the character of the single, dominant tone. Different individual tones can then be played together or in a series to form a pleasing chord or melody; and different melodies played by different instruments can be combined to form a single but infinitely variable symphony (think of Bach, Vivaldi, and Handel, who represented the dominant musical form of Leibniz's era). Thus, 'the general harmony of the universe', is analogous to the complexity, richness, beauty, and unity of a symphony – a *philharmonic*, so to speak. In this way, God's perfection can be seen to consist in his having created an infinite variety of elements forming a pleasing whole. Now it is also characteristic of a symphony that some of its passages are not at all pleasing, as during moments of dissonance and discord that provoke emotions and moods such as sadness, longing, fear, and displeasure. Also characteristic is that these moments are resolved by the restoration of the harmonic structure, restoring a sense of calm or producing joy. The difficulty arises when the dissonances and tragedies of life remain unresolved. From our limited experience, the world too often appears disordered and inharmonious; thus we naturally complain that things certainly could have been better, as when we find some tragedy impossible to justify.

As a result, we may never learn 'the hidden reasons for God's conduct'. We think that the world could have been better only because we have not understood how moments of pain and unease are resolved by their relation to the whole. This point requires careful attention. Leibniz is not declaring that God's reasons are mysterious and inscrutable, and so we should just accept them, as we are too often told to do. Rather, we can understand God's ways if we understand that imperfection and suffering are compensated by their inclusion in this 'best possible world'. If this point seems unconvincing, we shall have occasion to consider it further throughout the commentary, especially below and in §§5, 6, and 30. But for now, Leibniz maintains that it is a mistake to believe, just because we do not know what God's reasons are, that God has no good reasons.

Leibniz's other arguments against the view that God could have done better involve God's freedom, a topic of central concern in the *Discourse*. His opponents seem to hold, similarly to the voluntarists in §2, that God's freedom is preserved only if God is capable of exercising

---

[5] *Elementa Juris Naturalis* (1671), AA VI, 1, 484. For commentary, see Johns 2013: 59–60. For the Neoplatonic roots of harmony, see Mercer 2004: 208–52.

his will independently of his reason (ln 25). For Leibniz, however, this is impossible, and even if it were possible, it would not be praiseworthy and would detract from God's glory (ln 26). To counter these views, Leibniz maintains, in direct opposition to his opponents' view of free will, that 'the highest freedom' is 'to act in perfection following sovereign reason' (ln 24). Let us look more closely at these arguments, beginning with that of the opponents.

1. If the will is not determined by any reason, then it is free (assumption).
2. God's will is not determined by any reason (assumption).
3. Therefore, God's will is free (MP 1, 2).[6]
4. Since God's will is free, God could have willed to make things better than he did.
5. Therefore, God could have willed to make things better than he did (MP 3, 4).

This argument depends on what Medieval philosophers called the 'indifference of the will', a doctrine similar to the voluntarist's 'arbitrary judgment' we saw in §2.[7] This doctrine holds that the will is free since it remains in perfect equilibrium in regard to the objects of choice. In other words, the will itself is free to choose *for no reason* other than itself. If the will were determined to its choice by reason, then something other than the will would determine it and it would not be free. Thus, on this view God is free to make, or not to make, things better than he did.

How does Leibniz oppose this argument? Essentially, by denying its first two premises, as suggested in line 26, that a will without a reason 'cannot be'. He may have in mind, as we saw in §2, his *principle of sufficient reason* (PSR), which was understood there to mean 'all willing supposes some reason for the will' (ln 27). So, if God could have willed things to be better than they are, as Leibniz's opponents argue he could, then God must have a reason that determines his will to prefer one state of things over another (implied in §3, lns 27–8). But by his opponents' own premises, God has no reason. In effect, Leibniz turns his opponents' assumption on its head: rather than making freedom depend on a will indifferent to reason, freedom depends precisely on being determined by reason. Not only that, for it is 'the highest freedom to act in perfection following sovereign reason' (lns 23–24). In other words, God's freedom consists in his will being determined by the *highest* or most perfect reason. Thus, since God has already freely willed what is most perfect, things cannot be better than they are.

---

[6] 'MP' means 'modus ponens', the name for a valid form of argument.
[7] See §30 for a full discussion of 'indifference of the will'.

Now, this argument might still land Leibniz into trouble with his opponents, who might point out that God would *not* be free, precisely because he has no possibility of doing *otherwise* than he did in creating the best possible state of things. This objection would be based on what the contemporary 'free will' literature calls the 'Principle of Alternate Possibilities', which, stated roughly, is that free will minimally requires the possibility of doing otherwise than one did.[8] Accordingly, since for Leibniz God cannot will otherwise than what is most perfect, God would not be free. But for Leibniz, this principle is not required for free will. What is required is the ability to do what is best, or most perfect; and it is *this* principle (which we may call 'the principle of the best') that determines God's will. Accordingly, the will is free just in case it is determined by the best reasons. Thus Leibniz's opponents are mistaken to believe that *their* arguments preserve God's freedom.

Leibniz then presses an additional point against his opponents: If God did not act according to 'sovereign reason', the principle of the best, then his actions would not be *praiseworthy*. He would not be, as the contemporary literature would say, 'morally responsible.' If God must have no reason for his will, he could not be praised for his goodness (or perfection); he would not be capable of making a rational judgment over what is best. But if we understand that willing freely consists in the ability to deliberate over what is best and to choose it, then a will *completely* determined by reason is most free, precisely *because* it is completely determined by reason to do what is best. What matters for free will is not so much being free from constraints, reasons, causes, or being able to choose otherwise, but being able to will what is best. While questions may remain over whether *willing according to best reasons* is sufficient for free will, we should mark this point as only a first step in comprehending Leibniz's account of free will in the *Discourse*.

Leibniz's greatest concern, perhaps, with his opponents' position, is indicated in the last line of this article, that God's actions always deserve to be glorified. The preceding arguments serve to affirm this point: Since God's actions are free, rational, and perfect, they are praiseworthy and thus exceedingly worthy of God's glory. It is important, however, to understand what Leibniz means by 'God's glory', because we might mistake it to mean that God wants or needs to be glorified, as if God wants only to be admired, feared, and worshipped. Perhaps the best example of what Leibniz means by 'God's glory' can be found in *Theodicy*:

---

[8] See, for example, Frankfurt 1969.

107

One may say, with some, that glory is the satisfaction one finds in being aware of one's own perfections; and in this sense God possesses it always. But when glory signifies that others become aware of these perfections, one may say that God acquires it only when he reveals himself to intelligent creatures; even though it be true that God thereby gains no new good, and it is rather the rational creatures who thence derive advantage, when they apprehend aright the glory of God. (LT §109)

Leibniz makes a similar point in the *Discourse* (§35 lns 34–37). So, perfection is the glory of God; but when we recognise this perfection, it is not God who benefits, but us. Leibniz also continually reminds us that God's glory consists not in being feared for his power, but in being loved for his goodness and respected for his wisdom.

A final point for this article helps to foreshadow a most important principle that will be elaborated in subsequent articles. In line 22, we find a passage that Leibniz had struck from his first draft. It mentions a circle as the most perfect figure and an equilateral triangle as the most perfect sort of triangle. Why is he saying this? He is trying to explain to his opponents that absolute perfection is possible. But the remarks imply more than this. A circle is the most perfect of all figures because it is the *simplest*. That is, it consists of a single, continuous, symmetrical line. No figure could be simpler than it. Yet because of this simplicity the circle also contains an infinite number of sides. This makes it the simplest figure in conception but the *richest* in effects. This feature of simplicity combined with richness, as we will see in §5 and §6, is the principle of God's choice of the best possible world and a principle exemplary of God's perfection. Similarly, a triangle is the simplest figure that can be made with straight lines, and the simplest type of triangle is one having equal sides. Thus, if God were to make only one triangle, out of an infinity of possible triangles, he would make an equilateral triangle, since it is 'absolutely speaking the most perfect', which is to say, the simplest. This again suggests that *God creates according to the simplest laws productive of the richest phenomena*,[9] and that, against Leibniz's opponents, it is false that there is no absolute perfection in God. It is perhaps surprising that Leibniz struck from the *Discourse* these rather clear illustrations of this most fruitful principle.

---

[9] On this point AA refers us to Malebranche's *Search after Truth*, Elucidation XVII, §40: 'These laws are established as wisely as possible when their fecundity corresponds to their simplicity' (MS 743).

§4. The love of God requires our complete satisfaction in him; but this does not imply we should not strive to act for the best.

At this point, Leibniz appears to draw an important consequence from what we have seen thus far: God's perfection is the foundation of the love we owe to God. But it is also the foundation of the love we *have* for God. How so? This claim is, actually, fairly complicated and interesting, as it touches on Leibniz's conceptions of justice and love, especially as he defined love in various ways throughout his works. Let us start with the love we *owe* to God. Here, a principle of equity or reciprocity is involved: If you are beneficent to me, then I am indebted to you, thus obligated to be beneficent to you. It would be unjust not to be, since 'the just' is whatever is equitable.[1] And since God's love is shown by the felicity and perfection he seeks for us, we owe it to God to love him back. Now, it would be a mistake to expect that we could reciprocate an equitable felicity and perfection, as if we had the power to benefit or improve God in any way. But this is not what Leibniz means. The proper point would be that we owe it to God to promote felicity and perfection in ourselves and in all others, since we are God's creations, as well as to worship God and be thankful for all he does for us. In this way, the sort of love we owe God from the principle of equity amounts to having a kind of *respect* or *honour* for his works and all he does for us.[2]

The love that we *have* for God relates to the 'satisfaction' that is central to love, that is, to the affections of satisfaction or pleasure that result when we love someone or when someone loves us.[3] Why such affections occur is of course the most fascinating and wonderful aspect of love, at least in terms of its sensation. For Leibniz, the satisfaction of love does not consist simply, as is typically thought, in possessing the object of our desire or the thing we lack. Rather, pleasure and perfection are metaphysically correlated. That is, whenever a perfection is increased, a feeling of pleasure is the result; and whenever pleasure is felt, then some degree of perfection has been increased. So, in familiar terms, when I seek to increase another's well-being and virtue, I gain a sense of pleasure or satisfaction. At the same

---

[1] See *Elements of Natural Law* (LL 137) and Johns 2013: Ch. 2.

[2] It should also be kept in mind that the term 'felicity' has a quite specific meaning. It does not mean, as according to some translations, simply 'happiness', where we think of happiness as the satisfaction of desire (that is, a sort of utilitarian happiness). Felicity, rather, is the sort of happiness that results from virtue, that is, the satisfaction we get from being an excellent person, practically, morally, and intellectually.

[3] 'For we love him whose good is our delight' (*Elements* (1671), LL 137 / AA VI, 1, 464). 'To love is to find pleasure in the perfection of another' (*Felicity* (1694), LPW 83).

time, pleasure is increased in you as a result of the increase in your perfection. This has the overall effect of motivating us to love each other, since doing so increases both pleasure and perfection. Leibniz actually thought that the metaphysical connections among love, pleasure, and perfection could resolve the disagreement over whether love could be 'disinterested', that is, as having its sole object the good of another, without consideration of one's own good. But love involves both goods, he claims, since it means we find our own pleasure in the perfection of another.[4]

The love we have for God, then, is the satisfaction we feel toward him, as a result of the perfections he promotes in us and that we perceive in his works. The problem, as Leibniz indicates, is that we often do not have this love. Here he refers to the sort of love that is characteristic of true friendship, in which each party has the disposition to will what each find good. But this mutual disposition is 'difficult' to share with God, as we often fail to perceive God's perfections correctly. We are then naturally 'disaffected' from God when we perceive so much imperfection in the world. This is of course a central concern of Leibniz's – to defend God's justice and love in the face of imperfection and evil. Leibniz's suggestion appears rather uncompromising. The only resolution to our disaffection and 'rebellion' from God is to find satisfaction in *everything* God does. What we need to do then, in order to have the proper affection that accompanies the love we owe to God, is to perceive correctly the perfection he possesses. But this will be possible only if we understand the larger context in which God's perfection is distributed, which Leibniz will explain in subsequent articles. In the meantime, it should suffice to have 'confidence' (§5 ln 5) that God does 'everything for the best'.

At this point Leibniz has a more immediate concern: if we accept that God always acts perfectly, then everything is as it should be; and so why bother trying to change it? As the poet Alexander Pope concisely expressed his understanding of Leibniz's system: 'Whatever is, is right.'[5] But this might be taken to mean that we have no reason or ability to do anything but to accept the way things are. Against this, Leibniz says that our complete satisfaction in God does not mean that we should not nor cannot make the world and ourselves better. While we cannot change the past, we certainly must not sit patiently, like a 'quietist' (ln 17), in passive submission to God's will.[6] Nor should we act according to the sort of 'lazy reason' (ln 19),

---

[4] The relationship between pleasure and perfection will be discussed more intensively in §15 and §30. On 'disinterested love' in Leibniz, see Roinila 2013.

[5] *Essay on Man*, Epistle I.

[6] Quietism is the Christian doctrine that the soul can be restored to God through complete passive resignation of one's will to God's will. Its principal proponent was Miguel de Molinos (1628–96).

as Leibniz will argue later in *Theodicy*, which holds that we can do nothing against our determined fate.[7] Instead, we should act according to our best judgment of what we *presume* to be the will of God (ln 19).

With his notion of a 'presumptive will', Leibniz draws upon his early background in jurisprudence.[8] When a judge must make a decision without sufficient evidence for the motives behind the offence (which is often the case, since a person's true inner motives are impossible to inspect and may remain unknown, even to that very person), a presumption in favour of the weight of the evidence must suffice. Similarly, although we lack adequate knowledge of God's will and purpose, we can reasonably assume, through contemplation of his perfections, that God wants us to contribute to the general good as far as possible. Furthermore, acting on this presumption makes our strivings or intentions matter. For even if our efforts fail, or turn out not to conform to God's will, we will have done all we can by making our will accord with our best presumption of God's will.[9] Yet right intention is not simply a matter of what just anyone happens to presume God's will to be; the bulk of the evidence must rest strongly in favour of those actions that increase perfection in ourselves and others. In this way, Leibniz ties together several enduring elements of his thought – that we always act in view of what we judge to be best (see §13 and §30), and that the best judgments are rooted in true perceptions of the perfection in things and in the love that results from these perceptions. Whether this account of acting on presumption can truly escape the Quietist's or the Stoic's capitulation to fate, or the pre-ordinances of God, we shall have occasion to evaluate in the following articles.

---

[7] Leibniz speaks of this 'lazy' or 'inert' reason in *Theodicy* as a tendency 'towards doing nothing . . . and only following inclination for the pleasure of the moment' (LT, preface, 54–5). Also see LT Essays §55 and LCD §§106–7. Leibniz's probable source for the phrase is Cicero, *On Fate*, XII, p. 28, in which Cicero conveys the 'idle argument' that was given in an attempt to refute Stoic determinism, but which Chrysippus the Stoic criticises.

[8] 'We will always have to declare ourselves in favor of he who has the presumption unless someone else demonstrates the contrary. Such are most of the moral reasonings' ('On the Interpretation, Foundation, Application and System of Laws' (1678–9), LD 87). See also Laerke 2018, especially 632–34.

[9] 'For we must always presume that God is prompted towards the good we know, until the event shows us that he had stronger reasons, although perhaps unknown to us, which have made him subordinate this good that we sought to some other greater good of his own designing, which he has not failed or will not fail to effect' (*Theodicy* §58).

§5. On the rules of perfection: the simplest means and the richest effects.

In this article and the next Leibniz provides a much richer understanding of God's perfection. While we may have *confidence* that God does everything for the best (ln 5), we still lack understanding of what it means for things to be 'the best' and how God makes them so – especially in view of certain apparent inconsistencies. For example, if God is all-powerful and all-good, why should God allow sin and suffering? And if God is perfectly just, why does it seem that God dispenses 'grace' to those who do not deserve it while not dispensing it to those who most do? Indeed, Leibniz begins to touch on the theme for which he later became famous: *theodicy*, or a defence of God's justice. Put another way, we still lack understanding of the relationship between God's perfections and the world God creates. Part of the problem, as Leibniz points out here, is that our 'finite minds' simply lack sufficient knowledge of God, specifically of that 'vision of God' (ln 10), that is, the 'beatific' or blessed knowledge of the divine, alluded to in the philosophical and theological traditions.[1] But our ultimately insufficient knowledge of God does not mean we cannot attain a richer understanding of God's perfection and creation than we presently have. Thus, we find in 'the rule of divine perfection' the beginnings of the rather audacious idea for which Leibniz is most well known – that *this world is the best possible world* (*Theodicy*, 1710). But this idea is easy to misunderstand if you neglect the 'rule' that underlies it. Once you understand Leibniz in §5 and §6, you will see that Voltaire's *Candide*, the famous satire of Leibnizian optimism, rather misses its mark.

The essence of this rule is that God is a supremely efficient being, since God utilises *the simplest means* of bringing about *the greatest effects*. In other words, the laws of nature (the means of establishing order in creation) must be as simple as possible, yet productive of the greatest number and variety of beings. Moreover, the relationship between simplicity and variety must be one of 'balance', such that the means, that is, the laws, are neither deficient nor excessive in their production of the greatest variety.[2] But why

---

[1] In 'The Allegory of the Cave' Plato describes an ascent of knowledge from the shadows of the cave to the vision of *the good*: 'in the knowable the last thing to be seen, and that with considerable effort, is the *idea* of the good; but once seen, it must be concluded that this is in fact the cause of all that is right and fair in everything' (*Republic*, 517c). In 1 Corinthians 13:12: 'At present we see indistinctly, as in a mirror, but then face to face.' In *Summa*, Supplement, q.92, Aquinas discusses the beatific or blessed vision and whether we can receive it.

[2] Nicholas Rescher describes the rule as a trade-off between simplicity and variety: if the laws are too simple, then the world will not contain much variety; whereas if the

should we suppose that God must conform to some criterion of efficiency? First, the rule reflects the traditional notion of divine simplicity – which will be discussed below. Second, it reflects God's infinite variety or abundance, or what Leibniz often refers to as 'God's glory', as the source of variety or abundance in creation. Third, Leibniz thinks that the created world should resemble God's nature as abundant, as far as *possible*, without replicating God's nature (which God has no reason to do). Thus, the rule of divine perfection is not designed to produce a world that is *absolutely* perfect, as is God, but rather a world that contains the greatest variety of beings, under the constraint of greatest simplicity. Accordingly, not every *conceivable* possibility will be realised in the world. In §30 we will see how this rule is applied to the creation of individual substances.

The fourth reason for the criterion of variety and simplicity seems to consist in an appeal to our intuitions about rational beings: as Leibniz's examples serve to show, this is how a supremely rational being would operate. Consider, by analogy, the construction of a proof in geometry. It is possible to make a valid deduction by taking more steps than required; it is also possible to make an invalid deduction by leaving out a required step, definition, or axiom. But an expert geometer employs no more and no fewer steps and justifications than needed for a successful deduction. Or, consider that an expert architect makes the most efficient and attractive use of space and materials, in accord with the building's purpose. If, on the contrary, the architect were to design a building containing spaces entirely unsuited to their purpose, you would judge the architect to be irrational and incompetent. A skilled architect weighs various factors against each

---

variety is too great, then the laws cannot be simple. So, the objective is to find the right *compromise* between the two criteria, simplicity and variety, a combination in which the simplest laws produce the greatest variety (Rescher 1996: 151–2). This interpretation is attractive, since, as Rescher suggests, it is characteristic of Leibniz's tendency to combine and harmonise distinct and competing factors (for example, harmony is diversity compensated by identity, *Elements* AA VI, 1 p. 484). Lloyd Strickland (2006: 70–3), however, argues that simplicity and variety are not in competition, but rather that the rule specifies *both* 'the simplest in hypotheses *and* the richest in phenomena' *at the same time*, as indeed Leibniz says in §6 line 25. So, the two criteria must bring about a world in which both criteria are simultaneously maximal. This seems right; however, here in §5 (lns 2 and 28) Leibniz says that simplicity and variety ('richness') must be in *balance*. So, it seems to me more correct to say that, while the laws must be most simple *and* the phenomena most rich, the relation between the two criteria must be *parsimonious*, such that (i) the laws must be no more complex than they need to be to produce the phenomena; (ii) the phenomena must not be *so* rich that they cannot be regulated by a law. The Ptolemaic astronomy, for example, violates (i), while the absence of a law regulating complex weather patterns would violate (ii). I think this 'parsimonious' criterion best matches Leibniz's examples as well as Malebranche's, below.

other – costs, materials, spatial constraints, and of course the constraints of natural laws – all in order to produce the best building possible.[3]

This maximal balance of means and effects is perhaps best exemplified by what Leibniz says is the most perfect type of being, namely a *mind* or *spirit*, that is, an *intelligence*. Indeed minds, considered separately from bodies, are super-efficient since they occupy no space and yet are capable of contemplating the greatest things. More specifically, their perfection consists in their capacity for perfecting themselves, which, in human beings, is moral virtue. A great deal more should be said about moral virtue; but briefly it means the possession of excellent dispositions of character, like temperance, wisdom, honesty, compassion, courage, etc., dispositions that are conducive to a 'felicitous' or flourishing life. In this way 'the felicity of minds' is God's 'principal aim' (ln 23). The idea that minds 'impede each other the least' (ln 21) follows from the exercise of virtue: we may attain as much freedom and happiness for ourselves as does not conflict with the freedom and happiness of others – 'as much as the general harmony permits' (ln 24). In other words, through the instrument of minds, God brings about the greatest compatibility of competing desires, needs, and abilities, such as would be conducive to a harmonious society.[4]

If it appears that variety and abundance conflict with *simplicity*, we must keep in mind two conceptions of simplicity in God: (1) Simplicity means *unity*. God's essence is, of course, complex, consisting of all of his perfections: reasoning, goodness, power, and will. However, simplicity consists in these perfections being entirely integrated and unified. God's mind is most orderly and his overall purpose – the felicity of minds – is singular and unchanging. Unlike us, God does not possess competing wills and

[3] Leibniz is clearly following Malebranche: 'An excellent workman should proportion his action to his work; he does not accomplish by quite complex means that which he can execute by simpler ones; he does not act without an end, and never makes useless efforts. From this one must conclude that God, discovering in the infinite treasures of his wisdom an infinity of possible worlds (as the necessary consequences of the laws of motion which he can establish), determines himself to create that world which could have been produced and preserved by the simplest laws, and which ought to be the most perfect, with respect to the simplicity of the ways necessary to its production or to its conservation' (*Treatise*, Discourse I, §XIII). 'Now these two laws [of Descartes', namely, rectilinear motion and the proportional distribution of the motion of colliding bodies] are so simple, so natural, and (at the same time) so fruitful, that even if one were to have no other reasons for judging that it is they which are observed in nature, one would still have every reason to believe that they are established by him who always acts in the simplest ways – in whose action there is nothing that is not law-governed, and who proportions it so wisely to his work that he brings about an infinity of marvels through a very small number of wills' (*Treatise*, Discourse I, §XVII).
[4] On harmony see §3, §35, and §36.

desires, nor does God need to tinker constantly with creation in order to bring about his ends. God knows exactly what is best to do and his simple decree is sufficient to execute and accomplish it.

(2) The notion of God's simplicity also reflects a principle of scientific method to which Leibniz alludes at the end of this article: that the best explanation (or hypothesis) is one that accounts for all observations by means of the fewest laws. This principle, often called 'Ockham's Razor', is attributed to the fourteenth-century philosopher William of Ockham, who is supposed to have expressed the principle this way: 'do not multiply entities beyond necessity'.[5] Among contemporary philosophers the rule is often called 'the principle of parsimony'. This long-standing preference for methodological simplicity is motivated by historical developments within astronomy; but it may also be motivated by an interest in *theological* simplicity, since a simple universe reflects the simplicity of its creator.

This demand for both scientific and theological simplicity can be understood through the example of astronomy. Prior to the seventeenth century, under the Aristotelian model, the cosmos was understood to be *geocentric*, that is, all the stars including the Sun and the planets revolved around the Earth in perfect circles. This model was fairly simple and agreed with the way things naturally appear to us – and still does. However, closer observation revealed that planetary movements were more complex. At certain times, the planets appeared to move *backwards* (in 'retrograde') before resuming their forward course. To account for this oddity, astronomers in the Ptolemaic tradition (around 170 AD) proposed a new hypothesis, one in which the Earth remained fixed at the centre, while the other planets moved in a small circle of their own, called an 'epicycle', as they also orbited the Earth. When a planet entered one half of its epicycle, it appeared to move backwards; then as it entered the other half, it appeared to move forwards. The result was that the heavenly bodies appeared to move across the sky in elaborate but uniform swirls. This hypothesis had several virtues: it enabled astronomers to make more accurate predictions of planetary motion; and it remained consistent with the Church's cosmology, which the Church drew from biblical passages suggesting that the heavens revolved around the Earth.[6] It also reinforced a common religious conviction that the Earth and its creatures are natu-rally at the centre of God's care and concern.

---

[5] This expression appears nowhere in Ockham but is traditionally attributed to him. See SEP on Ockham.

[6] Many passages depict the Sun moving (rising, setting). But this passage, cited at Galileo's trial, suggests that the Earth is unmoving: 'Lord, my God, you are great indeed! [. . .] You fixed the earth on its foundation, never to be moved' (Psalm 104:1–5).

This 'Ptolemaic' hypothesis, however, had a major problem: there was no natural reason to explain why the planets should move forward and then backward. The only real motive for the hypothesis was to retain the geocentric model, which was, after all, consistent with tradition, observation, and Church doctrine. But its baroque complexity had no explanation on the order of physical causes. Eventually, when astronomers like Copernicus (1543) and Galileo (1630) with his telescope proposed the *heliocentric* model, they were in effect proposing a much simpler hypothesis. On this model, with the Sun fixed at the centre, the apparent backward (retrograde) motion of the planets is explained by the forward motion of the now-moving Earth, as it moves past those planets. Thus, this hypothesis had no need to posit some additional 'law of epicycles' to account for the 'retrograde' motion. The heliocentric hypothesis turned out to be much simpler and more efficient, because it relied on fewer means (laws) to explain the observations (effects); and, since it is simpler, it more likely represents the truth. As Copernicus said: 'But we should rather follow the wisdom of nature, which, as it takes very great care not to have produced anything superfluous or useless, often prefers to endow one thing with many effects.'[7] The wisdom of nature, of course, reflects the wisdom, simplicity, and abundance of God, who produces the richest of effects with the fewest laws.

Despite the appeal of the simplicity of natural laws, astronomers and theologians were reluctant for many years to adopt the heliocentric hypothesis, since it opposed Scripture, displaced the Earth from the centre of divine concern, and, most strikingly, did not conform to how things appeared in the sky to the plain and casual observer. (We still say, after all, that the Sun rises and sets.) For many, it was an unnatural and dangerous hypothesis. No doubt Leibniz had in mind Galileo's 1633 appearance before the inquisition, and subsequent house arrest, as he quietly drew this analogy between God's simplicity and that of astronomical laws. But Leibniz intends the analogy to show that the character of nature distinctly reflects the character of its creator.

§6. God's actions are most orderly. Nothing occurs without a determinable order.

This article further illustrates God's perfection (simplicity and richness) by focusing on 'order'. Its main objective is to explain how God's actions are never without reason, even where natural events seem to us as disordered or as miraculous. Miracles will be discussed in §7. Leibniz's explanation

[7] *On the Revolutions*, 24.

contains a number of terms that can be difficult to track. To begin, all of God's actions or volitions conform to a 'universal order', an order which is 'at the same time the simplest in hypotheses and the richest in phenomena' (ln 25). Included within this universal order are God's wills and actions that *we* distinguish as *ordinary* and *extraordinary*. In other words, God's ordinary actions are those we can identify as conforming to natural laws, that is, some 'particular order', such as the laws of motion. On the other hand, we take God's *extraordinary* actions to be inexplicable in terms of natural laws. Leibniz is concerned here to show that despite their seeming inexplicability, natural events, such as a violent storm, nevertheless conform to natural laws; thus, nothing 'absolutely irregular' happens in the world (ln 9).

As we saw in §5, Leibniz conceives of God's law for creation as consisting of the simplest means for producing the richest effects. This means that natural laws will be as few as will be productive of the greatest variety and order of phenomena. However, this also means that some particular effects, especially those that appear to be greatly disordered – such as earthquakes, floods, tragic accidents, or even the apparently random outcome of a roll of a die – might convince us that no law of nature, no simple decree of God's will, could account for them. We would be wrong, however, since any disorder is only *apparent*, conforming nevertheless to the 'universal order' that God has established according to the law for creation.

The examples that Leibniz offers are intended to show that no matter how much apparent disorder in the phenomena, there is a simple rule for their generation, a simple order in the cause. We can better understand what he means by considering a common but mistaken conception of a random event. If we take 'random' to mean an *uncaused* event, there can be no such thing, since, according to his principle of sufficient reason (PSR), every event has a cause. But if we take 'random event' to mean an event whose cause was unexpected, or whose explanation is too complex to understand or to make predictions from, then we are not really denying cause and order to the event; we just do not know the causal law involved in it. Chaos theory, for example, does not say that events are uncaused; it says that the initial conditions of events are so sensitive and fine-grained that we cannot make reliable predictions from them. This is an *epistemic* problem resulting from our lack of ability to identify all the relevant causes and their effects, not a matter of an effect lacking a cause. Similarly, God does nothing that is uncaused, even if we do not know what the cause is.

By asserting a law for God's perfection ('the simplest in hypotheses and the richest in phenomena', ln 25), Leibniz would seem to be asserting what many philosophers and theologians would decry as an unwarranted epistemic assumption, or worse, an anthropomorphism of God's will.

However, possibly having in mind such accusations, Leibniz does not say that this law expresses precisely how God's mind works, or that it implies God looks to a law and follows it, but only that the law reflects an 'imperfect resemblance to the divine wisdom' (ln 29), so that our minds may be elevated to a more adequate and praiseworthy understanding of God. This law provides at least the plausibly correct understanding that God's will is ordered according to the highest wisdom, even if we comprehend only a small quantity of that order and wisdom.

And yet a different and more difficult problem arises. This law places significant pressure on a positive account of God's *justice*, since it would seem to make God responsible for every natural disaster and moral evil. Leibniz will address this implication in the next article, with the notion of God's *permissive* will.

§7. That miracles conform to the general order, though counter to natural laws; and how God permits evil but does not will it.

The previous discussion of order sets the stage for confronting two problems in this article: (1) How miracles are consistent with the natural order (laws of nature). (2) How God *permits* evil but does not will it.

First, to understand the problem with miracles, we must clarify what a miracle is often thought to be. Most people today call 'a miracle' anything that appears to be wonderful, amazing, extremely desirable, fortunate, or unexpected. But for Leibniz, and any serious theologian today, a miracle specifically implies the agency of God or some God-appointed agent. In addition to being divinely caused, a miracle is considered to be a *supernatural event*, which means that it occurs as an *exception* to what Leibniz calls 'subaltern maxims', that is, to the laws of nature, such as the laws of motion. Leibniz's concern about miracles is that since they are exceptions to natural laws, they appear to be disordered, thus repugnant to God's perfection. Given that God's actions are most orderly (as stated in the heading of the previous article), Leibniz needs to explain how miracles conform to some type of order.

To solve this problem, Leibniz uses the notions of 'general will' (*la volonté generale*) and 'particular will' from Malebranche, who introduced them in his *Treatise on Nature and Grace* (1680). One of the problems Malebranche sought to solve was how to retain the simplicity and wisdom of God, given that certain natural events appear to be disordered. Consider, for example, the birth of a deformed child.[1] Malebranche says that while nature's laws always follow God's *general will*, which is always 'wise and

---

[1] MT Discourse I, §XVIII.

just', God does not directly, by a *particular* will, decree that a child shall be deformed. However, God's intervention by a particular will to prevent such misfortunes would detract from the wisdom and simplicity of God, as if the laws that he established were not otherwise most fruitful and simple.[2] Miracles, then, according to Malebranche, which may also appear to be disordered since they do not follow natural laws, can be ascribed to the order of God's grace.[3] Thus miracles are not cases of disorder, since they still conform to God's general will.

Now we can see how Leibniz employs Malebranche's terms. All events, whether natural or miraculous, conform to God's 'most general will' (ln 12). This will, as we have seen, is to bring about the best, in accord with the principles of simplicity, variety, and harmony. Miracles, however, conform to God's particular will, as exceptions to natural laws, while still conforming to the general will. This may seem puzzling: how can God make exceptions to natural laws while retaining a sense of order conforming to the general will? The answer is that natural laws, or 'the nature of things', are only the result of God's 'custom' (ln 8), a term implying a certain regularity, but a regularity that can be contravened in favour of a more suitable outcome. A miracle, then, is an exception to a natural law – but an exception that God has found to have greater value than the law to which the miracle is an exception. Thus, miracles remain in conformity with God's general will and order.

However, Leibniz must tread very carefully here. He wants to avoid the view, as does Malebranche, that God intervenes from time to time in order to make things better than he had already established, because that would imply an imperfection in God, and would conflict with his argument in §3 that God could not have done better. For example, suppose God sees that the effects of a drought are becoming very severe.[4] The land is parched, the crops will not grow, and the local population is starving and dying. God wants this suffering to stop, and he knows the rain will not come soon enough; so, he decides to make it rain, contravening the natural course of events. This miracle would even be consistent with God's general will, since it promotes the overall perfection by reducing suffering and increasing life. However, if God must intervene from time to time to 'correct' the course of nature, then God as much as admits that the world could be

---

[2] 'It is true that God could remedy these unhappy consequences through an infinite number of particular wills: but order would not have it so . . . And in consequence God is not to be blamed for not disturbing the order and simplicity of his laws by miracles which would be quite convenient to our needs, but quite opposed to the wisdom of God' (MT Discourse I, §XLIII).

[3] MT Discourse I, §XXI.

[4] Similar to an example Malebranche gives in *Treatise*, Illustration VII (MT 199).

better than he made it. Such an outcome would also detract from God's simplicity or constancy, since his will would change from time to time. So, while Leibniz wants to maintain the traditional view that miracles are divinely caused, it is hard to see how, as exceptions to God's own natural laws, their occurrence does not detract from God's perfection. Leibniz will provide a possible answer to this difficulty in §16.

The second problem for Leibniz is the worry that since God wills only what is best, and yet evil (moral and natural) occurs, it would seem to follow that *God wills all evil*. Thus Leibniz touches on the notorious 'problem of evil', which he famously claims to resolve in *Theodicy*.[5] One solution to that problem is anticipated here in the *Discourse*: that although God *permits* evil, he does not *will* it.[6] Similar to Malebranche, Leibniz holds that the laws of nature that God has willed can result in misfortunes and tragedies (natural disasters, deformed infants). He also recognises that humans commit evil against God's will (ln 22). However, while God always disapproves of evil, he *permits* it. Now the reason God permits it is twofold: (1) humans can become more perfect (less inclined to commit evil) through having to suffer natural punishments for the evils they commit (lns 23–4); (2) for any evil, God knows how to 'draw a greater good from it' (ln 28).

In sum, Leibniz wants to maintain that God wills only good actions and that only humans commit evil actions. So while God *could* prevent them, he permits them, and thus justifies them, *just in case a greater good can be derived from them*. To illustrate, consider Sarah, whose actions are (a) *good*, just in case they tend to promote 'the most perfect order'. God 'concurs'[7] with Sarah's good actions, even commanding them – even if they fail to occur (suppose an accident prevents Sarah from attending the charity function). That's because the character of such actions or intentions is 'good in itself', regardless of outcome. No problem here.[8] But now suppose Sarah performs (b) an *evil* action, by purposefully kicking an abandoned baby on her way to the charity function. Such an action is 'evil in itself'.

---

[5] Briefly, the problem of evil is that evil exists, and yet given God's attributes (omniscience, omnipotence, and omni-benevolence) God could prevent it, but does not; thus, God lacks one or more of those attributes. One attempted solution is to deny that evil is real (Augustine), or to show that evil is consistent with God's attributes. Leibniz in a way does both. See Michael J. Murry's entry in the SEP, 'Leibniz on the Problem of Evil'.

[6] On the permissive will see *Theodicy* I §25. Also see Echavarría 2010.

[7] Concurrence forms part of God's metaphysical influence on our actions. See §14 and §30.

[8] As we saw in §4, God approves of actions motivated by our best deliberation over God's 'presumptive will', even if such intended actions, after a sincere effort to realise them, fail to occur.

Now, an action evil in itself can be permitted, just in case God can derive greater perfection from it. So, suppose Tara, a witness to Sarah's evil, is as a result moved to establish an orphanage in which abandoned babies are well cared for and grow up to become rational benefactors themselves. Naturally, Tara's actions not only conform to God's general will, but more than compensate for Sarah's evil. Thus God 'concurs' with Sara's evil action, because of the greater perfection derived from Tara's actions. Thus Leibniz can say that God's *particular* willings (exhibited through the actions of his creatures) are not the evil willings of God, since he does not in fact will them, but merely permits them. The permission is justified, just in case 'in the end more perfection is found in the whole series' (ln 25) of events, than if the evil had not occurred.

The reader may judge for herself whether this distinction between willing and permitting absolves God from responsibility for the evil actions of God's creatures. In any case we must not mistake Leibniz's position here. God's permission of evil does not mean *approving* of evil in any way. It means that *in spite* of the evil we freely commit, God can derive greater perfection from it. (Leibniz will use this same reasoning in §30.) Nor must we take Leibniz to be saying that God permits evil *for the sake* of deriving a greater perfection. If he did, then harming babies for fun would be good, even recommended, *because* greater goods would result from it. Now, although Leibniz says that the natural punishments that result from our evil actions can serve to make us more perfect, this does not imply that it is acceptable to commit evils because doing so will make us better eventually. What Leibniz says is that evil actions are evil in themselves; so, they should never be done for the sake of deriving a greater good, even though God *does* derive a greater good from them.

Leibniz's justification for the permissive will may still need defending. If God could prevent an evil but fails to do so, then is he not responsible for it? Leibniz himself says, elsewhere, that if someone could prevent an evil done to us but declines to, we would have a right to complain against them.[9] And yet Leibniz is here suggesting that we do not have a right to complain; indeed, we are expected to acknowledge that God could not have done better or otherwise than he did.

So far in the *Discourse*, the reader cannot fail to notice that Leibniz is deeply concerned to defend and advance a positive account of God's perfections. We have seen how God creates the world according to the principle of the best, that is, according to the rule of simplicity and abundance; and that any *seeming* imperfections – natural disorders or intentional evils – can be overcome by even greater degrees of perfection. Leibniz is not by

---

[9] *Meditation on the Common Concept of Justice*, LPW 53.

any means finished with these arguments; but by bearing them in mind the reader is in a good position to turn to Leibniz's next major concern: the metaphysical nature of the individual human being.

§8. On the complete notion (concept) of an individual substance: the principal motive for the doctrine; the philosophical conception of substance; the problem of individuation; Leibniz's early conception of individuation; the complete notion of an individual in the *Discourse*.

Articles 8, 9, 13, and 14 are arguably the most important, if not the most difficult, in the *Discourse*, since they deal with one of the most central topics in the history of philosophy – that of substance – and since Leibniz's rather distinctive account of an *individual* substance developed out of certain complex and obscure difficulties tied to that history.[1] In addition, his conception of it, as expressed in the summary of §13, that 'the individual notion of each person contains once and for all everything that will ever happen to him', literally 'frightened' his correspondent, the philosopher-theologian Antoine Arnauld, for its implication that God and creatures are not free.[2] Thus, questions about substance and freedom formed the greater part of the Leibniz-Arnauld correspondence. So, what is the complete notion of an individual substance, and why does Leibniz need it? What follows is a lengthy and detailed exposition on some of the background needed to answer these questions.[3] The exposition is divided into five sections: 1. *The principal motive for the doctrine*; 2. *The philosophical conception of substance*; 3. *The problem of individuation*; 4. *Leibniz's early conception of individuation*; 5. *The complete notion of an individual in the* Discourse, which itself is divided into six brief sub-sections.

The principal motive for the doctrine
Leibniz's principal motive is expressed in the first line: to distinguish the actions of God from the actions of creatures like us. This distinction is needed to avoid the views of certain of his contemporaries implying that

---

[1] There is a vast literature on the topic of substance in Leibniz. Probably the best place to start is with Robert Sleigh's (1990) commentary on the Leibniz-Arnauld correspondence.

[2] See introduction, pp. 11–12. See Arnauld's first reply to Leibniz, 13 March 1686 (LAV 9 / LAM 9).

[3] Leibniz's *Primary Truths* (1689, AG pp. 30–4) is also recommended. For some of the logical aspects of the 'complete notion', written in the same year as the *Discourse*, see Leibniz's *General Inquiries on the Analysis of Notions and Truths* (LGI 2021).

God is the only truly acting being.[4] If those views are correct, then we are not the cause of our actions, thus, we do not have free will; nor are we moral agents, since moral agency requires being the cause of one's actions. However, if we are individual substances, then we are the cause of our actions. Leibniz will have more to say in other articles to establish that the will is free. But a necessary, if not sufficient, condition of freedom is to be the cause or source of one's actions. It cannot be that God is the only source of our ability to act.

The philosophical conception of substance

To begin to understand Leibniz's conception of an individual substance, we must trace the historical development of the philosophical conception of 'substance', a term that may be better translated as *primary being*.[5] The question 'what is primary being?' can be understood in various ways, such as: (a) What are the ultimately simple or fundamental constituents of reality? (b) What is the source and cause of everything that exists, or what is the being or beings upon which all being depends? (c) What retains its essential identity through time, while undergoing any number of 'accidental' changes? (d) What does it even mean to speak of 'being'?

An attempt to answer (a) was originally taken up by the Pre-Socratic philosophers, who, by noticing similarities among the multitude of things, claimed that all things were composed of one, or many, basic 'elements': Water, Earth, Fire, Air, or some combination of them; or that everything was composed of what Democritus called 'atoms', the 'unsplittable' material components of all things. Some of these natural philosophers posited non-material elements and principles as well – but the basic idea is the same: all that exists can be reduced to *something* not further reducible. Contemporary natural scientists have implicitly followed this Pre-Socratic approach, although of course refined methods and improved instruments have greatly expanded our understanding of the basic constituents. *Water*, for example, is composed of the elements *hydrogen* and *oxygen*, each of

---

[4] Leibniz has in mind Malebranche's doctrine of occasionalism, which is discussed in §33; and the doctrine of 'divine conservation' which is discussed in §14. Leibniz may also have in mind Spinoza's *Ethics* (Part I) in which God, the only substance, is the only acting being, of which creatures are only modes, thus not substances, thus not independently acting beings.

[5] That is, what Aristotle calls, in Greek, *ousia*, is translated into Latin as *substantia* and in English commonly as *substance*. Richard Hope translates *ousia* as 'primary being' (*Metaphysics*, Bk IV, Delta, Ch. 7, para. 8, 1017b10) and this strikes me as the best way to understand the term. I beg the reader to bear in mind that the following account of substance is a rough, impossibly brief, not uncontroversial, but hopefully not misleading, summary of 2,000 years of complicated ideas.

which consists essentially of a specific number of *atoms*. Atoms, as we now know, can themselves be further analysed into a host of elementary particles (electrons, protons, neutrons, and then further into quarks and leptons).[6] Thus, even from the contemporary scientific perspective, all sensible and material things consist ultimately of irreducible particles (although this point is also scientifically disputed), and these, so far as we know, are the primary beings.

For most philosophers of the Modern period (seventeenth century), the obvious answer to (b) is God. For Descartes, while everything depends on God for its existence, everything consists of only two *kinds* of substance: thought (mind, soul) and matter, each of which are conceived as having no properties in common with each other.[7] For Spinoza, there is only one substance, God or nature, conceived under two attributes: thought and matter; and every individual thing is considered to be a 'mode' (or way) of one or the other of these attributes. On this view, we are all just finite chips off the infinite block of the one substance, such that we are not individual beings distinct from God. The point here is that in answer to the question of substance, various conceptions have been put forward, each with starkly different metaphysical, physical, and theological consequences.

As we just saw, natural philosophers and scientists appeal to whatever basic constituents of matter as the 'building-blocks', so to speak, of every-thing else. However, Aristotle, most Medieval philosophers, and Leibniz are among those who maintained that *material* building blocks could not be primary, could not be substance. Their basic claim is that matter by its very nature cannot account for its *organisation*, that is, for the fact that bits of matter have any discernible organisation or shape at all; nor for how a multitude of individual atoms can come together to make up a single thing or organism.[8] So they maintained that something *not* material must account for the character of matter, and *that* something is called its *form*. Form determines (in some sense) specific *arrangements* of undifferenti-ated matter, resulting in individual things of distinct kinds. For instance, an animal and a human, each of which are made of the same elementary matter, differ only in how their form arranges their matter. Thus, an armadillo has the form ANIMAL while a human has the form ANIMAL plus the form RATIONAL – the latter marking the species difference between

---

[6] The contemporary 'Standard Model' is described here: <https://home.cern/science/physics/standard-model>

[7] See Descartes, *Principles* I, §52–4. Also, *Meditation* VI, p. 54.

[8] Some of these reasons for the inadequacy of matter to account for its organisation are indicated by Leibniz's critique of Cartesian physics throughout the *Discourse*, but especially in §10 and §12.

animals and humans. Forms can also determine species differences among minerals, chemicals, and plants. While it is difficult to explain clearly what a form *is*, it is fairly clear that form is the immaterial principle (or cause) that determines things to be the *kind* of thing they are.

So, to return to our question: what is primary being (substance)? From what has just been said, it would seem that *form* is primary being, since it distinguishes matter into distinct kinds, without which distinction we cannot say what matter *is*. On the other hand, some would say that *matter* is primary, since matter is what persists through all of the changes in form that a thing undergoes (something like the view expressed in (c) above). For instance, a caterpillar larva undergoes 'metamorphosis' (literally, a 'change in form') when it becomes a butterfly. Yet, we still want to say that the larva and the butterfly are the *same* creature, and it seems that the matter can account for this, since it remained while the form changed. Then again, it seems clear that the matter changes *along with* the form. The question is what, if anything, is ultimately responsible for the identity of the being as it undergoes change. The answer should lead us to *primary being*.

At this point, we can conveniently set aside the complex debate over the primacy of either matter or form, by admitting that all beings (except for God and angels) are *combinations* of matter and form (a view which Aristotle called *hylomorphism*). This would appear to give us what we want for a primary being: (a) a basic, although complex, constituent of reality; (b) the source and cause of all existing things, since everything can be explained in terms of matter and form; (c) a being that retains its identity through change; and (d) to speak of 'a being' is to speak of an individual of a certain kind.

The hylomorphic view may get us much closer to 'primary being' or substance, but not close enough; and that is because we observe that some beings have features that can be considered *more* primary. Plants, animals, and humans, for instance, unlike minerals and chemicals, have a greater degree of *independence* because they possess within them the source of their changes, motions, and activities, whereas minerals and chemicals are changed and moved by something external to them. As a result, we need to add another criterion for primary being: (e) a primary being contains its own principle of change and activity. While other beings such as minerals have a form (let us call it 'substantial form'), growing and self-moving beings have something more, which Aristotle called 'psyche' and which we call 'soul'. Thus, it is soul that gives beings their capacity for self-movement, or what we tend to call 'life'. Let us then call 'primary being', in the fullest sense, a being consisting of form and matter, *and* possessing an internal capacity for self-movement and change, that is, a soul.

125

Let us take a closer look at the features of living beings and why they are considered primary. First, it is important to note that primary beings are *not* irreducible building blocks of other beings, as on the scientific view, but are instead *indivisible wholes*. We say they are wholes for several reasons: they are each endowed, through their material constituency and form, with certain abilities and qualities, namely reproduction of their kind, growth, self-movement, responsiveness to their environment, sensation (in some) and thought (in some); but, essentially, they all possess internally an overall unity and distinctness of *function* – a kind of *life*. Their *form* or soul is the arrangement of their matter, and this arrangement endows them with the qualities and abilities they have according to their kind: a plant *grows*; an animal grows and *senses*; a human grows and senses and *reasons*. Moreover, while you can divide minerals without destroying their form, a functioning whole cannot be divided into other functioning wholes without being destroyed. This *indivisibility* makes, perhaps, the strongest case for primary being. Accordingly, we can characterise a primary being as an organic whole which acts (does things), suffers (actions happen *to* it), and which is the source and subject of the actions, passions, and changes it undergoes throughout its lifetime. Under this conception, primary beings (substances) are individuals consisting of matter-form sub-components of whatever kind, *plus* a determining form (plant-ness, animality, humanity), comprising a *whole individual*.

The question of individual substance can be expressed in another way (closer to Leibniz's terminology): What is the ultimate subject of predication? That is to ask, what is the *subject* to which all the *accidents* (qualities, properties, etc.) belong? This way of conceiving of substance can be found in Book V of Aristotle's *Categories*, in which Aristotle sets out all the 'predicaments' (categories), or ways of talking about subjects. For example, when we say, 'Socrates has wisdom', we assert that a subject, Socrates, has the *quality* of wisdom. When we say, 'Socrates is six feet tall', we attribute a certain *quantity* to his body. When we say, 'Socrates is sitting on a chair' we assert a certain *relation* or *situation* in regard to Socrates, namely that he is in a sitting-relation to a chair. In fact, as Aristotle holds, every time we make assertions or judgments, we are claiming that a certain *predicate* (indicating quality, quantity, situation, etc.) belongs to a certain *subject*. This will not be surprising when you notice that every assertion (every true or false statement) has a subject-predicate structure. But this indicates, for Aristotle, that *the subject* is the fundamental category of being – since it is that which every predicate is about. Now if this subject is not a predicate of any other subject (that is, if Socrates does not belong to any other subject as part of an organic whole) then the subject is an *ultimate subject of predication* – a *primary being*. So, a substance is said to be an ultimate subject of predication, and for Aristotle (as for Leibniz) Socrates is a substance, so are you, and so is every individual human. These points should be kept in mind when we discuss below the relationship between Leibniz's predicate-in-notion theory of truth and the complete notion of an individual substance.

The problem of individuation

We should by now have a more refined understanding of what 'substance' means in its philosophical sense. However, the above account glosses over at least one difficulty that Medieval philosophers and Leibniz had long sought to resolve. Since the difficulty is complicated and obscure but crucially important, a bit of stage-setting is required. Perhaps the reader has already noticed in the above account that while *there are* individuals, no account of their *individuality* has been given. While Socrates, for example, like all substances, cannot be predicated of any other substance, and he has matter and the form of humanity, just like every other human, what makes him *Socrates* as opposed to, say, Callicles? Aristotle himself pointed out the difficulty: any definition of an individual consists of *universals* (properties common to many things).[9] Thus, there are many humans, many of which have brown hair, brown eyes, and walk, talk, laugh, sit, run, have a soul, and can be wise; and so we define an individual in terms of properties that it shares with other individuals. But to say that *this* individual is distinct from *that* one requires a way to say that these common properties belong to *this* substance only, making her the *unique* individual that she is. How do we do that? Does individuation consist in some physical or mental characteristic, or some distinct subset of them? Is there a *form* of individuality? Is it the individual soul? The question here is not how do we *tell* one substance from another, but rather *what is it, what is necessary, for a thing to be the very individual it apparently is?* An answer to this question is not easy to come by; but understanding what is at stake in the question is crucial for understanding Leibniz's principle of individuation.[10]

To get a better handle on the problem, let us consider several possible principles of individuation. (Please bear with the following exposition, which is long, but will hopefully pay off.) We should begin by establishing

---

[9] *Metaphysics*, Bk VII, 1039a14–21.

[10] The reader should bear in mind that the question of individuation here will not be a question, again, of how we *discern* one individual from another (even though the principle of individuation *can* be what discerns one from another); nor is it a matter of finding *some efficient cause* for being an individual. It is a matter, rather, of what constitutes the individuality of the individual, which is a *metaphysical* question, as will be explained in what follows. The best source on the problem of individuation is Jorge Garcia (1984) by whose chapter 1 I am guided in this section.

a means for evaluating a possible principle. The 'principle of individuation', as we shall call it, must involve (1) some property or set of properties belonging to the individual alone, such that the individual is the *ultimate subject* of its properties (as Aristotle suggests), and (2) some property or set of them that *persists*, despite changes in other properties the individual may undergo – for we intuitively believe that while individuals change constantly in certain respects, they also remain the same in some respect. These two criteria make intuitive sense as basic requirements for individuation, whatever *the* principle of individuation turns out to be.

Now, let us consider probably the most intuitive of individuating principles: *space*, with which we must include *time*. It seems obvious that distinct individuals occupy distinct spaces simultaneously, as we can plainly observe. Right now, I am in my own space *here*, while at the same time Monique sits *to the left* of me, and our friend, Alia, stands to the right of us both. Thus, we have three distinct individuals, *because* each one simultaneously with the others occupies a space bounded uniquely by its own body. Distinguishing individuals in spatio-temporal terms works incredibly well for practical purposes, and we do it all the time.

But now consider that individuation in spatio-temporal terms does not fulfil the above criteria: (1) Space and time do not belong to the individual alone, since one's spatial location at a certain time depends on (is relative to) the spatial-temporal designation of other things. For instance (baring absolute spatial coordinates) my space-time designation (three feet between Monique and Alia) depends on the spatial designations of Monique and Alia. Thus, my spatial designation is relative to *other* things, rather than a property belonging solely to me. (2) Space-time properties do not *persist*, since spatial relations and quantities can change, as the individuals move about and change size, for instance.

Consider a harder case: Suppose you are the only object in the universe (your name is Monique) and your body never changes size, density, or location. You are an unmoving and unchanging quantity of matter. Thus, what belongs uniquely to you and persists is the portion of space your body uniquely occupies, such that, even if something identical to you in all apparent respects *did* exist (Phonique) it could not occupy your exact portion of space. So, it would seem that what makes you an individual is just your unique portion of body space. While this case appears quite convincing, consider that to occupy a unique portion of space, you would *already* have to *be* an individual. Thus, it is not space that individuates you; rather, it is *you* who occupies and individuates this space. In other words, your being has logical and metaphysical priority to the space you occupy.[11] If space

---

[11] Garcia 1984: 41.

was metaphysically prior and individuating, then your individuality would not be about *you*. So, while you indeed have a unique and persistent spatial quantity, it is your existence or presence that individuates you. Consider also that even if you insist that your quantity of matter individuates you, this principle cannot be applied to beings that are not material, such as God, angels, and souls (a key point for Leibniz, as we will see). It is for all these reasons that space and time *presuppose* rather than explain individuation; and so they cannot satisfy a metaphysical criterion of individuation.

But we have only scratched the surface of the problem. Leaving space and time behind, suppose now that the principle of individuation consists in some unique physical or sensible quality like colour or shape. For instance, that Socrates possesses a particular type of nose shape we call 'snub',[12] and further that the particular size and contour of his snub-nose belongs *only to him*. There are three good reasons why unique size and shape will not individuate Socrates. As Aristotle would point out, qualities like snub-nose are universals, meaning they can belong to many individuals. Second, like all physical qualities, size and shape can change, and so can the shape of Socrates' nose. Third, we can imagine two spatially distinct individuals (say, Socrates and Mocrates) having the same snub-nose contour and size, yet we would still insist that these individuals are, for some *other* reason, distinct.

If not one physical quality, then could a unique *set* of physical qualities serve as a principle of individuation? But all the problems we have encountered with single qualities obtain for a set of them. Here is Socrates (tall and knock-kneed) and there Mocrates (short and bowlegged). Anyone could clearly *tell* them apart. However, these qualities change over time, and we can imagine many other individuals having these same qualities, forcing us to seek a larger subset of features that would distinguish one individual from every other; and it is unclear what this set should be. So, let us then dismiss the possibility of finding a set of physical qualities sufficient for individuation.

It might make sense then to turn to *enduring* or *unchanging* qualities, such as those we typically attribute to the individual soul or personality, such as *wisdom* or some unique inner temperament. Surely your 'personality' individuates you. But here we run into similar trouble. Wisdom is a universal (sharable) property; so, more than one individual can have it. But suppose that what individuates Socrates is his *unique* wisdom, since he (as he himself tells us) is *most wise*.[13] This immediately raises questions: Would

---

[12] Plato, *Theaetetus*, 209a.
[13] Plato, *Apology*, 21. The Delphic oracle declares that no one is wiser than Socrates, which Socrates understood to mean, 'I do not think I know what I do not know.'

Socrates still be Socrates if he were *not* most wise? If Socrates had always been foolish, would he not still be Socrates? When Socrates was an infant, he was not wise at all. Does that mean that this infant was not Socrates? If, then, this one quality will not individuate him, suppose *a unique set* of character traits would do so: a measure of wisdom mixed with irony, irascibility, and quarrelsomeness, tempered by equanimity, bravery and soberness. Suppose moreover that these traits exist in the soul from birth to death. But here we run into familiar problems: an indeterminate set of shareable, changeable qualities, with no way to show how they belong to Socrates *uniquely*.

Having exhausted quantities and qualities, we might at last turn to *actions*. Individuals both perform actions and undergo them. Socrates defends his fellows at Delium, is sentenced to death for impiety, and drinks the hemlock, while Mocrates abandons his fellows, escapes from prison, and gets drunk. These actions belong to them alone. This seems to be on the right track, since action-predicates correlate with Leibniz's characterisation (below) of substances as *acting* beings and with his example predicates. But exactly how are action-predicates supposed to individuate? The answer will come in due course.

Hopefully by now, the reader should be able to see why the problem of individuation is a real problem and why a principle is needed: If we do not know what distinguishes individuals as substances in their own right, as substances capable of action, then we cannot distinguish the actions of individuals from God's actions; and if not, then all beings, as Spinoza held, are modes of the single substance, God, who would then be the only truly acting being in the world. Aristotle seems to have concluded that individuals are individuated by their particular *quantity of matter*, since a material thing is just a concrete instance of all of the abstract universal properties (essences and accidents) it may have. Even though his answer convinced many, the question of individuation remained a vexing problem.[14]

It is important to understand why it remained a problem. Many Medieval Christian and Islamic philosophers were not satisfied with

---

[14] Two problems with Aristotle's account immediately arise: (1) Since matter itself is undifferentiated, it has no distinguishing characteristics, unless it has form. So, it is hard to see how something with no characteristics can serve as a principle of individuation. (2) *Quantity*, we can recall from Aristotle's *Categories*, is an accident that can only *belong* to a substance, which, by definition, is a primary being. Again, it is hard to see how an accidental property can individuate a substance, since the latter has ontological priority and is presumably already individuated. On Aristotle's principle of individuation (and whether he actually had one) see Regis 1976 and Sfekas 2004. Note that contemporary philosophers typically hold that things are individuated by spatial-temporal properties; see, for example, Strawson 1959.

Aristotle's account for theological reasons, since it did not satisfy their concerns with the soul's identity after death and with an individual's moral accountability for sin.[15] So, while Aristotle went on to develop the notion of substance in terms of a combination of matter and form (or *hylomorphism*),[16] some Medieval philosophers sought to identify a principle of individuation that would account for the continuity of identity from birth, to death, and afterward. For the most part, they retained Aristotle's criteria: an individual is the subject of predication, an indivisible whole, in the sense that it cannot be divided into more basic individuals, even if it contains constituent parts. An individual is an organic unity, whose parts contribute to the functioning of the whole, and whose whole function is oriented toward a distinct end or purpose, such as life and moral virtue. Aquinas followed Aristotle's view of individuation as 'quantity of matter'.[17] But other Medievals diverged on this point, since this principle could apply only to *material* beings but not *immaterial* beings, such as angels which are considered to be 'pure intelligences' (pure souls). A material principle also could not clearly apply to humans, who possessed, in addition to a body, an immaterial soul and whose end was not only virtue but ultimately salvation and immortality. These complications thus brought on the need for a *single* principle that could individuate beings like us consisting of both matter and soul, from birth to afterlife. At this point, something like Aristotle's *substantial form* looked like a good candidate for individuation, since it could provide what matter could not: *unity*, *identity*, *persistence through time*, *source of action and purpose*. The idea of form as a non-material individuator was also readily transferable to the Christian idea of the individual soul. If there is anything that persists through all of the changes a human being can undergo, then it is the human soul. Still, it remained difficult for the Medievals to say exactly what the individuation of souls consisted in.

Leibniz's early conception of individuation

Leibniz's 'complete notion' (or complete 'concept' as it is often translated) of an individual substance in the *Discourse* can be more clearly understood as an attempt to solve the problem of individuation, as a problem having developed out of this Medieval response to the Aristotelian tradition in which he was immersed, and as both sharing in and rejecting key features

---

[15] For example, see Ogden 2016.

[16] See *Metaphysics*, Bks 4 and 7.

[17] 'For individuals are demarcated within species by dimensionally defined material, but species within genus by a defining differentiation taken from the form' (Aquinas, *On Being and Essence*, 95).

of that tradition. We can find Leibniz engaging intensively with that tradition in his bachelor's thesis in philosophy, *Metaphysical Disputation on the Principle of Individuation* (1663), composed, incredibly, at the age of seventeen.[18] A brief account of it will provide some clues to what Leibniz is doing in the *Discourse*.

In general outline, this precocious undergraduate considers four traditional theories of individuation and rejects all but one: (1) that individuation is determined *negatively*, that is, by the individual's in-divisibility into other things. Leibniz rejects this on the grounds that individuation must be something *positive* about the individual itself, not something depending on reference to its difference from other things. (2) That individuation consists in the concrete *existence* of the individual (as opposed to its abstract essence). The idea behind this proposal is that existence is an *action* which 'contracts' (reduces) the abstract essence into an individual thing. Since this is a *positive* feature, it has initial plausibility as a principle of individuation. Leibniz's reasons for rejecting it are complicated, but can be boiled down to this: for existence to individuate, it would have to be 'separable', in some sense, from *essence*; but, he argues, this is not possible.[19] Thus, since essence and existence are inseparable, the individuating principle must include both essence *and* existence, not merely one of them. This modification on (2) will be called the 'whole entity' principle which Leibniz will accept, below. (3) The idea put forward by Duns Scotus, that individuation consists in some metaphysical *part* of the thing called *thisness* (*haecceity*), its being *this very individual*, Leibniz rejects because it also treats only a part of the thing, in this case, its form. In any case, since the thing must *already* be individuated before it receives the 'this', the haecceity does not add anything to the individual. Thus *haecceity* cannot be a principle of individuation. The principle that Leibniz accepts is (4), the 'whole entity' principle, since it is positive, and since it can individuate beings having either matter or form, or both, and since it includes both essence and existence, which together comprise everything of ontological import. The 'whole entity' account also has the advantage of corresponding with

[18] AA VI, 1, 3–19. See McCullough 1996 for translation and analysis. McCullough explicitly argues for a continuity, despite certain differences, between Leibniz's account in the *Disputation* and that of the *Discourse*, while others deny any significant continuity. I wish only to point out useful connections. See Mates 1986; Bahlul 1992; Di Bella 2014; Rodriguez-Pereyra 2014.

[19] His argument depends on two types of distinction typically made in Scholastic philosophy: essence and existence are (a) conceptually or *mentally* distinct, but not (b) *really* distinct; that is, they are inseparable for existing, mattered things. Of course, other Scholastics disagree on how and whether essence and existence are distinct; but almost all agree on these two types of distinction.

Leibniz's metaphysical commitment to *nominalism*, that is, to the view that only individuals, not universals or accidents, really exist. On the nominalist view, universals and accidents are simply mental abstractions having no real existence apart from concretely existing individuals. Thus the 'whole entity' principle satisfies Leibniz's requirements for individuation: an ontologically independent, positive, whole, concretely existing being.[20] The other part of this principle, that existence is an *action*, no doubt contributed to his conception of individuation in the *Discourse*.

Before turning to the *Discourse*, we should note two important consequences of the 'whole entity' view in the *Disputation*: First, it implies that *every property* of a thing is essential to the identity of that thing.[21] As we will see, this idea resonates well with the 'complete notion' that Leibniz develops here. Second, however, this view does not by itself provide a criterion for individual *distinctness*. Thus, we can imagine two spatially distinct 'whole entity' individuals having all of the same properties. While this might make them distinguishable in space, it would not make them unique individuals, nor would it explain why there are two of them. As indicated above, spatial difference is not a sufficient criterion for individuation. We should want a principle that explains *what*, belonging to the individual alone, is distinct about it. Nor is it enough to say that what makes Monique's properties unique to her is her *existence*, for reasons that will be seen.

The complete notion of an individual in the *Discourse*

With this background in view, we can at last turn to the text of §8, and bear in mind several key features of substances that we have picked up along the way: an individual substance (1) is the subject of all its predicates, yet not the predicate of any subject; (2) remains the same individual through change; (3) is the source of its action; (4) is a whole, unified being, in the sense that all of its parts contribute to the performance of its overall function and end; (5) is distinguishable from every other substance.

Now we should recall the original question for §8: how are God's actions distinguished from those of his creatures? As the text indicates, some philosophers, like Malebranche, imply they are not, since his doctrine of 'occasionalism' has it that creatures are not the causes of effects, but rather God's will is (ln 6). Others, like Descartes, have said that God 'acts only to conserve the force he has given to creatures' (ln 7). Leibniz,

---

[20] Mugnai 2001.

[21] This is according to Benson Mates, who, like McCullough, argues for continuity between Leibniz's early and late views on individuation. See McCullough 1996: 133 and Mates 1986: 7.

however, insists that God contributes much less than everything to a creature's actions, but also much more than merely the conservation of their being. To strike a proper balance, Leibniz says, drawing from his Scholastic background, '*actiones sunt suppositorum*' (ln 10), that is, 'actions belong to substances', or, to be explicit, an individual substance is the principle or source of its actions.[22] We should also note that 'passions' (ln 9) also belong to individual substances, a term referring in this context to actions that happen *to* substances – a point to which we will return in §14. But the main point is that if creatures are individual substances, then they are the source of their actions and passions. Most importantly, if they are the source of their actions, then their actions are distinct from God's.

So, what is it to be an active substance or a source of action? Leibniz begins with a 'nominal' definition of substance as the subject of several predicates, and this subject is not the predicate of any other subject (lns 11–12).[23] In his example, Alexander is the subject who possesses the predicate 'king', *and* Alexander does not belong to any other subject. However, this nominal definition is not sufficient to determine an individual (ln 13). There are several reasons why, although Leibniz does not state them here. For one, with only a few predicates, the nominal definition is not sufficient to distinguish Alexander from other subjects, since 'king' can be applied to many. Nor does the nominal definition tell us much about Alexander himself, who was not only a king, but also vanquished Darius and Porus (ln 35) and did many other things as well. So now the question becomes: *which* predicates will be sufficient to constitute Alexander as an individual substance?

---

[22] Leibniz defines 'suppositum' in the *Catholic Demonstrations* of 1669–70: 'An entity which subsists in itself is the same as what the mass of Scholastics mean by *suppositum*. For a *suppositum* is a substantial individual – as, for instance, a person is a rational substantial individual – or a certain substance in particular. Moreover, the School has generally established it as a property of *suppositum* that it is itself denominated by action; hence the rule that actions belong to *supposita*. It is clear from this that the *suppositum*, substance, or entity which subsists in itself – which are all the same thing – is defined correctly in the Scholastic sense also as that which has a principle of action within itself, for otherwise it would not act but be an instrument of some agent' (LL 117). Loemker: 'The conception of *suppositum* as individual subsistent substance, was established in Suarez, *Disputationes Metaphysicae*, Disp. 34' (LL 119, note 11). However, the origin of this phrase can be traced back to Aristotle: 'Actions and productions are all concerned with the individual' (*Metaphysics*, Bk I, Ch. 1, 981a16); and to Aquinas: 'For universals are generated or moved only by reason of something else, inasmuch as this belongs to singular things' (*Commentary on the Metaphysics* 1, lesson 1, no. 21). Also see Barnes 2015.

[23] Leibniz could be following Aristotle from *Categories*, Ch. 5.

These questions involving predication may have prompted Leibniz to turn to a standard, Aristotelian, account of truth, namely, 'true predication' (ln 15); in other words, to an account of truth that should provide the required *essential*, as opposed to *nominal*, definition of an individual substance.[24] The basic idea behind true predication is that all propositions (or judgments) are of subject-predicate form. For example, *Alexander* (the subject) *vanquished Darius* (the predicate). The term *'inesse'* (ln 19) literally means 'in the essence', and it refers to the idea that a proposition is true, just in case the predicate is 'included in' the subject.[25] Leibniz also characterises this theory of truth as 'concept containment', according to which a proposition is true, just in case the 'concept' of the predicate is 'contained' in the 'concept' of the subject.[26] For example, 'Pat is a woman' is true, just in case the predicate 'woman' is contained in the notion of the subject, Pat. To say 'contained in' simply means that the predicate is true of the subject. Thus, the nature (essence) of the subject is described by the predicates that are true of it.

Now, then, the question becomes, which predicates will be sufficient to constitute the essential definition of Alexander? Traditionally, an essence is determined on the basis of a few predicates, such as 'rational animal', while all other predicates attributable to the subject may be designated 'accidents', because the subject may or may not have them and still retain its essence. But recall that Leibniz is interested in defining an *individual* substance; so, he needs a set of predicates that are not only shared by many individuals, but which pick out a particular individual. Now, which predicates are required to do that? Leibniz's surprising answer is *all of them*.

---

[24] A discussion of the distinction between nominal and essential definition can be found in Aristotle (*Posterior Analytics*, Bk II, Chs. 7–10).

[25] In *Primary Truths* (1689), Leibniz attributes this 'inclusion' theory of predication to Aristotle: 'Therefore, the predicate or consequent is always in [*inest*] the subject or antecedent, and the nature of truth in general or the connection between the terms of a statement, consists in this very thing, as Aristotle also observed. The connection and inclusion [*comprehensio*] of the predicate in the subject is explicit in identities, but in all other propositions it is implicit and must be shown through the analysis of notions; *a priori* demonstration rests on this' (AG 31 / LCO 518–19). However, it is not certain where in Aristotle this idea may be found – possibly *Prior Analytics*, I.1, 24b27. A similar idea can be found in Arnauld and Nicole's *Logic, or the Art of Thinking* (1662), a book Leibniz surely knew, since it was the standard logic book of the day: 'I call the *comprehension* of an idea the attributes that it contains in itself, and that cannot be removed without destroying the idea. For example, the comprehension of the idea of a triangle contains extension, shape, three lines, [etc.]' (Arnauld and Nicole, *Logic*, 39). See also LAV xxxiii and Di Bella 2005: 131, who opposes the Aristotelian similarities (Di Bella cited in LAV xxxiii).

[26] This is how he describes it in 'The Nature of Truth' (1686) LP 93. The Latin for 'contained' is 'continetur' and for 'concept' is 'notio' (AA VI, 3 N. 303, 1515).

> The nature of an individual substance, or of a complete Being, is to have a notion so complete that it is sufficient to understand and to deduce from it all the predicates of the subject to which this notion is attributed. (lns 23–5)

Thus, the essential, as opposed to the nominal, definition of an individual substance, such as Alexander, is *the complete set of predicates* that are true of the subject.[27]

Let us try to be clear on why Leibniz insists that an individual must be defined by its *complete* set of predicates, by its 'complete notion'. For one, the complete notion of an individual is a consequence of the traditional 'in-esse' theory of truth, as described above, which tells us what it means for any proposition to be true. As he writes to Arnauld, 'otherwise, I do not know what truth is'.[28] So, to know the truth about a subject or individual substance, we must know every predicate true of it. Furthermore, as he also writes to Arnauld, true predication follows from the principle of sufficient reason.[29] Since everything requires a reason for its being so, the subject is fully explained by the predicates it has, and, reciprocally, the predicates are fully explained by their belonging to that subject. Thus, the theory of truth and the principle of sufficient reason provide Leibniz with a most rigorous methodology for defining an individual.

Leibniz also has theological reasons to insist on a complete notion. Since God creates the world and all its individuals, God must know everything about each one in order to determine which individual notions are eligible for creation. This point will be illustrated further in §9 and §30. Furthermore, to distinguish God's actions from those of individual substances (the express main point of §8), each substance must be the *source*, in some sense, of all of its own actions. And since all of its predicates belong to it, and to it alone, Leibniz can say that the individual is the source of them. This reflects the idea of the 'spontaneity of the soul' that he mentions in §30.

A final point motivating the complete notion (the complete set of predicates) stems from the background history of substance and the problem of individuation with which Leibniz was specifically engaged. To recall the conclusion of his early *Disputation*, individuation must include the whole entity, its form and matter. This idea may have encouraged his mature contention that individuation must include every predicate true of the thing, and his theory of truth gives him a much more rigorous method for resolving his early solution to the problem.

To complete this theoretical picture, let us see how Leibniz's 'complete notion of an individual substance' compares to the criteria we derived from

---

[27] See §24 for more on the difference between nominal and essential definition.
[28] Letter to Arnauld, 14 July 1686, LL 337; LAV 111 / LAM 63.
[29] Ibid.

the history of substance and the problem of individuation: (1) the individual is indeed the subject of all its predicates and not the predicate of any subject; (2) it remains the same individual through change, precisely because all its predicates belong to it. This criterion is especially appropriate for entities that undergo a multitude of dramatic changes, from birth to death and afterward, while remaining the same individual; (3) the individual is the source of its actions, again because all of its predicates belong to it; (4) it is a whole, unified being, in the sense that all of its parts serve to perform its overall function and end, as we will increasingly see; (5) and finally, it is distinct from every other substance. *This* criterion, however, has not yet been shown. While the complete notion is the principle of individuation (every individual substance has a complete notion), Leibniz has not yet identified the respect in which each complete notion is *different* from every other. To do that, he will introduce, in §9, his so-called 'principle of the identity of indiscernibles'.

Now that we understand what motivates the complete notion doctrine, we can fill out the picture more fully by turning to several issues that arise in the text of §8:

(1) The complete notion consists of an *identity* of subject and predicate. In other words, Alexander, the subject, is identical to the complete set of predicates that belong to him. Therefore, it will be possible (for God, not for us) to 'deduce' (ln 24) all of Alexander's predicates. Now, only two types of deduction are possible: (a) strictly *logical* deduction of a proposition to an identity, and (b) 'virtual' deduction.[30] Regarding (a), Leibniz is not concerned to point out that the complete notion consists of strict identities such as 'P is P' or 'Pat is Pat'. Rather, he wants to show that we can logically deduce many of the subject's predicates, if we know where to start. For example, if Pat is a *woman*, we can logically deduce 'Pat is human', and 'Pat is a rational animal', since the predicates 'human' and 'rational animal' are logically entailed in the definition of 'woman'. If definitions are taken to be primitive (not further reducible), then 'Pat is a woman' is an identical proposition. But if definitions are *not* primitive, then each predicate of the definition would still need to be defined, until a primitive notion is reached. In the *Discourse*, Leibniz does not provide examples of primitive notions, although elsewhere he argues that there must be some.[31] In any case, logical deduction is only one means of revealing the notional content of an individual substance.

---

[30] This difference between identical and virtual predication is often explained in terms of *finite* and *infinite* analysis. See Sleigh 1990: 12. But the issue is complicated. See Blumenfeld (1985) and Leibniz 'On Contingency' (1686) AG 29.

[31] In §24, Leibniz says 'when my mind comprehends at once and distinctly all the primitive ingredients of a notion, it has an *intuitive* knowledge of it, which is very rare'

The second type of deduction is (b) 'virtual', which means that the predicate is *potentially* or *implicitly* (not expressly) included within the notion of the substance. More significantly, this means that the predicate cannot be *logically* deduced, nor reduced to an identity. For example, from 'Pat is a woman', it cannot be logically deduced that Pat is a mother, because it is not logically necessary that a woman is a mother. So, how is it determined whether Pat is or is not a mother? For that matter, how is it determined that Pat is a woman? To state the problem generally, what determines an individual, such as Pat, to have any predicate whatsoever? The short answer is that ultimately God considers an infinite range of possible complete notions, one of which includes all of the predicates of a possible Pat, and then chooses it to be actual. So, the notion of Pat ultimately depends on God's choice. But to understand this answer fully, we will have to go through §§13, 14, and 30. For now, it must suffice to say that virtual predicates can be known (to us) only through experience. In sum, to know the *complete* notion of an individual substance is just to know all of the predicates that both logically and virtually belong to it. This idea should become more clear as Leibniz further illustrates the notion of Alexander.

(2) The philosophical tradition, as noted above, takes 'accidents' to be non-essential predicates, that is, predicates that the substance could have or not and still remain that substance. In the *Discourse* Leibniz treats accidents a bit differently, since he counts them all as essential to the substance. In addition, he considers accidents themselves to have *incomplete* notions (lns 26–31). From the notion of an accident such as 'being a king', we cannot deduce the subject to which it belongs (Alexander, say), because the accident can belong to many subjects. Also, while we can deduce *some* predicates from the notion of king ('is a head of state', 'holds a monopoly on state power', and 'is not a princess'), many other predicates belonging to the subject are not deducible from the accident. This tells us that accidents are not sufficient to determine an individual (ln 29); that is, as Aristotle would put it, since accidents can be predicates of other subjects, they cannot be individual substances. The influence of Leibniz's nominalism in the *Disputation* can also be seen here: accidents are universals that cannot determine an individual; they can belong to anyone but have no existence unless concretised or instantiated by an individual. Substances are ontologically independent, positive beings, while their accidents are fully dependent on them.

(lns 18–20). Elsewhere, Leibniz seems to have held that 'being' and 'nothing' are primitive notions, since they can be understood in themselves, without any other notion (see Plaisted 2003). Leibniz seems also to have held that *perfections* are primitive, since they are unanalysable (see commentary on §24).

Another difference between things with complete notions and things without them can be found in the references to 'the ring of Gyges' that Leibniz had struck from his first draft (see §8 translation, footnote 12). While God certainly knows the series of changes that this ring will undergo, it cannot be that God knows this by examining the *notion* of the ring; and that is because rings do not have notions. From this we can infer that a complete notion is possible only in things endowed with *soul*, since only souls can retain the memory of the changes they undergo – a track record, so to speak, of their complete notion. Leibniz is clear that Alexander's soul contains a complete record (vestiges and marks) of everything that happens to him (ln 39). But since material things like rings do not have souls, they do not have complete notions. They are passive objects whose 'actions' must be determined by active subjects. Leibniz is also reluctant in the *Discourse* to say that bodies are substances in their own right (as we have seen); so, if they are not, then they do not have complete notions. But bodies like ours *do* have complete notions by virtue of the soul that accompanies our body. We can infer from this that only bodies accompanied by souls can be substances.

(3) An individual substance is not made up of a container of predicates. Predicates are words or concepts denoting the real properties and actions of substances.[32] This point is emphasised by Leibniz's assertion that 'actions belong to substances' (ln 10). Substances are capable of action, while their predicates describe what they do. It is correct to say, however, that the notion of an individual substance consists of a complete set of predicate notions. It is by means of notions that God knows what your *complete* notion is, so that God may decide whether your notion, your possibility, is worth making actual.

(4) It is important to understand that the complete notion is a *metaphysical* notion, not an *epistemic* one. That is, while the complete notion constitutes the individuality of a substance, individuality itself does not require knowing all of the predicates included in the subject. As Leibniz indicates, *if* one perfectly understood the notion of the subject, *then* one would know all of the predicates that belong to it. While only God possesses such knowledge, that knowledge is possible only because the substance is *already* individuated. *Knowing* the complete notion is not required for the substance to *be* an individual.

(5) Consider that the complete notion of an individual cannot consist simply of a *collection* of predicates, but that the collection must be *ordered*;

---

[32] It was common among certain Medieval philosophers to distinguish two types of predication: formal and material, the former being a word or concept and the latter a real feature of the thing predicated (Garcia 1984: 29).

otherwise, the substance would consist of a pointless jumble of notions. Leibniz indicates two ways that the predicates are ordered: teleologically and temporally. The teleological order is indicated in line 32: having rejected, in his *Disputation*, the individuating principle of 'haecceity' as an incomplete principle, Leibniz now finds the term suitable for referring to the complete notion.[33] But what the haecceity or 'thisness' contains, from God's point of view, is the 'foundation and reason for all the predicates' (ln 33). That is, Alexander's actions have a kind of goal-oriented coherence, since they stem from his birth, character, training, desires, choices, history, and future ambitions. Alexander was born in 356 BC to Philip II of Macedon; tutored by Aristotle, then became king, conquered other kings (Darius and Porus), and much of Persia, Phoenicia, Egypt, parts of India, and died at the age of thirty-three, likely as a consequence of his ambitions and excesses. Thus, Alexander's life does not consist simply of one event after another, but rather of a coherent narrative in which any one event is explained by both its history and its future. The teleological order then provides the basis for the *temporal* order: 'when we well consider the connection of things, we can say that there is from all time in the soul of Alexander vestiges of everything that happened to him, and marks of everything that will happen to him' (lns 37–40). While each event implies every other, each event follows a distinct, irreversible, order from past to future. Only God knows beforehand (*a priori* and not by experience) how this order will unfold through the course of time.[34]

(6) In addition to the teleological and temporal orders, each individual soul (or notion of the soul) has 'traces' or connections with 'everything that happens in the universe' (ln 40). This idea greatly expands and yet complicates the common understanding of 'an individual', which typically takes an individual to be defined by its spatial boundary. Consider: since Alexander's actions involve the actions of other individual substances (his family, his soldiers, and everyone he conquered), whose actions involve the actions of still others, and whose notions include all events that affect them, such as the weather, the changing seasons, and earthquakes, it follows that traces of every event involving everything in the universe will be found within every single soul. This is the ultimate result of the 'complete concept' and 'true predication' theories Leibniz has employed. Each individual substance is related in some way to everything in the universe. These relations are called 'expressions', as will be explained in §9.

---

[33] Nevertheless, I contend that 'haecceity' (thisness) is not Leibniz's principle of individuation.

[34] Note that by '*a priori*' Leibniz is not saying that God knows by *logical deduction* what the subject will do. Rather, God knows *prior to experience* what the notion contains.

Since the story in §8 is quite complex, let us briefly review 'the complete notion of an individual substance'. (1) Metaphysically, each substance has a certain ontological independence: each is the subject of all its predicates, and each, as a whole, is not a predicate of any other subject (nominal definition). (2) Each substance is a distinct individual, whose individuality or essence is determined by *all* of the predicates that are true of it (the *essential* or *real* definition). (3) Each individual substance contains a teleologically and temporally ordered set of predicates, a set which includes ordered relations to all other substances, things, and events. (4) An individual substance is *active*, and the source of its actions, since all of its actions belong to it alone and are not caused by any other substance. Thus, its actions are distinct from God's actions and from the actions of other substances, and yet *related* to them (in a way yet to be explained).

After all of this, the reader may rightly feel overwhelmed and bewildered by such a complex notion of *an individual*. The most puzzling aspect must be, after having arrived at a notion that includes 'everything that happens in the universe' (ln 40), what is any longer *individual* about it? And since this is true of every substance, what is distinctive and particular about any one of them? The complete notion does not really tell us. However, as noted, this puzzle will be solved in the next article by the claim that each individual substance expresses the universe in its 'own manner'.

Most importantly, however, given that the main subject of this article is the distinction between the actions of God and those of individual substances, does the complete notion really make us the *cause* of our actions, distinct from God's? The lurking danger here, which so alarmed Arnauld, is that all of a substance's actions, past, present, and future, appear to be fixed within the complete notion and cannot be otherwise than they are. Recall that since God created everything, including Alexander, according to what is best, God decided, or at least *permitted*, that it were best that Alexander do *everything* he did – and God knows this before creating Alexander. Thus, it is difficult to understand how the actions of individual substances are not simply God's actions; or how Alexander's actions could be otherwise than they are; and thus how God's rational creatures have *free will*. For that matter, it is difficult to understand how *God* could have chosen otherwise than in accord with the complete notion of even a single individual, since any given individual has infinitely many relations to every other. Despite his having so far established a rather novel and remarkable conception of an individual, it remains to be seen, in articles 9, 13, 14, 15, and 30, whether Leibniz can resolve all the difficulties now pressing upon it.

§9. Several 'paradoxes' following from the complete notion; and that 'each unique substance *expresses* the whole universe in its manner', that is, according to its unique degree of perfection.

This complex article deals with several 'paradoxes' resulting from the account of the complete notion of an individual substance given in §8. These are not paradoxes in the usual sense, as will be explained, but they include two of Leibniz's most well-known doctrines, that of the principle of the 'identity of indiscernibles', and that of 'expression', according to which each substance is like a mirror that 'expresses' the whole universe and God in its own way. Both of these doctrines will provide us with a way to determine what exactly the individuating feature of an individual substance is.

We will begin with the concept of 'expression', since it is key to understanding not only this article, but Leibniz's metaphysics generally. As was said in the previous article, the actions of an individual substance are distinct from God's actions and from the actions of other substances; at the same time, substances have *relations* of some kind with each other, and we noted that the nature of these relations was yet to be explained. We might expect substances to have *causal* relations with each other, but this is not what Leibniz has in mind (the idea that substances have causal relations will be discussed in articles 14, 15, and 33). The relation Leibniz has in mind in this article is that of *expression*.

The concept of expression is easier to grasp when we consider how *ideas* relate to each other, for ideas are mental expressions or representations of things.[1] Thus by 'expression' we can understand that substances relate to each other *ideally*, rather than physically. In another work, Leibniz offers several examples of expressive relations.[2] Generally speaking, two things are said to express each other when a one-to-one correspondence could be shown to hold between them. For instance, in geometry a circle may be said to express an ellipse. This can be illustrated by holding a light directly above a flat, round, disk, as the latter is held at an angle above a flat table. The shadow projected onto the table will form an ellipse, and a one-to-one correspondence can be found between every point of the disk's circumference and every point of the ellipse's perimeter. Thus, the two different shapes, the disk and the ellipse, 'express' each other. Or, consider how an algebraic equation such as $(x-a)^2 + (y-b)^2 = r^2$ expresses a circle on a Cartesian coordinate system. The correspondences between the

---

[1] See Leibniz, 'What is an Idea?' (1678), in LL 207.
[2] These examples are drawn from Kulstad 1977a: 57. Also see McRae 1976: 20–6. For the Neoplatonic roots of the idea of expression, see §14 below.

expression and thing expressed (and vice versa) convey precise relations between two very different things. The idea of expression is also commonly used to explain how language basically works, as when we say that a word expresses our thoughts or an idea. The relation between a word-sound and its idea is harder to conceive as a one-to-one reciprocal relation, since the relationship is conventional, rather than natural or mathematical; nevertheless, when a word is used correctly, it is said to 'express' its idea exactly. Similarly, each substance, each of which is in some respect different from every other, expresses every other and indeed the whole world. We do not of course express the whole world precisely or just as it is, but rather, in degrees more or less, as a painter might 'express' a landscape in a painting.

To take Alexander as an example, Leibniz is saying that Alexander's action-predicates are expressed in the notions of Darius and Porus, as he vanquishes them, and whose actions (or passions) are in turn expressed in Alexander's notion. Considered in relation to every other substance, Alexander expresses *the whole universe* (ln 18). The relation is ideal because it is a relation perceived by the mind, but not a relation produced by or involving physical causes. It is nevertheless a very *well-grounded* idea, based on actual relations, not on imaginary or coincidental ones.

For a clearer understanding of 'expression' we can resort to explanations that Leibniz does not employ in the *Discourse* but develops later. Accordingly, we can think of substances as essentially *perceiving* beings and thus as *representing* each other internally; for example, when you look at a landscape you are said to represent it in your mind. In this sense we can think of 'expression' as a *representing relation* among substances, as the way in which substances represent the world in their own way.[3] We should also think of 'expression' as a general explanation for how substances can be related notionally or ideally, rather than causally. In any case, we may bear in mind this working conception of 'expression' as we proceed.

Now let us turn to the 'paradoxes' that Leibniz says 'follow from this', that is, from the complete notion of an individual substance established in §8. Note first that these are not paradoxes in the familiar, logical, sense of a proposition having indeterminate truth-value, as in, for example, 'this sentence is false'. Rather, they are opinions (*doxas*) that lie outside (*para*) the norm. Thus, Leibniz aims to introduce new doctrines that his contemporaries like Arnauld may find hard to accept or even to understand, at first, but which could be understood upon examination and elaboration.

---

[3] 'Indeed, all individual created substances are different expressions of the same universe and different expressions of the same universal cause, namely God. But the expressions vary in perfection, just as different representations or drawings of the same town from different points of view do' (*Primary Truths*, AG 33).

(1) The first paradox is implied in the summary: 'That each unique substance expresses the whole universe in its manner' (ln 1).[4] Now, we know that each substance has a complete notion; the complete notion is what makes each substance an individual. However, we noted in §8 that the complete notion does not yet provide a criterion of *distinctness* – a way to say that each complete notion is *unique*, distinct from every other. What is implied, then, is the 'paradox' that 'it is not true that two substances entirely resemble each other while differing [only by number]' (ln 6). This statement represents Leibniz's mature formulation of what has come to be called 'the principle of the identity of indiscernibles'. It is a formal statement of his principle of individuation. It tells us *that* each substance is unique. It does not tell us, however, the precise respect in which each substance *is* unique (which we will come to below).

Meanwhile, let us gain some clarity on the principle of the identity of indiscernibles. It can be more simply stated as: no two individuals have all their properties or predicates in common.[5] To grasp the principle more clearly, imagine that yesterday you met Aaron and then today you meet Darren, who appears to be the same individual as Aaron, but you are not sure. Well, if Aaron and Darren have all the same properties (or predicates), then they really are the same individual seen at different times. But if there is at least one predicate true of Aaron that is not true of Darren (or vice versa), then in fact Aaron and Darren are distinct individuals.[6]

For even more clarity, consider some possible objections that may seem obvious. Suppose you think, against Leibniz, that two individuals can resemble each other entirely and *can* differ 'only by number'. To illustrate this, you conceive of two *amoebae*, which, as single-celled organisms, you can imagine have very few properties each: the same quantity of mass and size, the same quality of shape, and the same motions throughout their lives of blind striving for sustenance. In other words, all predicates true of

---

[4] When Leibniz says 'each unique substance', he is not saying that there are unique substances as opposed to non-unique (identical) substances. For Leibniz, every substance is unique.

[5] The principle is often interpreted as saying that substances (or things) are 'qualitatively' distinct, or that substances are distinguished 'intrinsically'. But since most of the properties of individual substances Leibniz cites in the *Discourse* are *actions*, not qualities (Alexander vanquishes, Caesar crosses, Peter denies, Judas betrays), it is more accurate to say that substances are generally distinguished by their *predicates*. The interested reader may consult the voluminous commentary on the principle of the identity of indiscernibles, and the SEP entry is a good place to start.

[6] In *Primary Truths*, Leibniz extends the application of this principle to include not only substances, but also single eggs, leaves, blades of grass, and portions of seemingly homogeneous matter (AG 32).

Amoeba 1 are true of Amoeba 2. But look, you say, they *are* distinguished *only by number*; so, Leibniz's indiscernibility principle is false.

Not so fast. We should recall from §8 that individual substances must be distinguished by predicates (or *a* predicate) belonging to them alone, in other words, by some *internal* predicate, not by some abstraction like a number. You might want to say that you are not distinguishing them by their names, '1' and '2', but simply by a *difference* in number. But again, a difference in number is a *relation* belonging to two things, thus not a predicate belonging to each thing alone (1 is different *from* 2, and vice versa). Therefore (if these amoebae will be more than merely imaginary) some *internal* difference must distinguish them. Suppose you then want to say that these amoebae are not conceived in your mind, but actually reside on a plate under a microscope, one on the left, the other on the right. Thereby you distinguish these otherwise supposedly identical amoebae by their respective *spatial locations*. But again, as we saw in §8, space cannot belong to substances as individuating properties (rather, substances determine spaces); so, spatial location cannot be what individuates them.[7] But then what *does* individuate substances, such that they are each distinct from every other? As Leibniz insists about the indiscernibility principle: 'For it certainly must be possible to explain why [substances] are different, and that explanation must derive from some difference they contain.'[8] That difference, I suggest, is the *unique degree of perfection* that each substance expresses, as explained in the 'final paradox', below.

(2) The second 'paradox' involves the prominent Aristotelian-Christian philosopher Thomas Aquinas's claim that every angel is a 'lowest species'.[9] The 'paradox' is that as a result of Leibniz's indiscernibility principle, the complete notion of an individual substance also designates a lowest species, as long as the term 'species difference' is understood correctly. This point may seem insignificant, but it is actually important, interesting and clarifying. According to the traditional (Aristotelian-Scholastic) classification of all beings (ontology), every being can be classified by its properties as a *species* under a *genus*. In turn, each species can serve as a genus for yet other species falling under that genus. However, a *lowest* or *ultimate*

---

[7] We could say the same about a difference in size or any quantitative difference. Note the passage Leibniz strikes out at line 10: 'Also if bodies are substances, it is not possible that their nature consist solely in size, figure, and motion, but that something else is required.' In general, following his critique of Cartesian substance (which we will encounter in several articles), Leibniz thinks that extended (quantitative) properties are abstractions and imaginary, but substances are real and basic. Of course, substances can have quantitative properties; it's just that they are not *individuating* properties.

[8] *Primary Truths*, AG 32.

[9] See footnote 7 in the translation of this article.

species (*species infima*) is an individual member of a genus, but which is not a genus for another species.[10] Thus, we can classify and distinguish every being, from spiritual substances (God and angels), to spiritual-corporeal substances (plants, animals, humans), to strictly corporeal beings (rocks), and geometric figures right down to their individuals.

Now, Leibniz is telling us that when we classify beings, we must distinguish two types of 'species difference'. The first type, which is more common, marks a *physical* or *quantitative* difference between individual members of a species. A mother and daughter, for example, differ by being physically distinct species of the genus HUMAN. Similarly, two equilateral triangles of different size are two species of the genus EQUILATERAL-TRIANGLE. These two individuals are each *lowest species*, since from them no further classification of individuals can be made (that is, no individual human is a genus for a further species of human; nor is an individual equilateral triangle a genus for a subaltern species of equilateral triangle or for anything else).

The second type of species difference is *essential* or *conceptual*, and this is key. For example, under the genus SUBSTANCE there are two species, body and mind, which are distinguished from each other by their essential attributes, respectively, *extension* and *thought*.[11] Similarly, under the genus TRIANGLE, a geometer distinguishes two species: *right* and *equilateral* (among others) which marks a *conceptual* but not a *quantitative* difference between the two species. Now, the species difference *equilateral* has no further *conceptual* divisions. That is, since equilateral is not a genus for another species, each individual is a lowest species (as we said above). Of course, equilateral triangles differ in size – but these species differences are *quantitative*, not *conceptual*. Now, the same classification pattern should hold for bodies and minds, which are two *conceptually* distinct species under the genus SUBSTANCE. But notice that while an individual body is a lowest species, it has a *quantitative* difference from other bodies; and while a mind is also a lowest species, it cannot be quantitatively distinguished from other minds, because minds are immaterial; therefore, minds must be distinguished from each other in a way suitable to their nature, and that is, *conceptually*.

What Leibniz wants to say is that his individual substances are lowest species just as angels are for Aquinas, but of the *conceptual*, not the *quantitative* type, just as geometers distinguish their figures, that is, conceptually,

---

[10] See Arnauld and Nicole, *Logic, or the Art of Thinking*, 41.
[11] This is Descartes' distinction. We should bear in mind that Leibniz does *not* distinguish mind and body as distinct *substances*.

not quantitatively.[12] For Aquinas, each angel is a (lowest) species of the genus SPIRITUAL SUBSTANCE. But since angels have no matter to individuate them, they can be individuated only by a formal difference (grade of being). Leibniz is pointing out that this is a *conceptual* species difference, certainly not quantitative. Just so, each complete notion of an individual substance is a lowest species of the genus HUMAN, but in the conceptual, not the quantitative sense. In sum, each complete notion marks a conceptual difference from every other, in accord with the geometers' understanding of conceptual species difference. Such a difference is markedly more robust than a merely quantitative difference because it is metaphysical. It is also precisely suitable to the object in question, namely a mind or soul.

As a result, Leibniz could claim another 'paradox' for the indiscernibility principle: that it is a *single* principle of individuation applicable to *all* types of beings, material and non-material. This reflects the 'whole entity' principle he had endorsed in his early *Disputation*. Since for Aquinas the principle of individuation is 'quantity of matter', a different principle for spiritual substances (angels) is required ('degree of being'). Leibniz's complete notion, however, is applicable to spiritual as well as to enmattered beings. Although Leibniz is undecided at this point whether bodies by themselves are substances (as seen in the passage struck out at line 10), it is clear he thinks that human beings having both body and soul constitute a single individual substance. Thus he can say that each person is its own species, a lowest species, considered conceptually or notionally.

(3) The third paradox (ln 11) says 'a substance can begin only by creation and perish only by annihilation'.[13] The sense in which this 'follows' from the complete notion is that a complete notion represents a *unity*, a unified thing, and Leibniz thinks that true unities cannot be created or destroyed (except by God).[14] Consequently, souls (since they are true

---

[12] Letter to Arnauld, 14 July 1686: 'If St Thomas could maintain that every separate spiritual substance [intelligence] differs in species from every other, what harm will there be in saying as much of every person, and in conceiving individuals as ultimate species, provided that species is not taken physically, but metaphysically or mathematically? [. . .] But in metaphysics or in geometry, we may say that things differ in species whenever they have a difference consisting of a concept explicable in itself [. . .]. For all that, we know that complete Entities cannot differ in magnitude alone' (LAV 79 / LAM 74).

[13] In *Primary Truths*, Leibniz says, '*corporeal* substance can neither arise nor perish except through creation or annihilation', but that they, or animate things, are only transformed (AG 34).

[14] In his *New System* (1695), in words nearly identical to those of the *Discourse*, Leibniz says:' 'For, since every substance which has a genuine unity can begin or end only by a miracle, it follows that they can come into being only by creation and end only by annihilation' (LNS 1, 12 / AG 140).

unities) must have been created at the beginning of time, along with the world. Traditionally, it is thought that God creates a human soul just as its body is generated from the pre-existing matter of its parents. But Leibniz holds, paradoxically, that all souls are created at the beginning of time, although human souls do not attain their full form until birth, through a special process he calls 'transcreation'.[15] Thus he also denies the transmigration of human souls.[16] Leibniz's view that God can annihilate substances at any time would also seem paradoxical, since it is an opinion out of step with Scripture, which nowhere says that God annihilates souls; Aquinas seems to say that God *could*, but does not, annihilate anything.[17]

(4) A substance cannot be divided into two, nor can two be made into one (ln 12). This paradox likely follows from the traditional doctrine of individuation, which requires individuals to be literally 'un-dividable' into further individuals. Nor can two become one, since to make one, two would have to be annihilated, and this is impossible. For these reasons, 'the number of substances does not naturally increase or diminish, although they may often be transformed' (ln 13). That is, upon death your soul does not dissolve but is transformed into a spiritual body (resurrection). Animal souls are eventually transformed into other animals.[18]

(5) The final paradox is complex and most important: that 'every substance is like an entire world, a mirror of God and of the whole universe, that each one expresses it in its own way' (ln 16). This follows from the complete notion and the doctrine of expression, wherein, as noted, each substance has an expressive rather than causal relation to every other substance. Most importantly, each substance expresses every other *in its own way*. This idea points at last to the *unique quality* that makes substances metaphysically and discernibly individuated. This quality, I argue, is the *unique degree of perfection* that each substance expresses of God and of the universe.

Consider several reasons why this degree of perfection must be unique and why it must express perfection. Each substance represents or expresses God and the world, which is to say that each has a *perspective* on the world.

---

[15] As he says in *New System*: 'So I had to recognize that (with the exception of souls which God still intends to create specially) the constitutive forms of substances must have been created with the world and must always continue to exist' (LNS 1, 12). On 'transcreation', see the entry on this term in *Historical Dictionary of Leibniz's Philosophy* (Brown and Fox 2006).

[16] On death and generation, see LNS 1, 13–15.

[17] *Summa*, I, q.104, a.3 and a.4. Also see next footnote.

[18] Leibniz's views on birth and death are complicated. See the entries on 'generation', 'preexistence', 'preformation', 'transcreation', 'transformation', and 'transmigration', in Brown and Fox 2006. Also see *Theodicy* §91 and §397; *Principles of Nature and Grace* §6 (AG 209); and Roinila 2016.

If identical perspectives *were* possible, then the two supposedly distinct substances would really be one. (This follows from the identity of indiscernibles.) So, each substance, if it is to be a unique individual, must have a unique perspective. Moreover, God has at least two good reasons not to create beings with identical perspectives: (a) Even if God could create two identical substances, God would have no reason to *prefer* that the one exist rather than the other. This point is important, for, as we will see, God determines which individual notions will be created. (b) God's primary motive for creating beings is to increase his glory by creating the greatest variety of beings expressive of his nature. For example, 'the universe is in some way multiplied as many times as there are substances, and the glory of God is even redoubled by as many different representations of his work' (lns 18–20); whereas the creation of identical perspectives would decrease rather than multiply the expression of God's attributes. Thus God's glory can be increased, only if God's creation is represented by as many substances as uniquely represent the world. For these reasons the unique perspective must be *of perfections*, since these are the attributes of God that substances express and multiply. In sum, the principle of individuation is precisely that *unique* degree to which the soul expresses, represents, 'imitates', or approximates God's perfections, namely, wisdom, power, and goodness.

Let us see how each perfection may be uniquely expressed. Regarding *wisdom*, each substance expresses its own degree of epistemic perfection. Naturally, God's omniscience expresses the world completely, while each individual substance expresses it much less completely, just as a map of a city represents an actual city less completely than the city itself. So, each substance, or soul, contains a more or less perfect epistemic 'map' of the world, which it draws relative to its own 'situation', character, and experience. Moreover, one's own soul expresses, represents, knows, its own thoughts, ideas, and affections more distinctly than it expresses the thoughts, etc., belonging to other substances. It expresses the passions of its own body, and its spatial and temporal relations with other bodies, uniquely and more distinctly than any other substance would express them. In fact, as Leibniz will maintain, one's own soul expresses some degree of knowledge of everything in the universe, no matter how epistemically remote (confused) one may be in relation to it (lns 22–24). But in whatever degree, the amount of epistemic perfection a given soul expresses must be its own.

The perfection of *power* is best understood as both moral and epistemic, rather than physical. This is indicated in the way Leibniz says that substances 'accommodate themselves' to every other substance and to God. In other words, since all other substances express my perfections to some degree, the more moral and epistemic perfection that I possess (that is, the more morally good and wise I am), the more perfection *they* will possess.

In this sense, my power 'extends over all the others in imitation' of God's omnipotence (lns 26–7). But for every degree of perfection that I lack, other substances extend their power over me. The particular expression of each substance nevertheless extends infinitely, as Leibniz indicates in his *Labyrinth of the Continuum* (1683):

> For every soul, or rather every corporeal substance, is confusedly omniscient and diffusedly omnipotent. For nothing happens in the whole world which it does not perceive, and it has no endeavor that does not extend to infinity.[19]

Although referring to 'corporeal substances', namely, substances possessing both soul and matter, again, each substance expresses the entire universe *infinitely*, but limitedly, according to its particular degree of perfection. For these reasons I suggest that we take Leibniz's principle of individuation, at least in the *Discourse*, to be the unique degree of perfection that each substance expresses.[20]

Let us draw the commentary on this article to a close by summarising the meaning and consequence of Leibniz's complete notion of an individual

---

[19] LC 265.

[20] As far as I know, Leibniz does not anywhere *directly* claim that a unique degree of perfection is the principle of individuation. However, consider again the following passage from 1689: 'all individual created substances are different expressions of the same universe and different expressions of the same universal cause, namely God. But the expressions vary in perfection, just as different representations or drawings of the same town from different points of view do' (*Primary Truths*, AG 33). While this passage does not entail that a substance's unique degree of perfection constitutes its principle of individuation, it strongly suggests this interpretation; and taking the principle this way permits us to understand more clearly the reason God chooses which individual notions to make actual, namely, those which contribute, in combination with all other possible substances, to the greater overall perfection. This passage from *Primary Truths* also suggests that the 'point of view' of a substance (also mentioned in §57 of *Monadology*) is a function of its difference in perfection. It should be borne in mind, however, that Leibniz may have eventually come to hold that what individuates a substance is *the law of the series of its changes*. A good expression of this view can be found in a letter of 1698, in response to some of Pierre Bayle's criticisms of Leibniz's system: 'But in my opinion it is in the nature of created substance to change continually following a certain order which leads it spontaneously (if I may be allowed to use this word) through all the states which it encounters, in such a way that he who sees all things sees all its past and future states in its present. And this law of order, which constitutes the individuality of each particular substance, is in exact agreement with what occurs to every other substance and throughout the whole universe' ('Clarification of the Difficulties which Mr Bayle has Found in the New System of the Union of Body and Soul', LL 493). Presumably, this law is unique for each substance, although Leibniz does not provide an example of such a law, nor does he indicate exactly how it individuates. But supposing substances could be individuated this way, God would still need a reason to choose one law of the series over another, and this choice would most likely have to be based on the substance's contribution to perfection.

substance: 1. The complete notion (the full set of predicates) is the essential or real definition of an individual. 2. Each individual substance must be unique (as specified by the principle of the identify of indiscernibles). 3. Each substance is unique by virtue of the unique degree of perfection that it expresses in its relation to the universe. These results are crucial. Since each substance has a complete and unique notion, God may then inspect each one in order to admit into existence only those substances that *in combination* contribute the most to the best possible world.[21]

If the picture Leibniz presents so far, in §8 and §9, seems extravagant and strange to our more austere modern sensibilities, it becomes less so once we draw together several seemingly disparate threads of the argument. In order for our actions to be distinct from God's, Leibniz needs to establish that individual substances are the sources of their own actions, that they are self-acting creatures. At the same time, each individual must somehow have relations to other individuals, to the world, and to God. Leibniz believes that all these requirements are met by the complete notion, complemented by the principle of identity of indiscernibles and the doctrine of universal expression. We are unique, self-acting, but not isolated individuals; we form a society of substances, all acting *with* each other, affected *by* each other, with each substance making its own contribution to the totality of perfection.

Still, the question remains whether the actions of individual substances are *free* actions, in a sense relevant to our common understanding of 'free

---

[21] This point must not be understood to mean that God admits into existence only those substances that exhibit the *most* perfection, but rather that God considers the perfection of each substance *in connection* with all others and chooses that total combination of substances constituting the best possible world. Thus it is possible that substances having very little of the perfections can still 'make it' in the best possible world, just in case God can derive greater perfection from them; and this may be accomplished through the actions of other substances. For this reason, it is all the more important that each substance be individuated by its unique degree of perfection, so that God can choose which total combination will indeed be most perfect. This point may become clearer in reference to §7 and especially in §30 in reference to the sin of Judas. I would also ask the reader to consider a section of *On the Ultimate Origination of Things* (1697). In this piece, possible things 'strive with equal right [*pari jure*] for existence in proportion to the amount of essence or reality or the degree of perfection they contain' (AG 150). In other words, all possible beings are simply, and equally, essences, but each expresses a certain degree or proportion of perfection. However, from the infinite combinations or possible series of essences (let's say the series of actions of all possible substances), the one series that *exists* will be 'the one through which the most essence or possibility is brought into existence' (AG 150). That is to say that the actual world is the one which contains the greatest degree of completion (perfection) of essence (possibility) given the comparative limitations of each substance. Thus each substance contributes its own proportion of perfection to the whole. I submit that each substance must do so *uniquely*.

will': that we are free to choose our actions. It is not enough to say that we are unique individuals distinct from God, and it is too much to say that we are entirely distinct from God's will, since God creates us based on the particular perfection we express. Furthermore, we have seen that God *knows* the complete contents of every individual notion. Thus, it remains for Leibniz to show how God's *foreknowledge* of our notion does not entail we are not free to determine at least some of our actions, especially those actions that make us morally responsible. Leibniz will address these matters in §13 and §14, after taking a detour through the relationship between physics and metaphysics.

§10. That substantial forms have their place in physics, but not as explanations of the details of phenomena.

With the matter of freedom yet to be fully addressed, it may seem puzzling that Leibniz should suddenly turn to a seemingly obscure discussion of the relationship between substantial forms and physical bodies. Likely, he has in mind to show that just as the true account of an individual depends on a metaphysical principle, namely, the individual notion contained in its soul, the true account of physical matter (or body-in-general) also depends on a metaphysical, soul-like principle. Thus, if Leibniz can convince us of the former, we might more readily accept a metaphysics of physics. But why does he need to convince us of the latter?

To make his overall argument for God's perfection in the *Discourse*, Leibniz must confront nothing less than the scientific revolution of the sixteenth and seventeenth centuries, of which he is very much a part, and its possibly dangerous consequences for theology. But Leibniz is not only interested in saving theology, but in saving physics from itself, that is, from its own faulty premises. By Leibniz's time the new 'mechanical philosophy' of Galileo, Bacon, Descartes, Gassendi, Hobbes, and Boyle had largely displaced the ancient (Aristotelian and Medieval) physics based on 'substantial forms', so-called 'occult qualities', and other non-material entities. The new physics had come to represent a general shift in method away from qualitative and toward quantitative analysis. In his youth, Leibniz had upheld the substantial forms of Aristotle, until around age fifteen (1661) when he had a kind of conversion to the mechanical philosophy. However, by about 1668, he definitively came to hold that the mechanical philosophy was unintelligible without proper appeal to the ancient substantial forms.[1]

---

[1] Leibniz writes of his philosophical development in *New System of Nature* (1695), AG 139, and in a letter to Nicolas Remond in 1714 (LL 655). See Mercer 2004: 24–7; 39–40; 67, for details on this development. See also Garber 2009: 3–10.

Thus, here in the *Discourse* (§11) he argues for a 'rehabilitation' of portions of the ancient physics. But it is not possible clearly to understand Leibniz's attempted rehabilitation without grasping at least some of the mechanical philosophy's critique of ancient physics. Thus, the following serves as important background for §10 and §11, as well as for Leibniz's influential criticisms of 'Cartesian mechanics' in articles 12, 17, and 21.

Personally, I used to doubt the value of studying obsolete physical theories. But in fact, it is very useful, not only for understanding more deeply a wide range of problems in the Modern period, but for gaining insight into problems in contemporary physics, such as the nature of matter, force, particles, and problems in scientific methodology. Also, the conflict between Modern mechanics and God's purpose provides useful background to current debates over 'intelligent design'.

We begin with Aristotle's account of matter and change,[2] although we must first take note of the ancient doctrine of atomism, as introduced by the Pre-Socratic philosopher, Democritus (460–370 BCE). An atom, according to its literal definition, is an ultimately 'unsplittable', that is, solid and undividable, portion of matter; and all things are composed entirely of an innumerable multitude of them. Aristotle was not an atomist, but he seems to have held that matter is fundamentally 'primary matter', an infinitely divisible, formless, and featureless stuff. In fact, it is hard to imagine what primary matter is, except in terms of some structure or definition. Thus (as we saw in §8), Aristotle supposed that a non-material principle, namely *substantial form*, was required to give primary matter whatever structure, organisation, and difference from other portions of matter it may have. In this way, matter and form, together and inseparably, could serve to distinguish matter into *kinds* of matter. Aristotle then adopted from Empedocles the idea that all of matter consists fundamentally, not of atoms, but of four basic matter-form combinations called the 'Elements': Fire, Air, Water, and Earth. Of course, Aristotle needed to explain how only these four elements could account for the multitude of different things we observe (such as vapours, ice, stones, animals, plants, humans, etc.). Thus, he needed a theory of *change*.

We can think of change in two ways: (1) as when one thing becomes another thing; or (2) as when a thing undergoes some change in itself. A change of the first kind is a change in *form*. Thus, the element of Fire can become Air; or the element of Water can become Earth. A change of the second kind is a change in *quality*, such as when a hot stone becomes cold, or a wet sponge becomes dry. But what causes these changes? Aristotle held that change always proceeds from an immediate state to a *contrary*

---

[2] I draw this rough account from Aristotle's *Generation and Corruption*.

state; thus he supposed that each of the elements consisted of (or was *known* through) one pair of *qualities*: Fire is hot-dry, Air is hot-wet, Water is cold-wet, and Earth is cold-dry. Note that these are *perceptible* (primarily *tangible*) qualities by means of which we perceive the Elements in varying degrees: Fire *feels* hot and dry, and Water *feels* cold and wet, etc. Thus, all changes among and within the Elements could be understood as changes among contrary qualities: human flesh, for example, which consists of a mixture of all the Elements, becomes bone (earth-like) when it becomes dry. The point is that a virtually infinite range of permutations of such changes could account for the multitude and variety of everything we observe, and thus could account for the form and quality of every material thing. Now, it matters little that these sorts of explanations seem to us simplistic, inadequate, and largely false. What matters is the role that *form* and the perceptible *qualities* play in subsequent developments, for these are the metaphysical properties of the physics with which Leibniz and the Moderns were concerned.

For the Medieval Aristotelians (the Scholastics), the natural world was populated by substantial forms, qualities, and a host of similar 'soul-like' metaphysical entities. The distinctions among things in terms of genus and species were distinctions made by substantial forms; for example, animals had the form of the genus ANIMALIA, while humans had that form plus the species difference RATIONAL. Gold, silver, and lead were species of the genus METAL, with each species difference determined by its gold, silver, or lead *form*. As for qualities, every species of thing had its characteristic qualities, such as, in the case of metals, hardness, softness, malleability, fusibility, etc. Thus, an infinity of forms and qualities determined every difference in matter, in the effects that matter had upon our senses and that matter had on other portions of matter. Where the form determined a difference in genus or species, it was typically called a 'substantial form'. When the form determined a property of a thing, it was typically called a 'sensible quality'.

It is important to understand that the forms and qualities are considered to be non-material entities or principles. On the ancient or at least Medieval conception, *primary* matter, conceived as formless and infinitely divisible, was thought to be essentially inert, unable to form, organise, or set itself into motion. In these respects, primary matter was entirely *passive*. Form, on the other hand, was the non-material *active* principle; it organised matter, set it into motion, accounted for the life and activity of plants and animals, and overall provided the unity of structure, function, and change throughout the life of an organism. In this way, the form was

---

[3] More on the final cause in §§19–23.

responsible for the *final cause* of a thing, that is, the function or purpose that the organism, by virtue of its organisation, was capable of performing.[3] Form did everything matter could not do, all without being matter itself. Thus, given the assumptions about the passivity and inertia of matter, it was quite reasonable to assume an active principle such as form. In this way, for the Medievals, form is the metaphysical explanation for the properties of matter, just as the soul is the metaphysical explanation for the unity of the human body.

What happened to this ancient-Medieval physics? After some 2,000 years, seventeenth-century natural philosophers like Galileo, Gassendi, Bacon, Descartes, and Boyle increasingly found that explanations of the properties of bodies in terms of forms and qualities proved rather empty, while other explanations proved more fruitful. To take an often-cited example, it was known that consuming poppy seeds could make you sleepy. The Medieval and Renaissance era explanation for why they made you sleepy was that poppy seeds have a *dormitive* quality, that is, a *form* that makes you sleepy. But for the Moderns, this does not explain how the form produces this quality, nor what its sensible, material properties really consist of. It conveys only what you already know, that these seeds induce sleepiness because *that's just what they do*. Such qualities were often called 'occult' qualities because they could not be explained by anything other than their effects.[4]

Increasingly, the Modern natural philosophers (physicists) and medical doctors (physicians) sought explanations in terms of the *mathematical-geometrical* properties of bodies, that is, in the size, shape, number, arrangement, and motion of tiny bits of matter they called 'corpuscles'. The appeal of these properties of bodies, often simply called 'mechanical', is that they could be precisely and objectively measured, and thus could be

---

[4] In 1673, the playwright Moliére (in the third Interlude of *Le Malade imaginaire* [*The Imaginary Invalid*]) mocked this *virtus dormitiva*: 'Opium makes you sleepy because there is a sleeping virtue in it, whose nature is to dull the senses.' While this kind of derision of Scholastic physics was common in the seventeenth century, the Scholastics were well aware of the difficulties they faced in trying to account for the hidden causes of a thing's properties and functions. Augustine (fourth century) for example, remarked on the qualities of quicklime (that they could be sensed, but not understood). The fifteenth-century polymath Cornelius Agrippa wrote: 'There are vertues in things, which are not from any Element, as to expel poison, to drive away the noxious vapors of Minerals, to attract Iron, . . . And they are called occult qualities, because their Causes lie hid [from our senses] and mans intellect cannot in any way reach, and find them out. Wherefore Philosophers have attained to the greatest part of them by long experience [and conjecture], rather than by the search of reason' (*Three Books of Occult Philosophy*, quoted from Hutchison 1982: 239). On substantial form in Aristotle, Scholasticism, and the Moderns, see Pasnau 2004.

155

convincingly characterised as the *real* properties of bodies *themselves*. On the other hand, the *sensible* qualities of things (colour, sound, taste, smell, and feel), that is, the *experience* of these qualities in the minds of perceivers, are *not* measurable in mechanical terms. These qualities are found only *in our sense perceptions*, not in things themselves.[5] Thus, the sensible qualities were thought to be *effects in us* of the size, shape, number, arrangement, and motion of the corpuscles, which were the causes. In effect, the natural philosophers returned to a version of ancient atomism, although most took corpuscles to consist of infinitely (or indefinitely) divisible bits of matter, rather than the indivisible ('unsplittable') atoms of the ancients.

A practical illustration of this shift from the old qualitative physics to the new mathematical physics is provided by the Irish chemist Robert Boyle, in his *Origin of Forms and Qualities* (1666). What accounts, for example, for the explosive quality of gunpowder? It was well understood that gunpower consists of nitre, charcoal, and brimstone (sulphur), and that an explosion occurs when the compound of these chemicals is forcefully struck. Now, the Scholastic-Aristotelian physicist would say that the cause of the explosion was a certain *form* (let us call it 'explosivity'), that is, a power or disposition of these chemicals in combination to explode when vigorously agitated. Were we to press for an explanation of what this form precisely consists in, the Scholastic physicist could say, 'since none of the chemicals individually have within them this explosive quality, it cannot be a property of *matter*. So, it must therefore be some *non-material* property somehow arising from the compound.' Yet, the explanation Boyle gives is different – and decisive: Each of these chemicals consists of tiny corpuscles of a certain size, shape, number, and arrangement, and which alone determine the particular qualities of these chemicals. The quality of *explosivity* results from nothing more than an *efficient cause*, namely, the vigorous agitation of these chemicals in combination – not in forms or anything inexplicably arising from these strictly material properties. Accordingly, the motions of tiny corpuscles, often beyond detection by the bare senses, constitute the quality, cause, and effect, of every material thing, living or inert.

In just this way, the ancient explanations were 'reduced' to the new 'mechanical philosophy', or *corpuscularianism*, as it was also called, since it

---

[5] This distinction between mathematical and sensible qualities is well known in philosophical literature as the distinction between primary and secondary qualities. But it is a distinction not easy to make. Of course, in contemporary terms, we do have ways of measuring sensible qualities objectively; for example, the note of A at 'concert pitch' can be given a purely mechanical description: a vibration of air molecules occurring at 440 cycles per second. But what you *hear* is the *sound* that those 440 cycles per second create in your head. It is the hearing, or the phenomena of sound, that does not have a mechanical description.

depended only on the mathematical-geometrical properties of tiny bodies.[6] Boyle had effectively reduced Aristotle's 'contrary qualities' to the properties of corpuscles, and showed that matter could indeed organise, differentiate, and move itself, or at least that chemistry had no use for the ancient explanations.[7] While the mechanical properties of bodies are still conceived of as *powers* or *dispositions* to produce some effect, either upon our senses or upon other material objects, there is nothing more to these powers than corpuscles in various sizes, shapes, arrangements, and motions – nothing metaphysical or non-measurable about them – and so explanations in terms of forms and qualities were gradually replaced in Modern physics by such mechanical explanations.[8]

What, then, is Leibniz's criticism of the mechanical philosophy? In his typical fashion, he argues that it is partly right but partly wrong. On the one hand, as he makes clear in §10, beginning on line 11, he agrees that form-like qualities should not be appealed to in physical explanations. His example is a bit inappropriate, since a clock is a manufactured rather than natural object. But a clock may be said to have a 'horodictic' (ln 18) or time-telling quality, which is not found in any of its material parts (springs, rods, and gears); thus, its quality must be something over and above its matter. As Leibniz remarks, however, the horodictic form does not at all explain how the clock actually works to perform its time-telling function, and so explanations in terms of forms and qualities are going to fall far short of revealing the inner laws of matter in motion. Rather, before resorting to forms and qualities, we should conduct our investigations as far as possible from the standpoint of corpuscles, their magnitudes, arrangements, and motions.

On the other hand, Leibniz maintains that the mathematical, corpuscular, properties of bodies cannot, by themselves, explain *all* of the properties of bodies and their interactions. As he says at line 21, explanations like 'horodicity' represent a 'misuse' of the forms that prevents us from understanding the true metaphysical principles on which matter depends and by means of which we understand 'incorporeal natures' and God. Is there,

[6] The word 'mechanical' comes from the Greek *mekhana*, meaning 'trick' or 'expedient' of nature. But the idea of a 'mechanical philosophy' derives from the 'simple machines' of the Renaissance: the lever, pulley, wedge, and screw, whose properties and functions were determined though strict analysis of their mathematical-geometrical properties. See Osler 2010: 94.

[7] Similarly, Descartes said that he had no use for substantial forms and so-called 'real qualities' in *any* part of physics, since he could account for all phenomena by virtue of the properties of extended matter and its motion. See *Principles* IV, §§187, 198, and 201.

[8] See Boyle 1991: 34. John Locke borrowed much of his corpuscular mechanics from Boyle.

then, a *proper* use of the forms? And what exactly are those metaphysical principles?

These questions are not easy to answer; but they have centrally to do with Leibniz's conception of matter and whether bodies have their own principle of difference, organisation, and, most importantly, unity. As we have seen, Aristotle and the mechanists agree that matter is *infinitely divisible*. While Aristotle resolves this divisibility by giving matter *form*, the mechanists came to believe that matter is *self*-forming. But for Leibniz, the mechanists' view cannot ultimately be sustained. The infinite divisibility of matter entails that matter cannot *complete* itself, cannot form a unified, definite thing; so, *something like* Aristotelian substantial form is required. What Leibniz is arguing in this article is that for matter to have structure and unity, it must, like the complete notion of an individual substance, have *substantial form*. This is what 'the Moderns' have failed to recognise.

It would seem then that 'substantial forms' (ln 1) are what Leibniz alludes to as 'so necessary in Metaphysics' (ln 22). However, it is not clear that Leibniz really thinks that bodies have substantial form and are thus substances. His edit on line 1 is quite revealing. He writes, 'the opinion on substantial forms has something solid', but then strikes 'if bodies are substances' from the final draft. So, *does* he think bodies are substances? Why doesn't he just say so? The best clue to his position comes in a letter to Arnauld, written several months after he had composed the *Discourse*:

> If the body is a substance, and not a simple phenomenon, like the rainbow, or a being united by accident or aggregation like a heap of stones, it cannot consist in extension, and there must necessarily be conceived in it something called substantial form, which corresponds in some way to what is called the soul.[9]

In sum, a body *can* be a substance *only* if it has a principle of unity, that is, a substantial form. Without such a principle, bodies are incidental collections of undifferentiated stuff, or they are the phenomena of something *else* that *is* substantial. But the real reason Leibniz does not say outright that bodies are substances is that he thinks they are *not* substances, at least not according to Descartes' conception of body as 'extended substance'.

---

[9] Letter to Arnauld, 14 July 1686, LAV 115 / LAM 66. Leibniz goes on to say: 'I have finally been convinced of this, as though in spite of myself, after having been far removed from it earlier. Nevertheless, however much I approve the Scholastics in this general and so to speak metaphysical explanation of the principles of bodies, I am as corpuscularian as one can be in the explanation of particular phenomena; and it is to say nothing to affirm qualities or forms of them. One must always explain nature mathematically and mechanically, provided that one knows that the principles themselves, or laws of mechanics or force, do not depend only on mathematical extension, but on a few metaphysical reasons' (LAV 115).

To understand fully Leibniz's contention against Descartes' conception of substance, we will need to go through §12.[10]

Until then, what is clear in this article of the *Discourse* is that Leibniz thinks that *some* sort of soul-like 'incorporeal natures' (ln 24) are involved in the structure and unity of material bodies, and if we can accept that, then we may more readily accept other incorporeal or metaphysical principles. Regarding the latter, Leibniz likely has in mind the principle of *force*, which in §17 he will argue is a metaphysical principle not explainable in material terms, but which is responsible for the motions of bodies. In mentioning 'the marvels of God' (ln 25) he likely alludes to God's 'final causes', which are needed to explain *why* material things have their characteristic structure and behaviour. The argument for final causes will be given in §§19–22. The final point, though, is that the physicist need not appeal to God's agency ('concourse') nor to any other extravagant metaphysics in order to do good physics. Leibniz is saying that in order to save the phenomena, stick with what you can observe and measure, and reach for metaphysics only when the phenomena can no longer explain themselves. In sum, Leibniz wants to maintain that, when understood properly, portions of the ancient physics, the new mechanical philosophy, and the old theology are collectively required to form a complete account of natural phenomena.

§11. The Scholastics, who upheld substantial forms, are not to be despised entirely.

Continuing with the previous article's theme of the revision or 'rehabilitation' of the Scholastic doctrine of substantial form, Leibniz recognises that he is again advancing a 'paradox', that is, in this case, a view out of sync with the mechanical philosophy of his day. Notice again his reluctance to say openly that bodies are substances (line 6, footnote 3). Substantial forms can be admitted 'on the hypothesis' that bodies are substances – but he strikes this hypothesis from the final draft because he is not ready to commit to it. We can assume, then, that if bodies *are* substances, there is all the more reason to permit the proper use of substantial forms – that is, as principles of unity of structure and function.

His mention of the 'nearly banished' substantial forms could be a direct reference to Descartes' *Principles of Philosophy* of 1644:

---

[10] Leibniz's remarks here in §10 are complicated by his developing notion of 'corporeal substance'. See the excellent analyses in Sleigh 1990, Chs. 5 and 6; and Adams 1994, Chs. 10 and 11. For a comprehensive view, see Phemister 2001.

When dealing with natural things we will, then, never derive any explanations from the purposes which God or nature may have had in view when creating them <and we shall entirely banish from our philosophy the search for final causes.> We should, instead, consider him as the efficient cause of all things.[1]

A 'final cause' is a description of the structure, design, and developmental 'goal' of an organism. Since the description cannot be given in completely mathematical terms, final causes are like substantial forms in being unmeasurable, unobservable causes that Moderns like Descartes also sought to banish from physical explanations. The reason Descartes gives for banishing final causes, however, is not that they are not measurable, but that since God is infinite, we can never fully discern God's purpose for giving the world the design and structure it exhibits. Thus, we should instead seek out the *efficient* causes (what we call nowadays simply 'causes') in nature because we can know them, both as the observable causes of the motions of sensible matter and as the cause by which God set everything into motion. Leibniz agrees with Descartes on the role that efficient causes should take in physical explanations, but thinks final causes must ultimately be included, as we will see in §19–22.

But more to the point of this article: while warning us against the misuse of substantial forms in physics, Leibniz also wants to defend the Scholastics who employed them.[2] For example, the Aristotelian-Christian philosopher-theologian Thomas Aquinas had usefully distinguished *substantial* form from *accidental* form, thereby generally distinguishing the essential properties of a thing from its accidental properties. On the one hand, every living creature possesses the substantial form of 'vegetative soul', which denotes the creature's capacity for digestion and growth, without which the creature would not be a living being. On the other hand, accidental form designates properties not essential to being a creature, such as colour, size, and particular design. Leibniz has much less trouble attributing substantial form to living creatures as a whole than he does to inanimate bodies themselves. But again, while essential and accidental forms are useful for distinguishing various beings and their particular functions, he insists that such forms ultimately lack explanatory power; we must investigate phenomena experimentally and mathematically, in order to understand them more completely. Indeed, his own experiments compelled him to admit that there is more than matter in the principle of bodies. Leibniz makes good on this claim in the following article.

---

[1] *Principles* I, §28. The angle brackets contain a passage from Descartes' 1647 French version of *Principles* added by the translators, CSM.

[2] Elsewhere and later Leibniz praises the 'Scholastics' for their erudition on a wide range of topics. See LRB IV.viii.9.431.

§12. Critique of Descartes' conception of extension: that extension involves imaginary notions and therefore cannot constitute the substance of body.

While Descartes is not named in this article, his famous account of body as 'extended substance' is clearly the target of Leibniz's criticisms. Thus, this article represents Leibniz's first direct attack in the *Discourse* upon Descartes' mechanical philosophy. The first clue that his target is Descartes is in the line he struck from the summary (see footnote 1): 'if there is nothing in bodies other than what consists in extension'. That there is nothing but extension (three-dimensionality) in bodies is precisely Descartes' view. Leibniz then continues in the main with his claim that 'the nature' of bodies cannot consist entirely of extension. In other words, since Descartes takes *extension only* to be what determines body in general to be *substance*, and since for Leibniz to be a substance requires something more than extension (supposedly, substantial form), Cartesian bodies are not substances. Leibniz's particular criticisms of Cartesian extension here are several and brief; so, to understand them, we will need to take a closer look at Descartes' conception of extension. The reader should keep these points in mind for §17.

Descartes' conception of body as extended substance forms one essential component of his famous and controversial 'mind-body dualism'. Like the other corpuscularists, Descartes holds that all of matter is indefinitely divisible; but Descartes' conception goes a bit deeper by characterising the *nature* of matter, its essence, as extended: 'Thus, extension in length, breadth, and depth constitutes the nature of corporeal substance; and thought constitutes the nature of thinking substance' (*Principles* I, §53). Thus, matter consists solely of spatial magnitude – *and nothing else* – no sensible qualities, forms, or forces; and 'thinking substance' is characterised as essentially non-extended, thus as a substance distinct in essence from matter. For our purposes, we do not need to engage the problem of mind-body interaction endemic to Descartes' conceptions; we need only to understand his conception of corporeal substance, because Leibniz argues it is mistaken.

Now, Leibniz indicates (at line 7) that 'size, figure, and motion' characterise extension. This is not, however, Descartes' precise view. While for Descartes size (or magnitude) is synonymous with extension, figure and motion are *modes* of extension, not essential properties of it. 'For everything else which can be attributed to body presupposes extension' (*Principles* I, §53). That is, *figure* presupposes some magnitude of matter, and *motion* presupposes some part of matter moving in relation to other parts. But the role of motion is key: since all of matter is simply extended, simply three-dimensional, it is not divided into *definite* parts, since any part of it is indefinitely divisible and, most notably, indistinguishable from any other part. Therefore, if there are to be parts of matter distinguished from other parts, there must be a principle of division of matter, and that principle is motion: 'All variation in matter, or all the diversity of its forms, depends on motion' (*Principles* II, §23). In other words, parts of matter are distinguished from each other when one portion is moving differently from another portion. So, while motion is not essential to matter itself, it is the principle of distinction in matter. But the key point, since motion distinguishes the parts of matter, is that Descartes has no need to appeal to substantial forms and qualities as principles of variation and diversity in matter.

Material objects are, of course, distinguished by more than their shapes, namely, by colour, odour, taste, and various tactile qualities such as cold and hot. Here, too, Descartes appeals to motion and extension rather than to mysterious 'occult' qualities to account for these sensible qualities. Take a green ball, for instance. Its roundness is explained by the portions of matter at rest (which is a mode of motion) maintaining a round shape. Its colour is the product of the shapes of numerous bits of matter that make up the ball and the way those shapes make particles of light strike the ball and then our retina. Similar accounts can be given of how all the qualities we sense are caused by the shapes and motions of small, often imperceptible, bits of matter.

It is also important to understand how Descartes distinguishes what are called the primary qualities (extension, shape, and motion) from the secondary qualities (those of the five senses: colour, odour, touch, etc.). Thus, the green ball has the primary quality of roundness and the secondary quality of greeness. The secondary qualities are said to be not in objects, but in perceivers. So, it is thought that the primary qualities are the *real* qualities of bodies, while the secondary qualities are only effects in us caused by the primary qualities. But how is this difference between the primary and secondary qualities determined? Aren't both the primary and secondary qualities perceived by our senses? Yes; but for Descartes there is an important difference, namely, that the primary qualities are most distinctly perceived, while the secondary qualities are perceived confusedly. In other words, we understand much more clearly 'what it is for that body to have [shape] than what it is for it to have colour' (*Principles* I, §69). We understand this for several reasons: primary qualities can be given objective measurement (the ball has a diameter of 20 cm), while secondary qualities cannot be measured in this way. Secondary qualities, furthermore, can be abstracted from extended properties; that is, I can think of the object as possessing no secondary properties whatsoever, but I cannot think of it as having no primary qualities. Descartes can maintain, then, that we have no reason to appeal to 'occult' qualities to account for secondary qualities, because they can be accounted for by extension and its modes of figure and motion – in short, completely by the measurable properties of things external to us, as these properties cause impressions on our mind. In addition, we can understand how material bodies have effects on our senses, but we cannot comprehend how supposedly non-material qualities, such as forms, could have effects on us or on other bodies.[1]

Now, from this understanding of the basics of Descartes' principles of body and motion, we can determine why Leibniz denies that they explain the substance of bodies. First, Leibniz insists, against Descartes, that for bodies to be substances (or for body in general to be a substance), matter must have *something* 'connected to souls', something metaphysical, *like* substantial forms – something that is not extended – that can account for the unity, structure, and variety of extended matter. His argument for this claim – not found in the *Discourse*[2] – is that if matter is completely uniform (as it is for Descartes, since it is nothing but extended) then not only does it have no principle of distinction itself, but motion cannot account for it. For example, imagine you are standing in front of a giant tank of absolutely clear, non-particulate water. Now imagine having visibly to distinguish one portion of the water from another. You could not do this, because everything is visually uniform. Suppose now that a roughly one-foot-wide stream of water in the tank was moving from the right of you to the left, at roughly head level, while the portion above and below this stream remained at rest. Could you tell that this stream of water is moving? You could not, because there is nothing visible to distinguish the moving portion of the stream from the portions at rest; no particles to see float by, no waves or swirls could appear in the water, since all is visibly uniform. This is just how it is with Cartesian matter. Since it has nothing in it to distinguish one part from another, motion cannot determine any differences in matter. 'And thus, everything would be just as if there were no change or discrimination in bodies, nor could we ever explain the different appearances we sense'

---

[1] Descartes: 'We cannot in any way comprehend how the same things (that is, size, figure, and motion) can produce something else of an entirely different nature from themselves, such as those substantial forms and real qualities which many Philosophers suppose to be in things; nor indeed how, subsequently, these qualities or forms can have the force to excite local movement in other bodies. [. . .]: It must certainly be concluded regarding those things which, in external objects, we call by the names of light, color, odor, taste, sound, heat, cold, and of other tactile qualities, or else by the names of substantial forms; that we are not aware of their being anything other than various arrangements of the size, figure, and motions of the parts of these objects which make it possible for our nerves to move in various ways, and to excite in our soul all the various feelings which they produce there' (*Principles* IV, §198).

[2] See *On Nature Itself* (1698), in AG 161–5.

(AG 164). One might try to object to Leibniz's claim by pointing out that you could *feel* the difference between the two portions of water by putting one part of your arm in the moving portion and the other part in the resting portion. But Leibniz's point here is not that the differences in uniform matter are not possible to sense; it is, rather, that if the senses are required to detect differences in matter, then the principle of distinction is not in matter *itself*. It is in the senses. Therefore, since the principle of distinction is not in matter, *matter cannot be substance*; nor can its properties be principles of distinction; and, therefore, if bodies are to be substances, then some metaphysical principle in matter is required to serve as its principle of distinction. And it must be metaphysical, since if it were something material, then we would be thrown back upon the problem of the uniformity of matter.

This 'something', however, 'changes nothing in the phenomena' (ln 10). This means that it would not *change* how bodies appear and behave but would *explain* their appearance and motion. For example, in line 9, Leibniz alludes to Descartes' contention that animals do not have souls but instead are machines or automatons whose actions can be explained mechanically, that is, solely in terms of the motions of their material parts.[3] Nothing would be changed in this explanation if we acknowledge that animals possess souls. Similarly, for Leibniz, whether matter has something soul-like changes nothing in the way we study phenomena. We should still proceed by way of observation and measurement and attention to the primary properties of things. What a metaphysical principle provides is the reason for the behaviour we observe and measure. It provides the reason why things move with a certain speed and direction. This point should become apparent in §17.

In another passing criticism, Leibniz remarks that the properties of extension contain something 'imaginary' and relative, just as do our perceptions of sense. His criticism is twofold. First, he is referring to the way Descartes distinguishes (as we saw above, in reference to *Principles* I, §69) extended (primary) qualities from the sensible (secondary) qualities, such as colour, heat, etc. For Descartes, our much clearer understanding of the former over the latter tells us that the former are properties of bodies while the latter are properties of perceivers. Leibniz contends, however, that this distinction cannot be so neatly drawn, because the primary qualities are also subject to the contributions of the senses. For example, as Descartes would agree, matter itself is infinitely divisible and imperfectly, minutely, divided; therefore, for Leibniz, any definite shape that some part of matter *apparently* has will in part be a construction of the perceiver, who, as it were, casts a cloak of unity over the object. Consider that we perceive a figure in

---

[3] See Descartes, *Discourse on Method*, Part V, CSM I, 139–41.

a pointillist painting as a continuous form, rather than as composed of discrete dots, unless we look very closely. The position of the perceiver can also make a difference in the apparent shape. A basketball viewed from two metres appears perfectly round; but up close we may observe a number of irregularities, especially very close up, where its round shape may not even be perceivable at all. The second part of Leibniz's criticism again relates to motion, but in a different way. According even to Descartes, motion is relative to states of rest among other parts of matter (*Principles* II, §25). For Leibniz, this relativity means that motion cannot determine a substance, since what determines something to be a substance cannot depend on its *relation* to something else. In sum, for all these reasons, the properties of extension, size, figure, and motion, cannot constitute the substance of matter.

Leibniz's final criticism of Cartesian substance is based on identity (ln 17). Without some metaphysical, unifying, form, all of the parts of matter would constantly change position; thus, no stable identity of any part of matter could be secured. But the issue of identity also relates to an important difference between substantial forms and souls. If there are substantial forms of bodies, they do not retain their perceptions, that is, they do not retain the knowledge or memory of what they are. Thus, there is a hierarchy of metaphysical principles. Only human souls retain this knowledge from life to afterlife, making them morally accountable and capable of community with God. More on this point in §34.

We can close the commentary on this article by noting, once again, Leibniz's reluctance to commit to a doctrine of bodies as substances. At line 6, Leibniz initially had written, 'either bodies are not substances, in metaphysical rigour . . . or', but then struck this from the final draft. The result of his criticisms is that bodies in a Cartesian sense cannot be substances, 'in metaphysical rigour'. But then if not, what should he say about them? If he says what he seems to want to say, that bodies have substantial form, then this might commit him to the reality of corporeal substances, and he is not ready to commit to this. The fact is, he is still working out the metaphysical relationship between the human soul and its own body. We get his account of that relationship in §32 and §33.

§13. On whether the complete notion entails a fatal necessity; on distinctions between necessary and contingent propositions and consecutions; on God's foreknowledge of future contingents; on inclination without necessitation.

With this article, Leibniz temporarily departs from his critique of the Cartesian conception of substance in order to head off a problem that may be implied by the complete notion of an individual substance introduced in §8. The problem is that since the complete notion contains the idea of every action of the individual, then every action is, in some sense, 'necessary'. Moreover, in §9 we saw that the individual notion has definite and actually infinite relations of expression with every other substance, such that each individual expresses every other and God 'in its manner'. As a result, it appears that everything in the universe happens by an unavoidable, invariable, inflexible necessity; and yet Leibniz had introduced the complete notion in order to distinguish God's actions from human actions, so that humans could be said to be the cause of their actions and thus to act freely.

Leibniz is well aware of the problem and believes he has a solution, as indicated in his summary of §13 and in the article itself: It is true that from the nature of a circle we can deduce, with *logical* necessity, all the properties of a circle (ln 14); and if we apply this same sort of necessity to the deduction of all the predicates contained within the complete notion of an individual substance, then indeed all its actions must follow with logical necessity as well, such that 'human freedom would have no place and that an absolute fate will reign over all our actions as well as over all other events in the world' (lns 16–18). Leibniz argues, however, that while the predicates of the complete notion are *certain* (assured to occur) they are not *logically necessary*; thereby, human freedom is not threatened.

Leibniz did not figure, however, that Antoine Arnauld, to whom Leibniz sent only the summaries of the *Discourse* (not the articles themselves), would misunderstand, or find unconvincing, this attempt to preserve freedom. Indeed, in his first response to Leibniz, Arnauld explicitly registers his 'fright' and 'shock' over the implications contained in the summary of §13.

> If this is so [that the individual notion of each person contains once and for all everything that will ever happen to him], then God was free to create or not to create Adam; but supposing that he did will to create him, everything that has happened since to humankind, and will ever happen to it, must have happened and must happen by a necessity that is more than fatal. For the individual notion of Adam contained his having so many children, and the individual notion of each one of these children, everything that they would do and all the children they would have; and so on.[1]

The problem, as it appears to Arnauld, is that even if God were free to create the first individual notion, that of Adam, God would not be free to create anything other than what followed from it – which is everything. This implies that neither God nor humankind would be free to act

---

[1] Letter of 13 March 1686, LAV 9, translation slightly adjusted.

otherwise than in accord with this very notion. Arnauld went on to say that the Church would not approve of such an opinion and to urge Leibniz to abandon these useless metaphysical speculations and to attend to the salvation of his soul by converting to Catholicism (LAV 11 / LAM 9).

While Leibniz did not go on to convert to Catholicism, he did try to convince Arnauld that the connection of predicates within the complete notion was not *logically* necessary (thus not fatally but only *hypothetically* necessary – a distinction which Arnauld, the author of *Logic, or the Art of Thinking*, would perfectly understand). Perhaps, if Arnauld had seen the entire contents of §13, he would not have been misled by Leibniz's summary. In any case, it is anything but obvious to many readers how Leibniz's distinctions among *certainty*, *logical necessity*, and *hypothetical necessity* suffice to establish the required freedom for God and his creatures. Leibniz's discussion in §13 is intensely complex – and even when clarified, the sense in which freedom is preserved remains doubtful. Thus, I think it best to clarify the most important and complicated terminology Leibniz employs, to reconstruct the argument I think he intends to make, and to let the reader judge its cogency for herself. Keep the following question in mind as you read the commentary and re-read §13: How is it that both God and his creatures are inclined, but not necessitated, to perform the actions they do?

A priori: In contemporary philosophy, '*a priori*' usually refers to the means by which the truth value (true or false) of some proposition can be known. That is, simply by knowing the *meanings* of the terms involved in the proposition, or by analysing them, one can know whether it is true. This mode of knowing is distinct from '*a posteriori*' knowledge, for which one must appeal to experience. For example, if I know that the meaning of 'cat' includes 'mammal', and that every mammal is a vertebrate, then I know *a priori* that any given cat has by nature a backbone, without having to check the cat. However, if I want to know the particular size and colour of the cat, I must investigate with my senses (*a posteriori*). Yes, we must appeal to sense experience in order to fix the meanings of 'cat' and 'mammal', etc. But once that is done, an *a priori* inference is a matter of logical consequence. In propositions involving strictly logical relations, appeal to sense experience is not needed at all. The point is, based on *a priori* knowledge we can make true inferences about many things by means of logically certain relations, without appealing to experience – and we do this frequently.

It is important to note, however, that this is *not* exactly how Leibniz is using '*a priori*' here (lns 2 and 81). He is following an older, Medieval, usage of the term meaning *knowing a truth from its cause prior to knowing its effects*, and these effects need not be known by strict logical inference – although God, by virtue of his omniscience, can know them independently of experience.[2] To use Leibniz's example, since the individual notion of

167

Caesar includes all of Caesar's actions, and God knows this notion, God has *a priori* knowledge of Caesar's actions, before causing this notion to become actual. Thus understood, the counterpart to *a priori* knowledge is *a posteriori* knowledge, which begins with knowledge of effects and infers *back* to causes, such as we typically do when we look for the cause of some effect or when we test a hypothesis. Thus, humans can have only *a posteriori* knowledge of Caesar's notion, while God has *a priori* knowledge. The main point is that when Leibniz says that individual substances have '*a priori* proofs of their truth', he is not saying that their truth is knowable by means of logical deduction, but rather by means of the (mostly) contingent relations within their notion, which only God can know completely. It helps to recall §8 where Leibniz distinguishes *identical* predicates from *virtual* predicates. The former can be known by logical deduction, while the latter can be known completely only by God because they cannot be logically deduced. Thus, where Leibniz says that the complete notion of an individual substance such as Caesar can be discovered solely by means of a 'demonstration' (lns 63 and 84), we can clearly take him not to mean a demonstration of logical necessity, as in a proof in geometry.

Necessary truths: These truths, and their counterpart 'contingent' truths, mirror the contemporary distinction between *a priori* and *a posteriori* truths, as explained above. However, the terms 'necessary' and 'contingent' designate propositions in terms of their *modal* character, that is, in terms of *necessity, possibility*, and *impossibility*. Their principle, or source of truth, is the principle of non-contradiction. A necessary truth is a proposition in which the denial of the predicate results in a contradiction. Now, contradictions are *impossible*, that is, always false; or rather, the object of a contradiction cannot even be conceived. For example, if I say, 'circles are square', I am asserting a contradiction because it is impossible to conceive of a square circle. So, the proposition is *necessarily* false. On the other hand, if I say, 'circles are round', then I am asserting a *possible* conception, but also a necessary truth. It is *possible* because the proposition contains no contradiction in conception; but it is also *necessary* because to assert that circles are not round, at least by definition, is to conceive of the impossible, that is, of a circle that is not a circle. There are millions of necessary truths in mathematics, geometry, and logic. A 'demonstration' in those sciences consists of a chain of necessary truths, each of which follows the other by

---

[2] 'These are subjects whose truth [the mind] is capable of finding and understanding, either by proving effects by their causes, which is called an *a priori* proof, or, on the contrary, by demonstrating causes by their effects, which is called an *a posteriori* proof' (Arnauld and Nicole, *Logic, or the Art of Thinking*, 233). However, in *Primary Truths* (AG 31), Leibniz describes 'a priori proof' in terms closer to contemporary usage.

a relation of logical consequence, such that the conclusion is a logically necessary consequence of its preceding truths. To deny the conclusion of a demonstration (provided the deduction has been performed correctly) is to contradict its relationship to the preceding truths. Another way to say what a necessary truth is: *it is logically impossible for a necessary truth to be false*. As we will see, Leibniz denies that the action-predicates within a complete notion follow with logical necessity – which means they are contingent.

Contingent truths: As indicated above, these are propositions that are true, but *possibly* false, because denying them does not result in a contradiction. Take for example the true statement, 'Julius Caesar was emperor of Rome.' We can imagine or conceive of its denial (whereas we cannot conceive of the denial of a necessary truth). So, a contingent proposition is *possibly* true or false. I have no idea whether 'Hank was a Roman general' is true or false. Its truth depends on *how things really are in the world*, namely, the reference of 'Hank', the meaning of 'Roman general', and whether the predicate truly belongs to Hank. If the statement is true but I deny it, my denial would simply be false, not contradictory. And if the statement is false (say, because the same Hank is actually a Roman senator) and I affirm it, then I am merely affirming a false statement. So, this shows that 'Hank was a Roman general' is a *contingent* statement. In other words, *it is logically possible for a contingent statement to be true or false*, its truth-status depending on how things are in the world. As we will see, Leibniz insists that the complete notion of an individual substance consists mostly of contingent truths.

Ex hypothesi: Latin for 'from the hypothesis'. We typically understand a hypothesis to be an explanation of some phenomenon, and that we confirm or disconfirm the hypothesis by experiment. But this is not what Leibniz means where he speaks of necessity '*ex hypothesi*' (ln 29). He means that a truth, condition, or decree is *put forward* (hypothesised) from which additional truths follow assuredly but *contingently*.[3] For example, from the hypothesis of my complete notion, it is not logically necessary that I perform every action included in it. That is because performing an action not included in my complete notion remains possible 'in-itself', that is, conceivable.[4] So, in every complete notion, each action-predicate follows another with hypothetical necessity but *certainly*, given the hypothesis. We will soon find out, however, whether a hypothetical necessity can preserve the measure of freedom Leibniz claims for created substances.

---

[3] As Leibniz explains in a later work, 'for the present world is physically or hypothetically necessary, but not absolutely or metaphysically necessary. That is, given that it was once such and such it follows that such and such things will arise in the future' (*On the Ultimate Origination of Things* (1697), AG 150).

[4] This claim may however be in tension with Leibniz's claim in §30 that a change in even one predicate of an individual results in a different person. See commentary.

These terms, *necessary*, *contingent*, and *necessity from the hypothesis*, as explained above, should now be compared with *certain* or *assured* (Leibniz uses the latter two interchangeably). For any given predicate belonging to an individual notion, God knows this predicate with *certainty*. However, Leibniz maintains, God's knowing this does not imply that the predicate belongs with logical necessity to the notion. If it is in my notion that I (a) eat lunch and then after lunch I (b) study the culinary arts, there is no logical necessity from (a) that I do (b); nor is there logical necessity that I *not* do (b). Thus, my study is a contingent predicate of me. It is, however, *certain* that I will study after lunch because this predicate is contained in my notion and God knows this. This *certainty* gives rise to the following problem.

God's foreknowledge of future contingents. Since the Medieval period it has often been argued that if God has *foreknowledge* of your actions, even if they are contingent, then you are not free to act otherwise (if God knows you will eat the doughnut tomorrow, then you will eat the doughnut tomorrow).[5] Thus, human freedom is threatened. Leibniz attempts to solve the problem this way: God knows your complete notion, as a possible notion

---

[5] This problem of God's foreknowledge, also called 'the problem of future contingents', likely originated with Aristotle's example of the sea-fight (*On Interpretation*, Ch. 9). Different interpretations of and solutions to the problem have been given, but the following will suffice for our purposes. In classical logic, the principle of Bivalence says that every proposition necessarily has one, and only one, truth-value: either true or false. No proposition can have a third or undetermined truth-value. For example, 'there is now a sea-fight', is true (or false) depending (contingent) on the way the world is now. A difficulty arises, however, with propositions about the *future*, such as 'there will be a sea-fight tomorrow'. As with propositions about the present, this looks like a contingent proposition, because we think it *could* be either true or false, depending on how the world will be. However, since the world that the proposition represents is *not yet*, its truth-value would be undetermined (neither true nor false), in violation of the principle of Bivalence. If we give up the principle of Bivalence, then classical logic does not work. To avoid that we might suppose that the proposition 'there will be a sea-fight tomorrow' *has* a truth-value, either true or false (even if we do not know which). This means, however, that if there is a sea-fight tomorrow, then *today* the proposition is true and cannot be false, and if a proposition cannot be false, then it is *necessary*. Therefore, the future will be necessary, rather than contingent (the same necessity holds if it is true tomorrow that no sea-fight takes place). This was Aristotle's worry, and it offends our natural sense that in spite of logic the future remains undetermined. For some Medievals, the problem acquires a different character with the introduction of God's foreknowledge of future contingents. If God knows that a sea-fight will take place tomorrow, well, that makes the proposition true (saving the principle of Bivalence); but then the proposition is *necessarily* true, just as before; and yet everyone wants to maintain that propositions about the future are contingent, or else free will is lost. While Leibniz accepts God's foreknowledge of future contingents (they are 'certain'), he denies this implies they are necessary, since, he claims, they are 'contingent in-themselves', that is, their denial does not imply any formal contradiction. See Murray 1995 for a more detailed account of the Medieval problem.

in his mind, before you are created. Thus, when God creates you, it is *certain* that you will act according to this notion. Leibniz denies, however, that this certainty entails that you are not free, on the grounds that since your actions are, in relation to each other, *contingent in themselves* (without contradiction), they are not logically necessary; and if they are not logically necessary, then you are free.[6] So, for Leibniz, God's foreknowledge does not entail that you are not free. But here is the sticking point. For even if the series of your actions are free of logical necessity, it remains difficult to see how you can act otherwise than in accord with your notion. Again, if your notion has you eating a doughnut at 11 a.m. on 7 April 2023, then you will eat it. And if free will depends on being able to act otherwise than your notion specifies, then you are not free not to eat it. Let us see if Leibniz can unstick himself from this point.

Distinction of consecutions: One more terminological clarification will be useful: a consecution (ln 26) is a type of connection or 'following' of propositions, of which there are two types: (1) absolutely necessary, such as we find in the truths of geometry (and of course logic), that is, followings whose denials are impossible; and (2) contingent followings, such as are found in hypothetical necessities and contingent propositions, whose denials do not imply a contradiction. Leibniz thinks that free will is possible, as long as we understand that the actions of a substance follow contingently, but not with absolute necessity.

With these definitions and distinctions at hand, we are ready to apply them to the text to see whether they can do the work for which they are designed: to preserve a sense of freedom for God and his creatures, despite the pressures of necessitation and determination that the complete notion appears to impose. In other words, let us see if Leibniz can mitigate Arnauld's initial fright and shock. We should begin with God's 'free decrees', since all of creation follows from them. The first is for God 'always to bring about what is the most perfect' (lns 66–7) or 'God always chooses the best assuredly' (ln 72). This decree is known as Leibniz's 'principle of the best'. Let us set aside for now any scruples over whether God has in fact created the best possible world. We need to know whether God is constrained by logical necessity to adopt this decree and to act in accord with it, in the same way God *is* constrained to adopt the properties of a circle that follow necessarily from its definition. Suppose that God does not always choose the best. Is this possible? While it would be contrary to God's will and action, it remains 'possible in itself' (ln 73). In other words,

---

[6] It must be kept in mind that, for Leibniz, *contingency* is not by itself sufficient for freedom; it is only one of three necessary conditions for freedom, the others being *spontaneity* and *deliberation*, as we will see in §30.

it is conceivable (not a contradiction) that God does not do the best.[7] Nevertheless, it remains that God *cannot* do other than the best – not because it is logically impossible, but because it would imply an imperfection in God's nature, which is, supposedly, conceivable. Thus, Leibniz's position is that God's decree to do the best is 'hypothetically necessary' (or contingent) since he is not logically constrained to adopt and act in accord with the principle – even though he will not fail to do so.

The second of God's 'free decrees' pertains to the human will, that 'man will always do (although freely) what would appear the best' (ln 68). Let us first make some sense of this decree before deciding whether anything of logical necessity is involved in it. This decree reflects a long-standing principle of human nature, going back as far as Plato, Aristotle, and the Scholastics: that we have a natural (or God-given) tendency to act according to our perception of the good.[8] On its face, however, this seems false, since we often exhibit opposite tendencies, for example, to pursue what is bad (excessive food and drink); to act for unknown reasons (I have no idea why I bought those pants); to perform deeds even when we *know* they are bad (such as planning and committing a crime); or when we pursue the bad simply through making mistaken judgments about the good. The decree has considerable plausibility, however, in this sense: The reason you take any *conscious* and *intentional* action at all is most likely that it *appears to* you be the best action to take at the time, all things considered. Even if you decide to do something bad, you may figure some good will be gained from it (great pleasure, great wealth) or some greater evil (pain and suffering) will be avoided. Of course, the decree recognises that you do not possess perfect knowledge and thus you can be mistaken about what is objectively good or best. We can set aside the question of what is objectively best for us. But the claim is that every conscious, intentional action results from your judgment about what *seems* best to you. In sum, God has implanted in us the inner drive or tendency to do what we perceive to be the best – even though we often fail to do it.

---

[7] This may be hard to see because it seems there *is* a contradiction here: If we conceive of God correctly, Leibniz maintains, then God is *necessarily*, by his essence or nature, a perfect being. Thus it would be a contradiction (and not merely false) to conceive of God as imperfect, or as having an imperfection, just as it would contradict the nature of a circle not to prescribe a circle. On the question of whether God's actions are logically necessitated by his nature, and whether some sort of 'necessitation' renders God's actions unfree, see Adams 2005. See also *Theodicy* §174, §§191–3, and §344: 'if the answer is given that God was constrained by supreme wisdom to establish the laws that he has established, there we have neither more nor less than the *Fatum* of the Stoics . . . This objection has been sufficiently overthrown: it is only a moral necessity; and it is always a happy necessity to be bound to act in accordance with the rules of perfect wisdom.'

[8] *Sub specie boni* or, 'under the guise of the good'. More on this in §30.

Now, the question is whether it is logically necessary for God to have decreed this nature for us. It seems not, for God could have decreed that we do *what appears wanton*; and while such a decree would imply an imperfection in God, it does not imply a contradiction for God to have given us a wanton nature. Therefore, God freely gave us an optimum-seeking nature. We should also note that *we* are not logically necessitated to act according to this nature. For one, the decree explicitly says that we will always do *freely* what appears best (ln 69). But the reason our actions are free is that they are contingent – free of logical necessity. Again, we must keep in mind that while freedom from logical necessity is, for Leibniz, a minimal (required) condition of freedom, it is not sufficient. We will encounter all of Leibniz's conditions for freedom in §30.

Now that we have established that God's decrees are free decrees, let us determine whether God is necessitated to create Caesar, based on Caesar's notion. From what has been said, the answer is fairly straightforward. God would create Caesar, if it were best; and if so, it would not be a contradiction for God not to create Caesar, but only an imperfection; therefore, God is free to create Caesar. The fact of Caesar's existence confirms *for us* that God saw, from Caesar's notion, that Caesar should be included in the best possible world. This makes additional sense in view of §9, where Leibniz determined that, by virtue of the unique degree of perfection comprising each individual notion, God knows exactly how Caesar's notion contributes to the best possible world (though this does not imply that Caesar is *more perfect* than other individuals – only that his notion contributes better than others to an *overall* scheme of perfection. Thus, very imperfect individuals can be included in the best possible world, as we will discover in §30). And in answer to Arnauld, Leibniz can say that God creates Adam and all that follows from his notion, not from logical necessity, but from the contingency of including his notion in the best possible world.

Now, since God has freely created Caesar, we must ask whether and how Caesar himself (or any individual substance) is free in regard to his complete notion. Leibniz is aware that this freedom is not easy to prove, so he responds to the following possible objections: (1) Someone might say that Caesar's actions are necessary because God has foreknowledge of them. Leibniz responds by saying that the same holds for future contingents, that they are *assured* because God knows them; but those who hold that God has knowledge of future contingents do not admit that they are logical necessities – and, as we saw, neither does Leibniz. (2) God's foreknowledge aside, a stronger and more complicated objection would be that the *notion itself* determines Caesar's actions 'necessarily', in some sense. The problem is that God has 'imposed' this notion onto this individual (ln 41), that Caesar has been given this form 'in advance', and thus he must 'answer to it' (ln 44–5). In other words, since the notion itself forms the very nature of Caesar (even though Caesar himself is contingently created), the created and existing Caesar cannot but act in accord with it. We can see that the *notion* must be responsible *in some sense* for an individual's actions – otherwise, God would have no reason to contemplate complete notions as the basis upon which he creates a world. So, to meet this objection, Leibniz needs to explain how the complete notion *determines* the actions of creatures, without their actions being determined *necessarily*. Here is how Leibniz believes he can do this.

Leibniz admits that on account of the individual notion, it is *assured/ certain* that Caesar will act in accord with his notion; indeed, on the *hypothesis* of this notion, it is 'impossible' for Caesar to act otherwise. This impossibility stems from the 'necessity of the hypothesis', which says that once a thesis (notion) has been put forward (created), what follows from it is 'necessary'. But the necessity here is not logical, because the actions within the notion follow each other *contingently*. This is explained by the distinction of connections or 'consecutions'. Suppose that two of the predicates in Caesar's notion are (a) 'crossed the Rubicon' and (b) 'became emperor of Rome'. The question is in what sense (b) 'follows' from (a), and the answer is *contingently*, since no contradiction obtains in the case that Caesar does not become emperor of Rome. Therefore, as in this action, all of Caesar's actions are non-contradictory followings, and so his actions are possibly free. If Caesar's action-predicates followed one another with the same necessity that 'the sum of the angles of this triangle = 180°' follows from 'this is a triangle', there would be no possibility of free will in Caesar. Presumably, Caesar freely chose many of his actions based on his judgment of what seemed to him best. We may still wonder, however, how it is possible for Caesar to act otherwise than in accord with his notion, given that the complete notion makes it 'certain and assured' that he will act in accord with it. But Leibniz is concerned here only to show that if the action is possible 'in-itself', that is, free of logical necessity, then it is a free action.[9]

Leibniz's arguments boil down to the claim that since all of God's and Caesar's actions (and the actions of every individual substance) are contingent, insofar as they are free of logical necessity, then free will is possible. However, we should not take this freedom, this contingency, to imply the absence of determinism. For Leibniz takes it as axiomatic that a reason of some sort determines every event and choice. Indeed, we can find here a version of his famous *principle of sufficient reason*: 'all contingent propositions have reasons to be thus rather than otherwise' (lns 79–80).

---

[9] We will return to this problem in §30.

This principle is crucial to the rationality of his system, because, if every consecution were equally possible, there would be no reason why things should be thus and not otherwise; but in fact, 'these reasons are founded only on the principle of contingency . . . on what is or appears to be the best' (ln 86). Thus, we are brought back to first principles, that is, to God's free decrees: (1) that God always chooses the best or most perfect; and (2) that human beings choose according to what appears to be best. The idea is that the actions of God and creatures are free since they are contingent, but they are nonetheless determined, in the sense of 'inclined' but not necessitated, by these first principles or 'free decrees' of action.

Thus, we are brought to the final term needing clarification in this article, and the one that succinctly expresses its main point. Speaking of both God and creatures, Leibniz writes: 'It is true that their choice always has its reasons but [these reasons] incline without necessitating' (lns 6–7). The idea of inclination without necessitation stems from an ancient astrological principle which says that the stars incline events without determining them necessarily – so that events can be said to occur from causes other than astral influence.[10] Thus, due to inclining reasons, Leibniz can strike a balance between (a) logical necessity (which he considers a blind or 'fatal' necessity) and (b) indeterminism (or absolute liberty of indifference, in which the will undergoes no cause or influence whatsoever, a condition he considers impossible and absurd). Accordingly, the actions of God and creatures are *determined* by reasons that do not logically necessitate the action, but nevertheless supply *sufficient* reasons for the action to occur. These reasons can be characterised as generally teleological or 'final causes', whose source is the nature of the substance itself. That is, God is contingently inclined, but determined, to create for reasons of *the best*, while creatures are contingently inclined, but determined, to act for reasons that *appear* best. In this way, the willing of God and of creatures *should* be both free and rational.

Despite these largely coherent formulations, the reader will likely retain doubts, as I have suggested, that they are sufficient to show that creatures are free from the pre-determination of the complete notion. For, despite the logical contingency Leibniz has built into the complete notion, if freedom requires the capacity to act otherwise than the complete notion dictates, it is not clear how an individual can do this. We will have to postpone judgment on this matter at least until we consider his arguments in §30. For now, we turn to the more abstruse components of Leibniz's metaphysics of substance.

---

[10] See *New Essays*, LRB II.xxi.8.175 and the note on 'incline without necessitating', lxix.

§14. That God produces diverse substances, each of which uniquely expresses God's view of the universe, thus increasing the glory of God. That substances do not enter into causal relations, but God makes all of their actions correspond.

Now that Leibniz has explained the sense in which the actions of individual substances are distinct from the actions of God and other creatures – that their actions are grounded entirely within their notion, that each action is a logically contingent consequence of its prior, and that each substance expresses every other – Leibniz now attempts to complete the picture, by explaining (1) how substances are *dependent* on each other and (2) the sense in which they 'act on' or have causal relations with each other. Substances are dependent on God mainly for their creation and for the 'correspondence' of their expressions or perceptions.[1] But on account of this 'correspondence', Leibniz puts forward a rather non-intuitive metaphysical theory: that substances do not have causal interactions, as typically conceived; rather, their apparent interactions are explained as 'correspondences' among substances that only express and perceive each other. In sum, this article complements Leibniz's account of substantial relations begun in §9 and that continues in §15 and §33. Let us begin with God's creation of substances and work through how their perceptions mutually correspond.

The creation of diverse substances: A good question not often asked is why God, a perfect being, lacking in nothing, should create anything. As we saw in §3, God creates in order to be glorified – not for *his* sake (God has no need to be glorified) but for the sake of his creatures who benefit from admiring and partaking in God's infinite perfections.[2] So, in order to express his perfections maximally and to benefit as many substances as possible, God creates as many *different* substances as possible – not *absolutely* possible, but as are together compatible with the sort of world God decrees himself to create: the best possible. Being epistemically infinite, God is able to consider all possible ways that a whole world could be and chooses the best one (lns 12–18).

The manner of God's creation – emanation and expression: Leibniz incidentally refers to the ancient Stoic (often called Neoplatonic) doctrine of 'emanation', according to which (although adapted to Leibniz's purposes) God, the Divine Mind (*Nous*), the source of all being, continuously radiates its essence (intellect) outward to produce all that exists. The process of

---

[1] In §33 Leibniz will use the term 'commerce' to explain the correspondence or 'union' of soul and body.

[2] *Theodicy* §109.

emanation is similar to the way in which the sun continuously radiates heat and light,[3] or, as Leibniz puts it, 'similar to how we produce our thoughts' (ln 11) from out of the depths of our soul. Accordingly, we should understand that all that exists is a manifestation of God's essence, and that each *created* substance is an *expression* of that essence.[4] Leibniz's conception of 'expression' as a correspondence or relation of similarity of one thing to another is key here (see commentary, beginning of §9). As an expression of God, each substance bears a degree of likeness to God's perfections and in turn expresses the world according to its own (limited) degree of perfection.

Emanation and conservation: All things, especially substances, are dependent on God's emanation as the cause of their creation and essence; but they are also dependent on God for their continuation, or what is called 'conservation' (ln 10). According to one version of this Scholastic doctrine, since creatures are created out of nothing, they lack the causal power to sustain their being. Thus, some portion of God's power, the power through which God created them, is required to sustain the existence of each created substance.[5] This may also explain the sense in which God 'concurs' with a creature's actions (see commentary, §30).

Every substance is like a world apart: Since God's essence is intellect or mind, and essential to mind is thought and perception, each substance, insofar as it is a soul, is an expression of God's intellect and in turn expresses the world. This means, remarkably, that each substance expresses, or represents, the entire world within its soul. From the fact that each substance is *unique* (as established in §9), it follows that each substance represents the whole world according to its unique degree of perfection. Thus, 'each substance is like a world apart' from every other (lns 21–2). Each substance, then, represents a whole 'system of phenomena' (ln 13), that is, a whole series of its relations to all substances and to the natural world, to the extent that, supposing the whole world were destroyed and nothing remained but God and oneself (ln 57), the entire course of the world – past, present, and future – could be discovered within one's notion alone. But a substance is not an *actual* world apart; nor could a world represented by a single unique perspective properly represent God's glory and perfection. For this, God creates a *multitude* of substances, each expressing a unique portion of the world and of God's perfections.

---

[3] See Armstrong, *Plotinus*, 33.

[4] Thus, as it is aptly put by Gilles Deleuze: 'the One manifesting itself in the Many' and thus 'the One remains in what expresses it, imprinted in what unfolds it' (1990: 16).

[5] See A. J. Freddoso, Introduction to Suarez 2002, sections 5, 6, and 7. See also McDonough 2007. For Descartes' version of conservation, see *Principles* I, §21.

Substances as perceiving entities: The terms 'perception', 'expression', and 'representation' are closely related. Each substance or soul is essentially a perceiving substance. The fact that each substance *expresses* the whole world means that each substance *perceives* the world in degrees more or less clearly and distinctly. Perceptions themselves are true insofar as they are clear, but false when we assent to judgments based on unclear perceptions (ln 20).[6] But what exactly does it mean for a substance to perceive or to have a perception? To perceive is to *represent* within the soul something external to it. As Leibniz later defined it, '*perception* is the expression of many things in a true unity, or in a simple substance; if it is combined with reflection of the percipient, it is called *thought*'.[7] So, a human being represents the world, through the perceptions occurring in its soul (its true unity). We are not, however, conscious of all our perceptions, since, Leibniz argues elsewhere, perceptions can occur below the level of conscious awareness (which he calls 'confused' perception). But when we have thought or cognition, we have 'clear' perception; and when thought is accompanied by the awareness that 'I am having this thought', Leibniz calls this 'apperception'.[8]

In sum, perception is a species of expression;[9] while both occur within the soul, expression more precisely captures the idea that perceiving beings represent the whole world in varying degrees within their soul. There is, however, a very curious problem here, since Leibniz also maintains that we do not *receive into our soul* the expressions of things external to it. Thus, Leibniz must explain how our perceptions 'correspond' with the world in the ordinary way we experience it.

The correspondence of perceptions: At this point the reader surely wonders why Leibniz is setting out such unusual ideas. Why does he repeatedly insist that substances 'express' and 'perceive' each other and the whole world? He has a number of reasons, but here we shall focus on two. First, it follows from the kind of beings we are: individual, expressing, perceiving, substances, whose nature it is to perceive the world according to their own measure. This establishes the *independence* of each substance from every other, except God. Second, to maintain this independence, Leibniz insists

---

[6] This is basically Descartes' argument in *Meditation* IV and *Principles* I, §30–3. That is, the will errs when it assents to a false judgment of the intellect; thus, the cause of error is our will, not the intellect.

[7] *New Method for Learning and Teaching Jurisprudence*, revision note to Pt. 1 sec. 34 (AA VI, 1, 286, ln 20 / LL 91). The note was inserted in 1699 (AA VI, 1, XVIII).

[8] See footnote 7 on 'apperception' in the translation. Also see §33 and especially Leibniz's doctrine of 'small perceptions' in the preface to *New Essays on Human Understanding*.

[9] McRae 1976: 24.

that what happens to each substance is 'a consequence only of its complete idea or complete notion alone' (lns 48–9). As he indicates in the heading, substances do not 'act immediately' on each other, meaning they do not enter into causal relations as we typically conceive of them); rather, God makes their *perceptions* of acting and being acted upon mutually *correspond* (lns 3–5) such that causal relations are only *apparent*. This point is also indicated where Leibniz says, 'a particular substance never acts on another particular substance, nor suffers from another' (ln 47). That is to say, in the traditional language of 'action and passion', or causal interaction, substances do not interact; rather, each substance perceives the other, due to the perceptions that each is having within its *own* soul.

This idea of a correspondence of perceptions, taking the place of causal relations, is perhaps the most difficult of Leibniz's doctrines to understand and accept. As we will see in §33, Leibniz utilises a similar explanation of correspondence (which he later came to call 'pre-established harmony') to explain the relationship between the soul and the body. We will also see how Leibniz's rejection of certain theories of causation motivates these non-intuitive (for us) explanations. But in the meantime, let us look more closely at how the correspondence of perceptions is supposed to work. Suppose, for example, you and I see each other approaching from a distance. The *usual* seventeenth-century explanation for our mutual perceptions would be that the motions of tiny corpuscles of light make impressions upon our senses (our eyes) and these impressions enter our soul. But according to Leibniz what is really happening is this: In accord with your notion, you perceive me approaching you; while in accord with my notion, I perceive you approaching me. But your motions are not causing me to have perceptions of you; nor are my motions causing you to have perceptions of me. Rather, our perceptions are occurring within each of us, independently of each other. But then why do we say we are perceiving *each other*? And how do we coordinate our actions so that we eventually meet? The answer, very generally, is that God, who has complete knowledge of our respective complete notions, sees that our perceptions *correspond* with each other and keeps them in mutual relation, so that our notions express the same external event, even though no perceptions will enter our souls. Thus, the perceptions occurring in me occur simultaneously and in correct correspondence with the perceptions occurring in you.

The result of this correspondence of perceptions, from the point of view of perceiving beings, is a 'system of phenomena' (ln 13), that is, a world of objects and creatures that *appear* to interact causally but which actually do not. This 'system' is a consequence only of the series of perceptions determined by each individual notion (ln 49) along with their correspondence.

'In fact', to put the whole matter quite simply, 'nothing can happen to us but thoughts and perceptions' (lns 50–1). In other words, the correspondence of perceptions means that we do not have causal interactions; nevertheless, the order of our perceptions is entirely consistent with our usual practice and understanding of the world in causal terms. We may still regulate our conduct, make successful predictions about the future in view of the past (lns 26–8), and coordinate our activities with others (ln 34). Sceptical doubts such as Descartes entertained about whether our experience is of an internal mental world or of an external extended world can make no difference, on Leibniz's account, because either way reality exhibits perfect accord with our clear and distinct perceptions (lns 28–30). Thus, by all appearances the world is governed by scientific laws, as we typically understand them. But again, this is a manner of speaking, a convenient but precise way of understanding how to get along in the world. Emphasising this point, Leibniz concludes that we attribute what happens to us as 'causes acting upon us' (ln 59), although the reality is quite different; for the correspondence of our perceptions is the real 'foundation' of our causal judgments.

This rather unusual view of a world of non-interacting, independently perceiving substances may impart the impression that 'the world' is quite unreal, as if it were a mass hallucination produced and coordinated by an omniscient puppet master. We would do well, however, to set such characterisations aside, until we have a more complete understanding of Leibniz's motives and grounds for his claims, as we will find in §33. These have mostly to do with his commitments to the kind of beings he believes we are (soul-substances dependent on *and* independent of God, each having their own perceptions) and with his considered views on the natures of soul, matter, and causation. In the end, we might find that even if we cannot accept this extraordinary view, it remains remarkably consistent with these metaphysical commitments, and consistency is the minimum we should expect from a metaphysical system.

At this point in §14, line 60, the final draft (l^2) ends. However, in the first draft (L^1), a long passage continues (from line 62 in the translation) without break, to the first line of what is now §15. Leibniz struck that passage, and we can speculate why. It appears intended to serve as an explanation for the 'foundation of this judgment', that is, for the judgment that causes act on us (ln 59). But judging from the first line of §15, Leibniz may have thought the passage too complicated or obscure for this purpose, and so §15 consists mostly of a revision of the struck passage. However, even though it was not Leibniz's intention, the passage is worth including, as it provides important clues to understanding §15.

The main objective of the deleted passage is to show how the causal language of 'action and passion' can be explained in Leibniz's metaphysical terms of perfection and perception. So, a little background into the terms 'action' and 'passion' is in order, especially since Leibniz employs them in various places in the *Discourse* (recall for example §8, ln 9, where actions and passions properly belong to individual substances). The source of these terms is Aristotle, for whom action and passion together constitute one of the 'categories' denoting change or motion in a substance. Accordingly, when a substance 'cuts' something, it is active; when it is cut *by* something,[10] it is passive. Generally speaking, a thing whose source of motion is *in itself* is the acting thing, whereas the thing that is *acted upon* by something external to it is passive.[11] In beings having both matter and form (that is, everything except God and angels), *form* is active while *matter* is passive. As we might expect, the mind or soul is the active principle in us, while the body, consisting of inert matter, incapable of its own movement, is the passive principle.

This basic picture is oversimplified, since some matter is capable of active motion such as nutrition and growth, and since the mind can be passive due to its imperfections. But from here it is easy to see which are the active and passive principles in Leibniz's passage. The *will* is active when it is the source of an action involving its own body, and it is passive when something else moves its body, as when someone pushes you. But the will can also be the active cause of something it did not will. Suppose I push you, intending only that you move away from me, and as a result you fall down. I did not will that you fall down, but since I contributed to your fall, I am the active cause of it.

At this point, the Aristotelian categories of action and passion become linked to the metaphysics of *perception*. Even though the body is the passive, acted-upon, principle, I distinguish my actions from yours through the perceptions I have of what occurs in my body. I *notice* (apperceive) that I am the cause of my bodily motions, because these motions are most strongly felt, while I perceive but do not feel the motions of other bodies. Even though my soul contains the whole world, and all bodies are in universal sympathy,[12] my body is the locus of the most 'strongly felt' changes it undergoes or suffers (lns 86-91). My *spatio-temporal* place is that

---

[10] Aristotle, *Categories*, 11b1.

[11] For an account of action and passion that focuses on the emotions, see James 2003, Part 1, Ch. 2.

[12] Leibniz may be alluding to Malebranche, whose spokesperson in *Dialogues on Metaphysics and Religion* (1688) asserts that 'there is "sympathy" between strings of the same pitch. This is certain since they act one on the other, and that is what the word signifies' (MD III, 48). Cited by Meyns 2018.

of my body, while my *metaphysical* place depends on the degree of activity and passivity of my perceptions. Also notable is that the mind undergoes both active and passive modifications: 'our wills, judgments or reasonings are actions', while 'our perceptions or sentiments are passions' (lns 93–4). Thus, a thought is an active perception, whereas a bodily sensation is a passive perception, since it happens *to* the soul.

Leibniz now links the Aristotelian categories of activity and passivity to the metaphysics of *perfection*. When a substance is the source of its action, it increases its perfection, that is, it acts in accord with its power, its proper function (thought) and purpose (for the glory of God). To be acted upon by another substance or to undergo an emotion would correspond with a decrease in perfection, power, and purpose. This is the basis for the widely held idea that the emotions are *passions*, in the sense that they are sources of bodily suffering and cognitive confusion. But the main point seems to be that the quantity of perfection (activity) in each substance is the measure of its contribution to the glory of God, and thus substances contribute to the very reason for which God creates substances at all.

Throughout the whole passage, one should notice that the language Leibniz uses is very tentative, as if he seeks to avoid any implication that actions, passions, or perceptions involve *causal* interactions among substances. For example, 'we say we have acted and are the cause' (lns 63–4); 'when it seems to me that by my will something happens' (ln 65); 'this would have happened to it' (ln 66); 'there are also some phenomena of extension . . . whose foundation is called . . . our body' (lns 72–4); 'we attribute all the passions of this body to ourselves' (lns 76–7); 'about the body we say that the change which happens to it. . .' (ln 95). The expression most indicative of causal interaction is 'when several substances are affected by the same change' (ln 98). These expressions, conveying how things *seem* and what we *say*, not so much how things *are*, likely indicate that Leibniz is not prepared to disclose fully his objections and solutions to the problem of causal interaction among substances, nor between souls and bodies. Again, we will get a more decisive understanding of these matters in §33. But more directly, these expressions serve to show how the traditional Aristotelian language of action and passion – language *suggestive* of causal interaction – can be described in the metaphysical terms of perfection and perception. Article 15 will extend this language by adding the 'accommodation' of substances, a claim from which some moral implications may be drawn.

§15. On the causal and moral implications of expression, perfection, and accommodation.

After having struck the long passage in §14, Leibniz revises his attempt to explain how the language of 'metaphysics', namely, of perfection, perception, and here, expression, can be reconciled with 'practice', that is, with the traditional Aristotelian language of motion and change, namely, action and passion. But the term 'practice' may have two meanings here. On the one hand, it refers to the usual practice of causal attribution, as just mentioned. On the other hand, it may have a 'practical', that is, a *moral* sense, related to how substances *ought* to conduct themselves. In this sense, the 'correspondence' of substantial perceptions in §14 becomes the 'accommodation' of substances to each other, as if they were 'obliged' to do so. Thus, Leibniz appears to be drawing out the moral implications of his metaphysics of perception, expression, and perfection, or so I hope to show.

Leibniz's first objective, following his intended revision of the passage cut from §14, is to show that the common language of activity and passivity can be understood in perfectionist-expressionist terms. The question is, in what sense do substances 'act on one another'? (ln 14); and the answer is something like this: 'we attribute to ourselves more, and with reason, the phenomena that we express more perfectly, and we attribute to other substances what each one expresses best' (lns 9–10). It is difficult to understand what this means, practically speaking.[1] Likely, it means that the most *active* substances are those which exhibit the most perfection in their actions (or, that the most perfect actions are those that exhibit the most activity – which is to say that perfection and activity are convertible terms). In other words, we attribute the action to the substance that best explains the phenomena. Consider, for example, walking on the pavement. You would attribute the action to yourself and the passion to the pavement – you are walking, while *it* is being walked on; and while the pavement could be said to 'act on' you by pushing back on your feet, it is your activity that imposes motion onto the pavement (thereby *limiting* the pavement's activity, as well).

But this phenomenon, this walking scenario, can also be explained in terms of expression and perfection. Consider what 'expresses' the phenomenon most distinctly (recall: an expression conveys a one-to-one relation between two distinct things; so here we have a relation between your motion and the pavement's). You are the one distinctly expressing movement and change, while the pavement much less distinctly expresses it.

---

[1] See Garber 2005 for a detailed interpretation, especially from p. 100. Also see *Monadology* §51.

To assert that the pavement is more distinctly active than me would be to say that it acts on my feet, pushing upward and causing *them* to move. This is not entirely false from the standpoint of physics, but it is not a *distinct* explanation of the phenomenon. A more distinct explanation is also more *perfect*, because it is more complete. Not only does my walking explain the phenomenon distinctly, but it allows for an explanation in terms of teleology and perfection: this phenomenon is *most distinctly* explained by my will and desire to take a walk.

Recall that the point of replacing the language of action and passion with the language of expression and perfection is to show that the activity of substances can be explained without depending on explanations in terms of *causal* interaction; Leibniz needs the latter type of explanation given his insistence that substances do not causally interact; at the same time, he wants to show how the two conceptions of substantial activity, Aristotelian and his own, are compatible. But let us work through one more example, because it might be objected that the pavement is not in any clear sense a substance (as Leibniz would surely say it is not) and thus the scenario does not illustrate a relation between *substances*. So, suppose two substances, you and I, are having a conversation (disregard the fact that we are *embodied* substances). We are having a conversation about rational proofs for God's existence. Insofar as we are *reasoning* about this matter, our souls are active. But since this is a conversation, it will involve both active and passive moments. For instance, while I am talking (active), you are listening (passive). Thus, I am acting on you while you are acted upon (although your listening is not entirely void of activity). These roles will naturally be reversed throughout the course of the conversation. Now, how might this phenomenon, the conversation, be explained in terms of expression and perfection? When I am speaking and reasoning, my degree of expression increases, and while you are listening, your degree of expression decreases. This does not mean that I am talking more, or more effectively 'expressing' my ideas; it means that while I am expressing my ideas, I am most distinctly expressing the phenomenon of conversation.

Again, the point is to explain how it is possible for distinct substances to be in relation without being in a *causal* relation. Recall that, metaphysically speaking, we should have to say that the conversation takes place entirely within each of us, independently of one another; that each of us independently expresses a portion of the world, a portion of its perfection; that God has arranged it so that our perceptions, our responses, 'correspond' with each other *as if* we are having a conversation. And yet the conversation, *not* metaphysically speaking, can be completely explained according to common practice, that is, in terms of action and passion, in terms of an exchange of ideas, of an exchange of sensory perceptions.

These scenarios (walking, conversing) are also apt for illustrating substantial relations in the terms Leibniz goes on to use, namely, 'accommodation' and 'limitation'. As stated in the heading, God has formed each substance 'in advance such that they accommodate themselves to one another' (ln 4). He then says in the main body, 'it is therefore in this way [in terms of expression] that one can conceive that substances impede or limit each other, and consequently one can say in this sense that they act on one another, and are obliged, so to speak, to adapt themselves to each other' (lns 12–15). Accordingly, my walking motions are accommodated to the 'push back' of the pavement (and equally, the pavement is accommodated to my walking motions). We could also say that my walking imposes a *limitation* on the pavement's expression of its motions, and vice versa. More appropriately, our conversation occurs through the mutual 'accommodation' between us both, an accommodation of subject matter, comprehension, and timing. A 'limitation' or impediment occurs within our respective notions when the one expresses the conversation less distinctly (more passively) than the other.

Explaining activity and passivity in terms of expression is not of course limited to the phenomena of walks and conversations, but applies to any scenario in which substances, indeed all substances, all the time, relate to each other, whether physically or mentally. But the explanation also extends to *moral* relations, if we pay attention to the moral implications of the term 'accommodation', or, as Leibniz also puts it, that substances are 'obliged, so to speak, to adapt themselves [*s'accommoder*] to each other' (lns 14–15). While Leibniz may intend for the moral implications to be drawn only by analogy, that is, 'so to speak', as if the accommodation is nothing other than metaphysical, the accommodation seems at times to be explicitly moral, as I will show.

As Leibniz continues his analysis, we find that 'the virtue of a particular substance is to express well the glory of God' (ln 17). The glory of God, we recall, consists in the maximal expression of God's perfections. It follows that a *passive* substance does not distinctly express God's perfections and is thus limited in perfection. The moral implications are clear: the *virtue* of a rational substance is its *power* – not simply its metaphysical power to act, but its *moral* power, that is, its power to regulate its metaphysical power; in other words, its power to accommodate itself to the good of other substances. The greater its moral power, the more active it is; the more its ends are adjusted to the ends of others, the more perfection it exhibits and the more it thus expresses the glory of God. Inversely, the less moral power it expresses – the less active, accommodating, and perfect it is – the more the substance is passive and suffers (ln 25).

185

To make these moral implications more concrete, we can explicate 'accommodation' in terms of Leibniz's earlier writings on jurisprudence. Rational substances can 'accommodate' each other in several morally relevant ways: by preventing wrongful harm to each other, by helping each other attain their morally virtuous ends, by disclosing the truth, by promoting the common good; and they can 'impede or limit each other' (ln 13) by doing the opposite.[2] Passivity (confused perception, excessive emotion) prevents substances from expressing their proper nature, which is their capacity to regulate their wills and desires *rationally* and in accord with the rights and advantages of universal justice.[3] Leibniz also maintains that the nature of substances is to tend in action toward perfection (where 'perfection' is understood as the *completion* of their rational nature); but *that very perfection* entails that rational substances accommodate themselves to each other in the ways just outlined.

In addition, the last few lines of this article indicate a close correspondence between metaphysical and moral perfection. Metaphysically speaking, a degree of pleasure or pain accompanies every perception – or better: every *action* is accompanied by pleasure, and every *passion* by pain – and 'vice versa' (ln 27); that is, every pleasure increases or encourages an action, while every pain decreases or discourages an action. The deeper background to this metaphysical formulation is likely Aristotle's argument that pleasure is the by-product of the exercise of a capability or process: digestion, sensation, physical vigour, and thinking are all natural processes that are good for the organism, and the fact that they produce pleasurable sensations is the immediate indication of their good.[4] The employment of our rational capacity produces the most pleasure – as counterintuitive as this may seem.[5] However, we must be careful here, because the *object* of a pleasure has moral import. As Leibniz notes, you may act for the sake of some perceived advantage, thereby gaining some degree of pleasure, and yet a greater evil may result. Suppose you murder someone out of revenge for their having 'stolen' your lover, and you thereby take pleasure in the uninhibited assertion of your will, passion, and physical power. There is

---

[2] These sorts of acts fall roughly under the 'three degrees of right' or justice that Leibniz borrows from the Roman jurist Ulpian: 'harm no one, give to each his due, and live honourably'. See Johns 2013: 12–14.

[3] See Riley 1996 and Johns 2013.

[4] 'Pleasure completes (*teleioi*) the activity, not as the inherent state (*hexis*) does, but as an end which supervenes (*epiginomenon*) [on the action] as the bloom of youth does on those in the flower of their age' (*Nicomachean Ethics*, Bk 10, Ch. 4, 1174b31–3).

[5] 'That which is proper to each thing is by nature best and most pleasant for each thing; for man, therefore the life according to reason is best and most pleasant, since reason more than anything else *is* man' (*Nicomachean Ethics*, Bk 10, Ch. 7, 1178a5).

perhaps nothing more pleasurable than the unrestrained expression of one's powers, but also nothing worse, morally speaking, than finding pleasure in the destructive expression of power. The virtuous person, on the other hand, finds the greatest pleasure in acts of virtue – in acts that increase perfection in oneself and others. Such actions are the best expressions of rational nature and of the glory of God. We are morally obliged, then, to *limit* the exercise of our power to finding pleasure in virtue, that is, in the mutual accommodation of our respective moral powers.[6]

§16. God's 'extraordinary concourse' is included in each individual notion, thus accounting for the compatibility of miracles with natural laws.

This article will seem disconnected from the previous, unless one considers that Leibniz aims to complete the account of an individual substance by explaining how miracles can be included in the complete notion.

As we saw in §7, a miracle is not simply an unusual or amazing event, but rather implies God's agency in the alteration of a natural law. Thus, natural laws can account for the unlikely survival of a baby being carried away by a massive flood and deposited safely on the bank of a river; but to attribute a miracle to this event requires attributing God's agency to it, in the absence of which the baby would have drowned. Miracles are also commonly said to be performed by humans through God's agency. Thus, God gives a holy person the power to heal the sick by the laying on of hands. We are also familiar with people who make dubious claims to have performed miracles and who may be mistaken or lying. In fact, the Catholic Church requires strong evidence that a presumed miracle could have occurred in no other way than through God's 'extraordinary' agency. The problem is, given that for Leibniz all events are extremely well ordered by God, and that all of our actions are the consequence of our complete notion, how can anything like a divinely ordained alteration of the laws of nature, or a change in our complete notion, occur? To put the problem of miracles in terms Leibniz utilises here, how is anything 'supernatural' even possible?

We can recall §7 where Leibniz says that miracles conform to God's general ordering of events, even though they 'may be above' a particular natural law, that is, a 'subordinate maxim'. Similarly, we can say that when you perform a miracle (through God), that event is included in your

---

[6] The relationship between pleasure and activity is quite complex in Aristotle, and the question of whether Leibniz was a motivational (or psychological) hedonist is also complex. I would argue against those commentators who maintain that Leibniz is an ethical hedonist (Johns 2013: 41–5). But see Jorati 2014.

individual notion. So, insofar as your individual notion conforms to God's general order, miracles conform to God's general order as well. In other words, if you include the event in the general order, nothing really 'supernatural' or miraculous occurs. Extraordinary events just seem extraordinary from our perspective, from the fact that they are unusual or unlikely.

At the same time, Leibniz wants to retain the common conception that there is something 'supernatural' in such events. To explain this, he says that our natures are unlimited in one sense but limited in another. They are unlimited because our nature expresses the whole universe, but limited because our power is limited. Whatever is beyond our power is thus 'supernatural'. Miracles can be said to be supernatural then, when God gives us the power to perform what is beyond our nature to perform. This power Leibniz designates throughout this article as God's 'extraordinary concourse'.

Let us consider an example to see how this 'extraordinary concourse' is supposed to work. Suppose that a baby lying on the train tracks is bound to be run over by a speeding train. You are 50 metres away, and given the speed of the train and your distance from the baby, you see that it is unlikely that you will be able to save it. But you run, and God provides you with extraordinary speed and agility to sweep the baby off the tracks just in the nick of time. Did God 'intervene' and give you the power *just at that time*? No – rather, your deed along with God's help (extraordinary concourse) was included for all time within your complete notion. So, all is in accord with God's general order. Now, a question might arise as to who is responsible for this extraordinary event, you or God? The answer should be both, because while you could not have moved as swiftly without God's power, God's power would not have been sufficient without your own effort and will. God simply provided that extra push to accomplish your will's desire; and yet the power may be called 'supernatural' because its exercise exceeds your natural power.[1]

---

[1] Sleigh argues that in this article Leibniz distinguishes 'between a substance's concept and its nature' (1990: 78), a distinction which conforms to the traditional distinction between 'essential (necessary) properties of an individual substance and its contingent (broadly construed, accidental) properties' (79). The purpose of Sleigh's argument is to sort out Leibniz's distinctions among various kinds of predicates, but also to deny 'super-essentialism', a characteristic some have attributed to Leibniz's complete notion. Super-essentialism says that all properties of a substance are essential and thus necessary to it. I agree with Sleigh that super-essentialism, so construed, cannot be correct, since, as we saw in §8, Leibniz maintains that the substance contains predicates (for example, 'crosses the Rubicon') that are contingent; that is, they are *certain*, but not *necessary*. Within the class of contingent predicates, Sleigh distinguishes the *natural* from those that are not, namely, the *supernatural*. My explanation for miracles in §16 is consistent with Sleigh's, since miracles are contingent predicates of the substance. However, I

The teleology of the event also exceeds the power of our understanding. Since we do not entirely comprehend God's general order, we do not know why God gave you the power to save the baby (nor do we know, for that matter, why God allowed someone to leave a baby on the tracks – although we can attribute that to the imperfection of the one who did). All that we can comprehend is that the general order of things is grounded on the principle of perfection; but we cannot fathom how any given event fits into that scheme. For this reason, nor can we fathom why miracles do not happen when we most wish they would.

So much for the account of the order of miracles. In the next article, Leibniz turns to an intensive study of a 'subordinate maxim', a law of nature, involving something metaphysical, but nothing like a miracle.

§17. God conserves the same quantity of force in the universe that he originally put into it, not the same quantity of motion, against Descartes.

This article, along with §§10, 12, and 18–22, forms a most influential part of Leibniz's critique of the Cartesian conception of extended substance. His argument in this article is that Descartes' account of matter and motion cannot explain the general law of the conservation of force. His criticism serves to provide additional evidence of the need to posit 'something metaphysical' to account for the agreed-upon conservation law. It also forms part of his efforts to 'restore' the Aristotelian 'forms' and 'final causes' that Descartes and others had sought to banish from physical explanations. In sum, Leibniz seeks to show that the mechanical philosophy cannot depend solely on the size and speed of bodies to give a proper accounting of the general law of the conservation of force.

suggest that, in §16, Leibniz is making a more distinct claim about the *metaphysical* character of these predicates, rather than their *modal* character. While utilising the traditional distinctions, Leibniz also indicates that the essential, natural, and supernatural predicates are distinguished by degrees of substantial *power*. Thus, the power of acting that God gives to every individual substance is *essential* to it, since no substance can be or act without it. However, the power of acting that substances contain within themselves, their *natural* power by means of which they cross Rubicons and solve equations, etc., is *contingent* to the substance; while the power to act supernaturally, also contingent, is a power God contingently adds to our natural limited power. Thus, the distinctions among predicates – essential (necessary), natural (contingent), and supernatural (contingent) – are made by virtue of the degree of power each substance contains; or more precisely, by the degree of perfection contained in each substance. Thus, while *all* predicates are *included* in the complete concept (notion) of the individual substance, only a portion are essential to it.

189

The 'demonstration' that forms the basis of Leibniz's criticism in §17 is nearly identical to that of an article he published roughly at the same time he composed the *Discourse*.[1] That article initiated a debate lasting nearly seventy years (the *vis viva* or 'living force' controversy) over the nature and measure of force.[2] The demonstration that Leibniz presents is brief and seemingly straightforward. However, to fully grasp its meaning and significance, we must elucidate its background and its several subtleties and implications. As in §10, we need a bit more of the Aristotelian-Medieval background on the 'causes' of motion, and we need to understand the basic premises of Descartes' laws of motion (the mechanical philosophy). The problem with which Leibniz is concerned may seem obscure, even obsolete, but its importance lies in his effort to advance a new and influential theory of force. It forms a part of his overall effort, once again, to provide physics with a proper grounding in both metaphysics and theology.

Let us begin with a review of some brief Aristotelian-Medieval background. As outlined in §10, the primary constituents of all bodies, according to Aristotle, are the four elements: Earth, Water, Air, and Fire.[3] Bodies consist of these elements in varying amounts, and all the variations of *kinds* of bodies (metals, woods, and liquids) are explained by differences in their forms and qualities such as dryness, moistness, and heat. But now in this article we are primarily interested in the *causes of motion* of bodies. Aristotle distinguishes three: the formal cause, the final cause, and the efficient cause. We need to say something brief about each.[4]

Usually, the *formal* cause is said by Aristotle to be the definition of a thing, or the formula for its essence. For example, the formal cause of a piece of gold is its essence, its 'gold-ness' (whatever that may consist of). The *efficient* cause is typically said to be the cause of motion. However, as it turns out, matters are much more complicated, since two types of motion can be distinguished: (1) natural motion, by means of which a body moves itself; and (2) violent motion, which occurs when one body collides with another. It may help to distinguish these types as *internal* motion and *external* motion. But to make matters even more complicated, natural motion

---

[1] 'Brief Demonstration on a Notable Error of Descartes and Others Concerning a Natural Law' (*Acta Eruditorum* 6 January 1686), in LL 296–301.

[2] The following articles offer helpful context for §17 and for the *vis viva* controversy: Arthur 2016; Glezer 2018; Iltis 1971; Papineau 1977; Shimony 2010.

[3] Aristotle, *On the Heavens*, Bk III, Ch. 3, and *On Generation and Corruption*, Bk II, 1–8.

[4] Nowadays we tend to think only of one type of cause, namely, that which is the cause of an effect. But for Aristotle, a cause is a type of explanation, and there are four types: material, formal, final, and efficient. Only the last is roughly equivalent to our contemporary sense. For Aristotle's full account of causes, see *Physics*, Bk II, Ch. 3. My discussion here may not exactly match up with Aristotle's, but it will suffice for understanding the problems Descartes and Leibniz were concerned to solve.

becomes identified with the *formal* cause, while violent motion is identified as the *efficient* cause. In addition, the formal and final causes *together* become responsible for natural motion. Let us see just how, before we deal with violent motion.

Here are two *formal* causes of natural motion: the forms of *heaviness* and *lightness*. The form of heaviness (*gravitas*, or what we now think of as weight) is the cause of a body's tendency to move downward, while *lightness* is the cause of a body's tendency to rise.[5] Bodies with more Earth in them have more heaviness and thus tend to move downward, while the heat (Fire) in a body (say, in a stone) has more lightness and thus tends to rise. Notice that this account says nothing about *mass* or the *force* of gravity as these ideas are conceived of today.

These forms, however, explain only *how* certain bodies rise and fall (by virtue of their forms), but do not explain *why* bodies should move these ways at all. Since we can imagine that the opposite occurs – that stones rise and fire falls – we need an explanation stronger than 'that's just what they do'. The reason *why* then calls for an explanation in terms of the 'final' or teleological cause. For Aristotle, Nature (*phusis*) is an inherently teleological, that is, end-directed, system. In regard to the natural motions of bodies, this end can be characterised in two ways: (a) as 'the movement of each body to its own place', where its own place is with other bodies possessing the same *form*, following the principle 'like moves to like'[6] (thus, heavy bodies will tend to move toward other heavy bodies, light bodies toward light); and (b), the endeavour of each body *to reach its final resting place*.[7] For the heavy elements, that place is the centre of the Earth, where all heavy bodies are at rest, while the natural place for lighter elements is in the heavens. A more comprehensive account of Aristotle's cosmology is needed to make sense of final cause explanations, but the final cause provides the ultimate explanation, since it explains *why* bodies move the way they do. Their motions reflect a cosmos thoroughly infused with function, purpose, and design (without, however, conscious intentions of any sort). We will have more to say about final causes later in relation to this article and §19.

So far, we can say that the formal and final causes explain the how and the why of natural motion; they are the *internal* causes of natural motion. We should keep this in mind, because Descartes will deny that these causes

---

[5] *On the Heavens*, Bk IV, Chs. 3 and 4.

[6] *On the Heavens*, Bk IV, 3, 310b.

[7] The resting place will be 'where their matter is nearest to being', and that will be where the element is no longer *becoming*, that is, no longer in motion, no longer tending *toward* its resting place, but having arrived at motionless *being* (*On the Heavens*, Bk IV, 3, 310b32–311a10).

explain motion. Now let us turn to the *efficient* cause, that is, to the *external* or 'violent' causes of motion. What causes a body to move after it is struck by another? It is not easy to say because we observe only the motion, not the cause. So, let us suppose that the cause is a *force*. Generally speaking, a force is considered to be the cause of a body's motion and of its continued motion, and we can identify two general types of force: (1) the cause of a body's motion is *its own force*; (2) the cause of a body's motion is *another body* with which it comes into contact.[8] As we saw, on Aristotle's account, the force of motion in a falling body could be explained in terms of (1), its internal form of heaviness and its final cause, while the force of an object thrown could be explained in terms of (2), something external to the body, that is, a thrower or another moving body. After Aristotle and the Medieval period, the concept of force underwent a number of changes, but the ancient conceptions did not disappear entirely. The conception we are most familiar with today, Newton's 'Force = mass x acceleration', is not devoid of ancient content or current puzzles.[9] In any case, this distinction between (1) internal, and (2) external causes of motion figures decisively in the problem at hand: force is the efficient cause of motion; but for Descartes force is the external and *only* cause of motion, whereas for Leibniz there are, in addition, *internal* forces, along the lines of formal-final causes. In sum, what is at stake is a proper understanding of the phenomena of matter in motion, and for this you must provide a proper accounting of force.

Now let us turn to Descartes' accounts of body, motion, and force, which are found in his well-known (certainly by Leibniz) *Principles of Philosophy* (1644). Regarding body, as we have already seen in §10: 'the nature of body does not consist in weight, hardness, colour, or other similar properties; but in extension alone', and extension consists only in length, breadth, and depth.[10] Thus, Descartes has no place for Aristotelian 'forms' such as gravity and levity – these being unexplainable in extensional terms.

---

8 Aristotle, *Physics*, Bk VII, Ch. I, 241b24. For the Moderns as well, bodies cannot transfer their force of motion without coming into direct physical contact with other bodies. A force that could move bodies without coming into contact (what is called 'action-at-a-distance') was thought to be impossible. From this perspective, Newtonian gravity is rather mysterious, as indeed Leibniz claimed it was. See the Leibniz–Clarke correspondence (LCC), Fourth Paper, and Attfield 2005.

9 In contemporary physics, force is the measure (in Newtons) of *work* needed to make a mass of, say, 1 kg accelerate at a rate of 1 metre per second, per second. So, 1 Newton = $1kg(\frac{m}{s^2})$, but does this *measure* of force tell us what force *is*?

10 *Principles* II, §4. The reader may detect something curious about Descartes' characterisation of body as extended. Can a body consist only of length, breadth, and depth? Length *of what*? Of body? Then what is body? Descartes goes on to say in §4 that a body is a 'thing', and that it 'consists solely in the fact that it is a substance which has extension'. But then the substance is not extension itself, though it is extended; it is *something*

As for motion: 'God is the primary [*efficient*] cause of motion; and that he always maintains [*conservare*] an equal quantity of it in the universe' (*Principles* II, §36). This principle must be understood properly. Since matter has extension only and no forms, it has no internal cause of motion. So, the cause must come from something external.[11] Normally, that cause is another body; but since the motion of *that* body will need a cause, and so on, eventually you must appeal to the cause of *all* motion, which is God. Thus, at the creation, in a moment we might call 'The Divine Shove', God set all of created matter into motion.[12]

Directly connected to God's act of creation is God's 'conservation' of matter in motion. As we learned in §16, Descartes held, in accord with the traditional Medieval view, that, due to the deficiency of matter, namely its inability to maintain its being and sustain its motion, God by his 'ordinary concourse' (*concursum ordinarium*) 'conserves' always the *same quantity of motion* he put into matter at the time of creation (*Principles* II, §36). What motivates this conservation principle is not only the deficiency in matter, but that 'it is one of God's perfections to be not only immutable in His nature, but also immutable and completely constant in the way He acts' (*Principles* II, §36). Consequently, God's immutability and constancy must be manifest in the unchangeable laws of nature and in his continuous conservation of the *total quantity of motion* he originally put into matter. Thus, the law of conservation of motion both displays God's perfection and explains why matter remains in motion. Keep this point in mind, because it turns out to be quite significant at the end of this article.

Since this conservation principle is at the centre of Leibniz's criticism of Descartes and of their respective accounts of *force*, let us be clear on how the principle works for Descartes. As a consequence of the above principles of extension and conservation, Descartes can determine, by measurement and calculation, the quantities of all motions of collision, fall, and rest of particular bodies.

• The quantity of motion of any given body is determined by the product of its extension (size) and speed (motion) (*Principles* II, §43).[13]

---

extended. This is the question motivating Leibniz's critique of Descartes. Well, *what* is extended? And the answer must be something that is not explained by extension itself.

[11] This is not entirely true, since Descartes recognises the internal resistance of bodies as well as their inertia (laws of motion). However, whatever these internal principles were, they could theoretically be explained in extensional terms.

[12] See Garber 1992: 278.

[13] What Descartes says here is actually a bit more complex, but speed (*celeritatis*) concerns Leibniz the most.

- Two or more bodies with the same proportions of size and speed will each have the same quantity of motion (*Principles* II, §36).
- If we could add up all the products of the quantities of motion of all bodies, we would get the total quantity of motion that God originally gave to matter. Thus, the conservation principle: the *total quantity of motion* will be exactly the same at all times, even though many particular motions will differ in quantity from each other (*Principles* II, §36).[14]

In other words, the conservation principle entails that particular motions will reflect *exchanges* of quantities of motion, while the same whole quantity of motion in the universe (that God originally put into matter) remains the same.

To illustrate, suppose a universe containing only two round and solid bodies, A and B, each with a diameter of 3 metres. A is moving at 6 metres per second, while B is moving at 4.

Body	Size × Speed	= Quantity of Motion
A	3 × 6	18
B	3 × 4	12

The total quantity of motion in this universe is 30. Now suppose that A and B collide. We may suppose that the faster body, A, will slow down by 2. Therefore, so that the total quantity of motion remains the same, the speed of B will increase by the same amount A decreased. Now suppose our current universe while comparing only two bodies, A and B. If the size of A is twice that of B, but the speed of B is twice that of A (that is, if the sizes and speeds are in proportional relation), then the quantities of motion will be equal.[15]

Body	Size × Speed	= Quantity of Motion
A	6 × 3	18
B	3 × 6	18

All this may appear to be an oversimplification of vastly complex phenomena, especially in light of our current physics.[16] But the point

---

[14] In contemporary terms we would say that energy is transferred from one body to another, but the total amount of energy in the universe is conserved.

[15] Following Descartes' example in *Principles* II, §36.

[16] It is important to bear in mind that 'size' and 'speed' do not conform to our present understanding of these terms (that is, *mass*, and *velocity*, which is speed + direction). However, if we understand 'size' to mean not simply *how large in dimension* or how much

is sufficient to show that Descartes' calculations are consistent with and derivable from his own principles (of extension and the conservation of quantity of motion). More to the point: Descartes maintains that the conservation of *force* can be measured by *quantity of motion*, that is, by the product of only the sizes and speeds of bodies, that is, again, only by their extensional and moving properties.[17] Anything that could be attributed to forces, such as the speed of falling, or the force of impact, could in principle be measured by the size and speed of bodies. And this is the very claim that Leibniz thinks he can refute.

It should also be emphasised that on this account Descartes has no use for Aristotelian *forms*, since they have no extensional properties. Nor does he have use for *final* causes. For the Moderns, final causes were determined, not by nature as in Aristotle, but by God. Yet, Descartes' express reason for banning final causes from physics is not that there *are* no final causes, but rather that such explanations are 'useless' for physics, since the infirmity of our nature is incapable of comprehending God's purposes.[18] Instead, everything that we can know about matter and motion is sufficiently discoverable through its extensional properties and the laws of motion.[19] These means of investigation were the essence of 'Cartesian mechanics' and were supposed to put an end to the old, mysterious, forms and final causes in physics. Leibniz, as we have seen, has other ideas.

We are now well prepared to see exactly how Leibniz claims to find a fatal flaw in 'the Cartesians'[20] account of force, measured in terms of quantity of motion. A 'subaltern maxim' (lns 1 and 5), we should note, is a law of nature, and all natural laws, such as a conservation law, are subject to God's general will. But what Leibniz sets out to demonstrate is that Descartes' 'quantity of motion' fails to measure quantity of force; thus, quantity of motion cannot be the measure of force.

---

it *weighs*, but rather *how much matter the object contains*, then it is not much different from mass. Furthermore, 'speed' means simply how fast that quantity of matter is moving, measured by its distance over time, but without direction (a scalar, but not vector quantity). So, the 'quantity of motion' of an object can be understood as the *quantity of moving matter*, calculated by the product of its quantity of matter and its quantity of motion over time. Nor need we worry whether the units are pounds, metres, or seconds, as long as we keep them consistent. Descartes' quantity of motion is close to but not identical with what we now call 'momentum' (Iltis 1971: 21). For *force*, we can think in contemporary terms as the energy required to do *work*, such as to throw an object or for an object to fall a certain distance at a certain speed. But to understand the problem here, our current understanding of gravity must be set aside.

[17] *Principles* II, §43. 'In what the force (*vis*) of each body to drive or to resist consists'.

[18] *Principles* I, §28 and *Meditation* IV, CSM I and II, 39 / AT VIIIA and VII, 56.

[19] *Principles* IV, §187.

[20] Followers of the Cartesian method in mechanics.

Leibniz's first point, to which the Cartesians would presumably agree, is that conservation of force is 'reasonable' (ln 14); for, if force were not conserved, then perpetual motion would be possible; but perpetual motion is impossible. Let us be clear why. First, if the conservation law is true, i.e. the total amount of force in the universe remains constant, then force can neither be created nor destroyed – only particular things can lose or gain quantities of force. Second, we observe that systems or machines performing work (such as clocks) eventually stop moving when their force (source of power or motion) runs out. Their force (capacity for acting) dissipates in the form of heat, unless a new source of power or force is applied. But suppose we could design a clock or machine that, once set in motion, could run perpetually (historically, many elaborate designs for perpetual motion machines have been attempted). This would be possible, only if the force could be created anew or imported from outside the universe; but by hypothesis, this is impossible. In other words, a perpetual motion machine would have to cause a greater *effect* (namely motion) than it has power to produce. As we will see, the deeper conclusion of Leibniz's demonstration is that effects must always be *equal* to their causes. But for now, Leibniz begins his demonstration by setting out two specific assumptions on which the Cartesians would agree, in order to show how they would measure force in their own terms.

First assumption: Think of a pendulum.[21] If the bob is released from an original height of 4 metres, with its chord taut, it will swing down along a steady curve, reach its low point, and then swing back up to its original height. For sake of experiment, any impediment or friction the pendulum undergoes along the way is ignored. This implies that the force required for the pendulum to elevate itself back to its original height should be equal to the force it gained from its fall. Force is conserved; so far, so good.

Second assumption: Force is also conserved in this example implicitly taken from *statics*, the mechanics of bodies in equilibrium. To illustrate, imagine placing body A weighing 1 pound at one end of a 6-foot plank (with a fulcrum in the middle) with this end resting on the ground. Then press down on the raised end of the plank until A reaches a height of 4 metres. The force required to elevate A would be the same as required to elevate another body, B, weighing 4 pounds, to a height of 1 metre.

---

[21] The diagram Leibniz draws at this point in the text does not quite match the scenarios he describes.

	Weight (pounds)	Raised to Height (metres)	Applied Force
Body A	1	4	Same as B
Body B	4	1	Same as A

While we do not know what the *quantities* of force are, the assumption that they are the same is reasonable, given the equal proportions of weight to height. More importantly, Leibniz has good reason to suppose that Descartes and the Cartesians would agree to this.[22]

Having set out these two agreed-upon assumptions, Leibniz constructs a third scenario that he says follows from both assumptions. Taking bodies A and B to be pendulums set in proportional relations of weight to height, it follows from the first assumption that each will acquire as much force in their fall to elevate themselves back to their original height. It follows from the second assumption that A and B will require the same force.

	Weight	Height of Fall and Return	Total Force
Body A	1	4	Same as B
Body B	4	1	Same as A

As Leibniz states, 'the force of these two bodies is equal' (ln 40). Given that the Cartesians would agree that force is conserved in these two scenarios (plus the one involving the denial of perpetual motion), Leibniz will now determine whether the quantity of *force* of these bodies can be measured in Cartesian terms of quantity of motion (size times speed).

Before we go on to the final scenario to see how Leibniz calculates quantity of motion, it is important to notice that the above scenarios are based on *height* or distance of fall, but not explicitly on *speed* (in fact, the second assumption is a case of pushing, not of falling speed). Thus, Leibniz must assume, on behalf of the Cartesians, that the falling speeds are proportional to the height, as depicted in the accompanying table.

Body	Size	Distance of Fall	Speed (metres/sec)	Size x Speed	Quantity of Motion
A	1	4 (from height C)	4 (at impact point D)	1×4	$= 4$
B	4	1 (from height E)	1 (at impact point F)	4×1	$= 4$

[22] See Papineau 1977: 124 and Iltis 1971: 24, fn. 10.

To make matters more clear, let us also suppose that the unit of speed is metres per second.[23] Accordingly, the speed of body A at impact point is 4m/s, while that of body B is 1m/s; and since the quantities of motion are equal, the quantities of force must be equal (given that quantity of motion = quantity of force). These assumed speeds are reasonable, given the prior assumptions. That is, since the Cartesians agree that bodies in proportional relations of sizes and heights have the same quantity of force, then bodies in proportional relations of sizes and speeds will have the same quantity of force – that is, if speed is indeed proportional to height.

Now, to discover whether force *can* be measured by Descartes' quantity of motion (which it is the whole point of Leibniz's demonstration to determine), Leibniz calculates the speed of each body according to Galileo's *law of falling bodies*. Accordingly, the speed of body A at impact will have only *twice* the speed of body B – not four times as much.

Body	Size	Distance of Fall	Speed at Impact	Size × Speed	Quantity of Motion
A	1	4 (from height C)	2 (at impact point D)	1 × 2	= 2
B	4	1 (from height E)	1 (at impact point F)	4 × 1	= 4

Thus, contrary to the Cartesian assumptions, the quantities of motion are *not* the same. Since the speed of A is now only twice that of B, while the size of B is still four times larger, B's quantity of motion is twice that of A's. Since it was agreed that the forces should be equal, but now the quantities of motion are not, Leibniz concludes, 'there is a great difference between quantity of motion and force, as was needed to be shown' (lns 51–2). The result is devastating for Descartes' laws of motion, because it implies that quantity of motion cannot be the measure of force; thus quantity of motion cannot be what God 'conserves' in the universe. As Leibniz had anticipated in the summary of §17, 'God always conserves the same force, but not the same quantity of motion'.

---

[23] The above table reflects Leibniz's diagram at this point in §17. Leibniz does not always indicate the units used in his example. Therefore, from here on, all units will be understood thus: size is in pounds (since he uses *livre* for *weight* and implicitly includes weight in what is generally referred to as size). Distance or height is in metres. Time is in seconds. Speed is in metres/second at impact point. Also, speed is to be understood as uniformly accelerating, but scalar, not vector. Quantity of motion and quantity of force have themselves as units.

To better understand this result, let us take a closer look at how it was derived. According to Galileo's law, the speed of a body in free-fall, at point of impact, is proportional, not to the height from which it falls, but to the *square root* of the height from which it falls, a law conveniently expressed as 's $\propto \sqrt{d}$ ' (where 's' is speed and 'd' is the height).[24] Thus if we know the falling distance, we can get the speed. To be confident in this calculation, we can check for several distances (although for ease of calculation, only the perfect squares):

If d = 1, and s = $\sqrt{d}$, then s = 1.
If d = 4, and s = $\sqrt{d}$, then s = 2.
If d = 9, and s = $\sqrt{d}$, then s = 3.
If d = 16, and s = $\sqrt{d}$, then s = 4.

And so on. Now that we know how to get the speeds using Galileo's law, we can calculate the quantity of motion, just as Leibniz does, for bodies A and B in his diagram. The accompanying table makes the calculation explicit.

Body	Size	Distance	$\sqrt{d}$ = Speed	Size × Speed	= QM
A	1	4	2	1 × 2	= 2
B	4	1	1	4 × 1	= 4

Based on the speeds calculated according to Galileo's law, the quantities of motion turn out unequal, as Leibniz showed; thus, quantity of motion cannot be the measure of force.

---

[24] Galileo's law is frequently expressed as d $\propto t^2$ (the distance of the fall is proportional to the square of the time of the fall). Mathematically equivalent to that expression is $\sqrt{d} \propto$ t (the square root of the height from which the body is dropped is proportional to the time of fall). From these expressions we can get the speed: $\sqrt{d}$ gives us t, and speed equals distance over time (d/t). For example, if d = 4, then t = 2; thus, the speed of fall = 2. From this, we get the convenient expression: s $\propto \sqrt{d}$ (speed is proportional to the square root of the distance or height). Galileo's law may be found in his *Dialogues [or Discourses and Mathematical Demonstrations] Concerning Two New Sciences* (1638), 'Day Three' on 'Natural Accelerated Motion', Theorem II, Proposition II: 'The spaces described by a body falling from rest with a uniformly accelerated motion are to each other as the squares of the time-intervals employed in traveling these distances' (174). It should also be noted that Descartes himself expressly, though reservedly, shared Galileo's view: 'The distance covered by a falling heavy body is proportional to the square of the time which the body takes to fall . . . albeit with many qualifications, for in fact it is never completely true, as [Galileo] thinks he has demonstrated that it is' (Letter to Mersenne, 1634, CSM III, 44). See Arthur 2016: 94–8, on Descartes' model of free-fall.

If this is correct, that quantity of motion is not the measure of force, the question that naturally arises from Leibniz's demonstration is: how then should force be correctly measured? While Leibniz does not say *explicitly* in the *Discourse*, his remarks immediately following his demonstration provide some important clues.

> One sees by this how *force* must be estimated by the quantity of the effect that it can produce, for example by the height to which a heavy body of a certain size and kind can be raised, which is very different from the speed that one can give to it. And to give it double the speed it must be given more than double the force. (lns 52–6)

Let us focus on the first sentence: 'force must be estimated', not by the speed of the body, but *by the effect it can produce*. From Leibniz's scenarios, we find that the *effect* is the height or distance to which a body can raise itself, or, as in the last scenario, the speed of the body at impact, while the *cause* would be the height or distance from which the body is dropped. (Keep this point in mind because I will return to it to make a final point.) This implies that the force of a falling body is proportional to the height of the fall, such that when the height is increased, the force is increased. But as the second sentence implies, the proportion is not 1-to-1 with height, as the Cartesian assumes. As Galileo proved, the correct speed is calculated as the *square root* of the distance. This implies that if the *speed* should be doubled, then the height will need to be *more* than doubled – in other words, squared.

The point of doubling the speed would be to show what it would take for the forces in bodies A and B to be equal. In other words, what would it take for the Cartesian to calculate the size times speed so that the two bodies have equal quantities of motion, and thus equal force? Leibniz is implicitly suggesting that you must raise the height of Body A by a factor of a square, to 16 metres, which, when Galileo's law is applied, makes the speed at point of impact 4, instead of 2. Then the quantities of motion will be equal. Simply stated, to make the quantities of motion equal between the two bodies, you must square the height of body A.

Body	Size	Height	Height^2	$\sqrt{h}$ = Speed	Size × Speed	= QM
A	1	4	16	4	1 × 4	= 4
B	4	1	1	1	4 × 1	= 4

The speed of A is now doubled, from 2. So now that the quantities of motion are equal, Descartes could say that force is conserved. But this means, against Descartes, that for falling bodies in proportional relations of size and speed to have the same force, the speed must be determined by the *square root* of the falling distance.

A simpler way to estimate the force is by squaring the *speed*. We can do this because Galileo's law, s ∝ √d, implies s² ∝ d, that is, the distance is proportional to the square of the speed. But again, the only way to increase the speed by a square is to square the height. Thus, as is often pointed out in the literature, *mv²* (mass x velocity squared) appears to be the correct estimate of force. In fact, almost ten years after the *Discourse*, in his most developed and important work on force, *A Specimen of Dynamics* (1695), Leibniz clearly identifies Galileo's law as the source for the implication of *mv²*: 'One can conclude . . . that in general the forces in bodies are jointly proportional to the size of the bodies and the squares of their speeds' (AG 128). The Cartesians seem to think, on the other hand, that *mv* is the proper estimation of force. As Leibniz has just shown, the Cartesians are wrong.

But is this the only lesson Leibniz wants to impart in his demonstration, that force is correctly measurable by *mv²*? Let us assess the deeper significance of Leibniz's demonstration. The difference between Descartes' quantity of motion and Leibniz's estimation of force (between *mv* and *mv²* as they are often characterised)[25] signifies more than the correction of a calculation error or a disagreement over the meaning of certain technical terms. It marks two very different conceptions of force. Descartes presupposes that force can be explained entirely by the measure of extension and motion, while Leibniz argues that, while force can be estimated this way (after all, he estimates force by the same means, size and speed), a correct estimation implies the presence of something in bodies *in addition* to the extended properties of matter and motion, and that something is force. That this appears to be Leibniz's position is evinced in his letter to the great polymath Pierre Bayle, written in 1687, one year after having composed the *Discourse*:

> I would like to add a remark of consequence for metaphysics. I have shown that force ought not to be estimated by the product of speed and size, but by the future effect. However, it seems that force or power is something real at present, while the future effect is not. From which it follows that we must

---

[25] Note that I am hesitant to use the terms 'mass' and 'velocity' because in the *Discourse* Leibniz does not use them and, as is widely known, size is not equivalent to mass. Also, velocity is currently understood to be a vector (directional) quantity, but nothing in Leibniz's demonstration includes a measure of direction. He needs only to calculate according to Cartesian, and then Galilean, assumptions. While these points do not affect the validity of Leibniz's demonstration, failing to recognise them could be misleading.

admit in bodies something different from size and speed, at least unless one wants to refuse bodies all power of acting.[26]

This passage may very well express Leibniz's contention in §17 that 'force must be estimated by the quantity of the effect that it can produce' (lns 52–3). The 'effect', as we saw in a pendulum, is the height to which the bob can raise itself after free-fall (ln 25), or the speed of the falling body at impact. While this effect is measurable, or estimable, as the square of the speed that the body acquires during fall, it is a *future* effect (or what we today might call *potential energy*). As a future effect, it must be present *in* the body, but cannot be measured until the effect has occurred. In other words, force is something present *in* bodies but is not an extended property *of* them; thus, bodies would have in themselves the power of acting; and this implies that force is a *metaphysical*, that is, a non-extended, principle in bodies. To put the matter in terms of causes: Leibniz's view would seem to be that the cause of motion of bodies is not only their sizes and speeds, but also their internal force.

However, as convincing as this answer may be to the question of what *in addition* to matter accounts for the motion of bodies (that is, metaphysical force), it arguably does not convey the deeper implications of Leibniz's demonstration in §17. So, let us bring the commentary on this article to a close by considering an alternative set of implications that follow from his claim that 'force must be estimated by the quantity of the effect that it can produce' (ln 53). In outline: First, Leibniz holds that this estimation is governed by the principle of *the equality of cause and effect* – and this is the metaphysical principle Leibniz is concerned to attach to his account of force.[27] Second, the ground for this principle is the principle of conservation of force, which, if violated, results in 'perpetual mechanical motion', which Leibniz maintains 'has no place' in physics (ln 17). This leads, finally, to an important *theological* implication: that the conservation of force cannot be violated, because that would imply an imperfection in God.[28]

---

[26] Letter to Bayle, January 1687, LGP III, 48, quoted by Garber 2009: 154 and Sleigh 1990: 118.

[27] Taking a cue from Garber 2009: 152, but also diverging.

[28] With the following line of argument, I am not claiming that Leibniz has settled his view on the matter of the measure of force. I only wish to give a plausible account of the background of Leibniz's thought in the *Discourse*, and specifically in §17, as an aid to understanding his demonstration and its significance. It is not possible here to set out a proper accounting of the development of Leibniz's theory of force and its influence. The interested (and technically proficient) reader is referred to the SEP ('Leibniz's Philosophy of Physics'); to his essays on dynamics in AG; to Garber 2009: 129–44; and to the articles mentioned above in reference to the *vis visa* controversy. My argument is

Let us start with the equality principle. Leibniz actually had been working through some version of an equality principle in his 'Conspectus Libelli', written nearly ten years prior to the *Discourse*:[29]

> There turn out to be certain things in a body which cannot be explained by the necessity of matter alone. Such are the laws of motion, which depend on the metaphysical principle of the equality of cause and effect. (LC 233)

Clearly, the equality principle is a metaphysical principle. That it entails the conservation of force is clearly indicated further down:

> Force or power [*vi seu potentia*] . . . must be estimated from the quantity of the effect. But the power [*potentia*] of the effect and of the cause are equal to each other, for if that of the effect were greater, we would have mechanical perpetual motion, if less, we would not have physical perpetual motion. Here it is worth showing that the same quantity of motion cannot be conserved, but that on the other hand the same quantity of power [*potentia*] is conserved. (LC 235)

Four points: (1) The first sentence is nearly identical to that of the *Discourse*, which says 'force must be estimated by the quantity of the effect that it can produce' (§17, ln 53), which strongly suggests that mv^2 provides the right measure of force, for Leibniz. (2) However, the measure of force must conform to, or is governed by, the principle of the equality of cause and effect, and this, in turn, rules out perpetual motion. Here is how: to say that the cause must equal its effect is just to say that the effect cannot be greater (or lesser) than its cause, because if it were, then you would get either perpetual motion (which would require the introduction of force from outside the universe) or, on the other hand, the universal force would eventually run out (see §17, ln 18), and these conditions are ruled out by the hypothesis of conservation. (3) Thus, the proper estimation of force is significant, because the equality of cause and effect implies the conservation of force. What is conserved in the end is not simply the quantity of force as determined by Galileo's law, 'size times speed squared', but rather the equality of cause and effect. (4) This in turn suggests that the 'something metaphysical' in bodies is not only force, but its principle or law. Since the principle of equality is a general law of embodied forces, but not a measure of extended things, it cannot be exhaustively explained by the extensional properties of matter and motion. Thus, what Leibniz *implicitly*

---

also aided by my understanding of Garber 2009: 145–55; Lodge 1997; and Sleigh 1990: 116–19.

[29] 'Conspectus for a Little Book on the Elements of Physics', in AA VI, 4 N. 365, titled *Conspectus Libelli Elementorum Physicae* and dated 1678–9. Translated in LC 231–5, and in LL 278 as 'On the Elements of Natural Science'. Cited by Garber 2009: 143.

demonstrates in §17 is the metaphysical principle of the equality of cause and effect.

The demonstration itself implicitly shows, moreover, how Cartesian quantity of motion violates the equality principle, while Leibniz's quantity of force does not.[30] This can be readily seen by focusing on the scenario depicted in Leibniz's diagram, wherein the speed of the bodies at impact, determining their force, is calculated from the height of their fall. Thus, the *cause* of the force is the height from which the bodies are dropped, and the *effect* of the force is the speed (times the size) that the bodies acquire at impact; so the effect must be equal to its cause. But is it?

Recall that, for the Cartesian, the height of body A, which is 4, causes the speed at impact to be 4. (This equivalence is merely coincidental and apparent.) But, as Leibniz showed, using Galileo's law, the proper speed is 2. Therefore, the Cartesian formula results in a greater speed, 4, resulting in a force greater than its cause can produce. In other words, *the effect is greater than its cause*. This is ultimately why the quantities of motion (and thus of force) of bodies A and B are not equal.

Now, how does Leibniz's quantity of force (size x speed²) maintain the required equality? As implied (ln 56), to make the quantities of motion equal for bodies A and B, you must increase the *cause*, that is, the falling distance of body A, by a square, from 4 to 16 feet, to get the *effect*, which is 4. This is why, then, the quantities of force of A and of B are equal after application of the law. They are equal because the cause produces exactly the amount of effect (force) contained in its cause. It should now be clear how these results imply perpetual motion for the Cartesian, but not for Leibniz: the measure of force by means of 'quantity of motion' generates an effect greater than its cause, and that implies perpetual motion.[31]

From this we can see how Leibniz's demonstration in §17 has important physical and metaphysical implications. The physical implication is that without the correct measure of force, your calculations and predictions will of course be wrong. More severely, you will demonstrate what has 'no place' in physical explanations, namely, perpetual motion. The *metaphysical* implications are that something unexplainable in extensional terms must be present and operative in extended bodies. That something is of course force; but it is also, more generally, the equality principle which regulates force. Since the principle of the equality of cause and effect is a general law governing all bodily forces, it is operative in bodies, without

---

[30] Again, taking a clue from Garber 2009: 148–9, but making the point differently.

[31] Of course, the inequality would apply, not just to the given example, but for all free-falling bodies in proportional relations of size and speed, as the Cartesians would apparently calculate them.

being an extensional property of them. (How it is possible for a non-physical law to be operative in physical bodies is for the reader to investigate.)

Finally, we can find an important theological implication. If effects may exceed their causes (if perpetual motion were possible), then force will be created anew. Not only would this result in a perpetual miracle, but to an increase in the total amount of force, leading to increasingly chaotic effects. It would imply that God would not have provided a conservation law sufficient for the universe to run or regulate itself – and this in turn implies an imperfection in God. Like Descartes, Leibniz is committed to the view that God's perfections consist in part of *simplicity, immutability, and constancy.*[32] But if God had constructed a system of unstable and mutable laws, or had periodically to add force to the universe, these perfections would be greatly undermined; and yet the principles of conservation and equality follow fittingly from them.

We have seen, then, that Leibniz's brief demonstration contains much more than the correction of a measurement error in physics. The theological implication is highly significant for the *Discourse*, since, as we will see, Leibniz seeks to maintain concurrently two types of causation, each of which can be explained independently of the other, but which are also interdependent. These are the *efficient* (physical) cause and the *final* (God's purposive) cause. As he claimed in §10 and §11, we can and should conduct our physical investigations as far as possible without appeal to final causes, and we should never resort to empty explanations in terms of 'occult' qualities. At the same time, to get the physics right, you must appeal to certain metaphysical principles; and once you do that, you should see that these ultimately depend on God's estimation of what these principles and laws should be – without which (to anticipate §21) 'the phenomena' would indeed be very different. Thus, final causes are built into the very causes of motion of matter as supplements for what efficient causes cannot explain. The role of final causes will take on increasing importance in the following sections. But for the moment Leibniz is not finished critiquing Descartes, for in the next article he brings forward yet another reason why Cartesian mechanics cannot explain force: it cannot even explain *motion*.

§18. Thus, to explain the cause of motion in bodies, 'one must have recourse to metaphysical considerations separate from extension'.

Whatever may be the precise physical and metaphysical import of Leibniz's demonstration in §17, he clearly considers it a decisive refutation of the Cartesian conception of matter as extended substance. More specifically, it refutes the claim that quantity of motion is the correct measure of the

---

[32] Descartes, *Principles* II, §36.

conservation of force. In article 18, Leibniz again criticises Descartes – not on the 'quantity of motion' principle, but on the nature and cause of motion itself. As we saw in §12, Leibniz attacked Descartes' contention that the parts of matter are distinguished by motion, by contending that motion is merely relative to our perception and cannot be located in the parts of matter itself. Here in §18, Leibniz claims that motion itself, on Descartes' account, is not even real, since the motion of one body is relative to the motion of other bodies. Thus, to give motion its required reality one must admit, taking a cue from §17, that bodies get their motion from some metaphysical reality, that is, their internal force.

Here is the Cartesian background to Leibniz's argument. Descartes defines motion as 'change of place', that is, the change of place of one body *from* its place among other bodies at rest, *to* its place among other bodies at rest (*Principles* II, §§25–30). So, imagine bodies A, B, and C, all of which are at rest. Motion can be discerned, only when the bodies change position relative to each other. If B, situated between A and C, moves closer to A and further from C, we attribute motion to B. This means that motion is always *relative* to the motion (or rest) of other bodies. This initially makes sense, because supposing a universe containing only one moving body, we could not tell whether it was moving, since its motion would need to be compared with the position of another body at rest or moving at a different speed.

For Leibniz, however, Descartes' relativity of motion implies that motion is 'not something entirely real' (ln 12), and he says that he could show this 'geometrically' if he wanted to (ln 16). Likely, he has this in mind: Suppose in the scenario above that body B remains at rest, while bodies A and C move to the left. A *change of place* has indeed occurred, but due to the motions of A and C, not B. But this scenario is indistinguishable from the previous. So, you could not know to which bodies motion should be attributed, B, or A and C. Therefore, for Leibniz, this implies that Cartesian motion is *apparent* or *relative*, not real.

A passage from his 'Critical Thoughts on the General Part of the Principles of Descartes' (1692) can serve to support and clarify this point. Addressing the relevant passage in Descartes' *Principles* (§25), Leibniz writes:

> If motion is nothing but the change of contact or of immediate vicinity, it follows that we can never define which thing is moved. For just as the same phenomena may be interpreted by different hypotheses in astronomy, so it will always be possible to attribute the real motion to either one or the other of the two bodies which change their mutual vicinity or location. (LL 393)

This allusion to different hypotheses in astronomy no doubt refers to the Ptolemaic and Copernican hypotheses, each of which purport to explain planetary motion consistent with observations made from the Earth. The Ptolemaic hypothesis places the Earth at rest in the centre of the system, with the planets and Sun revolving around it; while the Copernican places the Sun at rest in the centre, with the Earth and other planets revolving around it. Now, for each hypothesis you can equally account for the geometrical relations, that is, in terms of lines and spaces, between the bodies in motion and those at rest. The problem is that you cannot determine which bodies are in motion and which at rest. If the Earth is in motion in the Copernican system, it can equally be said to be at rest in the Ptolemaic, and vice versa. The geometric relations are the same. 'The consequence of this will be that there is no real motion' (LL 393).[1]

Leibniz does not mean that there *is* no real motion, but rather that, due to Descartes' rules of motion, the real *cause* of motion cannot be assigned to one body or another; for what gives reality to motion is the *cause* of motion, not the relative position of bodies. 'We require not only that [the body] change its position with respect to other things, but also that there be within itself a cause of change, a force, an action' (LL 393). Thus, if bodies have forces in them causing their motion, we could say in the one hypothesis that it is the *Earth* that is in motion, or in the other, counterfactually, that the *Sun* is in motion. According to Leibniz, then, an explanation for the reality of motion is possible: the *force of the body itself* is responsible for its motion, at least in part.

The problems with Descartes' laws of motion are, as in §12, that they cannot explain how bodies can be distinguished from each other; nor, as in §17, can they explain the proper estimation of *force*; nor, as in this article, can they explain the cause of *motion*. In all cases, Leibniz's criticisms point to the need to posit something metaphysical or immaterial – either the 'banished' substantial forms or a metaphysical 'force' – in addition to the extended properties of bodies. That something immaterial is required also means that something of religious piety can be brought to bear upon physics, since immateriality implies the nature of God. Leibniz will take this latter suggestion to a more explicit level in the next four articles, as he argues for 'final causes' as fundamental, metaphysical explanations for the laws of physics.

[1] Leibniz makes the same point quite clearly in an essay of 1689: 'Since we have already proved through geometrical demonstrations the equivalence of all hypotheses with respect to the motions of any bodies, it follows that not even an angel could determine with mathematical rigor which of the many bodies of that sort is at rest, and which is the center of motion for the others' ('On Copernicanism and the Relativity of Motion', AG 90). Angels, it may be noted, were often called 'intelligences'.

§19. On the utility of final causes in physics.

In conformity with Leibniz's initial premise in the *Discourse*, that God is perfect, it must follow that God always wills the best and most perfect physical laws; thus, for us fully to understand physical laws, God's will or 'final causes' must be included as part of our physical explanations – even though we need not appeal to them while doing physics. For Leibniz, the usefulness of final causes consists primarily in their aid to the *discovery* of physical laws, as we will see. Descartes, however, has maintained that final causes are 'totally useless' because we cannot know what God's reasons are;[1] nor can we admit into our physics the knowledge of anything that is not measurable in terms of extension and its modes. Leibniz is not so circumspect. He thinks that God's reasons can at least be approximated, since they are apparent in the ends (goals) of natural laws themselves. He also worries that the physics of 'our new philosophers', the Cartesians and Spinozists, will lead to impiety, if final causes are left out of account. While this article is concerned primarily with a general defence of including final causes in physical or natural explanations, it does not make an argument for a particular final cause exemplified by some physical law. That argument will come in §21 and §22.

First, let us be sure that we have a clear conception of the difference between a 'final cause' and an 'efficient cause', for, although we met the Aristotelian causes early in §17, we now need to distinguish these two causes more precisely. In his *Physics*, Aristotle distinguished *four* 'causes' or 'whys' which must be taken into account in order to understand the nature of things: the material, formal, efficient, and final causes.[2] In brief, the material cause is the matter out of which something is made, for example, wood, stone, or metal. The formal cause, of which we have seen a great deal in the *Discourse*, is what determines or defines a thing to be the kind or individual that it is, which can be anything from an angel, a human, an animal, as well as a thing made of wood, stone, or metal. The *efficient* cause is what we typically think of nowadays as the cause of motion or change in a thing, such as when one body 'causes' another to move, fall, break, or to change shape by pressing against it. We tend to think of all events as having efficient causes, or quite simply 'causes'. The *final* cause is often not easy to distinguish from the formal and efficient causes, but it explains the function of the thing (what it is made to do), or the natural development of a thing – what it is designed to become; for example, that an acorn develops into an oak tree, or that an embryo develops into an adult human. When

---

[1] *Meditation* IV, CSM II, 39 / AT 56 and *Principles* I, §28.

[2] *Physics*, Bk II, Ch. 3; *Metaphysics*, Bk I, Ch. 3 and Bk V, Ch. 2.

such a thing develops into its fully mature form, it is said to have reached its *end*, *telos*, *completion*, or *perfection*. Thus, the final cause can be conceived of as that which brings a thing to its perfection which is the completion of what the thing contains in its essence to become. The final cause can also be applied to nature as a whole, as when we say that nature strives to maintain a state of equilibrium, or to support life. Nowadays, most physicists have no place for final causes, largely because physical explanations (efficient causes) sufficient for predictive purposes can be given without appealing to what appear to be non-physical causes, namely, goal-orientation, perfection, or intelligence. On the other hand, the case for final causes among organisms such as plants, animals, and humans, is much harder to dismiss. While the theory of evolution does not depend on final causes to account for the diversity and development of species and individuals, most biologists acknowledge that teleological-functional explanations are very useful for understanding the relations of the parts of an organism.[3] Humans and animals often guide their actions in view of goals and purposes, more or less self-consciously. For the most part, however, the general idea of 'final cause' presupposes some sort of agent (or soul) possessing some degree of thought or intelligence as an active principle.

In the seventeenth century, philosophers or natural scientists like Descartes increasingly sought to dismiss final causes as unknowable and focused instead on physical, measurable causes, namely, efficient causes as the causes of change and motion. Spinoza dismissed final causes in nature as 'anthropomorphic', that is, as an example of the sort of human prejudice that places humans at the centre of God's concern.[4] Leibniz argues, however, that final causes must be included among and supplemental to efficient causes. While his reasons for retaining final causes are largely theological – final causes are exemplary of God's intelligence and perfection – he also thought that a final cause account was *useful* because it contributed to our understanding of nature. On the assumption that the Architect of nature is perfect, the scientist can expect natural laws to exhibit perfections such as simplicity, efficiency, and *good purpose*. As Aristotle stated in his *Metaphysics*, 'the science which knows to what end each thing must be done is the most authoritative of the sciences . . . and this end is the good of that thing, and in general the supreme good in the whole of nature'.[5] Thus, nature is best understood by assuming its aim is to complete or perfect itself. While Aristotle did not conceive of a perfect god directing all things to their perfection, Leibniz believes that to assume the

---

[3] See the entry on 'Teleological Notions in Biology' in the SEP.

[4] Spinoza, *Ethics*, Part I, Appendix.

[5] *Metaphysics*, Bk. I, Ch. I (982b4–7).

good in nature is to assume a good and intelligent cause of nature, separate from nature, and thus to assume that nature is governed by the best laws. This means, most importantly, that the laws of nature, *conceived* as efficient causes, are ultimately *governed* by the final causes of God.

And so we find Leibniz expressing this ancient idea in a seventeenth-century theological context: 'God always intends the best and most perfect' (ln 11). Now, Leibniz is mindful that the world does not seem to be the best, but he maintains that this impression is due to our limited perspective. If we proceed from an egoistic perspective and insist that God's perfection reflect our own conception and desire for how the world should be, we will be disillusioned as soon as things go badly. But if we take a universal perspective, we will understand that the good does not necessarily aim at *one's own* perfection, but at everyone's and in the long run (at least, for every *human* – thus Spinoza's criticism still holds). Nor can we reasonably assume that the (efficient) causes of natural events are too complex for God to have thought through, nor too unimportant to be left to chance. There is *much* to question in Leibniz's assumptions here, but it is important to know what they are.

The contrast Leibniz makes here between efficient and final causes is similar to the contrast made in current debates between evolution science and intelligent design, where the former says that natural developments and designs occur through efficient causes only, whereas the latter says that these must have intelligence as their cause. For example, to say that 'we see because it so happens we have eyes' (lns 33–4) is to suppose a universe of chance, of only efficient causes, absent of intentions, purposes, design, and intelligence. Such a world makes no sense – if God exists and is perfect. Furthermore, without a sense of purpose, it is difficult to conceive what the eyes do. A thorough explanation of the laws of optics can tell us *how* the eye sees, but they cannot reveal that the eyes are *designed for seeing*. On the other hand, to say that the eyes *were* designed for seeing – a final cause explanation – allows us to understand that the laws of optics not only cause certain reflections and refractions, but that they are conducive to their end, namely, sight. We can also understand their greater purpose: that *seeing is good* for us, because it makes us capable of a greater range of perception, intelligence, and action. These perfections of our nature, we may call them, provide clues to the character of the universe as a whole: the world is *good*, the world has value, and without a *coordination* of multiple purposes the world would not exhibit the goodness and rational order that it has. The laws of nature are just such a coordination, that, Leibniz assumes, could not have come about without intelligence. In the seventeenth century, it was much easier to accept intelligence as a design element than it is now.

The fact that the world exhibits a great amount of order and apparent purpose is evidence that the 'effect must correspond to its cause' (ln 39), or in other words that the *cause* can be found in the *effects*. Once we understand that the cause, God, is perfect, then we can look for those laws of nature that exhibit the most perfection, as an aid to their discovery. A focus on the strictly 'efficient' (that is, mechanical) causes cannot tell us why the world is so ordered. Leibniz's analogy of the historian shows that history makes little sense when told from the mechanical perspective, without the intentions of intelligent agents. Similarly, natural laws make little sense without the supposition of a good and intelligent designer. As the following article illustrates, it also makes little sense to assume intelligence in the designer, and yet not to look for intelligence in the design.

§20. The passage in Plato's *Phaedo* explaining the difference between efficient and final causes.

The difference between efficient and final causes is illustrated in this passage from Plato's *Phaedo* (97c–99c), which Leibniz had translated from the Greek, around the year 1680, and then at the time of the *Discourse* instructed his copyist to insert at this point (see details in the translation, §20, fn 3). The passage depicts Socrates' initial approval of Anaxagoras, a Pre-Socratic philosopher who postulated that Mind or Intelligence (in Greek, *Nous*) created the world, and then his subsequent disappointment, when he finds Anaxagoras making no use of Mind in his explanations for physical phenomena – thereby postulating final causes only to resort to efficient causes.

The context for the passage is the series of Plato's dialogues forming the famous account of the trial and death of Socrates. In the *Apology*, Socrates defends himself against charges of impiety and corruption of the youth (for supposedly believing in unofficial gods and teaching unorthodox ideas about official gods). Found guilty and sentenced to die by self-ingestion of hemlock, the *Crito* presents Socrates awaiting his punishment while his friends exhort him to escape and go into exile. Socrates provides several reasons for why he is willing to accept his unfair death sentence rather than to escape.

The passage in the *Discourse* is taken from the final dialogue in this series, *Phaedo*, shortly before his death. Socrates and his friends are discussing – as only philosophers would, at a time like this – two types of *causes* and which type should be considered the principle of creation or action. The causes can be classified in Aristotelian terms as *efficient* and *final*. The former involves no intelligence, while the latter does. Socrates aims to show how ridiculous it would be to suppose that what is keeping him in prison is some

211

physical state of his body, as opposed to the *reason of the good* he finds in remaining in prison. It would be just as ridiculous to suppose that Mind did not put final causes to use in its creation of the universe.

In addition to the implied contrast between efficient and final causes, the passage alludes to a few other points close to Leibniz. (1) While Mind creates according to the greatest perfection possible, lesser minds (humans) act on the basis of what they perceive to be best. (2) The mind operates independently of the body yet is dependent on the body (on physical conditions) for the exercise of its will. (3) Assuming that the world could have been different, there must be a final cause for why things are so as opposed to some other way. In other words, Mind decides what is 'suitable to each thing in particular' and 'what would be the best in general' (lns 33–4). Finally, (4) since Mind is intelligent, purposeful, and good, we can assume that nature's laws exhibit those same qualities. Anaxagoras understood Mind, but he failed to convey its teleological relationship to nature's laws.

The second passage comes from the same place in *Phaedo*, and I include it because it contains some interesting differences from the previous. Translated/paraphrased in 1676, Leibniz appears to have had a different purpose in mind; namely, to show that the reality of things is explained ultimately by their *formal* cause (Platonic Forms); but furthermore, that the Forms lend proof to the immortality of the soul.[1]

§21. If the laws of nature depended solely on Cartesian mechanics, without Metaphysics, the phenomena of nature would be entirely different.

Leibniz's argument in this article is twofold: Cartesian mechanics cannot explain the phenomena of nature, since, once again, it cannot account for what is metaphysical in nature. In this case, it cannot account for the forces of resistance and inertia. These forces are, in addition, ultimately regulated by the law of conservation of force. Secondly, since the law of conservation of force is a decree of divine wisdom (since it is assumed that metaphysics requires a divine source), we must recognise that efficient causes (mechanical laws) require final causes. Thus, we must ultimately appeal to God, without whose wisdom/final causes the phenomena would indeed be entirely different.

---

[1] In the *Phaedo*, Socrates offers two arguments for immortality: (a) the argument from the soul's substantial affinity (the similarity of its nature to that of the Forms) and its dissimilarity to the composite nature of the body (78b–80e); (b) the argument from recollection (73b–76c). On the recollection (*anamnesis*) argument see §26 of the *Discourse* and commentary.

To see how Leibniz's argument works, we first need to review some basic Cartesian premises. Lines 8–11 of the article imply the following premises, familiar to us by now, from Descartes' *Principles of Philosophy*:

1. The nature of body in general consists solely of extension in length, breadth, and depth (*Principles* II, §4).
2. Motion is change of place of a body from one vicinity of bodies at rest to another vicinity of bodies at rest (*Principles* II, §25).
3. Whatever is deduced from these premises follows with mathematical/ geometrical necessity (*Principles* II, §64 and IV, §206).

Before we come to Leibniz's conclusion about these premises, it would be best to have some idea of what Descartes concludes from them; the answer is *a lot*. Along with the premise of 'quantity of motion' we saw in §17 (from *Principles* II, 36), Descartes derives three 'laws of nature' and seven 'rules of impact'. These laws and rules govern all motions as well as all causes and effects of bodies in collision (*Principles* II, §§37–53). Take for example his fourth rule of impact (*Principles* II, §49), which can be paraphrased thusly: Suppose body B, moving at a certain speed, collides with C, a larger body at rest. B would be driven back without losing any of its speed, thus retaining its full quantity of motion. Now, the sense in which this rule of impact follows from the premises with 'geometrical necessity' is this: given the nature of matter and motion, and given the sizes and speeds of the given bodies, the resulting collisions are necessary consequences (cannot be otherwise). But the most important point to grasp, for Leibniz's argument, is that there can be no consequence that is not already given in the premises. This is quite simply how a geometric argument works. You cannot conclude anything *more* than you put into it.

Now, here in the *Discourse* Leibniz describes a scenario that he claims would follow from Descartes' premises: 'it would follow, as I have shown elsewhere, that a smaller body, upon contact with a greater body at rest, would impart its speed to that body, without losing any of its own' (lns 11–13). Whether or not this scenario actually *would* follow from Descartes' premises, we can, for the sake of a deeper point, assume that it would. Leibniz's concern is that a collision law of this kind would run 'completely contrary to the formation of a system' (ln 14).

Why does Leibniz think so? Following his clue in line 11, 'as I have shown elsewhere', we are led to an earlier paper called 'On the Nature of Body and the Laws of Motion' (1678–82),[1] in which Leibniz sketches a

---

[1] AG provides the reference to this paper and it is translated in AG 245–50. The original is in AA VI, 4 N. 362, where it is titled 'Principia Mechanica Ex Metaphysicis Dependere'. That paper contains several phrases that appear here in §21.

number of scenarios that are *supposed* to follow from 'purely mechanical principles', that is, from Descartes' principles. One scenario in particular most resembles the scenario in the *Discourse*. It would follow, for Descartes, that 'a larger body at rest would be carried off by the smallest colliding body, with the same speed it has, however little that may be' (AG 249). Now, this may seem unlikely, since we would expect the smaller body to de slowed by the collision and the larger body to be moved only slightly. In fact, Leibniz takes Descartes' result to be 'utterly absurd', for, if it were true, 'the slightest bit of work would produce maximal disorder' (AG 249). This remark recalls the problem in §17: if effects are greater than their causes, then perpetual motion would result. We could imagine, then, if the Cartesian law were correct, a pool table on which a lightly struck cue ball would send its object, an 8 ball, into a series of perpetual collisions with the cushions and other balls at ever-increasing speeds. And if a *system* of such Cartesian laws were in place, then universal disorder would quickly ensue. This is likely why, Leibniz says in §21 of the *Discourse*, laws of this kind would run 'completely contrary to the formation of a system' (ln 14).

It is not likely, however, that Descartes would have failed to see such a problem with his laws. After all, as Leibniz indicates in 'On the Nature of Body', Cartesian laws have ways to prevent such outcomes. For instance, in the scenario Leibniz describes, Descartes could say that the larger body at rest would *resist* the motion of the smaller body, and thus would not be carried off by it (AG 249). This outcome would follow from Descartes' first law of nature, the law of inertia: 'that each thing, as far as it is in itself [or in its power] always remains in the same state; and that consequently, when it is once moved, it always continues to move' (*Principles* II, §37). Thus, the inertia of the body at rest would provide a measure of resistance to being moved by the colliding smaller body. Moreover, the body's inertia is measurable since inertia is a function of the body's size (*Principles* II, §43). Thus, the motion of the larger body at rest would be a function of its size, plus the speed and size of the colliding body. What would actually happen, following Descartes' laws, is that the smaller body would immediately deflect backwards, imparting *some* motion to the larger body, while losing some of its speed. Moreover, all motions could be calculated to show that the quantity of motion is conserved; thus, no absurdity of an effect greater than its cause should result.[2] The key point however is that for the laws of motion and collision to work properly, that is, to work under the general law of conservation of force, a *law of inertia* must be included as a basic principle.

---

[2] Descartes' third law of nature (*Principles* II, §40) and the fourth rule of impact (§49) are good examples of how the law of inertia is applied to colliding bodies.

But now here is the problem Leibniz finds with all of this: *from what in the nature of body* (extension) and the quantity of motion (size times speed, including direction) do you get *inertia*? While inertia is a function of a body's size (or better, density) and speed, inertia itself is not something having length, breadth, depth, or speed. It is something that *accompanies* a body's density and motion but does not have corporeal properties. The extended properties of bodies can tell us only which effects we can expect, but cannot tell us the cause of those effects, and that cause cannot be put entirely in extensional terms. Simply put, what Leibniz came to realise is that when you consider what is strictly contained in the notion of 'extension', you cannot get 'resistance to motion'. It simply does not follow. And since it does not, the Cartesian scenario cannot be 'deduced from the initially assumed notion of matter and motion' (AG 249).

Leibniz's conclusion, then, in 'On the Nature of Body', is that we must assume something 'over and above' the nature of body:

> We must recognise in bodies certain notions or forms that are immaterial, so to speak, or independent of extension, which you can call powers [*potentia*], by means of which speed is adjusted to magnitude. (AG 249–50)

To say that 'speed is adjusted to magnitude' is to say that some metaphysical force or power is required to explain how a smaller body may be slowed by a larger one, so that the effects correspond with their causes. And the explanation must be one that implies a metaphysical law: 'it is not the same quantity of motion (which misleads many) but the same powers that are conserved in the world' (AG 250). As he showed in §17, quantity of motion cannot account for the conservation of force. But the point is that the law of inertia plays the same regulatory role as the conservation law. Without the force of inertia, natural collisions would be chaotic and disordered; but with inertia, understood as a non-corporeal force, we can understand why the world *is* so well ordered, since inertia contributes to the overall conservation of force. Moreover, as we have learned, the law of conservation has theological import, since the laws of motion 'must be understood as having been produced and conserved in things by God' (AG 250). Thus, the law of the conservation of force points in the end to God's wisdom and final causes, because no other cause could explain why there should be a conservation law at all.

We can now make better sense of Leibniz's remarks in §21 of the *Discourse*. The laws of motion cannot be deduced by geometrical necessity from Cartesian notions of body and motion, because these notions do not account for the forces of inertia and resistance. Absent those forces, mechanical laws would result in absurdities and disorder. Thus, the mechanical rules run 'completely contrary to the formation of a system' (ln 14). Leibniz then concludes that 'the decree of divine wisdom to conserve always the same force and the same direction in sum has provided for this' (lns 15–6). That is, God gives to nature what Descartes does not – a system of orderly laws. Leibniz also recognises that 'direction in sum', or what we now call 'linear momentum', is conserved as well. That is, the total changes in directions of motion, such as when one body collides with another and is driven in the opposite direction, are accounted for by the conservation of force. Descartes' law of inertia cannot properly account for direction in sum. For Leibniz, conservation of force and direction can only be explained metaphysically and thus instituted by God for the purpose of maintaining order in nature.

So, yes, the 'phenomena' would certainly be entirely different (ln 2) without the wisdom of God's final causes.[3] This does not mean, however, that we should banish Cartesian mechanics and simply follow the wisdom of God. As always, Leibniz will insist that we take experimental and theoretical physics as far as we can. But at some point we will need to appeal to something metaphysical in nature, and something *purposeful*, some explanation for why the laws of nature are *this* way and not some other. And that explanation ultimately leads us to divine wisdom.

As for Leibniz's final remark, that 'the several effects of nature can be demonstrated doubly' (ln 17), that is, by efficient *and* final causes, this is shown in the following article through the example of a particular law of optics.

§22. Reconciliation of final and efficient causes, as exemplified by the laws of reflection and refraction.

In §21, Leibniz showed that the phenomena would be very different without final causes in nature, implying in fact that without them the natural world would be a much disordered place. Here in §22, Leibniz's concern is not so much to show that nature *needs* final causes, as if they must be superimposed onto efficient-mechanical causes in order to regulate them, but rather that physical laws – in this case having to do with

---

[3] There is another way to show why Leibniz thinks that Cartesian laws are 'contrary to the formation of a system'. This concerns Leibniz's principle of continuity, described in a paper written in 1687, only one year after the *Discourse*. The full title is 'A Letter of Mr Leibniz on a General Principle Useful in Explaining the Laws of Nature Through a Consideration of the Divine Wisdom: To Serve as a Reply to the Response of the Rev. Father Malebranche' (LL No. 37). The piece explains how Cartesian laws violate that principle. A more extensive account of the principle of continuity as forming the principal criticism of Descartes' laws of motion can be found in 'Critical Thoughts on the General Part of the Principles of Descartes' (1692), LL No. 42, specifically in the articles corresponding to §§40–53 of Descartes' *Principles* II.

optics – can be 'reconciled' by describing them in both efficient-mechanical and final-teleological terms. Leibniz also argues that thinking of physical laws as final causes facilitates the discovery of efficient causes.

Initially, Leibniz brings to mind a number of biological processes that are typically understood both mechanically and teleologically. The 'first tissue of an animal' (ln 7) refers to a seed's development into an embryo, while the 'whole machine of its parts' refers to the animal as an organism. The fluids that 'fortuitously' form a variety of members likely refers to the Galenic theory of physiology, in which the 'humours', the four bodily fluids (blood, yellow bile, black bile, and phlegm) play a role in the formation of various organs.[1] Thus, it is quite natural, even for us today, though having moved well beyond the theory of humours, to assume that teleological processes are responsible for the formation of animal and human organisms – their complete teleology being to maintain life. The enormous complexity of the human body, the 'divine anatomy' (ln 13) of its 206 bones and forty-two organs, is a sure indication that nothing less than intelligent design is at work. It would surely be difficult to understand this organisation strictly mechanically, that is, in terms of the sizes and motions of its various parts, without recognising how those motions contribute to the life of the organism; reciprocally, having a conception of the function of the parts facilitates an understanding of how they work mechanically. The heart pumps blood and oxygen through the body *so that* it may distribute oxygen and nutrients throughout the body, *so that* we may have life; and life is possible by means of the cardiovascular system.

Leibniz, however, wants to move beyond the sort of explanation that excludes the one or the other of these causes, since it might encourage the idea that those who maintain mechanical causes are *impious* while those who look for final causes are *superstitious*. Both causes are really one and the same, under different descriptions. He makes this case by considering two laws in the field of optics: *catoptrics* – the reflection of light in one medium against a reflecting surface, usually a mirror; and *dioptrics* – the refraction of light using lenses, or the propagation of light from one medium to another. Traditionally, optics held a great deal of interest for understanding how the eye works, accounting for optical illusions, and for understanding the very nature of light. These phenomena could increasingly be explained mathematically, geometrically, mechanically, or, as is generally put, by efficient causes. In his *Optics* (1637), Descartes explains the laws of reflection and refraction in just such terms, while Leibniz argues that their laws

---

[1] See the SEP entry on Galen.

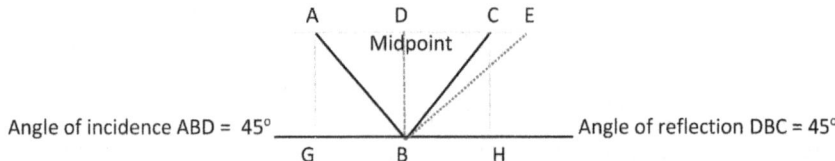

Figure 1 Reflection

can be explained as both efficient and final causes, but also that the latter provide strong evidence for the intelligence of the creator.

To see how the two causal explanations may be 'reconciled', as Leibniz claims, let us start with a brief look at Descartes' explanation of catoptrics, i.e., the reflection of light through air onto a surface (Figure 1).[2] Consider a light ray coming from point A at a 45° angle relative to the surface of a mirror (GBH). Striking point B, the ray will then reflect upward at a 45° angle to reach point C, which, incidentally, is the same height as point A. It turns out that the angle of incidence (the angle formed by ABD) is equal to the angle of reflection (DBC). This is the law of reflection. The question is *why*, since it is conceivable that from B the ray reaches some point to the left or right of point C, which would make the angle of reflection unequal to the angle of incidence. For example, if the same ray were to reach point E instead of C, the angle of reflection would be greater than 45°. The problem can be posed more generally: why, for any angle of incidence, is the angle of reflection equal to it?

Descartes' answer can be derived from his first two laws of nature: 1. 'that each thing, as far as is in its power, always remains in the same state' (*Principles* II, §37); 2. 'that all movement is, of itself, along straight lines' (*Principles* II, §39). Thus, in this case, the motion of the ray from A to B is simultaneously composed of two straight lines (which he calls 'determina-tions'): straight down from A to the surface at G; and straight across from A to the right toward C. These lines describe the tendencies of direction due to the second law of nature. An object on a left to right trajectory will continue in that direction, while an object in a downward trajectory will continue downward. When the ray is pointed at a 45° angle to the surface, the two directional tendencies combine to determine the ray to strike point B at 45°. As for the angle of reflection, since the mirror's surface prevents the ray from continuing in its downward determination, the ray contin-ues in its rightward determination. But why should it continue at 45°?

---

[2] See Descartes, *Optics*, Discourses 1 and 2. To simplify the explanations that follow, I change Descartes' scenario from that of the trajectory of tennis balls to rays of light.

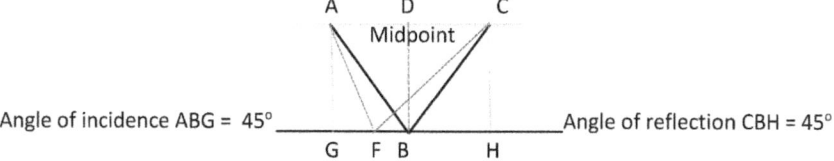

Figure 2 Reflection

Descartes' answer is that the ray will advance from B to C with the same speed it had from A to B; thus, 'it will continue to move as far as is in its power' (*Optics* II, 77); that is, in accord with the first law of nature. Thus, since the ray can travel only upward, it will travel as far from midpoint D as A is from D, making the angle of reflection 45°. From this we get the law of reflection, that the angles of incidence and reflection are equal. This is a strictly mechanical, efficient causal, explanation of the phenomenon of reflection, according to Descartes.

Descartes' explanation of refraction (dioptrics) is a bit more complex; but we need to have some idea of it, since Leibniz says that its demonstration by efficient causes is not as good as Snell's demonstration from final causes (ln 52). Descartes claims (correctly) that when light travels from air and enters into a denser medium (in this case, water), the ray will not continue in its determination, but will decline toward the vertical line (see Fig. 3). He accounts for this downward refraction by postulating (mistakenly) that light travels with less resistance and thus faster through a denser medium. We can ignore Descartes' mistake. All that matters for our purposes is that his explanation is purely mechanical. It does not suppose any qualities, substantial forms, or, most importantly, goals, purposes, or intentions. Light behaviour is explained strictly by its extensional and motive properties and those of the media through which it passes.

Leibniz gives his own accounts of reflection and refraction in a paper published in 1682, four years prior to the *Discourse*.[3] For reflection (catoptrics), light will take the 'easiest', which turns out to mean the 'shortest', route. But Leibniz proves this claim both mechanically and teleologically. Suppose that a light ray is to travel from its source at A to its end point C, by way of some reflection point on the surface of mirror

---

[3] *Unicum Opticae Catoptricae et Dipotricae Principiuum* (A Unitary Principle of Optics, Catoptrics and Dioptrics), *Acta Eruditorum*, June 1682. Trans. Jeffrey K. McDonough (LU). For more about teleology in physics see Leibniz's *Tentamen Anagogicum* ['Anagogical Testament'], LL No. 50, and McDonough 2009. For analysis see McDonough 2022, especially Ch. 1.

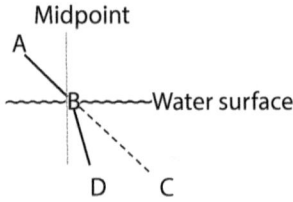

ABC = Path of light through only one medium
ABD = Path of light through air and water

Figure 3 Refraction

GBH (see Figure 2). The question is: where on the mirror will the light strike in order to reach C? Only one route is the shortest, ABC, and that is the path the light actually takes. In fact, any other reflection point will result in a longer path, as for example AFC. Now it just so happens that for the shortest path the angle of incidence (ABG) is equal to the angle of reflection (CBH).[4] Thereby the path of light reflecting off a hard surface and through one medium such as air can then be expressed in efficient-mechanical terms as a general law: the angles of incidence and of reflection are equal. But the 'final cause' explanation for the path is that light always takes the shortest path. Both expressions are equally valid expressions of the law of reflection. The sense in which the 'law of the shortest' expresses a final cause is that light naturally tends to complete the path in the most efficient or parsimonious way. That is, light, and nature in general, will do no more than is required, and certainly no less, to achieve a certain effect. Moreover, Leibniz seems to think that you could discover the law sooner by first considering the likely final cause. From there, you can derive the efficient-mechanical cause.

In refraction (dioptrics), shown in Figure 3, if the light ray were to pass through only one medium, say, air, it would maintain its trajectory (ABC). But passing from air into water, the water's thicker density resists the ray, pitching it downward toward the vertical (midpoint) line (ABD). This is why we see an oar 'bend' in the water. In answer to the question, why does light bend toward the vertical?, Leibniz simply says that it takes the 'easiest' or least difficult path. But this can be given a mechanical explanation: the easiest path is the length of path AB times the resistance coefficient of air, *plus* the length of path BD times the resistance coefficient of water. Leibniz however is not clear on how or why this path is the least difficult. He simply concludes that the laws of both reflection and

---

[4] Leibniz locates the angles of incidence and reflection in his figure differently than Descartes does; however, this makes no difference because the angles are still equal.

refraction can be reduced to one principle 'taken from final causes' (LU); namely, the law of the easiest path; *and* they can be explained equally well *mechanically* – as he thinks they should be.

The demonstration of the laws of catoptrics and dioptrics shows that the phenomena can be explained by both final and efficient causes. We should not take this to mean that light itself somehow has the intention or knowledge to take this path, or that God, by some magical intervention, made the light behave this way. Rather, 'the creator of things created light so that from its nature that most beautiful event would arise' (LU).

As indicated, Leibniz argues that consideration of final causes facilitates the discovery of efficient causes. He cites the method of 'the ancients' (namely of Heliodorus of Larissa, a fourth-century Greek mathematician, whose *Optics* may have been the first to posit the law of reflection in final cause terms, specifically in terms of economy and uniformity[5]) as having facilitated the discovery of the laws of refraction. In 1621, Willebrord Snell also used this method to compose a mechanical law of refraction now known as 'Snell's Law', and in 1662 Pierre Fermat postulated that light will take the path of 'the least time', thereby discovering Snell's Law independently. Finally, Leibniz suspects, Descartes also utilised this method, deriving it (or borrowing it without attribution) from Snell in order to develop his own mechanical account of refraction. Thus, even Descartes, by 'borrowing' from Snell, has made good use of final causes.

Perhaps a more convincing case for final causes in optics can be found in Leibniz's 'Anagogical Testament' of 1696 (LL No. 50), although his interest in the reconciliation of efficient and final causes ranges far beyond his interest in optics, as is well expressed in this passage from his 1695 *Specimen of Dynamics*:

> In general we must hold that everything in the world can be explained in two ways: through the *kingdom of power*, that is, through *efficient causes*, and through the *kingdom of wisdom*, that is, through *final causes*, through God, governing bodies for his glory, like an architect, governing them as machines that follow the *laws of size* or *mathematics*, governing them, indeed, for the use of souls . . . through *laws of goodness* or *moral laws*. These two kingdoms everywhere interpenetrate each other without confusing or disturbing their laws, so that the greatest obtains in the kingdom of power at the same time as the best in the kingdom of wisdom. (AG 126–7)

Thus, final and efficient causes are described as reigning in two distinct kingdoms, each having independent validity but also a strict correspondence or harmony with the other, such that every efficient cause

---

[5] Eastwood 1970.

has a final cause description, and every final cause has an efficient cause description.[6]

§23. The nature of ideas; how God acts on the understanding; and how ideas can be illusory: a critique of Descartes' supposed proof for God's existence.

As made clear in the opening passages of this article, Leibniz's case for final causes is important both for restoring natural philosophy to its theological place, and for elevating the minds of natural philosophers to a metaphysical place, specifically, to the place of immaterial principles in physics. In articles 23 to 29, Leibniz offers a similar restoration and elevation – though not having to do with natural philosophy but instead with knowledge. These articles comprise the 'epistemological' part of the *Discourse*, since they are concerned with the nature of ideas, the degrees of knowledge, and how knowledge may be acquired. Leibniz's positions implicitly engage his contemporaries Descartes, Nicolas Malebranche, and Antoine Arnauld on the idea of God, on the relationships among ideas, the senses, and God, and whether and in what sense we possess *innate* ideas prior to experience or whether all knowledge is gained from experience. The questions raised at line 15, 'whether we see all things in God, and how God is our light', will not be answered until §28 and §29. In this article, his objective is similar to that of §1, where he was concerned to determine whether the idea of a *perfection* is a coherent idea; but now he aims to determine whether the idea of God as *having all perfections* is a coherent idea.

First of all, what is an idea? Leibniz does not answer this question directly in the *Discourse*, but we can derive an answer from his brief essay called 'What is an Idea?' (1678). 'First of all, by the term *idea* we understand *something which is in our mind.*' It is not a part of the brain, 'but something other than the brain or a more subtle part of it' (LL 206). Neither are ideas identical with thoughts, perceptions, and affections, although these do not occur without ideas. Notably, Leibniz does not define 'idea' as we might expect, simply as *an object of thought*, or a representation of something. He emphasises rather that an idea is a *faculty* or power of thinking; thus, 'we are said to have an idea of a thing even if we do not think of it, if only, on a given occasion, we can think of it' (LL 206).

This last statement could relate to his doctrine of 'innate ideas', which will be discussed in §26 and §27. Nevertheless, ideas are *expressions* or representations of other things when they have 'relations to the thing expressed'. In §9 we saw that two things are said to 'express' each other

---

[6] See also *Monadology* §79; *Principles of Nature and Grace* §3; and McDonough 2008.

when a one-to-one correspondence could be shown to hold between them. But how can we find corresponding relations between ideas and things, or between ideas? Perhaps Leibniz's conception of ideas is best summed up here:

> That the ideas of things are in us means therefore nothing but that God, the creator alike of the things and of the mind, has impressed a power of thinking upon the mind so that it can by its own operations derive what corresponds perfectly to the nature of things. Although, therefore, the idea of a circle is not similar to a circle, truths can be derived from it which would be confirmed by investigating a real circle. (LL 208)

This passage expresses what is characteristic of how he treats ideas in articles 23–29: as a power of thinking dependent upon God to some degree, but also belonging to us alone. This also means that our ideas, or thinking power, can be made more clear and distinct by investigating the relations between ideas and things. Now, this may work very well for our ideas of *sensible* things, such as circles, but how shall we investigate the ideas of *insensible* things, such as God? Such an investigation can only be *intellectual*, and this is exactly the sort of investigation Leibniz intends to carry out in this article.

Let us recall that in §1 Leibniz was most concerned with whether the ideas that we suppose we have of things can be ideas at all – ideas of things that *could* exist but may not. As he points out there, and here, we may mistakenly believe we have an idea of a perfection, just as we mistakenly believe we have ideas of the greatest number or figure (§1, lns 13–14), or, here at lines 25–6, 'the ultimate degree of speed' and 'the intersection of the conchoid with its base'.[1] These ideas are inherently contradictory; thus, while at first they may seem to be ideas of real things, they cannot be ideas of anything.

Leibniz is similarly concerned with the idea of *a being having all perfections*, as well as with how this idea functions as a premise in a well-known argument for God – an argument that still garners a fair amount of attention today. It is commonly called the 'ontological argument' because it claims that God's existence (*ontas* in Greek) is demonstrated (proven) from the *very idea* (essence) of God, in this case, the idea of a being having all perfections. Now, Leibniz wants to determine whether this idea of God is a *possible* idea. To put it more precisely, he wants to determine whether it is even possible for such a being to exist; for if not, then of course the ontological argument fails. But if such a being *is* possible, then the argument shows, not only that God exists, but, rather surprisingly, that God *necessarily* exists. That we can prove the possibility of a thing through its

---

[1] The intersection can never occur. See footnote 6 of §XXIII.

idea may initially appear dubious, while the claim to derive necessity from mere possibility looks like a mistake, if not a logical trick. But let us take a closer look at this famous argument for God, the version of which Leibniz has in mind from Descartes' *Meditations*:[2]

1. I have an idea of God.
2. This idea is that of a being having all perfections.
3. Existence is a perfection.
4. Therefore, God exists.

This is a deceptively simple argument. A common initial reaction is that something is obviously wrong with it: it uses circular reasoning, wishful thinking, or it is simply incredible. Can you really prove that God exists with a few brief statements? These are good questions. But note that the argument is structurally valid – *if* the premises are true, the conclusion cannot be false. So, the crucial question is whether the premises are in fact true – or at least, as Leibniz insists, logically coherent. If one of them is incoherent or false, then the conclusion cannot be certain.

Examining premises 2 and 3 will help us understand the argument and give it its due.[3] As for 2, to speak of an idea of a thing means, in this case, to speak of the *essence* of a thing, that is, the attributes that make the thing what it is, such that if the thing did not have those attributes, it would not be that thing. In this sense, an idea contains the *necessary attributes* of the thing. For example, the essence of a triangle is that of a three-sided, enclosed, figure.[4] If the figure did not have this essence, it would not be a triangle. In the same way, it is said to be essential (necessary) to the idea of God that God have all perfections. To deny this would be to misunderstand what the essence of God is – just as to deny the essence of a triangle would be to misunderstand what the essence of a triangle is. You may want to dispute this conception of God, but it is a traditional and well-considered conception, and Leibniz accepts it. He just wants to show it is a coherent conception.

---

[2] The most well-known versions of the ontological argument are given by Anselm (*Proslogion*) and Descartes (*Meditation* V and *Principles* I, §14).

[3] For the sake of brevity, I will set aside premise 1, since the question of whether one can even have an idea *of God* is complicated.

[4] Descartes' comparative example is actually that of a property of a triangle: 'It is quite evident that existence can no more be separated from the essence of God than the fact that its three angles equal two right angles can be separated from the essence of a triangle [. . .]. Hence it is just as much of a contradiction to think of God (that is, a supremely perfect being) lacking existence (that is, lacking a perfection)' (*Meditation* V, CSM II, 107 / AT 66).

Now, what is a perfection? As we saw in §1, a perfection is a quality or attribute *capable of a highest, or maximal, degree*. At this point, we need only mention three perfections typically attributed to God: omniscience, omnipotence, and omnibenevolence. These perfections, among others, are said to constitute God's essence. Again, this idea is not something that theologians and philosophers simply made up to suit themselves; rather, when you seriously think about what God is *in essence*, you will be hard-pressed to deny that these perfections must be included. Now consider one more.

As for premise 3, it may seem odd to think of *existence* as a perfection, and while this premise is often disputed nowadays, several seventeenth-century philosophers, including Descartes and Leibniz, thought it perfectly acceptable. The simplest way to understand it is to say that if something lacked existence, then it could in no way be perfect, since it would lack the very attribute that would allow it to *be*; so, if a thing is to be perfect, it must at least exist. But this does not really capture the sense in which existence is thought to be a perfection. As said above, a perfection is a quality or attribute *capable of a highest, or maximal, degree*. We should add that existence is a *positive* quality, as is, for example, *omniscience*, as opposed to a quality that is the negation of a positive quality, such as ignorance or non-being. The thinking here is that only positive qualities can be perfections, because only they can have maximal reality (negations are considered not to have reality). In this way, existence can be understood positively, as a higher degree of *reality*. Bear with me.

Recall from §1 and §13 that a thing *possibly* exists if it is conceivable, that is, if we have a non-contradictory idea of it.[5] For instance, you can conceive of a one-horned horse (a unicorn). Thus, while a unicorn does not exist, it *possibly* exists, since there is no contradiction in its idea. Notice, however, that your idea or conception of a unicorn has a certain *reality* to it – in other words, possible things have a certain degree of reality, namely *as ideas* existing in our mind. However, possible things do not have a *maximal* degree of reality; they do not *exist*, in the sense that, as imaginary beings, they have neither causal interaction with nor presence among things external to the mind.[6] Such 'possibilia', or 'possibly existing things' as we may call them, thus have *less reality* than actually existing things, while actually existing things have *maximal* reality.[7] Now consider that a perfection,

---

[5] As Leibniz says in his well-known essay, 'Meditations on Knowledge, Truth, and Ideas' (1684), 'an idea is true when its notion is possible and false when it includes a contradiction' (AG 26).

[6] It is difficult to say what it means for something to exist, but I find this way of distinguishing mental things from extra-mental things rather plausible and clarifying.

[7] Strictly speaking, not everything that exists has maximal reality, since some existing things have more reality than others. While God is said to have maximal reality because

according to Leibniz, is a positive quality capable of a maximal degree of reality, and that existence is a quality having a greater degree of reality than possibility. Therefore, existence is a perfection.[8] Now, this is not to say that every existing thing is perfect, but it is to say that anything that exists has, at least, the perfection of existence.

So, the 'ontological argument' can be understood like this: God, having all perfections, with existence being one of the perfections, necessarily exists – necessarily, because existence is an attribute of God's essence, and a thing cannot be what it is without its essential attributes. As is often pointed out, this argument depends on the claim that existence is inseparable from God's essence, and some have raised the objection that by this argument anything could be said to have existence as part of its essence and therefore anything could be proven to exist, which seems crazy and pointless. For example, I might claim that I have an idea of 'the greatest island', and for something to be the greatest, it must at least exist; therefore, the greatest island exists.[9] Arguably, however, this objection falls flat when you consider that it is arbitrary, rather than necessary, to attach the idea of 'greatest' to the idea of 'island'. There is nothing in the conception of an island *itself* that requires or implies 'greatest'. A triangle necessarily has three sides; a unicorn necessarily has one horn; an island necessarily is a body of land surrounded by water. Granted, the reality of any of these things would be increased by bestowing them with existence. But nothing in the conception of these things, nothing in their essence or nature, implies 'the greatest', 'perfect', 'having all perfections' or 'exists'. These things remain what they are *in idea* without having 'greatness' or existence. Yet the very idea of God is exactly that of a being having all perfections, one of which is existence. No idea of anything else has existence included in its very conception. So only God necessarily exists.

It is worth pursuing by all means any conceivable scruple against this argument – as many thinkers have for centuries. But at this point this version of the ontological argument should at least appear more convincing than it did at first, and we are now prepared to examine Leibniz's own scruple, for while he ultimately accepts the argument, he warns that is it 'very imperfect' (ln 20). His reasons for this scruple have already been suggested, but to see exactly what they consist of, let us recall the argument:

God has all of the positive attributes in their maximal degree, the following beings have progressively fewer attributes and thus lesser reality: angels, souls, humans, animals, plants, and rocks.

[8] See Leibniz's Letter to Arnold Eckhard (1677) for some clarifying remarks on this proof (LL 177 and Adams 1994: 120–1).

[9] This is roughly Gaunilo's objection to Anselm's argument.

1. I have an idea of God.
2. This idea is that of a being having all perfections.
3. Existence is a perfection.

Therefore, God exists. But while Leibniz accepts 2 and 3 in principle, he suggests, though not explicitly, that premise 2 has not been proven. And here is his problem: it has not been shown that the idea of a being having all perfections is an idea of a *possibly existing being*. As he remarks, we may believe we have the idea of 'the ultimate degree of speed' (ln 25), but we actually do not, because the idea is contradictory. So, if the ontological argument will stand as a true demonstration that God exists, we will need to show that the idea expressed in premise 2 contains no contradiction, because contradiction is the mark of impossibility (as non-contradiction is the mark of possibility).

Let us be sure we understand what it would take to determine whether premise 2 contains a contradiction. Consider the three theistic perfections cited above: omniscience, omnipotence, and omnibenevolence. Leibniz is asking whether it is logically possible for a being to possess these perfections, plus any others, simultaneously. To know this, we must (1) first inspect each of these ideas to make sure that none are contradictory in themselves; and then (2) see whether they contradict each other. So (1) how might 'omnipotence', the idea of an all-powerful being, contain a contradiction? Well, just as there can be no 'greatest number' we might have to admit that there can be no greatest power, for some *greater* power may always be conceived. If so, the attribute is contradictory (impossible) and therefore nothing can have it – end of story. But for sake of argument let us suppose, as Leibniz does, that 'omnipotence' does not contain a contradiction (and neither do the other perfections – after all, we should know from §1 that omnipotence and omniscience can each be understood in a way that does not admit of a contradiction).

Now that we are sure that these ideas are not internally contradictory, we still need to show (2) that none of God's perfections contradict *each other*, such that God *could* have all perfections. In fact, in a paper written in 1676, ten years prior to the *Discourse*, Leibniz claims to demonstrate, on behalf of the ontological argument, or what he calls the argument from 'the most-perfect being', that all perfections are logically compatible, and thus that such a being is possible.[10] This demonstration, I submit, is what he has in mind when he says here in the *Discourse*, 'one can boast of having an idea of the thing, when one is assured of its possibility' (lns 29–30). This demonstration is not simple, but runs as follows:

---

[10] The paper is titled 'Quod Ens Perfectissimum Existit' [That a Most-Perfect Being Exists] (LGP 7, 261–2), translated as 'Two Notations for Discussion with Spinoza', in LL No. 14, 167.

1. A perfection is an absolutely simple, positive, and maximum quality.
2. Thus, insofar as perfections have no negation or limitation (implied in premise 1), *all perfections are compatible.*
3. Therefore, it is possible that all perfections co-exist in the same subject, and this subject is God.

Leibniz explains the proof this way: Premise 2, 'all perfections are compatible', would be false if the proposition, 'perfections A and B are incompatible', were necessary. For this proposition to be necessary, it must either be *proven*, or known through itself (*per se notae*, or self-evident). Proving it would require that both A and B be analysed. But by premise 1, perfections are un-analysable ('absolutely simple' entails no further constituents to analyse); so, the proposition cannot be proven. But then neither is the proposition self-evidently true. Therefore, the proposition is not necessarily true. Therefore, since it is not necessary that A and B are incompatible, it is *possible* that A and B are compatible (according to the logic of modality, if a proposition is not necessary, it is possible); furthermore, the same result obtains for any combination of perfections. Therefore, since it is possible that 'all perfections are compatible', 'there is or can be conceived to be a subject of all perfections or a most perfect being', namely, God (LL 167). In other words, it is possible that God, understood as having all perfections, exists.

It should be pointed out, however, that the move from the possibility of compatibility to the possibility of a *subject* of the compatibility is not explained. For while all perfections may be compatible, nothing in the premises gives us a *subject* of all perfections, nor that this subject is God. Nevertheless, we can assume that a subject of all perfections is at least possible. In any case, Leibniz believes that his argument for the compatibility of all perfections makes the ontological argument valid and sound: since the idea of God is possible, 'it is obvious that he also exists, since existence is included in the number of perfections'. He says he showed this proof to 'Mr Spinoza' who agreed it was sound (LL 167).

Now that we understand how Leibniz can more firmly claim that the idea of God (in the ontological argument) *is* the idea of a possible being, we can see how in the *Discourse* he takes the final step. If the idea of God is *possible*, then God necessarily exists (ln 31). But how can something that possibly exists necessarily exist? From what has been said we should be able to figure it out. Once it is shown that the idea of God is possible, and we accept that these perfections constitute God's essence, and that existence is a perfection, God necessarily exists. If God did not have existence, then this idea would not be an idea of God. The import of this conclusion is that, unlike every other being, which only *possibly* exists,

God necessarily, unavoidably, exists, because God is the only being whose existence is included in his essence. And yet, this necessity is proven from the logical possibility of God's essence. In sum, as Leibniz says, 'this is in fact an excellent privilege of the divine nature, to have need only of its possibility or essence to exist actually' (lns 31–3).[11] Thus, God is the only being that exists necessarily from itself, by virtue of its own nature, not by any other being.

I encourage the reader to work through any problems she may find with these ideas, proofs, and their presentation. Leibniz's more general point is that doing so will result in better ideas than will simply taking their truth or falsity for granted. If we are to reason properly with ideas, we must inspect them carefully – by demonstrating their conceptual possibility – to make sure that they are at least ideas of possibly existing things. If we do not, we risk reasoning with nonsense.

§24. The degrees and varieties of ideas and knowledge: Ideas clear, confused, distinct, adequate, intuitive, and suppositive. Definitions: nominal, real, causal, and essential.

Leibniz has just shown us how to reason with ideas of *possible* things, especially things of which we do not have sense experience. Now he will show us how to reason with ideas we obtain from sense experience. This article deals with epistemology (the theory of knowledge) more generally, since it presents a kind of taxonomy of 'varieties' of knowledge, or rather, a scale of degrees of cognition, ranging from 'confused' to 'clear' to 'intuitive'. The article is largely taken from a more comprehensive work, 'Meditations on Knowledge, Truth, and Ideas', published two years prior to the *Discourse* and cited by him many times throughout his career.[1] In that work, Leibniz alludes to a dispute between Antoine Arnauld and Nicolas Malebranche on the nature of ideas,[2] and explicitly identifies Descartes' view on ideas as 'not altogether satisfactory' (AG 23). Thus, Leibniz's purpose in that paper and this article is to set the record straight on what ideas are and how they function in our thinking and knowledge. Since Descartes' notion of 'clear and distinct ideas' forms the starting point of the problem – indeed, it forms the starting point of Modern epistemology, it would help to know something of Descartes' famous formulation.

---

[11] On this point see Leibniz's letter to Seckendorff, May 1685, translated in this volume.

[1] *Meditationes de Cognitione, Veritate, et Ideis* (AA VI, 4 N. 141, 585), published in *Acta Eruditorum*, November 1684, translated in AG and LL.

[2] Arnauld's *On True and False Ideas* (1683), a rather prickly rebuttal to Malebranche's theory of ideas in *Search after Truth* (1678). The nature of this dispute will be described in §28.

In his *Discourse on Method*, Descartes' first rule of method for reasoning in the sciences is this: 'to include nothing more in my judgments than what presented itself to my mind so clearly and distinctly that I had no occasion to doubt it' (CSM I, 120 / AT VI, 18). Throughout *Meditations* II and III, Descartes argues that he (or the meditator) has a clear and distinct idea of himself as a thinking, existing, being, as well as a clear and distinct idea of God, whereas, he argues, he does *not* have a distinct idea of the objects he perceives through his senses, including his own body. In *Principles of Philosophy*, he offers an important definition, which generally states the condition in which a 'certain and indubitable judgment' must be drawn, namely, from a perception that is both clear and distinct:

> I call a perception 'clear' when it is present and accessible to the attentive mind – just as we say that we see something clearly when it is present to the eye's gaze and stimulates it with a sufficient degree of strength and accessibility. I call a perception 'distinct' if, as well as being clear, it is so sharply separated from all other perceptions that it contains within itself only what is clear. (*Principles* I, §45)

For example, the perception of a pain is clear, since it is present and accessible to the conscious mind; however, it is not distinct, since in a judgment we often 'confuse' the sensation of pain with the wound that caused it (*Principles* I, §46). That is, we tend naturally to assume that bodily states are identical with mental states like pain. However – and this is part of a larger and deeply consequential argument for Descartes – bodily states are quite *distinct* from the sensations we have of them. In any case, his definition amounts to this: to have a clear and distinct idea is for all perceptions to be 'clear' to consciousness. The reader need not wonder why Leibniz finds Descartes' formulation unsatisfactory. From the beginning it has been criticised for being less than clear and distinct.[3]

Now that we have some sense of the problem, let us turn to Leibniz's attempt in the *Discourse* to provide a more rigorous account of knowledge. It helps to think of concepts (notions) as 'containers' of other concepts, or rather as sets of embedded conceptual entailments, which require clarification through definition and analysis of the logical relations between these concepts. As a brief example, the concept of a ring contains the concept of a circle, and the latter in turn contains the concept of shape. It will be seen that cognition begins with a clear but confused sense experience and increases in clarity by degrees, by means of the logical analysis of

---

[3] See Mersenne in Descartes' *Objections and Replies*, 'Second Set of Objections' (CSM II, 90 / AT VII, 126). For a recent and thorough attempt to explain Descartes' formulation, see Paul 2020.

concepts, until an 'adequate' cognition is attained.[4] But there is very little we can claim to know fully, simply by declaring it very well present to consciousness.

1. *Clear, but confused cognition*: On this level, we have a clear sense impression of something, yet an impression insufficient to distinguish the thing from other things of the same type; or, the thing contains internal properties not present to consciousness. For example, I am looking at a glistening rock which I believe is a piece of gold. Thus far my cognition is *clear*; but it is *confused* because I do not have either sensual or notional (definitional) knowledge of the properties of gold. Thus, I do not know how to distinguish gold from, say, fool's gold (pyrite). Similarly, I clearly sense that some poem or painting is good (or bad), but confusedly, because I cannot articulate exactly why. Similarly, I recognise a word like *entelechy* as having something to do with Aristotelian substances, but I do not really know *what*.[5] On this initial level, cognition appears to be not much different from Descartes' clear perception, which contains indistinct perceptions yet to be made present to consciousness. But in his 'Meditations on Knowledge' Leibniz is a bit more informative. We have 'clear enough' cognition when we recognise colours, smells, and other objects of the senses; however, this knowledge is confused when we lack 'explicit marks' to distinguish the constituents of these senses. In the case of colours, such 'marks' would be intellectual: descriptions of light spectra, reflectance values, and the laws of optics. It is important to note, however, that no amount of marks will be sufficient for a clear cognition of an object of sense, without sense experience. The only way to know what the colour red looks like is to have a sense experience of it (AG 24).

2. *Clear and distinct cognition*: I can attain a distinct cognition by refining and acquiring additional sense perceptions and notional marks, as suggested above. Beyond sensations, I can have a clear and distinct cognition of things sufficient to identify a thing as a certain kind. For example, an assayer (an expert in metals) possesses the marks, both sensual and notional, such as 'heaviness, color, solubility in [nitric acid]' (AG 24), to discern gold from pyrite. But the non-expert may be able to obtain a distinct *nominal* cognition (as opposed to a *real* definition – see below). For example, I may recognise a certain plant confusedly as a flower,

---

[4] In the translation, *connoissance* is rendered as 'knowledge'. However, in the commentary I prefer to use 'cognition' rather than 'knowledge', since the former more accurately expresses the sense in which cognition is a *degree* of knowledge, whereas 'knowledge' implies certainty.

[5] Leibniz uses this example in 'Meditations on Knowledge, Truth, and Ideas'.

but with sufficient marks I can identify it as a *petunia* as distinct from a *surfinia*, or a certain tree as *coniferous* as distinct from *deciduous*, while a botanist could recognise these distinctions immediately. Regarding a poem, while I might initially, confusedly, judge it to be 'bad', I may come to judge distinctly that it is bad because the poet, say, uses mixed metaphors or bungles the meter. These differences in distinct cognition indicate that distinctness is a function of the complexity of the object. But distinctness is also relative to the level of knowledge of the perceiver. While an assayer has a nominal definition of gold, she may lack cognition of its more basic marks and definitions.

3. *Adequate cognition*: This occurs when all notions are defined down to primitive or 'indefinable' notions. Primitive notions do not require, nor can they have, any *more basic* notions to define, because they are simple – they have no parts to define. Typical examples are *being*, *substance*, *thought*, *number*, and as we saw in §23, *perfection*, understood as 'absolutely simple'.[6] Of course, additional words are used to define, understand, amplify, and elucidate these notions, but they are still considered basic because they underlie all other definitions. In 'Meditations on Knowledge', Leibniz says that primitive notions are indefinable, hence understood *intuitively*, that is, through themselves (AG 24). By 'intuitive' Leibniz likely means an immediate or non-inferential cognition for which we need no other notion in order to understand. While I may not have an explicit or discursive understanding of the terms *being*, *substance*, and *thought*, I can be brought to understand them, at least nominally, through the elucidation of other terms. But no amount of elucidation can make 'I am a thinking being' any clearer than the immediate apprehension of that truth. The point is similar to that of the cognition of a colour. As Leibniz had said, the only way to know the colour red is to experience it; similarly, the only way to know these other terms is to *be* and to *think*. But as we will see in §26 and §27, intuitive understanding depends on innate ideas.

4. *Intuitive cognition*: The only difference between adequate and intuitive cognition is that we have the latter only when the complete set of definitions, down to primitive notions, are grasped 'at once' or immediately in a single comprehension. Such a level of cognition is 'very rare' (ln 20) and Leibniz likely reserves it only for God. What is interesting but difficult to understand about intuitive cognition is that it is involved implicitly in every perception or thought, and yet it is at the same time an achievement. Every perception carries with it the implicit understanding that 'I am a thinking being' and 'here now is

---

[6] See Plaisted 2003.

a thing', while at the same time this thing in our perception is known confusedly. To have a fully intuitive cognition, however, I must have a simultaneous comprehension of every sensation and notion involved in the experience.[7] The idea is similar to Leibniz's argument in §14 that each substance expresses (confusedly) the entire universe. On the one hand I have the clearest, immediate, intuitive, cognition of myself as a thinking substance; and yet truly to understand the depth of my substance, truly to intuit my 'complete notion', would require a complete and simultaneous comprehension of my relation to everything in the universe. While of course such a comprehension is not humanly possible, a constant *increase* in cognition certainly is.

Leibniz names one more variety of cognition, although he says almost nothing about it. *Suppositive* knowledge is cognition by means of symbols, that is, through language. The likely reason it is not indicated among the degrees of knowledge is because it is most certainly involved in all of them – but also because it involves both positive and negative qualities. The *Discourse* cursorily assigns to it a rather deflated status: most of human knowledge is 'confused or merely suppositive' (ln 21). But in his published essay, the suppositive is paired with intuitive cognition as a type of *adequate* cognition: 'adequate knowledge is either symbolic or intuitive'; and then *symbolic plus intuitive* cognition is called 'absolutely perfect' (AG 23). But then symbolic thinking is also considered 'blind' (AG 25). What is going on?

The tension between the characterisations of suppositive cognition as 'confused', 'intuitive', and 'blind' can be clarified by considering that suppositive knowledge is a matter of degree. That is, the quality of suppositive knowledge depends on how well we understand the notions that we symbolise – and for the most part, we simply do not fully cognise what the symbols represent. In 'Meditations on Knowledge' (and in the next article), Leibniz illustrates this with the idea of a chiliagon, a figure having a thousand equal sides. When we use the term without considering its constituent notions such as 'side' and 'figure', or indeed whenever we use a term to stand in place of an idea, we use it 'blindly' (AG 25) – which of course we do all the time. But then it follows that blind thinking becomes distinct cognition as soon as we reflect and become cognisant of the implied notions, right down to the primitives. The implication seems to be that language can both facilitate knowledge and lead us astray. As Leibniz argued at length in the previous article (and in the 'Meditations'), ideas, or notions, must be examined to determine their possibility. If we reason with

---

[7] On intuition in Leibniz see Picone 2008.

impossible notions, we reason with nonsense – but once we have defined our notions down to primitives and cleared away any impossibility, we can reason with perfect intuition.

Leibniz makes some additional refinements in his taxonomical epistemology by adding a taxonomy of definitions. (1) A *nominal* definition, as indicated above, is one that is sufficient to identify a thing, but not sufficient to determine whether the thing is *possible*. A subtle dig is made at Hobbes (lns 35–7), whom Leibniz takes to be a nominalist about ideas. As Leibniz claims in an earlier work, Hobbes maintains that truth, or the ideas and notions representing it, depends on definitions, which is fine. But since definitions depend on human will, the content of ideas is determined by whatever we conventionally decide it is.[8] For Leibniz, this is not fine, since ideas possess a reality in themselves apart from how we define them. Thus, for a definition to count as an item of true knowledge, its content must ultimately be brought to light through a *real* definition.[9]

(2) A real definition involves three degrees of possibility: (a) a thing can be defined as *merely* possible when it actually exists, since existence is a sure mark of possibility; (b) a definition is both *real* and *causal* when the possibility of the thing is given by experience *and* we have *a priori* proof of its possibility; for example, as when we have experience of a triangle and a demonstration of its properties; (c) finally, we have a *perfect* or *essential* definition when every notion has been analysed down to primitives (as, for example, in the possibility of a being having all perfections). It is notable that the highest degree of real definition is the one most removed from concrete existence. The implication is not that concretely existing things have lesser ontological value, but rather that *knowing* what they are is a matter of pure intellection. One notable exception to this scheme, as indicated above in regard to colours, is that it is not possible to have intellectual cognition of sensory experiences themselves. One must actually have those experiences to know the object's sensible properties. But to understand what those experiences are *of*, the object itself, one must have full intellectual cognition of its discursive notions, right down to primitives.

Here in §24, Leibniz does not provide a comprehensive account of his epistemology (it is not clear that he formulated a comprehensive account, anyway), but is concerned only to construct a workable taxonomy of cognition types in response to Descartes' famous, influential, and unclear

---

[8] 'Preface to an Edition of Nizolius', LL No. 6. Leibniz makes Hobbes out to be a 'super-nominalist' for making ideas identical to their names, as if numbers could change value according to a change in notation. But the charge against Hobbes is not accurate.

[9] The distinction between nominal and real in 'Meditations on Knowledge' is somewhat different from his account in §VIII, where nominal is the basic ostensive description of the thing, while a real definition gives us the essence.

criterion for truth as 'clear and distinct' perception. As Leibniz says in 'Meditations on Knowledge':

> Nor do I see that the people of our day have abused any less the principle that they have laid down, that *whatever I clearly and distinctly perceive about a thing is true or is assertable of the thing in question.* For, often, what is obscure and confused seems clear and distinct to people in careless judgment. Therefore, this axiom is useless unless we use criteria for the clear and distinct, criteria which we have made explicit, and unless we have established the truth of the ideas. (AG 26–7)

In sum, knowledge (or cognition) begins with a relatively raw experience that is nevertheless always imbued with a degree of intellectual cognition, and proceeds through both experience and definition, down to primitive notions. What is distinctive about Leibniz's account is its inclusion of a comprehensive definitional structure, which reveals that knowledge requires much more than what is present to an attentive mind, since what is present contains an infinite multitude, which, to be *known intuitively*, that is, non-inferentially, must be fully defined. In this way, Leibniz, rather than Descartes, clearly and distinctly sets out the possibilities and limits of our knowledge.

§25. Symbolised ideas require contemplation.

This article adds little to the previous, except to elaborate a bit on suppositive cognition. Leibniz repeats his observation from §23 that we have no notion of impossible ideas (ln 3), but also suggests that suppositive cognition makes us all the more susceptible to being misled. The likely reason is that since suppositive cognition is subtended by abstract and arbitrary symbols (for example, language), we do not actually cognise all of what is included in the whole idea, as when we think of a chiliagon without counting its sides, or of an equation without checking whether its constituents actually sum up. Cognition consists rather in 'contemplating' the ideas supposed to stand for those signs. *Contemplation*, in turn, consists not only in clearing the notion of any internal or external contradictions, but in examining its *compatibility* with other notions. Incompatibility is not, however, identical, logically speaking, to contradiction. For example, justice can be incompatible with happiness, but does not contradict it. Telling a lie for personal gain is compatible with pleasure, but not with ethics. A slanted rhombus cannot be inscribed within a true circle; physics without law is incompatible with order, but still possible – and a thousand other incompatibilities. Compatibility requires much more nuanced criteria potentially involving an infinity of considerations. On a simpler level, lack of contemplation may leave us mistaken about the true content of an idea. Only when we have intuitive cognition do we grasp the whole of what is quietly assumed as underlying the symbolic representation of notions.

A line struck from the very end of the original manuscript provides a hint to what follows. But it is consistent with what has been said in several places: that the soul is confusedly omniscient. Let us see just how so.

§26. That we already have all ideas in us; and on Plato's doctrine of reminiscence.

Articles 26–29 focus on (a) whether we already have ideas within our soul; (b) whether they are acquired through experience; and (c) whether they are objects of thought in our mind *or*, rather, in the mind of God. On each of these positions Leibniz takes his characteristically eclectic stand, by finding a bit of truth and falsity in each one. Yes, we do possess all ideas already, but not explicitly; yes, ideas are acquired through experience, but our understanding of them depends on the ideas we already possess; and yes, we understand all things through the ideas that are *in God*, but also through the ideas we already possess. In this way, too, Leibniz takes a position between and among Plato, Aristotle, Malebranche, and Arnauld, and depends largely on the doctrine of expression he broached in §14 (that the soul contains and expresses God and the whole universe). His discussion also provides some insight into the debate over 'innate ideas' as it concerned his contemporaries Descartes and Locke, but it also anticipates contemporary linguistic theory. While Leibniz does not argue for anything like a universal grammar, as contemporary linguist Noam Chomsky has, he does argue that we implicitly or 'confusedly' possess ideas that form the basis of knowledge that we do acquire and express distinctly – and this relationship is analogous to the relationship between the 'deep structure' of linguistic knowledge and the 'surface structure' of the language we speak.[1]

---

[1] See Chomsky's *Cartesian Linguistics* (2009a [1966]). Chomsky cites §26 of the *Discourse* specifically for having indicated the fundamental feature of language and thought – that the surface structure of language (or what we think distinctly) depends on a deep structure, which is known unconsciously, or confusedly (see 2009a: 63 and note 111). In *Aspects of the Theory of Syntax*, Chomsky cites passages from Leibniz's *New Essays* he takes to make the case for innate ideas (1965: Ch. 1, §8). Chomsky's basic supposition is what he calls the Poverty of Stimulus argument, or Plato's Problem (Chomsky 1988: 3–4), which is that experience supplies insufficient data for learning the complex grammar (of sounds, syntax, and semantics) that constitute knowledge of a language.

To begin his complex argument, Leibniz distinguishes two ways of conceiving of an idea. (1) An idea is the object of thought only when we think it. Consider for example that you now have the idea of an elephant. This idea contains both sensory and conceptual elements (greyish, has a trunk, is a mammal, etc.). Each time you have that idea, you have a new but similar idea of the elephant. Ideas may also contain only abstract elements, such as *justice* and *beauty*, or both abstract and sensory elements, such as *the beautiful elephant*. The main point is that ideas exist only insofar as they are thought by a mind. In contemporary terms, this may be called a conceptual or psychologistic account of ideas.

(2) Others say that the object of thought is a permanent idea, which exists without us even when it is not thought. Leibniz thinks this is mostly right, since ideas have their reality and permanent residence in the mind of God. But he also thinks that our soul contains permanent ideas already, whether we are thinking them or not. This is because according to his doctrine of expression, our soul expresses to some degree God and everything that exists. So, the idea of the elephant, or of justice, is in your soul whether you are thinking it or not. The thought you are now having of an elephant is the idea you have in (1), except you are having a thought that resembles a more abstract or general idea of an elephant in your soul (or, if not of an elephant, then some more basic ideas the mind employs to construct the idea of an elephant – more on how this may work, below). Thus, it is possible that your conscious thought of an elephant is a confused, inadequate, or mistaken idea of the general, and true, idea of an elephant. The same holds for abstract generalisations, such as the idea of justice. I may believe, like Plato's Thrasymachus, that 'justice is to serve the interest of the stronger' (*Republic*, 338c–347e). But through a process of reflection, discussion, and logical refutation I can arrive at the true idea of justice that is contained in my soul.[2] The true ideas of things lie within my soul and yours; we need only experience and reflection to bring them to the light of consciousness.

To account, then, for the efficiency with which humans acquire language, given this poverty, we must innately possess some basic, however abstract, linguistic structure that enables us to learn whatever particular language we are exposed to. This basic, implicit, unconscious, knowledge is evident in the way children express linguistic forms to which they were never exposed or instructed to correct, but which clearly indicate the mind's active background construction of a grammar, a capability that can only be explained, Chomsky claims, by pre-formed (innate) linguistic structures. Chomsky also cites Plato's *Meno* as an example of how the boy innately understands the principles of geometry, without which he could not be led by experience to solve the problem at hand (1988: 4).

[2] Thus, for example, Plato describes the true idea of justice as a harmony of elements within the State corresponding to a harmony of elements within the soul (*Republic* IV).

Leibniz has several metaphysical reasons for adhering to the latter view of ideas as *in the soul* yet in a way mind-independent. For one, since 'nothing enters the mind naturally from the outside' (ln 16), every idea must already be in the soul – although, as we recall from §9, every substance expresses the universe confusedly. Secondly, this view coincides with the identity conditions of an individual substance (in §8), namely, that a substance is an individual just in case its notion contains all of its predicates, such that a change in any one of its predicates entails a different substance. Third, and for that reason, Leibniz rejects a Scholastic doctrine of perception, according to which images or copies – called 'intentional species' or 'simulacra' – emanate from objects, strike the senses, and enter the soul (lns 17–8). His rejection of this doctrine stems from his rejection of a certain theory of causation, called 'physical influx', which will be discussed in §33. But roughly, since nothing can enter our soul, the ideas we have of things and our ability to construct them by means of the faculties of imagination and understanding are already in our soul. It is not that prior to experience we have the sensible ideas of colours, sounds, or objects of the other senses, but rather that the mind is capable of producing these ideas on the appropriate occasions of experience.[3]

For these reasons, Leibniz claims that 'nothing can be learned whose idea we do not already have in the mind, which [idea] is as the matter from which that thought is formed' (lns 21–3). This statement requires a bit of unpacking. In one sense, nothing can be learned or taught to us whose idea we already possess, since *to be taught* presupposes learning something we do not already know. But what is not obvious is the sense in which we have ideas in our mind without knowing that we do, and how they can be brought to distinct, conscious, knowledge. As a possible explanation, Leibniz alludes to Plato's account of 'reminiscence' (or better 'recollection' – Greek *anamnesis*) in the dialogue *Meno*. To understand how Leibniz likely thinks Plato's account explains how the ideas in us may be brought to light, I offer the following interpretation.

The initial question in the *Meno* is whether virtue can be taught. When Socrates and Meno confess that they do not even know what virtue is, the question becomes whether inquiry into anything at all is possible, if one does not really understand what the inquiry is about in the first place.[4] Otherwise, how would you know you have found the answer? Inquiry

---

For Leibniz, justice is ultimately defined as 'the love (charity) of the wise person' (LR 118). Of course, a great deal of reflection goes into developing these ideas.

[3] For a brief explanation of how this works, see Descartes' *Comments on a Certain Broadsheet* (CSM I, 304 / AT 359). For further discussion of the points in this paragraph see Jolley 1988.

[4] Fine 2014: 1, 7.

would be possible, however, if the answer were already contained within your soul; all you would need is a way to discover this knowledge in yourself by having it drawn out of you. Socrates then claims to elicit from a boy, through a series of questions, the answer to a complex geometric problem – though the boy has no explicit knowledge of geometry beyond the nominal definition of a square and an ability to count.[5]

Rather than go through the entire demonstration, it will suffice to show how Socrates prompts the boy's implicit understanding of the idea of *equality*. Socrates first draws a square, which the boy already knows is a square, but then forms four smaller and equal squares within it by drawing two lines across the middle of the square: one horizontal (a) and the other vertical (b). He then asks the boy whether these lines, (a) and (b), are equal to each other, and the boy immediately replies, 'yes'. Now, provided the boy is not simply guessing, how does he know that lines (a) and (b) are equal to each other? It is more complicated than it seems. First, we might suspect that the boy could have learned 'equals' from having learned the definition of a square as a figure having four equal sides. However, that answer simply assumes what is in question, namely, whether an idea, in this case 'equals', can be taught or inquired into without knowing what it is in the first place. Therefore, Socrates has good reason to suspect that the boy possesses prior knowledge of 'equals' in order even to understand the definition of a square he supposedly learned.

But let us test Socrates' suspicion by using the evidence at hand. Supposing that the boy already understands 'equals', he would understand that the idea applies, not only to sides of squares, but to lines independent of squares. He would know, in other words, that the idea could be applied universally, that it is applicable to many instances of a similar nature, instances on which he has never been specifically instructed. What evidence do we have that the boy possesses such understanding? Consider how the boy could be said, not merely to guess, but to know, that the lines Socrates draws, (a) and (b), are equal to each other. Suppose he visually compares the horizontal line (a) with a horizontal side of the square and then infers that (a) is equal to it. He then must make the same comparison of (b) with the vertical side. He would then have to infer that if (a) is equal to the horizontal side, and (b) is equal to the vertical side, and since the vertical side *is* equal to the horizontal side (which he knows from the definition of a square), *then (a) and (b) must be equal to each other*. In other words, the boy appears to exhibit knowledge of what Euclid specifically

[5] The problem is, given a square whose area equals 4 feet, what is the length of the side of a square whose area is twice 4 feet? The answer is the square root of 8. See Klein 1965 for a detailed account of the process.

239

called a 'common notion', namely, 'things which equal the same thing also equal one another' (*Elements*, Bk 1). Socrates, therefore, has strong reason to suspect that the boy already understands the idea of equality, without having learned either geometry or this common notion; because if he did not understand the idea already, he would not have been able to make such a complex set of inferences about equality without explicit instruction.

While someone who rejects this view (see next article) might claim that the boy could have derived the idea of equality by abstracting it from the experience of many similar instances, Socrates could point out that Equality, in its perfection, is never given to us in sense experience (*Phaedo*, 74c–76). All we are ever exposed to are imperfect approximations of, or tendencies toward, an idea that exists only in thought. Therefore, the boy must already possess the idea of equality in order to apply it to similar cases. Without prior knowledge of the idea of equality, the boy would not be able to determine that the two lines before him, (a) and (b), count as instantiations of the abstract idea of Equality. It may be granted, however, that experience and the promptings of his teacher are required to draw this implicit knowledge out of him.

The above scenario illustrates the sense in which an idea we already possess, in this case, 'equality', has a relation to the 'matter' of experience, as Leibniz suggests in line 22. But the scenario also illustrates the way in which ideas function as *relations to other ideas*, as explicitly expressed in the very last line of the article: 'One can even say that [the soul] already possesses these truths, when one takes them for relations of ideas.' Recall the Euclidean 'common notion' above: 'things which equal the same thing also equal one another'. This self-evident proposition actually expresses a fairly complex set of inherently relational ideas – equality, identity, and difference – that the boy could not have abstracted through sense experience. The boy would then not only require prior knowledge of these relational notions but must also possess the unlearned ability to make inferences between them and the lines and spaces forming the matter of his sensible experience.

As Leibniz indicates, something like this Platonic view of recollection is correct, minus the accompanying idea of reincarnation,[6] which Leibniz, in accordance with Christian doctrine, rejects. He also rejects Plato's idea that at some prior point we know and think distinctly what we learn and think now (lns 26–7),[7] likely because that would only beg the question as to how we were capable of acquiring and recognising these distinct thoughts without already having ideas of them. For Leibniz, all

---

[6] As depicted, for example, in the tale of Er, *Republic*, Bk X, 614 to end.
[7] Described in *Phaedrus*, 247c–250b and *Phaedo*, 79d.

that is required is that our attention be 'turned toward' (anima-adverted) the knowledge that we possess 'virtually', that is, potentially, within our soul, and be prompted by experience to combine those ideas into relations corresponding with experience. This is the sense in which all ideas are already in us, both as ideas ready to be consciously thought and as ideas capable of constructing other ideas. The opposing view, that we have no such ideas, is considered next.

§27. Thus, the soul is not a 'blank tablet'.

What does it mean to say that the soul is a blank tablet? It means that the soul has no innate ideas, no ideas prior to birth to recollect, and no concepts prior to experience by means of which it may organise experience. The 'blank tablet' or 'blank slate' is a frequently used metaphor for an empiricist theory of the mind according to which all ideas and knowledge come from experience. As Aristotle is supposed to have said, 'nothing is in our understanding [our intellect] that does not come from the senses' (lns 5–6). While Leibniz holds the opposite view, as seen in §26, he wants to maintain, in his typical fashion, that his opponents' views may serve as convenient explanations, but do not express metaphysical truth.

In order to be clear on Leibniz's position, it is useful to trace the history of the statement Leibniz attributes to Aristotle in line 6. First, it does not occur in Aristotle, but probably originated with Aquinas.[1] But while Aristotle could, arguably, agree that the mind does not contain ideas prior to experience, he still reserves for it an innate *capacity* to construct abstract ideas from sensory input.[2] Yet, a number of Scholastics,

---

[1] Aquinas, *De veritate* [On Truth] (q.2, a.3, argument 19), where the question is whether God knows things other than himself: 'Nothing is in the intellect that was not previously in sense. But in God there is no sensitive cognition, because this is material. Therefore, He does not know created things, since they were not previously in His sense.' In the 'answers to difficulties' for arg. 19, Aquinas says: 'That axiom is to be understood as applying only to our intellect, which receives its knowledge from things. For a thing is led by gradual steps from its own material conditions to the immateriality of the intellect through the mediation of the immateriality of sense. Consequently, whatever is in our intellect must have previously been in the senses. This, however, does not take place in the divine intellect.' Leibniz probably understood the phrase as coming from Aristotle's *On the Soul*, Bk III, Ch. 4, 430, where Aristotle speaks of the mind as a blank writing tablet.

[2] The relevant passages in Aristotle are listed in footnotes 3 and 4 in §27 of this translation, but see especially *Posterior Analytics*, Bk II, Ch. 19, the most relevant part of which is: 'We conclude that these states of knowledge are neither innate in a determinate form, nor developed from other higher states of knowledge, but from sense-perception. It is like a rout in battle stopped by first one man making a stand and then another, until the

241

apparently following Aquinas, took the statement (that there is nothing in the understanding. . .) as a kind of epistemological axiom and proof of Aristotle's empiricism. Descartes, however, cites it as one of his *former* beliefs (*Meditation* VI, CSM II, 52), and argues instead for the knowledge of various innate ideas.[3] John Locke, on the other hand, as is well known, while he does not cite the axiom directly,[4] invokes the 'blank slate' to present what appears to be a staunchly empiricist denial of innate ideas:

> Let us then suppose the mind to be, as we say, white paper, void of all char-acters, without any ideas; How comes it to be furnished? [. . .] Whence has it all the materials of reason and knowledge? To this I answer, in one word, from *Experience*. In that all our knowledge is founded; and from that it ultimately derives itself. (*Essay*, Bk II, Ch. 1, §2)

But what does 'experience' consist of, for Locke? Initially, material from the senses:

> The senses at first let in particular ideas, and furnish the yet empty cabinet, and the mind by degrees growing familiar with some of them, they are lodged in the memory, and names got to them. Afterwards, the mind proceeding further, abstracts them, and by degrees learns the use of general names. In this manner the mind comes to be furnished with ideas and language, the material about which to exercise its discursive faculty. (*Essay*, Bk I, Ch. 2, §15)

This is by any measure a persuasive explanation for how ideas develop from the matter of the senses. Locke is clear, however, that experience does not consist only of matter from the senses.

> Secondly, the other fountain from which experience furnisheth the under-standing with ideas is – the perception of the operations of our own mind within us, as it is employed about the ideas it has got; – which operations, when the soul comes to reflect on and consider, do furnish the understanding with another set of ideas, which could not be had from things without. And such are perception, thinking, doubting, believing, reasoning, knowing, willing,

---

original formation has been restored. The soul is so constituted as to be capable of this process' (100a9–14).

3 'Even the scholastic philosophers take it as a maxim that there is nothing in the intellect which has not previously been in the senses; and yet it is certain that the ideas of God and of the soul have never been in the senses' (*Discourse on Method*, IV, CSM I, 129 / AT 37). Additional examples of innate ideas cited by Descartes are himself as a think-ing thing (*Meditation* II, CSM II, 21–2 / AT 31–3), and 'my understanding of what a thing is, what truth is, and what thought is, seems to derive simply from my own nature' (*Meditation* III, CSM II, 26 / AT 38). Also see *Optics*, 'Fourth Discourse'.

4 Although Locke does invoke something like it: 'We have nothing in our minds which did not come from [senses and reflection]' (*Essay*, Bk II, Ch. 1, §5). What this means should become clear in what follows.

and all the different actings of our own minds; – which we being conscious of, and observing in ourselves, do from these receive into our understandings as distinct ideas as we do from bodies affecting our senses. This source of ideas every man has wholly in himself; and though it be not sense, as having nothing to do with external objects, yet it is very like it, and might properly enough be called internal sense. (*Essay*, Bk II, Ch. 1, §4)

On this account, it is difficult for Locke to maintain that the mind is *simply* a blank slate written upon by the material of the senses, since it is also capable of reflecting on its own 'operations'. In his *New Essays on Human Understanding*, his constructed dialogue with Locke, Leibniz is keen to agree with Locke's concession to the operations of the understanding we find in reflection. He expresses his agreement by citing and yet modifying the (misattributed) Aristotelian axiom:

Someone will confront me with this accepted philosophical axiom, that there is nothing in the soul which does not come from the senses. But an exception must be made of the soul itself and its states. *Nihil est in intellectu quod non fuerit in sensu, excipe: nisi ipse intellectus [Nothing is in the intellect that was not in the senses, except the intellect itself]*. Now the soul includes being, substance, one, same, cause, perception, reasoning, and many other notions which the senses cannot provide. That agrees pretty well with your author of the *Essay*, for he looks for a good proportion of ideas in the mind's reflection on its own nature. (LRB II.i.2.111)[5]

Thus, Leibniz has Locke agreeing on this much: that the intellect itself (the rational part of the soul) possesses – within its capability to reflect on the matter of experience – a number of ideas that do not derive from experience. Leibniz would, however, make the case for much more knowledge on the side of the intellect, when one considers how certain axioms (such as contradiction and identity, and certain moral axioms) are understood – not explicitly, but implicitly and pervasively throughout all of our reasoning.[6]

And so goes the debate on innate ideas, as it stood between Locke and Leibniz in the early 1700s. But Leibniz in the *Discourse* in 1686 already held that all these empiricist ways of speaking about how the mind learns

---

[5] Leibniz at this time (1706) may have derived the idea of adding 'except the intellect itself' from Johann Joachim Becher, *Appendix Practica* (1669): 'But the right Method of Knowing already knows the reason for things often before it has the word to reveal the truth it recognises, such that nothing sensible issues from the mouth that is not first decided in reason, and this axiom is more certain than the one which runs: *nothing is in the intellect which was not first in the senses*, when one understands externally, that is, when knowledge is recognised' (p. 49, my translation). Also see Schüssler 1991.

[6] See the whole set of arguments between Leibniz and Locke in Leibniz's *New Essays* (LRB) Bks I and II.i. The reader should not take my characterisation of Locke and this debate as definitive, but only as basis for further investigation.

and accesses ideas are largely beside the point – they are practical ways of talking about how the mind knows, thinks, and operates, but they do not convey the real metaphysical truth. He makes his point by analogy. As he remarks in §14, we *say* that substances act on each other (have causal relations), but this is only a practical way of speaking about the underlying metaphysical reality, which is that substances do not have causal relations, but rather *express* one another more or less distinctly. In the same way, speaking practically, we say that knowledge of external things comes to us through the senses; however, the metaphysical reality is that things express themselves in more or less distinct ways, which determines the clear or obscure manner by which we perceive them. Since the underlying metaphysical truth is that each soul is causally independent of every other (each is an independent substance), and that all of its experiences and knowledge lie within it, *everything* is innate; therefore, for the substance to know external things it need only look inward. This looking inward is not easy to do, since below the level of conscious awareness, ideas and expressions are not easily accessible (more about this in relation to Leibniz's doctrine of small or 'confused' perceptions in §33). However, conscious experiences by means of the senses can serve as occasions for reflection upon ideas that lie deep within the soul, ideas that do not immediately come with experience, but which make experience possible.[7]

With this distinction between the obscure depths of the soul and the clarity of conscious awareness, Leibniz distinguishes two general types of ideas: (a) ideas always present within our soul of which we are largely unaware; and (b) ideas that we are currently thinking. The latter are called *notions* or *concepts*, which we 'apperceive more manifestly', (lns 20, 25), that is, with full reflective awareness of what we are thinking. The claim is that while all ideas are contained within us, we *think* only with the concepts sufficiently clear to us.

This distinction of ideas also allows Leibniz to maintain the sense in which, according to accepted doctrines, we distinguish ideas not derived from the senses from those that are. Examples of the former include the 'I' that is thinking, as well as the ideas of *being*, *substance*, *action*, and *identity*. The generality of these ideas cannot come from the particulars of sense, but rather serve to organise the data of sense. The 'I' just is that internal cognition of a consciousness having an experience; it is the cognition of that same consciousness remaining *identical* over different experiences. Over time, this identity attains a kind of comprehensiveness that calls up the notion of *substance*, that is, the idea of oneself as an independent, enduring

---

[7] A dispositional account of ideas (as tendencies to arise under certain conditions) is possible here as well. See Jolley 1988.

thing among other enduring, and fleeting, things. We have, furthermore, the mental sense that this substance is capable of *action*; indeed, as Leibniz has shown, substances are fundamentally *beings* that *act* and *perceive*. These ideas are not linguistic entities, but rather ideas themselves to which we attach linguistic labels through experience, as Locke indicates. But without the unity that these ideas provide, without an organising ground upon which experience can be written, it would be difficult to explain how experience itself would even be possible.

Finally, as a way of clarifying this relationship between ideas within the depth of the soul and conscious thinking, we may return to the point Leibniz made in the last line of the previous article: '[the soul] already possesses these truths when one takes them for relations of ideas'. As I suggested, this line can be understood as expressing a relationship among several ideas, such as equality, identity, and difference. But 'relations of ideas' can also be understood in contemporary terms as expressing the relationship between ideas deep within the soul and ideas in explicit awareness. An interesting and plausible explanation of this relationship is suggested by Noam Chomsky, who identifies the *Port-Royal Grammar*, co-written by Antoine Arnauld, as the first work to present the relationship between the deep structure of thought and the surface structure of language.[8] The Port-Royal Grammarians take the standard view that the general form of a proposition is that of a judgment, according to which an attribute, or predicate, is asserted or denied of a subject. For example, 'God invisible created the visible world' is a proposition consisting of the subject 'invisible God' to which the attribute 'created the visible world' is connected. However, this proposition (or judgment) actually consists of a combination of three simpler judgments:

1. God is invisible.
2. God creates.
3. The world is visible.[9]

The Port-Royal Grammarians go on to explain that the second of these, 'God creates', is the basic judgment, while the other two are subordinate judgments. That is because the first is a modification of the subject, God, while the third is a modification of the attribute 'creates'. The novel idea presented by the Port-Royal Grammarians is that these three judgments form the 'deep structure' of the proposition. They are subsequently, through the medium of language, transformed by a series of rules to form

---

[8] Arnauld and Lancelot, *General and Rational Grammar* (1753).
[9] Chomsky 2009a: 80; Arnauld and Lancelot, *General and Rational Grammar*, 64.

the surface structure judgment, 'Invisible God creates the visible world'.[10] The main insight here is that language is expressed and understood on the basis of a more fundamental set of ideas and an innate capacity for structuring them.

We could make this Chomskian, Port-Royal, analysis a bit more Leibnizian by reducing these three judgments to their component ideas: *God, visible, create, world, negation,* and *being.* We could further decompose *visible* into *able to be seen,* or more abstractly into *experience. Create* might be reduced to *cause to exist.* At this point we have a set of ideas typically identified as innate, since they are not derived from experience: *God, existence, negation, sensation, cause,* and *experience in general.* The analysis here is all too brief and requires further elaboration, but it is consistent with Leibniz's sense of how ideas of which we are already in possession are accessed and combined to form new notions or concepts, as well as whole propositions. The mind not only possesses these ideas within its depths, it also possesses the capacity to rearrange them into novel judgments, or into ideas of which it had previously no conscious experience. And when one encounters in experience a complex idea as expressed above, one can readily understand it in terms of more basic ideas.[11]

§28. The sense in which God is the immediate object of our perceptions.

In §28 and §29, Leibniz takes a position on a dispute between Malebranche and Arnauld on the role of ideas in our perception. The dispute originates with Malebranche's claim in *Search after Truth* that we 'see' everything in God (MS III, 2, 6), a claim which Arnauld in *True and False Ideas* strongly rejects. In this article, Leibniz agrees with Malebranche, while in the next he agrees with Arnauld, all the while maintaining his position that all ideas are contained within the soul and thus contribute to our ability to perceive, think, and know.

To understand Leibniz's position, it helps to have some understanding of what is at stake in the dispute between Malebranche and Arnauld. By the seventeenth century, the role that ideas play in our ability to perceive external things had undergone a significant development since the ancient

---

[10] 'Now these subordinate propositions are often in our mind, without being expressed in words, as in the example cited' (Arnauld and Lancelot, *General and Rational Grammar,* 68; quoted by Chomsky 2009a: 80).

[11] I suggest that this ability to form novel ideas constitutes what Leibniz refers to in 'What is an Idea?' as 'a power of thinking upon the mind so that it can by its own operations derive what corresponds perfectly to the nature of things' (LL 208).

and the Medieval periods.[1] This development begins with Aristotle's conception (in *On the Soul*) that our sense perceptions are 'veridical', meaning that under optimal conditions they convey to us the nature of things. Augustine, however, within Neoplatonic and Christian frameworks, introduced the idea that true perception and cognition (apprehension of ideas) requires 'spiritual illumination'; in other words, God is the source of the light of truth, just as the sun is the source of the light which enables us to see.[2] By the seventeenth century, this move away from Aristotelian veridicality and toward spiritual illumination faced increasing scepticism due to the 'mechanical philosophy', which, as should be familiar by now, maintains that certain sense perceptions (the secondary qualities of colour, sound, smell, and taste) are not perceptions of the real qualities of things, but are productions of the mind caused by a thing's primary qualities (shape and size). Scepticism about the reality of secondary qualities reached its radical terminus in Descartes, who argued that sense perceptions cannot provide us with any certainty about external things – indeed, the former are nothing like the latter – and, furthermore, that no ideas are more veridical than those provided by the soul itself – that it thinks, exists, imagines, and senses the *apparent* qualities of things. We may be certain, however, with assurances provided by God, that our 'clear and distinct ideas', such as the nature of body as extended, *represent* the true nature of external things (*Meditation* II). According to this 'representationalist' view, commonly attributed to Descartes, when we perceive the sun, for example, the immediate object of perception is not the sun itself but an *idea* of the sun as it exists *in the intellect*.[3] This idea would include both the sun's sensory qualities (about which we cannot be certain) and its extensional, mathematical properties (about which we can be certain).

Malebranche largely follows Descartes on the veridicality, or lack thereof, of the senses; however, regarding extensional properties and other intelligible ideas, Malebranche is distinctly Augustinian. Like Descartes, he defines an idea representationally, as 'the immediate object, or the object closest to the mind when it perceives something, i.e., that which affects and modifies the mind with the perception it has of an object' (MS III, 2, 1, 217). He also maintains that the soul contains its own proper thoughts, namely sensations (such as the warmth and colour of the sun), imaginations, and natural inclinations (218). However, the soul does not

---

[1] See Gaukroger's introduction to Arnauld's, *On True and False Ideas* (1990). My account follows Gaukroger very generally and not always.

[2] For the sun analogy, see Plato's *Republic*, VI, 508a–509b; Augustine's *Soliloquies*, VIII.15; and *The Teacher*, 140–1.

[3] 'First Set of Replies', CSM II, 75 / AT 103.

have ideas of the primary qualities (shape and size) of things, nor ideas of the essences of things (formal qualities, such as kinds). Rather, to perceive these the soul depends wholly on *divine illumination*. In this way the dispute between Malebranche and Arnauld comes down to a dispute over the perceivability of what are generally called *intelligible* ideas and whether they require divine illumination.

Malebranche's argument for divine illumination is roughly this: (1) the human soul does not possess the power to *create* the intelligible ideas of things, since such power is reserved for God; (2) nor does God create these ideas in us, since, due to the infinity of ideas (an infinity of shapes, for example), it would be extremely inefficient for God to create every possible shape-idea in every soul; (3) since the soul is not perfect it cannot comprehend the *essences* of things. The only plausible conclusion, for Malebranche, is that *we see* [perceive] *all things in God* (MS III, 2, 6, 230), such that the immediate object of perception is not an idea (a representation) in our mind, but rather an idea (a representation) in God. Note that Malebranche's argument entails that there are no innate ideas.

In other words, human cognition requires God, who has both the *power* to create all ideas as well as the *infinite* and *perfect* nature to contain them. Thus, by virtue of God's idea of the essence of triangle, we can perceive an infinite variety of triangles or any other shape. Our 'minds perceive everything through the intimate presence of Him, who comprehends all in the Simplicity of His being' (MS III, 2, 6, 235). God is thus the light, as Augustine argued, that we depend on to 'see' in an intelligible sense. This means that the human soul is not sufficient unto itself to understand, but is epistemically deeply dependent on God, who is 'the true light that illumines everyone who comes into the world' (MS III, 2, 5, 231; John 1:9). Without God, we would have no way of comprehending the variety, essence, and truth of things.

Arnauld's principal objection is that Malebranche misunderstands the nature of ideas. On Malebranche's representational account, we have a *perception* of an *idea* of a thing; this is misleading, because it makes the idea into a thing (a representation) apart from our perception. It would be as if in order to perceive a real triangle a painting of a triangle must be placed between the perceiver and a real triangle, such that what is perceived is the painting rather than the real triangle. We could, then, suppose that since we are not capable of creating such a painting (presuming we do not have the materials), nor could such a painting perfectly represent the intelligible idea of a triangle, we must thereby depend on God to provide us with the right sort of painting (idea) as the object of our perception. Arnauld's contention, however, is that representations do not stand in place of things in *this* way. For him, the act of perception fundamentally involves a 'perception-idea', which is a single entity that does not stand in place of external things but rather is the means by which we perceive them.[4] The appropriate analogy would be the way in which we perceive some object through its image reflected in a mirror. To be sure, we perceive the *image* that is reflected in the mirror; however, the image is not a *representation* of the object, not the immediate object of our perception; rather, the image is the *means* by which we perceive *the object*. The upshot is that our perceptions, or perception-ideas, are perceptions *in our own mind* of the object. There is no need, then, to place God's ideas between our soul and external things in order to establish a proper epistemic relation between subject and object. This relation is sufficiently accomplished (however imperfectly) by the relation between the mind's representation of the object and the object itself.

Now that we see what is at stake in the debate, where does Leibniz stand? He does not take an explicit position on the specific role of ideas in perception, as Malebranche and Arnauld conceive of it. What he does, however, is show how his doctrine of expression can be understood to agree with Malebranche's doctrine that 'we see all things in God'. Recall from §27 (ln 17) that in order to state, in metaphysical rigour, whether the soul is either a 'blank tablet' or innately endowed with ideas, we had to realise both the 'extent' and the 'independence' of the soul. Souls are independent of each other since, on account of the notion of an individual substance, nothing external can enter the soul or cause it to change in any way. Nevertheless, due to the 'extent' of the soul, namely its internal and practically infinite trough of ideas, the soul expresses the entire universe – including God. Now, here in §28, Leibniz modifies that position somewhat by maintaining that the soul is not *completely* independent of God, since, again, in full metaphysical rigour, it is in continual dependence on God.

This dependence can be understood to hold in two ways: ontologically and epistemologically. First, Leibniz is explicit that God, and only God, acts continually on us, by virtue of his continual 'concurrence'. As we saw in §7 and §14, God's concurrence (or concourse) stems from God's single act of creating-and-sustaining our being. Thus, by virtue of our individual notion we are ontologically independent of every substance, except God. Second, by virtue of this ontological dependence, we are *epistemically* dependent on God. Through God's continual concurrence and action upon us, God communicates his being to us, and thus in varying degrees communicates all things *to* the ideas within our soul. In this sense only, as the source of all our ideas, God is the immediate object of our perception. It is, moreover, by these means of 'communication' that the ideas within

---

[4] Arnauld, *On True and False Ideas*, 66.

our soul are brought to awareness on the appropriate occasions of experience. When we see the sun, for example, God determines our senses to be 'disposed' (ln 17) to see the sun, just as when we say that our sense of sight is disposed to convey certain colours to us when it is presented with certain objects. It is also in this sense that God is the light of the soul, since God's operations on the soul bring the objects of experience to awareness.

But none of this implies the sort of dependence upon God to perceive the ideas themselves, as Malebranche would have it. Nor can we ignore the fact that, for Leibniz, the soul contains an infinity of ideas (which Malebranche denies), and that the soul is essentially an expressing-representing substance, as all things are represented in it. Thus, the metaphysically rigorous explication for 'we see all things through God' would be that we *express* all things through God, who is the immediate object of our expression. But our ordinary capacity to perceive and to grasp the intelligibles does not depend on perceiving them 'in God'. While I may very well depend on God for the existence and 'communication' of ideas, I still have an internal capacity to think them myself, by virtue of the ideas belonging particularly to my soul and its power to think them. Leibniz will explicitly assert in the next article that we think by these means.

Leibniz's concluding remarks serve to further qualify his approval of Malebranche's views. Yes, God is the light of the soul, but for Leibniz it is a light that God has provided for each individual soul. It is what the Scholastics, following Aristotle in *On the Soul* (Bk III, 5), called the 'active' or 'agent' intellect, which is the soul or mind's capacity to form abstractions and derive essences from the sensible material of the 'passive' intellect. In this way, the active intellect is characterised as a 'productive' and 'positive' power: just as light makes potential colours visible, the active intellect makes potential intelligibles (essences) explicitly perceived and understood. In view of the active intellect, Malebranche's claim that the soul lacks the capacity to derive the requisite essences does not hold up.

Leibniz's reference to the 'Averroists' serves to distinguish 'the active intellect' from controversial views associated with it. Averroes (Ibn Rushd, 1126–98), the famous Arabic-Islamic philosopher, whose commentaries on Aristotle greatly influenced Aquinas, interpreted Aristotle's active intellect as eternal, immortal, separable from the body, and ultimately as a single *universal* intellect.[5] The Averroists were Renaissance-era Christian followers of Averroes who, Leibniz asserts, gave the active intellect a

---

[5] It is not easy to distinguish Averroes' own interpretation of Aristotle from interpretations of Averroes' interpretation. One might start with his *Middle Commentary on Aristotle's De Anima*. Aquinas provides his critique in *On the Unity of the Intellect Against the Averroists*.

'bad sense' (ln 25) by maintaining that upon death the individual soul becomes one with (or dissolves into) a single universal mind, which is God's, thereby dissolving the soul's individuality, and, effectively, its immortality.[6] The Church understandably banned their views as inconsistent with official doctrine. But they are also inconsistent with Leibniz's insistence that the soul is an individual substance, distinct from God, and which maintains its individuality for eternity. By raising this controversy over the Averroists, Leibniz may have wanted to emphasise that, while he agrees with Malebranche that we see all things through God, this cannot entail that the individual soul is not distinct from God, in both an ontological and epistemic sense.

§29. The sense in which we think immediately through our own ideas.

Leibniz now indicates more explicitly the sense in which he disagrees with Malebranche and agrees (implicitly) with Arnauld: however much we depend on God for our being and nature, we perceive and think by means of the ideas within us. While each substance expresses God and the whole universe, it does so *in its own way*, as the doctrine of substance should remind us. Malebranche's position would also seem to entail that the soul does not even think its own thoughts; but this is 'inconceivable' Leibniz insists (ln 9), likely for two reasons: it is epistemically constitutive of thinking that the thinker be in an immediate, non-inferential, relationship to her own thoughts; otherwise, the thinker could not even know that it is having its own thoughts. Second, and again, it is ontologically constitutive of an individual substance that it think its own thoughts; otherwise, it is not a unified being.

Leibniz's main reasons for saying that we think with our own ideas have already been given in the previous article, regarding the independence and expressive extent of the soul. Here he offers another reason that is less than clearly asserted, but which hinges on the distinction between the passive and active powers of the soul (as in Aristotle's *On the Soul*, III, 5). The soul is passive insofar as it is capable of being affected representationally by external things; yet it also possesses the active power, in the form of a

---

[6] Leibniz gives his version of Averroes' argument and a critique of it in *Theodicy*: 'Preliminary Dissertation on the Conformity of Faith with Reason' (§7–11). He also expresses his opposition to the Averroists in 'Reflections on the Doctrine of a Single Universal Spirit' (1702, LL No. 58, 554). In these texts Leibniz names several so-called Averroists, prominent among them, Pietro Pomponazzi (1464–1525). Leibniz's characterisations of Averroism and Averroists are indirect however, and should be taken with caution. For more on the Christian Averroists see Brown 2010. For more on the interpretation of Aristotle's active intellect see Caston 2006.

disposition or tendency, to produce the essences of those things on the occasions of experience. To perceive the sun, for example, the soul has the passive power of receiving its sensible forms. Based on them it has the *active* capacity to produce ideas of the sun's intelligible essence and properties (roundness, power, heat, substance, duration). In this sense, the soul contains 'in advance' (ln 13) the power, both passive and active, of thinking, that is, of acting and producing its own thoughts, rather than having to depend on God for the object's perceptibility and intelligibility. Leibniz's overall argument in articles 28 and 29 could be summarised as maintaining that while God, as the source of everything, is the source of all our ideas, it must still be the case that we think them by means of the passive and active powers of our soul.

§30. On divine concurrence; on the spontaneity of the soul; that the will should always tend to the apparent good; on the indifference of the will; on precautions against the surprises of appearances; on the assurance from all eternity that the soul will not make use of this power; on whether you can act contrary to your notion and remain the same individual; on Judas' sin – and possible worlds; on the metaphysics of sin and evil: the original limitation of creatures; on the degrees of grace.

This is the most philosophically dense article and among the most important in the *Discourse*, since it completes the account of the 'complete notion of an individual substance' established in §8, by addressing potential threats to free will and by placing it within the scheme of the best possible world. It also touches on what we might call the theodicy of sin and some of Leibniz's psychophysiology. In sum, it describes God's role in human creation, life, and salvation. Due to the high number of allusions Leibniz makes to his solutions to various theological and philosophical problems, each topic is indicated by a bolded heading. The order of topics follow the order presented in the article summary above.

Divine concurrence

As the first line of §30 indicates, Leibniz is still concerned to distinguish God's actions from those of his human creatures. This concern is implicitly tied to the sort of causality God has in relation to them, as well as to the sort of causal powers they possess. As we saw in §14, in bare outline, God *creates* each creature out of nothing; but being created out of nothing, creatures have no power to sustain their own being; thus, through the same act by which God creates, God *conserves* the being of each creature. Then as creatures become themselves the causes of certain effects, God *concurs* with the actions of each creature. The doctrine of concurrence is motivated by an effort among certain Scholastics to keep God within the causal picture, to maintain the simplicity of his actions (creation and concurrence are together a single act), but also to avoid making God the sole cause of all creaturely actions. To say that God 'concurs' (literally, 'runs together') with our actions means that, from actions as mundane as getting out of bed, to the extraordinary series of actions resulting in the conquering of an empire, God contributes a portion of his causal power to the action.[1]

But the concurrence of God raises a troubling dilemma: who is the *sufficient* cause of my action, God or me? If God's causal contribution to the action is greater than mine, then I am not the sufficient cause; and if God's concurrence is not the sufficient cause, then what efficacy does his concurrence have? In other words, either I am not responsible for my actions, or, if I am, then God's concurrence is superfluous. One solution to this difficulty may be to maintain that God's concurrence is necessary but not sufficient for my action, while my actions are both necessary and sufficient. That is, I cannot get out of bed without God's concurrence, which is necessary but not sufficient for my getting out of bed. My causal power is also necessary, but moreover *sufficient*, for getting out of bed. Thus, even though our actions depend on God's concurrence, we can still be the sufficient cause of them.

The spontaneity of the soul

Leibniz, however, can contend with the above difficulty by means of his doctrine of the complete notion of an individual substance. Even though God continually conserves our being and 'concurs' with our actions (and thoughts), they are nevertheless 'spontaneous' because they flow from our individual notion (ln 13). The term 'spontaneous' does important work in the *Discourse*, so it must be correctly understood. For Leibniz, it does not mean what it typically means for us today, namely, that our actions are impulsive, unplanned, incidental, or uncaused, but rather that they have no *external* cause. The individual substance itself is the principle (*arche*) of its actions.[2] As Leibniz later explains, 'God originally created the soul (and any other real unity) in such a way that everything must arise for it from its own depths [*fonds*], through perfect spontaneity relative to

---

[1] On divine concurrence see Freddoso's introduction to Suarez 2002, section 7.

[2] The notion of 'spontaneous' stems from Aristotle's *Nicomachean Ethics*, where the Greek *ekousios* is translated into Latin as *spontaneum* but in English often as 'voluntary'. 'Since that which is done under compulsion or by reason of ignorance is involuntary, the voluntary would seem to be that of which the moving principle is in the agent himself, he being aware of the particular circumstances of the action' (Bk III, Ch.1, 1111a20).

itself, and yet with a perfect conformity relative to external things.'[3] In other words, the power of acting, the innate inclination for 'the good', lies within the individual. Since metaphysically for Leibniz the individual has no causal relation to other substances (only a representational or expressive relation) and its actions are the consequence of its complete notion, the individual is the sufficient cause of its actions. In this way, God's conservation and concurrence detract not at all from the spontaneity of the individual substance. Spontaneity is not, however, sufficient for *free will*. It is only one of Leibniz's three necessary and jointly sufficient conditions for freedom, the others being *choice* (resulting from deliberation), and *contingency*, which is freedom from logical necessity.[4] Leibniz defined the conditions of contingency in §13, while choice will be explained below. Spontaneity will also play a key role in §33, in his doctrine of the 'commerce' or 'perfect conformity' between the soul, the body, and external things, a doctrine that serves as a precursor to his later doctrine of 'preestablished harmony'.

That the will should always tend to the apparent good

Having addressed concurrentism and spontaneity, thus reaffirming both our dependence on and independence from God, Leibniz declares that God has 'decreed' that 'the will should always tend to the apparent good' (ln 16). We first met this decree in §13, as expressing the classical psychological view that rational action is taken *sub species boni*, or 'under the appearance [or guise] of the good'.[5] There, we saw that God has decreed

[3] *New System of Nature* (1695), AG 143.

[4] In 'The Confession of a Philosopher' (1672), Leibniz outlines spontaneity and choice as conditions of freedom, while in *Theodicy* (1710) he adds the condition of contingency, that is, that the action be free from logical necessity. 'Indeed, Aristotle defined *spontaneity* as obtaining when the principle of action is in the agent, and *freedom* as spontaneity with choice. From which we may conclude that each person is all the more spontaneous the more his acts flow from his nature, and the less they are altered by external matters, and all the more free the greater his capacity for choice, that is, the more he understands many things with a pure and tranquil mind. Therefore, spontaneity comes from power, freedom [comes] from knowledge' (LCP 69). In *Theodicy*, Leibniz states that, in addition to the combination of spontaneity and intelligence, 'which are found united in us in deliberation [. . .] freedom must exclude an absolute and metaphysical or logical necessity', whose exclusion he calls simply 'contingency' (§302).

[5] See Plato's *Meno*, 77c. Also, Aristotle, 'the good has been rightly declared to be that at which all things aim' (*Nicomachean Ethics*, Bk I, Ch. 1, 1094a). Aristotle also marks the difference between the true good and the apparent good: 'For each state of character has its own ideas of the noble and the pleasant, and perhaps the good man differs from others most by seeing the truth in each class of things, being as it were the norm and measure of them. In most things the error seems to be due to pleasure; for it appears a good when it is not' (Bk III, Ch. 4, 1113b).

this natural tendency in us by which we may be said to act contingently. But here, since Leibniz's concern is with the conditions of choice, it will be useful to look more closely at its traditional conception.

In *On the Soul*, Aristotle identifies two principles by means of which the soul originates movement: *appetite* (desire for the good) and *thought* or cognition. Appetite has *pleasure* for its object, while the object of thought is the means of attaining the ends established by appetite. So, while appetite provides the initial movement or *impetus* to action, the action taken is determined by the intellect's final calculation of the means for attaining the end.[6] Admittedly, this is an over-simplistic account of human psychology, but the basic idea can explain a lot. For one, it can explain why we make bad choices by making false or inadequate calculations about the means for some end. Also, the work of the intellect is not restricted to finding the means of attaining whatever object of appetite; it is also determined to seek the *true* good, that is, the ends truly worthy of choice. So, we make bad choices when we take, say, a selfish pleasure as the end worthy of choice when a non-pleasurable choice would have been more worthy. The intellect also plays a part in *training* the appetites to have as their object the ends established by the intellect. This work of the intellect in relation to appetite and desire is called *deliberation* and results in *choice*, the *excellent* and habitual exercise of which constitutes *virtue*.[7] In any case, the degree to which we successfully attain *the* good rather than the apparent good is the degree to which we have properly deliberated over the options available to us.

So, how does this practical principle ('practical' because action-guiding) work for Leibniz? As in Aristotle, the soul's initial impulse comes from appetite and its action is completed by thought, or in Leibniz's terms, by *perception*; thus, we act according to what the soul (which includes the intellect) perceives to be good. But Leibniz also characterises the principle as a decree given to us by God, as a principle of our nature; and this is the sense and extent to which God *determines* our will, by having made us capable of pursuing the good. How successfully we attain the good depends on how well we understand God's will and how strongly our will is disposed to follow this understanding over the impulses of appetite.

---

[6] *On the Soul*, Bk III, §10, 433a9–20

[7] 'Now thought is always right, but appetite and imagination may be either right or wrong. That is why, though in any case it is the object of appetite which originates movement, this object may be either the real or the apparent good' (*On the Soul*, Bk III, §10, 433a30). Also see *Nicomachean Ethics*: 'so that moral virtue is a state of character concerned with choice, and choice is deliberate desire, therefore both the reasoning must be true and the desire right, if the choice is to be good, and the latter [desire] must pursue just what the former [reasoning] asserts' (Bk VI, Ch. 2, 1139a25).

This implies, of course, that much can go wrong, such as when we sin (see below). Thus this principle, this decree, *inclines* (determines) the will toward the action without *necessitating* that we take it. As we learned in §13, for Leibniz, there must be a sufficient reason for our action, but this reason cannot compel us necessarily. In fact, Leibniz even maintains that the soul has the power to counter the totality of inclinations pressing upon it, by virtue of 'the indifference of the will'.

On the indifference of the will

At line 21, Leibniz refers to the will being in a state of 'indifference', a state opposed to necessity and by virtue of which the will has the power to 'do otherwise' and to 'suspend its action altogether'. But what does this 'indifference' really consist of? It has nothing to do with being in a passive state of apathy nor with actively suppressing the emotions. Rather, among Medieval philosophers what is often called 'the liberty of indifference' refers to a power of the will to choose a course of action or object independently of anything that might determine it, such as a desire, inclination, external stimulus, or even a good reason. For example, suppose I present you with two identical slices of your favourite pie, stipulating that you can choose only one. Since they are identical, there is no reason to favour one slice over the other. What do you do? Since you have the 'liberty of indifference', you choose one *arbitrarily*, that is, without reason – or, you may choose neither, again for no reason, but strictly by virtue of the will's power of indifference. Other Medievals argued, however, that an unmotivated choice is impossible, that the will must always be determined by some cause or reason. Jean Buridan, for instance, argued that faced with a choice of equal goods for equal reasons, the agent would choose to *suspend judgment*, rather than make an undetermined choice, which is impossible anyway. His argument follows the traditional moral psychology: since *the will always chooses what the intellect perceives is best*, and since each choice is equally good, no choice can be made – except to suspend or defer judgment until conditions enabling a preference should obtain. In such cases, the intellect judges that a choice to suspend is *better* than making no choice at all.[8] One can see a problem arising here: for either the will is determined

---

[8] Buridan's scenario (fourteenth century) prompted a critic to propose the case of a hungry donkey ('Buridan's Ass') situated at equal distance between two identical bales of hay. It was claimed that the donkey, having no reason (or cause) to prefer one bale over the other (and lacking the ability to suspend judgment), would become immobilised and eventually starve. See the SEP entry on Buridan. Similar earlier scenarios demonstrating indifference problems had been devised by Al-Ghazali in the eleventh century and by Aristotle (see Kaye 2004). In *Theodicy* (§49), Leibniz argues that the Buridan's Ass scenario is impossible, since, following the identity of indiscernibles, some difference

by *nothing*, which seems absurd, or it is determined by *something*, and thus it is not free. Buridan tries to resolve both extremes by characterising indifference as the suspension of judgment, so that the will is not wholly undetermined, but neither wholly determined by its options.

Leibniz's understanding of 'indifference' is a bit more complicated; although for him, similar to Buridan, indifference occupies a middle ground between absolute determination and absolute indetermination. Indifference is a *contingent* state of the will, since it excludes *logical* necessity, but also because it excludes *physical* necessity.[9] This is quite interesting because Leibniz has not said much in the *Discourse* about this type of necessity. Physical necessity (also contingent because not logically necessary) occurs by means of *efficient* causes, which are the God-decreed but unchanging laws of nature. Thus, a ball dropped from a certain height is *determined* by efficient causes to fall to the ground. A 'determination', Leibniz says, 'is produced when a thing comes into that state in which what it is about to do follows with physical necessity' (LP 103). Intelligent substances, however, are not bound by efficient causes, since they are capable of acting 'on the sole initiative of their own power', that is, 'by looking towards a final cause they interrupt the connexion and the course of the efficient causes that act on their will' (LP 100). So, my choice of which piece of pie to consume, which vocation to take up, with whom to partner, and so on, are influenced but not determined by physical laws and events, unless I allow desire to take its natural course. Thus, my choices can be determined by my deliberations over future ends. In this way, intellectual reasoning about ends is a cause distinct from efficient causes, and its guiding principle is the appearance of the good or best.

Thus far, the will is indifferent to physical causes. Leibniz maintains, however, that the will, in tandem with the intellect, is indifferent even to its very tendency to choose the best: 'although it is most true that the mind never chooses what at present appears the worse, yet does not always choose what at present appears the better; for it can delay and suspend its judgment until a later deliberation, and turn the mind aside to think

in the soul or in the world, even if consciously unperceived, would always influence the choice. The background interest in this question is the voluntarist-intellectualist debate (see *Discourse* §2). The voluntarist insists that God has the 'liberty of indifference' to create the world for any reason whatsoever, or for none, whereas the rationalist insists that God must always have reasons. For history and analysis of the problem see Rescher (2006), 'Choice Without Preference: The Problem of "Buridan's Ass"'.

[9] I am drawing from Leibniz's 'Necessary and Contingent Truths', an essay likely written around the same time as the *Discourse*, from the end of 1685 to the middle of 1686 (AA IV, VI, 1514, No. 303 / LCO 21. Translated in LP 100–3.

of other things' (LP 101). Thus, along with Buridan, Leibniz holds that it is possible for the will to suspend its choice (ln 22) just in case the soul perceives it would be best to do so. The only choice the will cannot make is for the worse, when the intellect knows what is best. Leibniz thus denies what is called *akrasia* or 'weakness of the will'.[10]

On the other hand, Leibniz denies that this freedom of indifference includes an 'absolute metaphysical indifference'; that is, the sort of undetermined 'liberty of indifference' insisted upon by some Medievals (and some current libertarians about free will). This metaphysical indifference places the mind in a state of perfect equilibrium in relation to its objects of choice (LP 102). This state can never obtain, Leibniz insists, since, due to the soul's 'complete notion', there is always some future predicate true of the soul inclining the soul's present state toward that future choice (LP 102). For example, as Leibniz says in §8 (ln 39), the soul (of Alexander) contains 'marks' of everything that will happen to him. Thus, a future satisfaction inclines the will to choose in the present the pie on the left; a future military conquest inclines a current military exercise; and an eventual heart attack inclines prior excesses. This may seem strange, as if the future were to cause the past. But it makes both natural and metaphysical sense: natural, since every future effect must have a prior cause, and metaphysical, since every future predicate is already contained in the individual's notion. Thus the soul can never be in a state of absolute indifference to its future actions, since every prior state of the soul is inclined in the direction it will eventually realise – certainly, but not necessarily.

The upshot of all this is that the soul, while capable of indifference to physical determination, is not indifferent to the determination of its complete notion. Since the complete notion is forever true in God's mind, whatever it contains must infallibly occur. Thus, despite the absence of necessitation, in both logical and physical senses, Leibniz is hard pressed to explain how the soul might have done otherwise than its complete notion determines, such that the soul may determine itself and act freely. The purpose of the next two sections seems to be to explain how the soul can nevertheless act freely.

---

[10] Akrasia (weakness of the will) is specifically the condition in which the agent knows the good action but does not choose it (choosing the worse). Note that while Leibniz denies cases of *strong* akrasia (as when the agent is consciously aware of the good but *at the same time* chooses the worse) he does not deny a weaker form, in which the agent consciously knows the good (or bad) *initially*, but whose judgment becomes occluded by a strong passion leading her to act wrongly, in relative ignorance of her initial judgment. For a superb account of Leibniz's view on akrasia, and his moral psychology in general, see Davidson 2005. For a comprehensive source on the problem of akrasia see Hoffman 2008.

On precautions against the surprises of appearances

Despite this qualified freedom and the indifference of the soul, we often lack the ability to respond constructively to unexpected difficulties, that is, in ways that are other and better than we are currently capable of. The expression 'surprises of appearances' sounds awkward, but it reflects the fact that we are often confronted with situations we are unprepared for. These typically take the form of *appearances* of the good that are not actually good, or when we are struck by hardship and sadness, such as when we lose a job or loved one. Leibniz suggests that while we cannot predict these occurrences, we can prepare ourselves to master their effects ahead of time. The idea is not original with Leibniz, since it was expressly practised by Stoics, such as Epictetus: 'Try, therefore, in the first place, not to be bewildered by appearances. For if you once again gain time and respite, you will more easily command yourself' (*Enchiridion*, XX). Similarly, Leibniz suggests that we should develop the habit, or 'firm will', to divert the flow of inclination, to suspend judgment, to reflect on what is best (or your *duty*, as he says below), and to refrain from action until having 'deliberated well and fully' (ln 26). Leibniz had removed 'to fortify [the will] through practice' from line 24 of the first draft, but it sums up his whole point, namely, the idea of virtue: the practice of developing excellent states of character, so that we may face future situations with equanimity. We can also prepare ourselves by imagining painful or fearful events, such as the loss of a loved one, and reflecting on how we can best face them, thereby preparing ourselves for their inevitability.[11] These preparations are not going to ease every difficulty, of course; but insofar as they interrupt the normal course of events – that is, the normal course of impulse, habit, and other physical causes – Leibniz believes they will provide a certain measure of freedom. Thus, he establishes, in part, one of his three necessary conditions of freedom: rational deliberation upon causes and choices.

On the assurance from all eternity that the soul will not make use of this power

Even though we are able to prepare ourselves for the 'surprises of appearances', it often happens that we fail to act rightly. The real difficulty, however, is that it is *assured from all eternity* that we will fail to act rightly on a given occasion, that we will fail to use our deliberative powers.

---

[11] Epictetus: 'Let death and exile, and all other things which appear terrible, be daily before your eyes, but death chiefly; and you will never entertain any abject thought, nor too eagerly covet anything' (*Enchiridion*, XXI). 'Begin by prescribing to yourself some character and demeanour, such as you may preserve both alone and in company' (XXXIII). See Seidler 1985 for numerous examples of moral preparations in Leibniz.

How, then, can we be free and responsible for our actions? Leibniz sets before us a real paradox: we cannot do otherwise than our complete notion dictates, *and* no one but ourselves is responsible for our sinful actions. But how can we be responsible if we cannot act otherwise?

Leibniz is well aware that the complete notion doctrine threatens to become incompatible not only with free will but also with some important theological doctrines. If we are not responsible for our sins, then God (who created us) will be responsible for them, in which case it would be unjust for God to punish us for them. Leibniz must also allow for the conditions of human salvation: since we are inclined to sin, we are subject to be damned, unless we may be saved. The metaphysical aspects of sin and grace will be addressed in the last two sections of this article. But the problem facing Leibniz at the moment is to explain how we are responsible for sins we cannot avoid committing; and he insists we cannot blame God. Employing the terminology of jurisprudence (in lns 2 and 30), if we do not have the 'right to complain' of God for the sin we are about to commit, it would be unjust to complain of God after having committed it. Thus, if we know we are about to sin, we alone can avoid it. But given it is 'assured' by God that we will sin, how can we avoid it?

To grasp Leibniz's solution, we must first recall the problem of God's foreknowledge of future contingents from §13. Leibniz had argued that God's foreknowledge of our actions implies, not their logical, but only their *hypothetical* necessity. This means that while our action will certainly (or assuredly) occur, it remains a logically contingent, and thus possibly free, action. The difficulty we encountered there, however, remains: given it is assured that we will sin on some future occasion, how can we act otherwise? His answer is that while God knows we will sin, *we* do not know we will sin; thus, we must, and can, act on what we *do* know, namely, on the duty not to sin (ln 40).[12] And if we do sin, that is on us, because we *could* have acted on the duty. The basis for this reasoning would seem to be this: it is human nature always to aim for the apparent good; and since we do not know what will happen, we must always *strive to do what appears best*, that is, to do that which brings about the greater perfection. But how is it possible to act *freely* on what is best, in this case on your duty, when it is assured that you will sin regardless? The following scenario may help to answer this question.

---

[12] Some ten years later, Leibniz will make the same argument in 'Dialogue on Human Freedom': 'But a future sin can be prevented, if the man does his duty, even though God foresees that he will not do it' (AG 112). But then Leibniz denies that the foreseen action *must* happen, for the reason that since we do not know what is foreseen, we must make an effort to do the right thing regardless, especially since God will be content with our sincere and ardent good will (AG 113).

Suppose you've just had a mildly pleasant conversation with Pat, whom you have just met at a busy café. She leaves, and while reflecting a bit on the conversation, you notice she has inadvertently left a thick wad of cash on the table. You casually pocket the cash, pay the bill, and on your way out consider your own financial straits and whether you will try to catch up with Pat. Soon enough, you encounter Pat on her way back to the café, expressing distress and urgency over her missing rent money. Have you seen it? Now, God knows from eternity what you will do. You could really use the money, you know too little about Pat to care much for her troubles, and you feel the sin coming on – a sure sign that your notion has been fixed for eternity: 'So sorry about your money; hope you find it!' You walk away satisfied that you are not responsible for the sin, because you could not have done otherwise.

But surely you could have done otherwise, Leibniz believes, and so do we.[13] Sure, you do not know what your notion contains, until you have acted. But before then, right through the moment you feel the sin coming on, you could reflect on what you *do* know: that you ought to treat others as you would wish to be treated, that you are to be truthful and return rightful possessions, and that you ought not harm those who do not deserve it. These are reflections on the *true* good, on what is best, on what constitutes human perfection, and as such they are disposed to call up in you the motives, sympathies, and desires sufficient to move you to act according to duty rather than selfish inclination. This is one way, as Leibniz describes above, that we may disrupt the chain of efficient causes of desire and act for the sake of ends, that is, for final causes that are not immediate links in the causal chain.

Let us look more deeply at how acting from duty rather than from habit or sensuous impulse is possible, according to Leibniz. As we have seen, we are naturally disposed to pursue what we perceive to be good. So, our good actions depend greatly on *how well* we perceive what the good is. What we most readily perceive to be good is *our own pleasure*, or the objects of our desire that give us pleasure. Leibniz defines pleasure, however, as *a sense of perfection*, or more specifically, as the sense of an increase in our power (*potentia*).[14] In the metaphysical terminology of the *Discourse*, pleasure is the sense of an increase in the soul's *activity*, as opposed to its *passivity*. Thus, pleasure is the *result*, the by-product, of a sense of perfection.

---

[13] The above scenario could be counted as an incidence of 'weak akrasia', as described above in footnote 10.

[14] I am drawing from a piece Leibniz wrote in 1678 called 'Aphorisms on Felicity, Wisdom, Charity, and Justice' (AA VI, 4, 2830), translated in Johns 2013: 88–9. A similar set of definitions is also found in LGR 137–8, and in Leibniz's letter to Duke Ernst August, August 1685, translated in this volume.

Now, since our nature endeavours to increase perfection, pleasure indeed motivates us to act – not least because we perceive pleasure to be *good*. However, feelings of pleasure are insufficient to lead us to higher degrees of perfection since they can also keep us mired in momentary and selfish pleasures. So, to increase the soul's perfection, we must reflect on higher perfections, that is, on practical principles (duties). Reflecting on duty abstracts us from our immediate pleasure and allows us to see how others are affected by our actions. This perception of a *good for others* motivates us, since it involves the perception of ourselves as the cause of a greater, more encompassing, degree of perfection. This perception is also accompanied by pleasure for oneself, since pleasure *results* from the perception of these perfections. Thereby the cognitive perception of one's duty can move the soul to act in accord with duty, overcoming the force of immediate and selfish pleasures. A soul particularly disposed and attuned to such intellectual perfections as duty would, then, in the scenario described above, find motive and pleasure in saying, 'Ah, no worries, I have your money!', and thus would turn away from its initial inclination to sin. This is how deliberation about ends (final causes), or *ends that we ought to have*, namely duties, can motivate us to act.[15] If there is anything to the 'ability to act otherwise' it is only the ability to respond to situations by means of reasons that you know, can know, or can reasonably be expected to know. *But I did not know of my susceptibility to certain temptations!* As a child, you are excused. But at some point, through experience, reflection, and practice, you can be expected to know and to master yourself. As a fundamentally imperfect being, you will of course make mistakes. But from them you are able to learn how to act rightly in the future. So long as you take active measures to perform your moral duty, by deliberating and preparing ahead of time, your actions are responsible and yours alone. Leibniz is saying that what you ought to do is strive to perfect your nature, that is, to do the best, and what is best is to act according to duty; and that means, at least, to refrain from harming others and, at most, to love them. These are duties of both natural justice and Scripture.

Now, here is a strong objection to all of this: The scenario presupposes just what is in question, that you *are* able to reflect on your duty to avoid the sin. But how are you able, if it is not in your notion to reflect on it? And supposing it were, how then are *you* responsible for reflecting? Thus the problem returns: there is not and cannot be any sense in which you acted otherwise than according to your complete notion. You are no more responsible for your virtue than you are for your vice.

---

[15] A duty, Leibniz says, is 'whatever is necessary with regard to the perfectly just' (LGR 140).

I see only one way Leibniz has out of this impasse, though the way remains uncertain. The difficulty with seeing how we can be free and responsible, on the complete notion account, lies in our tendency, encouraged by Leibniz no less, to think of the complete notion as the *cause* of an individual's actions.[16] Accordingly, God conceives in his mind the complete notion of a *possible you*, with all of your predicates, and then decides to create an *actual* you, based on the relative perfection of your notion. Thus, from this complete notion, all of your actions unavoidably follow. In short, since God conceived of your actions, God is the cause of them. However, it is not necessary to think this, and it would arguably be a mistake, given several implications of Leibniz's commitments.

To begin with, Leibniz is fundamentally committed to the idea that individual substances (living beings) are the *cause* of their actions. This is implied in the very idea of an individual substance: an entity is not a substance unless it is the subject and cause of its actions. But 'being a cause of action' needs further specification in terms of Leibniz's conditions for freedom, which include *contingency, spontaneity*, and *deliberation*. We understand by now that the *contingency* (the absence of logical necessity) of our actions means that our actions are not determined by the strongest sense of necessity. Therefore, it is at least *possible* for us to be the cause of our actions. We also understand, from *spontaneity*, that a substance has no other cause than itself – no cause external to itself. Of course, humans can in no sense be the cause of their being and material nature – we do not create ourselves. But even though God is responsible for this, it does not follow that all of our actions flow inevitably from this dependence on God. More to the point, spontaneity pertains to our passive and active relation to other substances. We are *passive*, since we are the cause of our reactions to actions that happen *to* us – actions that reduce our active power. This makes us the cause even of actions we do not consciously will. But what makes an individual's actions truly its own is its capacity for *deliberation over ends*, the capacity for choice and responsibility. Due to your deliberative capacity (which can be specified in more detail), you can be the active cause of your conscious choices, thus of an increase in your active power.

When we include all of what constitutes your complete notion, what God initially *conceives* of is a notion that is uniquely and completely *yours*. Your actions constitute the notion that God conceives of you and by means of which decides to give you existence. God *foresaw* that a being with exactly your character would sin at one moment and act according to duty in another. It is thus not necessary for Leibniz to establish that you have

---

[16] See especially §13 lns 40–5.

'the power to do otherwise' than your notion dictates (ln 21). All that is needed is to establish that *you are the cause* of your actions. Whether your deliberated choices subsist as ideas in God's mind or are expressed through a living, sensing, thinking individual, you alone made them. Thus, instead of conceiving of the complete notion as the cause of your actions, we should consider it as their effect. Conceiving of the complete notion as the effect rather than the cause should also help us make sense of what follows.

On whether you can act contrary to your notion and remain the same individual

In yet another effort to quash a possible threat to freedom in view of the complete notion, Leibniz makes a brief remark, but one with paradoxical implications for substantial identity: 'But another will say, from whence it comes that this man will assuredly commit this sin? The reply is easy, that otherwise it would not be this man' (lns 41–2). This reply is very different from the one given in §13, where he says that God knows all 'future contingents' (future actions) *assuredly* because they are included in your complete notion, of which God has complete knowledge. Here, however, the answer, given without elucidation, is that if someone, 'this man', did not commit the sin contained in his notion, then 'this man' would have to be a different individual. In other words, if even one predicate of your notion were different, you would be altogether a different individual. But why should we think this? For we commonly believe that we might have done any number of things other than we did, and yet we would still say we are the same person. We believe this because we can easily imagine it. If, in the scenario above, you had acted according to duty instead of sinning, you would still be you, right? However, if acting according to duty was not in your complete notion, then you would become a different person. But of course it *was* in your complete notion, and so you were not free to act otherwise than in accord with it. But now, not only does this seem absurd to us, it becomes impossible to act otherwise while remaining the same individual.

These problems stem from the fact that we must take the continuity of identity seriously, given Leibniz's strict requirements for individuation. According to Leibniz's definition of an individual substance, since the individual is defined by its *complete* set of predicates – its actions and qualities – a change in only one predicate entails a different individual altogether. In his correspondence with Arnauld, over the question of whether he is free not to take a certain journey, Leibniz puts the matter this way:

> Since it is certain that I will take it, there surely must be some connection between myself who is the subject and the execution of the trip which is the predicate (for the [notion][17] of the predicate is always in the subject in a true

proposition). There would therefore be a falsehood if I did not take it, which would destroy my individual or complete [notion], or what God conceives or conceived of me, even before resolving to create me.[18]

Here, we find Leibniz's continued commitment to the 'predicate-in-notion' theory of truth introduced in §8. Thus, no change in the complete notion can be admitted, because if even one predicate is changed, then the notion, while not *literally* destroyed, becomes false for that individual. Secondly, if even one of your predicates is not true of you, then God cannot know your complete notion; and then he cannot decide, in combination with other complete notions, whether you should be created. We should keep in mind that, strictly speaking, God does not *create* notions; they are ideas in his mind that he *contemplates* as possibly existing individuals; he considers the perfection they would contribute, in combination with other complete notions, and then on that basis decides whether to give them existence (more on this below). For God to be able to do this, however, every notion of an individual must be complete and remain fixed. Leibniz's answer to whether he is free not to take the trip is not that the predicate 'takes the trip' should become false (thus making his complete notion false) but that the decision to take the trip is already a free decision (LAV 103 / LAM 58).

But perhaps Leibniz's answer is unconvincing, since we have yet to clarify fully the respect in which a decision can be already free. So, let us return to the question: How can a change in only one predicate make for a different individual? A more convincing answer is that a single change entails many changes. Recall from §8 these additional features of the complete notion: that it contains all predicates within both a logical and rational order, such that God could 'deduce', in a sense, the entire notion from just one predicate; and that God understands the 'foundation and reason' for each predicate (§8, ln 33).[19] This is to maintain, in sum, a *sufficient reason*

[17] Leibniz uses the Latin *notio*, as he renders the whole parenthesised phrase in Latin.
[18] Letter to Arnauld, 14 July 1686, LAV 103 / LAM 58. Voss translates the French *notion* as 'concept', but I prefer to translate it as 'notion' because there is a difference in French between notion and concept, as is apparent where God conceives (*conçoit*) my *notion*, but not my concept: ('Il y auroit donc une fausseté si je ne le faisois pas, qui detruiroit ma notion individuelle ou complete, ou ce que Dieu conçoit ou concevoit de moy. . .', LAV 102). While the terms are indeed very similar, I understand conceiving to be a mental act while notions are objects of thought.
[19] As Leibniz again puts it to Arnauld, 'there must always be some foundation for the connection of the terms of a proposition, which must be found in their [notions]. That is my great principle . . . one of whose corollaries is the common axiom that nothing happens without a reason . . . why the thing turned out this way rather than otherwise' (Letter to Arnauld, 14 July 1686, LAV 111)' On identity, see 'Leibniz's Remarks on a Letter from Arnauld', June 1686, LAV 57–77. See also MB 128 and AG 69–81.

for each predicate. This means that each predicate has a reason that can be inferred *from* its prior predicate and a reason inferable *to* its subsequent predicate, such that the whole series will have rational and purposeful coherence. Thus, God sees that each predicate implies and is implied by every other, such that a change in one predicate would entail a change in all of them.

Here is a simple way to understand how such a dramatic change could occur. First, imagine we have an individual consisting of only three predicates, {1, 2, 3}, and that we have an 'arrangement law' (a sufficient reason) for the order of the predicates, namely that each predicate has a natural predecessor and/or a natural successor (except for the first and last). Now suppose we change the middle predicate from 2 to 5. In keeping with the arrangement law, predicates 1 and 3 must also be changed to 4 and 6, respectively, resulting in a completely new set {4, 5, 6}, as a consequence of changing only one predicate.

Now, to understand how this might work for a complex entity like a real human being, consider the 'sufficient reasons' for you not to have sinned in the above scenario. The sufficient reason for the change from the predicate 'kept the money' to 'returned the money', could be that you perceived a higher degree of perfection in the duty to return the money. But what is the sufficient reason for that perception? We can suppose that you possess the sort of psychophysiology that inclines you to pause and reflect before acting. The sufficient reason for your psychophysiology is that you have an innate disposition to pause and reflect before acting. Good for you. But this means that you would have done many things differently, not only this one, such that you would effectively be a different person.

Alternatively, we may suppose that you were born with a rather selfish disposition, but through experience and training you found it useful and pleasing to cultivate patience and other-regarding desires. Either way, you would have done many things differently. We can also suppose that your returning the money is a sufficient reason for future actions, such that if you had not done this, many future predicates would not be true of you. Your acquaintance becomes a friend. You understand yourself in a new light, others come to know you as trustworthy and kind, and so on. Therefore, for this one change in you to be possible, many predicates, many sufficient reasons, would have to be true of you as well, such that you really would be a different person.

Despite these examples, the reader might retain the nagging sense that you would not be a different person – that despite all these changes something of *you* would remain the same. Sure, you would be different, in the sense that you would have done different things and had different experiences. But you would not altogether be a different person. But are you sure about this? What is it about you that would remain the same, some unique and essential features of your soul? What are they? Is there anything to the soul other than the entire set of its predicates and their order? Leibniz thinks not. Certainly, this issue raises philosophical puzzles about the continuity of personal identity over time; it also places increasing pressure on Leibniz's account of free will. This becomes more apparent when we recall that each substance is related (by expression) to every other, such that a change in one substance implies a change in all of them. You can understand Arnauld's initial alarm in §13 over the complete notion: that it imposes a 'fatal necessity' over the whole world, rendering both God and creatures unfree.

It is apparent, then, that Leibniz's insistence on the unique, unchangeable identity of an individual substance presents a serious impediment to his other metaphysical commitments: If an individual substance is to be defined by all of its predicates, such that a change in one entails a different individual, it is unclear how an individual can act otherwise than according to the very notion that defines it. Consequently, the respect in which an individual is 'free' becomes untenable. However, as I have suggested, if we consider the complete notion as the *effect* rather than as the *cause* of the individual, then the problem of 'acting otherwise' ceases to obtain: it is through the individual's contingency, spontaneity, and deliberative capacity – the very conditions that define its freedom—that it *becomes* a distinct, complete, individual. Thus, the individual's notional identity is not predetermined for it, since the individual *makes* itself through its free actions. This is the best sense I can make of Leibniz's response to Arnauld, above: He is free to take the trip without doing otherwise than his notion specifies and without destroying his notion, because that decision was caused by him.

On Judas' sin – and possible worlds

At this point, Leibniz becomes concerned to explain why God would allow great sins to occur at all, given that God has the goodness and power to prevent them. Thus, he will touch upon the doctrine for which he is most famous, *theodicy*, or God's justice, and his claim that this world is the best possible. As such, this section requires a lengthy and detailed explanation.

Leibniz broaches the problem of sin through the example of Judas, a disciple of Jesus. As the well-known biblical story goes, Judas arranges to have Jesus turned over to the political and religious authorities, some of whom wish to prosecute him for sedition and/or blasphemy and put him to death – which, of course, he was (Matthew 26 and 27). But we can render the story in Leibnizian terms: the notion of Judas contains the predicate 'betrays Jesus', since the predicate is true of Judas. Since Jesus is considered not only a model of virtue, but the very son of God, this particular betrayal (a violation of loyalty, friendship, and trust) qualifies as a most egregious sin. The question Leibniz needs to answer then is: why would God allow it, presuming he could prevent it? He puts the matter this way: 'only this question remains, why such a Judas the traitor, who is possible only in God's idea, exists actually' (lns 45–6).

Leibniz's direct answer is that God saw that this great sin must and could be 'compensated with interest in the universe', or that, in other words, 'God will derive a greater good from it' (lns 49–50).[20] We must not mistake this to mean, however, that sins are allowed *for the sake of* bringing about a greater good; but rather that *if* a sin is committed, then God knows how to compensate for it. Still, this answer is initially puzzling, because the first question we might ask is why does God not simply prevent Judas from betraying Jesus? If he had, then Jesus might have been able to bring his rightful and beneficent mission to even greater fruition. On the contrary, as Leibniz argued in §7, God does not prevent sins from occurring, but has good reasons for *allowing* them: he takes sins as constraints imposed by human imperfections that must then be rectified through a more perfect series of human actions. Presumably, then, God saw that Judas' sin would be compensated, since as a result of it Jesus would become the instrument of human salvation, an outcome that God freely chose, from among other possible outcomes, even though human imperfection conditioned the choice. Leibniz will have more to say about the cause of imperfection and sin in the next section.

But we need to understand the 'possible ways' implication of Leibniz's answer to the problem: Judas is 'possible only in God's idea' (lns 45–6), as distinct from *existing actually*; and the 'series of things' in which Judas is included 'is the most perfect among all the other possible ways' (lns 51–2). These remarks indicate the difference between two modes of being: *possibility* and *actuality*, and they allude to Leibniz's doctrine that *this world is the best possible world*. The following serves to explain these remarks in outline.[21] Before anything is created, God's mind contains an infinity of possible ideas. These ideas consist of generally three types: (1) eternal truths, such as those of mathematics, geometry, and the laws of justice and morality; (2) possible and distinct sets of general or primitive laws of physics and

---

[20] See §7, ln 22. Leibniz may be drawing from Augustine on these points: that God would not 'in any way allow anything evil to exist among his works were he not so omnipotent and good that he can bring good even out of evil' (*Enchiridion*, 3, 11). And speaking of Adam's sin: 'But because God foreknew that he would make evil use of his free will, God prepared his design to bring good even out of one who did evil, so that man's evil will might not be made of no effect but nevertheless the Almighty's good might be fulfilled' (*Enchiridion*, 28, 104).

[21] Drawing from 'Necessary and Contingent Truths', LP 103–5.

human natures (we have seen that God has decreed that it is human nature to pursue the apparent good, though God can conceive of other possible natures); (3) every possible complete notion of an individual, including that of Judas and of infinitely many other possible but non-existing individuals. God then conceives of unique possible worlds, each of which is comprised of some combination of the above three types of ideas. Thus, World A is distinct from World B, because it has a different configuration of primitive laws and individuals, and so on for each conceivable world.

Now, while there is an infinity of distinct possible worlds, the number of possible candidates for *creation* will be greatly limited. Here we should recall from §5 and §6 God's general criterion for the best possible world: that it contain the simplest laws in balance with the greatest variety of beings. This criterion rules out many possible, that is, conceivable, worlds. Of course, no world will contain true contradictions, since the object of a contradiction cannot even be conceived. But the eternal truths of mathematics and geometry, presumably in every possible world, will form a world having a greater quantity of order and stability than without them.[22] Laws of motion and force will be consistent with the truths of mathematics and geometry, and, once given specific form, will determine the behaviour, character, and variety of that world's physical nature. Worlds whose laws tend to make matter collapse immediately instead of forming into organic wholes are not going to be good candidates for creation. Thus, only worlds containing a persistent optimum of simplicity and variety are going to be viable candidates for creation – and finally there will be *a* world that, in Leibniz's terms, 'is the most perfect among all the other possible ways' (lns 51–2). This is the world God creates.

But we are most concerned about worlds involving complete notions of individual substances: For each possible world, God must consider a complete (that is, bounded infinite) set of individual notions, with each notion (in accord with the principle of the identity of indiscernibles) distinct from every other. And, as we know from §14, since each individual substance expresses the whole world, each notion expresses every substance in varying degrees of activity. For example, if Pi 1 (possible individual 1) gets the job, then Pi 2 cannot; if Pi 3, or a class of like individuals, plunders the country's treasury, then many other Pis will suffer. God must then inspect each individual notion to determine its contribution to the overall perfection. The configuration of possible individuals contributing most to the greater overall perfection will be most eligible for existence, while

---

[22] Usually, in the literature on possible worlds, eternal truths are naturally included in all possible worlds, since they are logically necessary truths. But it seems possible to conceive of a world in which these truths have no application, or do not govern anything.

those contributing less will not be created and will eternally remain ideas in God's mind.[23] When all possibilities are taken in sum, there will be only one possible world for God to create, and that will be the one containing the greatest amount of perfection.

This brings us to the matter at hand. There is a possible (conceivable) world that does not include Judas. As a result, 'Judas betrays Jesus' would be false for that world, and so (conceivably) 'Jesus was crucified' would also be false. But now we are talking about a very different world, a world populated with different individuals having very different histories – a world which, for reasons beyond our ken, God saw would be less perfect than this one. So then God must have foreseen that a world which includes 'Judas betrays Jesus' should be included in the best possible world, and the most we can know about what makes this world the optimum is that God foresaw that the crucifixion of Jesus (not to mention all of the conditions in addition to Judas' betrayal that contributed to making the crucifixion possible and significant) would more than compensate for the sin of Judas, since this outcome would result in more perfection than any other *possible* outcome.[24]

That this world is the best possible world is no doubt hard to believe, given even a cursory glance around the neighbourhood, let alone a survey of history; so, some brief qualifications should be kept in mind. The word 'possible' must not be taken in an absolute sense, to mean 'the best world conceivable', as if all sentient beings should always be happy and never have to struggle and suffer. It means the best world that could be created, under the required limitations, constraints, and complex combinations. Since the best possible world must contain the simplest laws and the greatest variety of beings, we can expect many of its items and creatures to be far from perfect in an absolute sense. If the world is to consist largely of *matter*, then the world must unavoidably contain things that disintegrate on the one hand but generate on the other. If there are to be creatures with souls attached to material bodies, they will naturally be beset with a whole range of physical, epistemic, and moral imperfections. Thus, a world full of blissfully happy sages and saints is not possible, under the criteria of order and variety. In general, any world not maximally expressing God's glory (lawfulness and richness) is conceivable but will not be chosen. Let us state it thus: the best possible world is one that is well ordered and abundant,

---

[23] As noted in §9, this does not mean that the best possible world contains the most perfect individuals; it can contain, rather, very imperfect individuals, just in case God can derive greater perfection from a given imperfection. The case of Judas, as explained just below, is a prime example.

[24] Leibniz anticipates and responds to the objection that God's foresight results in an absurdity, since it implies that God foresees the very decrees that he makes (LP 103–5).

and contains the greatest happiness possible for rational creatures, given the necessary imperfections of their nature.

It is apparent from this account that Leibniz is defending God against the charge that God is responsible both for human sin and for the sorry state of things. And this defence, this 'theodicy', will appear far from convincing. Was Christ's suffering and death necessary for our eternal salvation? Other ways of salvation are certainly conceivable. Was it not possible for God to have created some *other* world – ever so slightly better than this one, if not a lot better? In the end, at least in the *Discourse*, Leibniz rests his case on the claim that we are not capable of comprehending 'the admirable economy of this choice' (ln 52), and that we can never fathom, following St Paul, the 'depth and abyss of the divine wisdom' (ln 56). But I think we should be careful not to take Leibniz to be appealing here simply to God's incomprehensible or inscrutable nature. God is comprehensible enough, in terms of his attributes – it is only that, as finite creatures, we cannot comprehend a virtually infinite range of possible notions and worlds, nor fathom the reasons for their relative value. We can have no idea of why *this* world is exactly *this* way and not some other – except that since God is perfect, God must have good reason. We may speculate on God's reasons for permitting a given sin, but ultimately these reasons remain beyond our ability to grasp.

On the metaphysics of sin and evil: the original limitation of creatures

Perhaps the above explanation makes sense as a theodicy for sins having profound theological consequence but may seem far removed from our everyday intuitions about sin. It will seem to many that if God 'permits' sins to occur, presuming God is able to prevent them, and despite God's compensation for them, God really ought to prevent them. Imagine that you stand by while a stranger brutally beats your friend, even though you could intervene. Are you justified in saying 'these things must be permitted – after all, God will compensate in due order'? Are you not rather an accomplice to a crime and all the more wicked for permitting it? Leibniz must sense that he has not said enough to absolve God from responsibility for sin, for he assures us that, despite the above theodicy, God is not the cause of evil (sin being one type of evil).[25] He then offers a few brief but profound remarks centred on the claim that the root of evil lies in 'nothingness' (ln 64). While these remarks do not inspire confidence

---

[25] 'Evil', in this context, refers to moral evil, either the transgression of a law, or the intentional infliction of undeserved suffering on another, as contrasted with physical evils, such as natural disasters and diseases.

that Leibniz will appeal to our everyday intuitions about sin, they do point to a compelling response to our everyday questions about responsibility for sin, both God's responsibility and ours.

To understand Leibniz's remarks, it will help to have in mind the biblical story of Adam and Eve (Genesis 2–3) and its common interpretations. As is well known, God forbids the primal couple, in their state of innocence in the garden of Eden, from eating from the Tree of the Knowledge of Good and Evil. A serpent (or the 'Devil' on some accounts) persuades or tricks Eve into eating the fruit of the tree, and Adam follows Eve's promptings to do likewise. Consequently, God expels them from the garden and punishes them and their progeny with pain, toil, and mortality.

Interpretations of the meaning and significance of the story of course vary, but we are most concerned to understand the cause of Adam and Eve's disobedience, since, whatever the cause, it is generally held that we (all of humankind) have inherited the tendency to sin from them. While the Hebrew scriptures say little else directly about Adam and Eve's transgression, several passages attribute the cause of 'wickedness' to an inclination of the heart (Genesis 6:5) or to the influence of Satan (Wisdom 2:24). The Gospels and Letters contain numerous references to Adam's sin (for example, Romans 5:12–21), and depict a struggle, as Paul puts it, between the law of sin in his body and the law of God as understood in his mind (Romans 7:23). Scripture on the whole frequently attributes the cause of sin to man's rebellious nature or to sensual lust, but the most commonly cited cause is *pride*.[26] It is through pride that we exalt ourselves to the level of God, so that, as the serpent says to Eve, 'you will be like gods who know what is good and evil' (Genesis 3:5). Since pride makes us believe we do not need God, it further corrupts human nature and provides a continual impetus for lust, crime, and other transgressions. It wasn't, however, until Augustine that Adam's sin was referred to in terms familiar today as 'original sin' (*peccatum originale*), which refers not to the first sin, disobedience, but to the cause and nature of sin, or more specifically, to the human soul in its original condition.

At this juncture, a problem arises: whatever the cause of sin, it is in our nature; and since God created us, it appears that God is responsible for the sins we commit. Of course, theological tradition generally maintains that despite our corrupt nature we have freedom of choice, by means of which we sin *willingly*, thereby making us, not God, responsible for sin.

---

[26] Pride ('haughty eyes') is the first of the seven vices or abominations (Proverbs 6:17); it is the desire to be like God (Isaiah 14:12–14), or to have excessive self-regard: 'That he may not become conceited and thus incur the devil's punishment' (1 Timothy 3:6). Luther connects pride to unbelief in and rebellion against God (*Lectures on Romans*, 76).

Still, we may wonder why God should be the cause even of our inclination to sin. It seems unfitting for a being supposed to be all-good, all-powerful, and all-knowing, to create beings capable of sin and evil. To address this problem, we need to follow Augustine a bit more deeply into the soul's original condition.

In his *City of God*, Augustine, quoting from Scripture, identifies pride as 'the beginning of sin'[27] and as the condition of 'a soul that is inordinately in love with its own power' (*City*, 12:8). But it is Augustine's characterisation of pride as a *defect* in our nature that leads to the conception of original sin as grounded in 'nothing'. Accordingly, a defect is not a being, cause, force, or presence, but rather the *absence* of them. Evil is thus a *deficient* cause, rather than an *efficient* or moving cause (*City*, 6). In this sense evil is an absence of reality and goodness, just as darkness and silence are absences of the positive realities of light and sound. As an absence of reality, evil is 'nothing', and nothing is the original and unavoidable condition of creatures who are 'made from nothing' (*City*, 12:8). Thus, God does not create evil; he creates beings who necessarily 'participate in nothing', and nothing is, if it is anything, simply a defect in being. While it may seem obscure and false to characterise evil as nothing, it just means that all of God's creatures are necessarily lacking in reality, goodness, and, generally, in perfection, by virtue of having been created from nothing.

To grasp the metaphysical picture more fully, we need to understand the Neoplatonic background on which Augustine is drawing.[28] Here, Being (or reality) and Goodness are convertible terms: a change in the quantity of one entails a change in the quantity of the other. Thus, the more reality a thing (or substance) has, the more goodness it has; and if it lacks goodness, then it lacks reality. The reality of a thing is a function of its ontological independence and ability to act. God has the most reality, since God does not depend on any other being to exist; and since God has all the perfections in their highest degree, God is the most active substance. Substances other than God – for instance, humans, animals, and plants, as well as strictly corporeal beings – have, in that order, lesser degrees of perfection, reality, activity, and goodness. It follows that since evil is a *lack* of goodness, it is a lack of reality. As Augustine puts it, 'whatever is, is good; and evil, the origin of which I was trying to find, is not a substance, because if it were a substance, it would be good' (*Confessions*, Bk VII, 12). This means not only that evil is not a substance, but also that it is not *in* a substance.

---

[27] *City*, 12:6, quoting from Sirach or Ecclesiasticus 10:13.

[28] A good place to start is Plotinus, *The Enneads*, First Ennead, Eighth Tractate, <https://www.sacred-texts.com/cla/plotenn/index.htm> (Plotinus 2018). Also see Armstrong 1953.

Evil is a natural absence in the substance's ability to act, comprising its ontological dependence, limitation, and imperfection.

Along these lines, it is helpful to think of evil as a *privation*, which is the absence of some quality or feature that is natural to a thing. For example, blindness and deafness are absences of sight and hearing in creatures that naturally have these faculties; accordingly, evil is a privation of the goodness that creatures naturally have by virtue of their *being*, which God gave them. Now, all of this may sound wildly wrong. By conceiving of evil as an absence, do we not risk losing sight of the positive reality of evil? After all, evil, moral evil, is the intentional infliction of harm upon the undeserving, and it would be crazy to deny it occurs. Are we to maintain that the intentional actions of the prideful, avaricious, and inordinately lustful are literally caused by nothing? Not at all. But what this doctrine is telling us is that these evils result from the privation of the positive faculties of the understanding and will, in the absence of which the soul is misdirected or overwhelmed by other causes. A deficiency in the *understanding* regarding the *truly good* will lead to the pursuit of unworthy goods; a weakness in the *will* makes us vulnerable to the forces of raw desire and the temptations of pleasure; the blows of misfortune and the indifference of privilege may reduce the power of both faculties and lead us into anger, apathy, or excessive self-love. The real and common cause of moral evil, then, is the privation or inability of the will and understanding to overcome these very real causes of sin.

To put the matter in terms of an evil as opposed to a good will, Augustine tells us that, on the one hand, the will is good because it is an active reality within us, and the Good cannot be the efficient cause of the Bad (*City*, 12:6). However, a deficiency, imperfection, or privation of the will makes us susceptible to turn toward the bad, that is, to pursue and indulge in objects of lesser value. The good will, however, endeavours to pursue the immutable things – God, first of all, and then the proper love of self and neighbour. If the will should turn away from these higher goods, concupiscence takes over. But while pursuit of the true good is difficult, the will always has, Augustine insists, the freedom to choose the good over the bad. The will is not bad to begin with, but it *becomes* bad by choosing the bad, and it chooses the bad because it is a deficient cause (*City*, 12:6).

We may now understand Leibniz's views on sin as informed by this Augustinian-Neoplatonic background.[29] Accordingly, Adam and Eve were

---

[29] For a detailed account of Leibniz on original sin, see Bobier 2016 and Newlands 2014. See also Leibniz, *Dialogue on Human Freedom*, 1695 (AG 114) and 'The Confession of a Philosopher' in LCP.

'evil' before they ate from the tree, not because their soul contained some suppressed wicked tendency urging to be expressed, but because of the 'original limitation or imperfection connatural to all creatures' (lns 59–60). This limitation explains how they could have been susceptible to Satan's persuasion before having sinned, and it is rooted in their having been created from nothing (ln 64). As Leibniz writes in 'Dialogue on Human Freedom':

> There was no positive evil in created things at the beginning, but they always lacked many perfections. Thus, because of a lack of attention, the first man was able to turn away from the supreme good and be content with some created thing, and thus, he fell into sin. That is, from an imperfection that was merely privative in the beginning, he fell into a positive evil. (AG 114)

Whatever motivated Judas to betray Jesus (whether greed, envy, or political stratagem), it was not on this account that Satan entered him (John 13:27). A weakness in Judas' faculties, namely his mistaken perception of the objectively good and his susceptibility to these motives, lead him to take the latter to be more worthy. More mundanely, the weakness in one's perception of what is truly good will stand as the deficient cause of actions that benefit oneself at the expense of others.

Leibniz's conception of moral evil as an imperfection rooted in the substance's deficiency and nothingness will, again, be difficult to square with experience.[30] For no one can ignore the reality of sensual desire, the mis-directions of the passions, or the distressing quantity of wilful corruptions, vile intentions, and monstrous crimes we have witnessed throughout history. But one advantage of this conception is that, rather than identifying the cause of sin with some 'evil urge' within us, we can, with a bit more work, bring together the following doctrines: (1) God is not responsible for sin, since the ultimate cause of sin is our necessary imperfection. (2) Although as a result of our imperfection, not caused by us, we will unavoidably sin, we are still responsible for sin. (3) That we are responsible stems from our capacity to improve ourselves through moral virtue. Thus, instead of being punished or damned, we may be reformed and saved. (4) That we are responsible also makes punishment for sin, whether in this life or after, just. (5) By recognising that we are inherently imperfect and weak, we may make ourselves and each other better through the positive realities of love, empathy, serving the public good, and promoting universal justice. These possibilities make us active rather than passive beings

---

[30] Echoing Augustine: 'If they are imperfect, one can only blame their limitation on their boundaries, that is to say, the extent of their participation in nothingness' (AG 115).

and fortify our independence from external factors that would otherwise determine us. (6) Try as we might to do well and good, we will often fail, and no amount of our own effort can repair the damage we have caused nor prevent the damage we will inflict. This makes us susceptible to damnation, for which we require the remedy of grace.

On the degrees of grace

Grace (*gratia*) is God's freely given gift of assistance or favour; it is a kind of power, a moral power, added to human moral and physical power, to encourage the performance of salutary actions.[31] It may also be given, through Jesus Christ, in the form of forgiveness of sins, and thus lead to our salvation (an eternal, heavenly life), rescuing us from damnation. Like *concurrence*, grace gives the recipient a certain power to act; but, unlike concurrence, which is constant, grace may be given at one time or another (unless you are in a state of grace). Though the recipient may pray for God's favour and forgiveness, grace is given solely at God's discretion, as a 'remedy' (ln 65) for our inherent imperfection, which is ultimately due to our origin from nothing.

The traditional doctrine of grace is highly complex and typically involves the following problems: (a) the *efficacy* or power of grace, whether grace is sufficient in itself to bring about its effect, or whether its effect depends on the will and disposition of the recipient; (b) the *distribution* or dispensation of grace, regarding who receives it, how much is given, and why; and (c) whether humans, through their salutary acts, can oblige God to give grace. In this section, Leibniz addresses the efficacy of grace, while §31 deals with its distribution and whether God's grace can be obliged.

Leibniz's discussion begins with a standard classification of the means by which grace is given, though the means may also distinguish types. God gives *ordinary* grace through revelation, prayer, worship, confession, and the sacraments; while *extraordinary* grace is given through miracles, prophecy, conversion, and the redemption of the soul. This distinction of means need not be exact or all-inclusive, since nothing much depends on it for Leibniz, but it bears keeping in mind.

More important is the traditional distinction between (a) *sufficient* grace (*gratia mere sufficiens*) and (b) *efficacious* grace (*gratia efficax*). While this distinction figures into the debate over the dispensation of grace, it is central to the debate over the power of God's grace to have its effect in the recipient. The debate stems from passages in the Gospels indicating on the

---

[31] My discussion of grace in §30 and §31 is guided by Echavarría 2017, Rutherford 2006, and <https://www.catholicculture.org/culture/library/dictionary/index.cfm?id=33281>.

one hand that *God wills everyone to be saved*, and yet on the other that *many will not be saved*.[32] So, why are many not saved? Arnauld, representing one set of theologians, maintains that the power of God's grace is absolute (efficacious in itself). Thus, if God grants you the grace for your salvation, then you are saved. Those who are not saved did not receive God's grace, for whatever reason of God.

The opposing view, represented by Malebranche, claims that God's grace is 'sufficient' to have some effect on the recipient, but not sufficient for salvation, as the efficaciousness of the grace will depend on the will and disposition of the recipient.[33] God's grace can be annulled, for instance, by the recipient's excessive lust (concupiscence).[34] Thus, while it is God's 'general will' that everyone be saved, our own will can save or damn us. This position has the virtue of making the recipient's will a key component of the efficacy of grace, but it does so by reducing God's power. Arnauld's position retains God's power, but loses the contribution of the recipient.

In the *Discourse*, Leibniz's exposition of the traditional distinction is a bit confusing; however, characteristically, he accepts both positions, while leaning toward Malebranche's. Accordingly, *sufficient grace* is efficacious 'in-itself', but only to 'produce a certain proportioned effect' in the recipient (ln 68). Whether the grace is sufficient to bring about the intended effect (a salutary action, salvation, or to prevent a sin) depends on whether the recipient joins his own will and disposition to it.[35] In other words, the efficacy of grace depends on 'the congruity of the circumstances' (ln 74).[36] For Leibniz, then, it is important that the recipient be given the grace

---

[32] 1 Timothy 2:4 and Matthew 22:14 in the parable of the wedding feast: 'Many are called, but few are chosen.' See Patrick Riley's introduction to MT 3–4.

[33] I am characterising the debate as between Arnauld and Malebranche in order to simplify the exposition. However, it is more accurately represented as between the Báñezians and the Molinists, after the Dominican theologian Domingo Báñez (1528–1604) and the Jesuit Luis de Molina (1525–1600). For the Báñezians, the efficacy of grace depends solely on the intrinsic nature of the grace – that it comes from God and does not depend on the will of the recipient. For the Molinists, efficacy depends on 'the circumstances that God foresees to be congruous with the dispositions of the person receiving the grace', <https://www.catholicculture.org/culture/library/dictionary/index.cfm?id=3 3281>.

[34] Grace, or 'preventative delectation', 'is always efficacious in some way; but it does not always produce the whole effect which it could cause, because concupiscence opposes it' (MT, Discourse III, XIX).

[35] Malebranche similarly compared sufficient grace to the weights on a scale. A weight has a definite effect, but its *net* effect will be proportional to the weights in the other bowl (MT, Discourse III, XX).

[36] This expression (lost in the AG translation) comes from Molina by way of Augustine's remarks on Matthew 22:14. 'It is true, therefore, that many are called but few chosen. Those are chosen who are effectùally [*congruenter*] called. [. . .] He calls the man on

sufficient to perform some salutary act, but also that she *strive* to make it efficacious. Having to make an effort provides an extra incentive to commit the action as well as demonstrates the recipient's moral strength and perfection. It remains possible, however, for the grace to be insufficient, in case it is incongruent with the recipient's will. Either way, the recipient will be responsible for the results of her actions, salutary or not.

Despite the potential insufficiency of grace, Leibniz reserves for God an *absolutely efficacious* grace that does not depend on any congruency of circumstances, for it is 'always victorious' (ln 73). On this point, Leibniz concedes to Arnauld. An example might be St Paul's (Saul's) conversion from persecutor of Christ to apostle, since there the grace must have been able to oppose all will and disposition to the contrary.[37] While it remains possible for some to render God's grace ineffective and thus not to be saved, in the end God's grace is supreme. The reason why God gives grace, whether sufficient or absolute, to some and not to others is dealt with in the next article.

With this distinction between sufficient and absolutely efficacious grace, Leibniz concludes §30 by resolving a theological dispute. But his position also reflects his overall effort in the *Discourse* to show that God's creatures are both independent from and dependent on God. They are independent insofar as they can and ought to perfect themselves through their own efforts, but their being and salvation depend ultimately on God.

§31. On God's dispensation of grace; on middle knowledge and God's reasons for admitting a possible individual into existence – thus resolving all the difficulties.

As indicated in the translation, Leibniz's discussion of grace in §30 had originally continued through to the end of (what is now) §31. But he went back and decided to end §30 with his discussion of the *efficacy* of grace and to begin §31 with the *dispensation* of grace. This article, then, is concerned to resolve certain 'difficulties' with the doctrine of dispensation. The central difficulty is why God gives grace to some and not to others. Leibniz claims to resolve it 'in one blow', by appeal to his doctrine of possible worlds and individuals. Let us trace Leibniz's argument along with some of the theological background that informs it.[1]

whom he has mercy in the way he knows will suit [*congruere*] him, so that he will not refuse the call' (Augustine, *To Simplician, on various questions*, Bk I, Q II, par. 13). Reference from <https://www.newadvent.org/cathen/06710a.htm>.

37 Acts 9:1–19; 22:6–21; 26:12–18.

1 For this explanation, I am guided by Georges Le Roy's (1957) commentary on §31 and by Echavarría 2017.

The problem of the dispensation of grace has its roots in a theological dispute between Pelagius and Augustine.[2] Pelagius held that creatures do not require God's grace in order to have faith and to do good works, since their capability for them resides in their own nature. God dispenses grace not in order to *cause* salutary acts, but only to endorse, or, perhaps, to encourage them. But whatever grace God gives, it is *earned* by the creature through faith and works.

Augustine, on the other hand, argued that Pelagius' view rendered creatures grossly independent of God and undermined the supremacy of God's will. He maintained rather that creatures cannot have faith, do good works, or attain salvation without God's grace. This makes creatures wholly dependent on God's will for their goodness, but also means that grace cannot be *earned*.[3] Thus, the gift of grace is *sola gratia*, completely *gratuitous* (freely given), even if undeserved.[4] Leibniz agrees with Augustine on this point, as is apparent in lines 7–8 of §31: 'the graces of God are wholly pure graces over which creatures have no claim'. However, this leaves the central difficulty over dispensation untouched. For one, God does not act arbitrarily; he must have some reasonable motive for grace (ln 10). Second, while Leibniz acknowledges the Augustinian-Calvinist[5] understanding of Scripture, which holds that God has elected for salvation 'only those whose faith and charity he foresaw' (that is, only those whom God knows will be good), this does not tell us why God has predestined some to be good but not others (lns 12–15).

Luis Molina's (1535–1600) doctrine of God's 'middle knowledge', alluded to in line 15 (*la science moyenne*, or *scientia media*), provides a sophisticated, compelling, and fairly Leibnizian solution to these difficulties over dispensation.[6] Accordingly, 'middle knowledge' is one of three types of knowledge constituting God's omniscience, the other types being *possible* and *actual*. We need not enter into all of the subtleties of these types. But characteristic of middle knowledge is that it consists of *counterfactual* knowledge, that is, knowledge of what some individual *would* do,

---

[2] Pelagius (AD 354–418) was a Christian theologian whose doctrines on free will, sin, and grace were attacked by Augustine. Pelagius was condemned and excommunicated by Pope Innocent I in 417. His views on grace can be found in his *Expositions*.

[3] See Augustine (1887), *Against Two Letters of the Pelagians*, Bk. I, Ch. 6; Bk. II, Chs. 12 and 21.

[4] 'For by grace you have been saved through faith and this is not from you; it is the gift of God; it is not from works, so no one may boast' (Ephesians 2:8–9, CSB).

[5] French Protestant theologian John Calvin (1509–64) was known for his doctrine that God predestines some for salvation and others for damnation.

[6] On Molina, I am drawing from a variety of sources. My account should not be taken to be exact, especially as I thought it best to keep it short and simple.

given some non-actual situation. For example, *if the people of Tyre had witnessed the miracles of Jesus* (which they did not), *they would have repented.*[7] As applied to the problem of dispensation, God's knowledge of counterfactuals allows him to consider, prior to creation, not what the individual *will* do, but how the individual *would* respond to the aid of grace, *if* God gave it, in order to decide *whether* it should be given, that is, whether the effect *would be* fitting to his providential plan for creation. We can set aside any difficulties with accounting for how God knows counterfactuals. But this account would appear to solve the Pelagian-Augustinian dispute, as well as the central problem: by virtue of his middle knowledge, God *could* take the creature's foreseen faith and works into account, without being required to give grace; thereby, God could dispense grace gratuitously, differentially, and rationally, according to his providence. Some individuals will be suitable for God's plan, while others will not.

As appealing and as Leibnizian as this Molinist solution is, Leibniz does not quite accept it; because it *still* does not resolve the central difficulty over why God dispenses grace disparately. And the reason it does not is subtle but important: it does not tell us how the creature is able to perform salutary acts at all. As Leibniz rightly characterises it, middle knowledge provides God with 'the foresight, not of faith and good acts, but of their matter and predisposition, or of what the man would contribute to them from his side' (lns 16–18). In other words, counterfactual analysis reveals not so much what God knows the creature *will* do, but rather what God knows about the *predispositions* of the creature, specifically her tendency to do the good in any situation. This shows that what is missing from Molina's account is the *cause* of this tendency, which is God, who endows all creatures with their original predisposition for the good. This 'ordinary grace' as Leibniz puts it, serves as the natural motive for God's 'extraordinary assistance', that is, future gifts of grace (ln 29). But the key point to be taken here, the reason he does not accept the Molinist doctrine, is that the central question of grace must ultimately come down to why God granted natural advantages (ordinary grace) to some but not to others (ln 27).

Before answering this question, Leibniz draws another point from his critique of middle knowledge. Since the question of dispensation comes down to a question about the natural advantages of the creature, this means that the question of grace 'reduces' to God's mercy (ln 30). But why? Leibniz does not say, but I think the reason is likely this: Consider the literal meaning of mercy (*misericordia*), that is, 'suffering of the heart'. Now, God does not literally suffer for us, but having created us he knows

---

[7] To paraphrase Matthew 11:21–2, a passage often cited as an example of middle knowledge.

that our nature is weak, vulnerable, prone to suffering, error, and sin. As we saw in §30, this is our 'original limitation', the unavoidable consequence of our having been created from nothing. Thus, to counter that weakness, it is an act of mercy on God's part to endow our nature with a predisposition for the good, however imperfect that disposition may be. If this is right, then the gift of grace is indeed completely gratuitous, as Leibniz insists it is. For, a created nature cannot in any way deserve its predisposition for the good; any good it has originally can be freely given only on account of God's mercy, not on account of the creature's actions, since clearly the creature has not acted before being created. In this way God's mercy fully reveals the gratuitous, 'wholly pure', nature of grace.

And yet, after all this, the central question remains: why does God endow more natural grace to some than to others? Having pushed the question back to an originary moment of grace, the answer is that, prior to creation, God examines the full range of possible beings, every complete substance, including everything that will happen to it – all of its ordinary and extraordinary graces, *faith and charity*, circumstances, sins, fortunes and misfortunes – and chooses those individuals whose exclusive configuration conforms to his providence (lns 34–8). Only in consideration of the complete notion and its relation to all others do 'all the difficulties vanish' (ln 39). God's reasons for dispensation do not depend on individual merit (*solo gratia*), but neither are they without it. Rather, *each* creature's merit must be measured against a complex scheme of dispensation and chosen on the basis of its contribution to that entire scheme.[8] Put another way, while 'it is very true that God has elected only those whose faith and charity he foresees' (ln 13), this does not entail that he elects them only because *they* deserve it. Rather, since God sees how their qualities fit within his entire scheme of perfection, it is possible that even some of the good ones will not be elected.

Despite this answer, Leibniz in the end maintains that we do not really know why it would please God to include one individual in the scheme of creation rather than another (ln 43). Appealing again to St Paul (Romans 11:33), the awesome depth of God's wisdom and goodness is ultimately 'inscrutable' to us. At the same time, however, our lack of comprehension extends only to the details within the unfathomable depths of this scheme – but not to the general picture, which we can comprehend in outline quite well. As Leibniz has maintained throughout the *Discourse*, and at the beginning and end of this article, God does not make decrees without grounding them in reason. The motives of election are those of

---

[8] Echavarría 2017: 295.

God's glory, justice, mercy, and grace, all of which reduce to the general order: 'the greatest perfection of the universe' (ln 49).

§32. The utility of metaphysics for piety and religion; on the accommodation of all substances; on the immortality of the soul.

As the *Discourse* nears its end, Leibniz indicates that his overall purpose has been to show – through the resolution of a number of disputes and difficulties – that a proper understanding of God and substance should increase one's respect, love, and admiration for God. Let us make a brief survey of that effort, before turning to the particular concerns of this article.

So far, we have observed Leibniz taking a number of positions that are challenging both to theological orthodoxy and to the natural philosophy of his day. For example, §1 and §23 show that the very idea of perfection must be properly understood, so that we may appreciate God's perfections properly. In §2, Leibniz argues that the 'voluntarist' conception of 'the good' leads to conceiving of God as a despot and tyrant. To refute that conception, he argues that the respect and love owed to God comes through understanding that God's will is consonant with his reason. In §3, Leibniz opposes certain 'moderns' (namely Malebranche and Arnauld) who claim that God could have created a world better than the present one; he refutes this 'impious' view by arguing, in §5, that God creates the best possible world according to the rule of simplicity and variety. In §4, Leibniz denies that his views imply quietism and fatalism. In §6, he explicitly states his intention to 'elevate our minds' to God, by showing that cases of apparent disorder are actually resolved by the law of order and variety. Similarly, in §7, Leibniz opposes the usual view of miracles as disruptions in the natural order of things, by arguing that all events occur according to the order God establishes for all time. In §8, Leibniz contends with an entire history of the concept of 'substance', in order to establish the independence and freedom of rational creatures; thus follows, in §9, a number of 'paradoxes' opposing the usual metaphysical and theological orthodoxies. Article 13 establishes the distinction between necessity and contingency as a defense against those who maintain that God creates and administers the universe by an unavoidable necessity. In articles 14 and 15, Leibniz contends with the orthodoxies of natural philosophy, by displacing the received notions of causal interaction with his own account of substantial expression and accommodation. Similarly, in §§10, 11, 12, 17, 18, 19, 21, and 22, he criticises the prevailing 'mechanical philosophy' of Descartes and others for its elimination of final causes (God's purposes) from physics, and in order to show that something incorporeal (force and substantial forms) must be included in mechanical explanations. In articles 24 to 29 Leibniz takes a middle position on the nature of ideas, in opposition to Malebranche and Arnauld, who argued, respectively, that we understand everything through God or that we think only with our own ideas. Article 30 argues that we have no right to 'complain' against God for our sins, and §31 concludes, against a number of traditional views on grace, that God's reasons of dispensation are grounded ultimately in his glory, mercy, and unfathomable perfection.

The particular concern of article 32 follows suit in its aim to motivate the piety of metaphysics. It shows the relationship of all substances to God and to each other, the independence of substances from all things, and finally, as a consequence of the latter, the immortality of the soul. The particular difficulty of this article, however, is to explain all of these things without depending on the usual account of 'efficient causes' among substances. As noted, Leibniz initially attempted to solve this difficulty in §14 and §15, by introducing the notions of 'expression', 'correspondence', and 'accommodation' of substances. In this article and the next, he treats the difficulty more extensively.

It is important to Leibniz, as it was to most thinkers in the seventeenth century, to emphasise our *dependence* on God, especially in view of the new physical hypotheses, namely Copernicanism and the mechanical philosophy, that threaten separation from God. Leibniz conveys this dependence by returning to the metaphysical summary in §14: like Plotinus' One, God is the inexhaustible, emanating, source of all being – of all order and diversity in nature, with whom our creation begins and on whom our continual existence depends. While the precise nature of 'emanation' remains obscure (ln 10), we can understand it by analogy with our own thoughts, which, as it seems, continually arise from within us. St Paul's idea that God is 'all in all' (1 Corinthians 15:28) expresses our unity with God, that God's essence pervades the whole of creation and resides within each of us, in distinct proportion to our own perfections.

To say that God alone 'determines' his creatures 'from the outside by his influence' (ln 13) means that only God can act upon us in any direct, quasi-causal way. God's influence consists in the universal distribution of his essence, specifically that of goodness, which 'obliges [substances] to accommodate themselves to one another' (ln 18). But this needs clarification. On one hand, God obliges substances to accommodate each other, simply by actualising those substances that together best express his essence. As I suggested in §14, however, Leibniz may have in mind that God's influence consists in his imposition of an obligation, that is, a *moral necessity*, upon intelligent substances to act benevolently. This is further suggested where Leibniz says that although God alone 'operates on me', the other substances contribute the reason for God's determinations (ln 17). In other words, each intelligent substance is obliged by God actively to accommodate itself to others, which should be possible by virtue of their mutual perceptions. Substances perceive each other as goal-directed beings, in view of which they are obliged to refrain from harming each other and actively to promote their mutually beneficial ends. Nevertheless, it is God alone who, in consideration of the actions of each individual substance, 'makes the liaison or communication of substances' (ln 20).

This 'communication of substances' raises, again, as in §14, the matter of how substances relate to each other without *causally* interacting. As difficult as it may be for us to accept, Leibniz maintains that, rather than having 'efficient cause' relations with each other, substances 'express' or represent their relations through their own perceptions. For example, as individuals in a dense crowd pass each other on a busy street, and as they desire to avoid collision, their respective movements are the consequence of perceptions and anticipations occurring within themselves – not through their perceptions of each other. But all perceptions correspond, since God has chosen that configuration of substances in which 'the phenomena of the one meet and agree with those of others, and consequently that there is reality in our perceptions' (lns 20–2). We give 'particular' reasons for these movements and collisions in terms of *causes*, but these are not the sorts of relations substances actually, metaphysically, have with each other. Specifically, we can see in the deleted references to 'occasionalism' (§32, footnotes 9 and 10 in translation) Leibniz's reluctance even to admit Malebranche's widely recognised explanation for causal interaction; but in the next article he offers his own explanation for the phenomenon of body-soul interaction, in implicit opposition to occasionalism.

So far, Leibniz has focused on the dependence of all substances on God for their creation and mutual relations. But the driving force of his argument is to assert the *independence* of each substance, ultimately for the sake of establishing the soul's immortality. For, ultimately, the substance itself is the source and cause of its actions and passions. This is asserted in the doctrine of 'spontaneity', discussed in §30, as one of the necessary conditions of freedom (here in line 25). While the being of the substance depends on God, its complete notion belongs to it alone. Now, while Leibniz has made it clear that no substance can be causally affected by another substance, he has not made clear precisely how substances cause their own actions. From what he has said, however, we can assume that substances are driven from one state to the next by their nature, that is, by their perception of the good and their desire to attain it, or more generally, by their inclination to perfect or complete their nature. Substances are active to the degree that their perceptions are clear and lead to increased perfection, and passive to the degree that their perceptions are confused and lead to decreased perfection. The accommodation of their perceptions with the actions of all other substances is sufficient to establish the appearance of causal interaction. Substances must, however, remain causally independent, if they are to be conceived in their most basic sense as *active, independent, beings* – and, most pertinent here, if they are to be immortal. Given the substantial soul's isolation from all external causal influence, *even from its own body*, nothing can destroy or corrupt it. Leibniz finds the sentiment of St Theresa of Avila (1550–82) most appropriate here: 'that the soul must often think as if there were only God and itself in the world' (ln 30), that is, nothing but God and one's immortal soul.[1] As the soul is causally isolated even from its own body, it cannot perish when the body does. How then is the soul related to its body? Leibniz's initial solution to this perennial perplexity is given next.

§33. On the metaphysical 'commerce' of soul and body; and on the source of confused perceptions.

This article focuses on two topics of major import and interest: (1) the 'commerce' or relation of mind/soul and body, a relation which Leibniz later came to call 'pre-established harmony';[1] and (2) the doctrine of confused perception, which results from the 'impressions' of all things made on the body. Both topics have centrally to do with the relationships among mind, body, and world. But the doctrine of 'commerce' is most important because it attempts to resolve a serious problem that Leibniz thought his contemporaries, Descartes and Malebranche, could not. The problem is to explain '*the great mystery of the union of the soul and the body*' (ln 6) – or what philosophers today call the 'mind-body problem'. As the problem is normally understood, we have no intelligible way to explain how two substances utterly distinct in nature, (1) mind or soul and (2) body, causally interact – and yet we feel very certain that they do. Although something like the problem arose earlier in the *Discourse*, Leibniz attempts to address it directly here.

As we have seen (§§14, 15, and 32), Leibniz denies that causal interaction between substances occurs – and here we may fully understand why. But his position is complicated by the fact, easy to overlook, that he is unclear in the *Discourse* about whether bodies, apart from their souls, are substances at all. The evidence indicates that he thinks they are not, as can be seen in numerous deleted passages suggesting or hedging the idea

[1] See footnote 11 in translation.
[1] For the development of Leibniz's doctrine of 'pre-established harmony' up to 1695, see LNS 18–19, 26 and 51.

that bodies are substances in some sense.[2] But the strongest evidence is found in Leibniz's criticisms of Descartes' conception of body as 'extended substance' (see §§12, 14, 17, 18). Thus, if bodies are not substances, we might wonder whether Leibniz has a mind-body interaction problem at all. Nevertheless, an explanation for the interaction or union of mind and body is still needed, since, as we have seen, the complete notion of an individual substance, while it includes the body, precludes anything external to the soul as a cause of its changes. So, we still need an explanation for the relationship of mind and body. In sum, to understand Leibniz's position on the 'union' or 'commerce' of mind and body, we need to understand (1) what the mind-body problem is; (2) why Leibniz denies several causal theories that address or purport to resolve the problem; and (3) what his own solution to the problem is.

It is often said that the mind/soul-body problem begins with Descartes. While many philosophers since Plato had claimed the soul was separable from its body, they were not generally concerned to explain how the two could causally interact. But Descartes' conception of the mind and body as *distinct substances* decisively turned this relationship into a problem. Conceived of in this way, the mind and body appear to be two radically different sorts of things, one material and the other non-material, such that it is difficult, if not impossible, to explain how they have causal interactions with each other.

Let us go through the problem as Descartes conceived of it. The nature (essence) of matter, of which the human body is composed, which Descartes calls 'corporeal substance', is *extension*, that is, a certain quantity in length, breadth, and depth.[3] The nature (essence) of mind, on the other hand, is *thought*, and thought is non-extended. Therefore, Descartes concludes, mind and body are really two distinct sorts of substance.[4] The problem, which Descartes admits, is that since thought and extension have no essence or property in common, we cannot conceive of how these substances causally interact; and yet they must. To illustrate the problem more

---

[2] See the correspondence with Arnauld (LAV) for more discussion on this topic. Eventually Leibniz came around to maintain definitively that bodies are not substances, although they are made up of substances and in this sense we can speak of corporeal substances.

[3] *Principles* II, §4. As mentioned in §17, Descartes' formulation is a bit curious. He says that 'the nature of body consists . . . simply in extension'. But what is it for something to consist simply of length, breadth, and depth? These are measurements or quantities *of something*, presumably of a body, not the essence of body itself. The body is *something extended*. So, then what is body? To say it is 'extended matter' doesn't answer the question.

[4] 'Thus extension in length, breadth, and depth constitutes the nature of corporeal substance; and thought constitutes the nature of thinking substance' (*Principles* I, §53).

fully, consider these two examples of interaction provided by Arnauld (a Cartesian) in his correspondence with Leibniz.[5]

(1) I am stabbed in the shoulder and feel a pain. There are two events, one bodily and the other mental. On the one hand, the knife enters my flesh and cuts my muscles, tendons, and nerves. These are motions of extended parts of matter. On the other hand, the pain I feel is a mental event. Even though the pain does not occur without the motions in my body resulting from the stab, the pain has no extended properties whatsoever. It is a mental experience, a sensation, and cannot at all be explained as the motion of parts of matter (just try it). Nevertheless, the stabbing in my shoulder *causes* the pain that I experience; therefore, an interaction between body and mind must have occurred somehow.

(2) I desire or will to raise my arm and remove my hat. Here we have a simple causal interaction running in the opposite direction, from the mind to the body. My will, which is a modification of my mind, a strictly un-extended substance (again, having no conceivable material properties), moves a material object, my arm. I perform interactions such as these all of the time, even though I do not understand how the interaction occurs.

Given the radically different natures of mind and body, it seems impossible for them to have causal interactions – hence the problem. One of Descartes' most trenchant correspondents, Princess Elisabeth of Bohemia, pointed out that, according to Descartes' own physics, for one thing to move another, each had to come into physical contact; but on his account of mind and body, physical contact is impossible.[6] While Descartes had no doubt about the union of mind and body, he never provided an explanation for it that satisfied his sharpest critics.

Arnauld's examples illustrate the typical sort of causal interactions we are sure must take place between mind and body. Let us now consider an alternative explanation for their interaction, called occasionalism, adopted by Malebranche, but which originated among Islamic theologian-philosophers during the tenth and eleventh centuries. Occasionalism was not initially intended to explain the mind-body problem at all, but to explain how causal relations among physical things could occur. Here are two ways to understand the doctrine and its motive: When we conceptually examine the essences and properties of things, we find nothing that explains a cause among them. For example, if you did not already know that cotton will burn when placed in fire, and you examined all of the properties of

---

[5] Letter of 28 September 1686, LAV 123.

[6] See the correspondence between Descartes and Princess Elisabeth of Bohemia (Shapiro 2007: 61–72).

cotton, you would find nothing in it suggesting that it will burn.[7] We learn only from experience that it burns. But there must be, it is supposed, a conceptual or logical connection that explains how fire could cause cotton to burn. Secondly, matter has long been conceived as inert and unable to move itself. Descartes' conception, for example, of matter as extended contains no idea of force or motion. Thus, nothing in matter can be the cause of motion.[8] In sum, since we find no logical connection or natural cause in the relation of cause and effect, and yet we find the connection of events so regular and purposeful, we are compelled to conclude, as Malebranche does, that *God* must be the cause of the connection. The same may be said for the causal relationship between mind and body. Thus, whenever I will to take a walk, God makes my body move. Whenever my body is damaged, God makes it so that I feel a pain. In this way, causal events are said to be 'occasions' for God's actions.

Now, let us see why Leibniz rejects causal interaction between mind and body. First, we should note that he does not deny causal interactions (efficient causes) among physical things (as should be clear from his account of conservation laws in §17). He maintains, however, that efficient causal relations among *substances* are a different matter – that they do not and cannot occur (as in §14, where he says that substances 'express' each other). The reason they cannot occur, while not mentioned explicitly in the *Discourse*, stems from his rejection of the Scholastic doctrine of 'physical influx'.[9] According to this doctrine, for one substance to have a causal influence on another – say, for me to push you over – something of my substance must enter yours. This something need not be physical, but rather some property or predicate of me (I *push* you), which then becomes some property of you (you are *pushed*). Thus, I lose something of my substance and you gain something in yours. No doubt this view seems strange to us, but Leibniz rejects it on account of the nature of the complete notion of an individual substance. As he states here, and similarly in *Primary Truths* (AG 33), 'everything that happens to the soul and to each substance is a consequence of its notion' (lns 12–13), and so all of its perceptions 'must arise [spontaneously] from its own nature' (ln 15). Thus, it is not possible for a substance to lose or gain any predicates or properties it does not already possess, without destroying its nature and unique identity. It follows that if the

7 Al-Ghazali gives this example in *The Incoherence of the Philosophers*, 17th Discussion (on causality and miracles).
8 'By nature [matter] has a passive capacity for motion. But it does not have an active capacity, it is actually moved only by the continuous action of the creator. Thus one body cannot move another by an efficacy belonging to its nature' (Malebranche, MD VII, 119).
9 See O'Neill 1993. Also see Leibniz, *Primary Truths*, AG 33.

doctrine of physical influx were true, substances would not be causes (or reasons) for their changes, which opposes the doctrine of 'spontaneity' on which Leibniz insists. So, if Leibniz were to apply this doctrine explicitly to the mind-body relation in the *Discourse*, he would say that a physical influx, which says that a body (substance or not) causes an internal change to the soul, would be inconsistent with his doctrine of substance.

Leibniz's rejection of Cartesian dualism and Malebranche's occasionalism is alluded to at lines 8–11: 'For there is no way to conceive that the one should have influence on the other, and it is not reasonable simply to have recourse to the extraordinary operation of the universal cause in an ordinary and particular matter.' In other words, as made clear by Descartes himself, given the respective natures of mind and body, no interaction can be conceived. The second clause in the above sentence alludes to occasionalism, which Leibniz rejects because he holds that it appeals to a miracle, that is, an 'extraordinary operation', to explain a rather ordinary operation, namely, the motion of matter. For one, Leibniz denies that matter is incapable of motion, since, as he has argued, forces are inherent to matter. Thus, occasionalism supposes that God was unable to endow material nature with its own ability to carry out its operations, and so God must continually perform miracles of intervention to make causal connections. For this reason, Leibniz holds that occasionalism diminishes the wisdom and simplicity of God and makes the natural operations of nature unintelligible. What is needed is an account of causation that elevates rather than diminishes God's perfection, but one that can also lead to the discovery of empirical laws.

So, how does Leibniz solve 'the great mystery of the union of the soul and the body'? First, by denying that interaction takes place at all; and then by asserting the 'commerce' of their respective actions. In other words, mind events and body events operate in precise *parallel* to each other, without interacting. Near the beginning of §33, Leibniz articulates the mystery of the union in terms of the actions and passions of both the body and soul. As he had explained in §14, the actions of the soul are reasoning, will, and judgment, while its passions are its perceptions and sensations. The actions of the body are the 'consequence of a preceding change' in the body, while a passion is the effect of an external cause upon the body (ln 96 in the deleted passage). So, the actions and passions of the one occur independently, but synchronically, with the actions and passions of the other, such that causal interaction only *appears* to occur.

As applied to Arnauld's above illustration, Leibniz could say (1) that when I am stabbed in the shoulder, a number of motions occur in my body (displacements of flesh, muscle, and tendons), but these motions do not cause any sensation of pain in my soul; however, at precisely the same time as these motions occur, I have a sensation of pain. (2) that my desire or will to raise my arm and remove my hat does not cause my arm to move; rather, at the precise time of my desire, the appropriate motions occur in my arm. From this, it follows that the body is not attached to 'our essence', that is, to the soul (ln 21). We know, however, that our body belongs to us, because the perceptions we have of it are more distinct than the perceptions we have of other bodies or other external things appearing to cause motions in our body (lns 16–20). Thus, again, the independence of the soul is preserved, since nothing has a causal influence on it, while its relations with bodies and the external world are maintained, without God having continually to coordinate these relations (in opposition to occasionalism). The correspondence or commerce of mind-body relations occurs on its own, due to the complete notion of the individual substance, wherein each body predicate corresponds with a mental predicate. Thus, the soul-substance undergoes changes according to its own laws, while the body undergoes changes according to the laws of mechanical causation – and never shall the two sets of laws change each other.

This doctrine of the commerce of soul and body, which, as noted, Leibniz later came to call 'pre-established harmony', is no doubt difficult to accept; for, while it solves the interaction problem by *eliminating* interaction, maintains the independence of substances, the independence of laws of nature, and the free will of creatures (so Leibniz believes), it does so at a heavy metaphysical cost. For it requires the assumption that God, at the time of creation, understands and concurs with every single mind-body correspondence for every single complete notion, and moreover that the motions of each independent substance correspond perfectly with every other. Furthermore, the parallelism of mind-body does not solve the 'union' of soul and body as much as it separates them to a degree that even Descartes did not imagine. It also runs counter to our deepest intuition that the mind and body interact in complete causal relation, even if we do not understand how. The doctrine preserves intelligibility, however, since the parallelism is at least intelligible, while Cartesian dualism is arguably not (or it has no explanation). Be that as it may, Leibniz's hypothesis appears more extraordinary than the problem it attempts to solve.

In their correspondence, Arnauld himself had trouble making sense of the doctrine and how it differed from occasionalism.[10] After some prodding by Arnauld, Leibniz offers, in part, the following clarification:

> It is therefore infinitely more reasonable and more worthy of God to suppose that he first created the machine of the world in such a way that without

---

[10] Letter of 28 September 1686, LAV 125.

violating at every moment the two great laws of nature, namely those of force and direction, but rather by following them perfectly, except in the case of miracles, the springs of bodies turn out to be ready to kick into action on their own exactly as needed at the moment when the soul has a suitable volition or thought, which it also had only in conformity with the preceding states of the bodies; and that in this way the union of the soul with the machine of the body and the parts that enter into it, and the action of the one on the other, consist only in this concomitance, which evinces the wonderful wisdom of the creator much more than any other hypothesis.[11]

Leibniz thus offers here a richer explanation of the idea he had broached in §14, that 'nothing can happen to us but thoughts and perceptions, and all our future thoughts and perceptions are only consequences, although contingent, of our preceding thoughts and perceptions' (lns 50–3). But his main concern in clarifying the doctrine is twofold: to show that it provides an *intelligible* explanation of both God's wisdom *and* the laws of nature. Given the conceptions of causality, body, and substance Leibniz had available, which he also attempted to reconfigure, his theory of the commerce of mind and body may reasonably be said to form an explanation both most natural and most theological, even if not the most intuitive.

The second main topic in this article concerns the source of confused perceptions, and it is important to understand their role in relation to the mind-body parallelism explained above. It is also important to distinguish this type of 'confusion' from the type discussed earlier. Recall from §24 and §26 that 'confusion' is an epistemic matter, having to do with the clarity of our *ideas*, ranging from confused to clear and distinct. For example, I have a clear perception of a flower (I know it's a flower) but a confused representation of it, since I do not know its particular kind. Here, however, the account focuses on the nature and source of perceptions and the relationship between mental perceptions and bodily senses.

The source of confused perceptions lies in the relationship that bodies have to each other. As Leibniz explains, all bodies, all material things, have a certain 'sympathy' with each other (ln 27), which means that any one body can cause motion in any other (or in any part of the same body). For example, when a guitar string is plucked, its motions will cause motions in the other strings – and in turn their motions will be conveyed back to the source and to each other.[12] But more characteristic of this universal sympathy is that all bodies affect each other by *degrees*, depending on their strength and distance from a source of motion. This idea is well expressed in *Primary Truths*:

[11] Letter to Arnauld, 30 April 1687, LAV 197.
[12] See §14 commentary, footnote 12, on 'sympathy'.

> For in a vessel filled with a liquid (and the whole universe is just such a vessel) motion made in the middle is propagated to the edges, although it is rendered more and more insensible, the more it recedes from its origin. (AG 33)

This universal sympathy would seem to be a simple consequence of the fact, for Leibniz, that since the universe is a *plenum*, all bodies are in either direct or indirect contact; so, if any one of them moves, they all move, no matter how remote. This is true, then, for our own body, which 'receives the impression of all the others' (ln 28). But the key point is that the nearly 'insensible' impressions that the body receives correspond to the 'confused perceptions' in our soul.

So how exactly do these bodily impressions correspond to the confused perceptions in the soul? We must be careful here, since, given the parallelism, the motions in the body cannot *cause* the perceptions in the soul. Rather, the parallelism (correspondence or commerce) requires that every motion of the body is accompanied by an appropriate perception in the soul – and every perception of the soul is accompanied by an appropriate motion in the body. Thus, the phrase 'perceptions of our senses' (ln 25) cannot mean that the soul perceives *the motions of the body*, but rather that the soul has perceptions *corresponding* to the motions in the body. A 'confused perception', then, is a perception (or a set of perceptions) in the soul corresponding to a multitude of motions occurring in the body. More precisely, a confused perception occurs when the soul does not *consciously* distinguish one perception from another, which is actually quite common. As Leibniz says, 'it is not possible that our soul should attend to everything in particular' (ln 30). Whatever is not perceived consciously is perceived below the level of conscious awareness as a confused perception. Leibniz's example of the waves crashing onto the shore provides a fitting illustration (ln 32). The 'murmur' of the waves we hear is composed of innumerable motions; just so, the soul contains, along with its distinct perceptions, confused perceptions of the motions occurring in those waves, indeed, of all motions in the universe. This reflects Leibniz's repeated assertion that every soul is confusedly omniscient.[13]

It is interesting and appropriate to compare this account of confused perception in the *Discourse* with Leibniz's doctrine of 'petites (small) perceptions' in his *New Essays* (1706). In that text, against Locke's contention that knowledge is acquired only through *conscious* experience, Leibniz

---

[13] LC 265 (1683), and *Principles of Nature and Grace* (1714), §13: 'Each soul knows the infinite – knows all – but confusedly. It is like walking on the seashore and hearing the great noise of the sea: I hear the particular noises of each wave, of which the whole noise is composed, but without distinguishing them' (AG 211). The ocean wave example also appears in Leibniz's preface to *New Essays* (LRB 54).

argues that we also acquire knowledge unconsciously; for example, when we adopt the customs, mores, and habits of a people, simply by being exposed to them over a period of time.[14] Leibniz thus distinguished three types of perception: petite, conscious, and self-conscious or 'apperception'. Conscious perception is the simple awareness of a thing or sensation, whereas apperception is the awareness of oneself as having a perception.[15] Most interesting is that petites perceptions can explain how states of mind such as anxiety, sadness, or joy can arise for no apparent reason, that is, without consciously thinking about the objects of such states. They result rather from unconscious perceptions that have grown in quantity and strength to become consciously perceived.[16] This shows that the soul is always active and thinking, that it is never in a state of absolute indifference, and thus that our desires are always inclined in one direction or another: 'we are never completely in equilibrium and can never be evenly balanced between two options' (LRB II.xxi.36.188).[17] In sum, the petites perceptions of the soul reflect 'the immeasurable fineness of things, which always and everywhere involves an actual infinity' (LRB Preface 57). The doctrines of confused and petites perceptions make Leibniz one of the very earliest of philosophers to theorise about an unconscious level of mental activity.[18]

---

[14] 'All our undeliberated actions result from a conjunction of minute perceptions; and even our customs and passions, which have so much influence when we do deliberate, come from the same source; for these tendencies come into being gradually, and so without minute perceptions we would not have acquired these noticeable dispositions' (LRB II.i.15.116).

[15] 'I would prefer to distinguish between *perception* and *being aware* [*s'appercevoir*]' (LRB II.ix.4.134). 'I have shown above that we always have an infinity of minute perceptions without being aware of them. We are never without perceptions, but necessarily we are often without *awareness*, namely when none of our perceptions stand out' (LRB II.xix.4.162).

[16] 'Besides, there are hundreds of indications leading us to conclude that at every moment there is in us an infinity of perceptions, unaccompanied by awareness or reflection; that is, of alterations in the soul itself, of which we are unaware because these impressions are either too minute and too numerous, or else too unvarying, so that they are not sufficiently distinctive on their own. But when they are combined with others they do nevertheless have their effect and make themselves felt, at least confusedly, within the whole' (LRB Preface 53).

[17] 'It would not be adding much to that if I said that it is these minute perceptions which determine our behaviour in many situations without our thinking of them, and which deceive the unsophisticated with an appearance of *indifference of equilibrium*' (LRB Preface 55–6).

[18] For more on perception see Kulstad 1977b; McRae 1976; Simmons 2011; Smith 2003.

§34. On the differences between spirits (minds), animal souls, and substantial forms; and that immortality implies continuity of memory (or, why it is pointless to wish to become the King of China).

This article helps clarify the similarities and differences among soul-like entities that Leibniz has mentioned in the *Discourse*, namely, substantial forms, animal souls, and spirits (minds). He begins by supposing something he has hesitated to admit, that bodies are substances. Notably, this was not his first thought, since in the original manuscript (L¹) he wrote, then crossed out: 'There is one thing that I do not undertake to determine, whether bodies are substances (to speak in Metaphysical rigour), or whether they are only true phenomena as is the rainbow' (ln 5 fn 1). A 'true phenomenon' is the appearance of something, but not an illusion. It has a *certain* reality, but its reality depends on something else. A rainbow, for instance, does not appear unless certain conditions obtain (the sun shining through water molecules). This dependence means that a rainbow cannot be a substance, but it nevertheless has a degree of reality. This would seem to be the case for bodies, too, according to Leibniz, since his criticisms of Cartesian substance as 'extended' amount to the claim that bodies themselves do not provide the reality that they are purported to have. What would give bodies the reality required to make them substances? The answer given here is *unity*. To make the supposition that bodies are substances, we must assume the definition of substance as an *unum per se* (ln 5), that is, as having *unity through itself*.

We know what 'unity through itself' means from Leibniz's account of an individual substance, whose unity consists in its complete notion, in its indivisibility, in being the source (*sponte*) of its actions, in its causal independence from other substances. But we know that bodies do not have these unities: they have no complete notion, they are divisible, their motions depend on causal relations with other bodies; nor do they have any self-unifying, self-organising principle. But wait – they *do* have a unifying principle: substantial form. As we saw in §§10, 11, and 12, substantial forms distinguish bodies into specific kinds, such as metals, wood, chemicals, flesh, and bones. So, then, it makes sense to suppose that bodies are substances, or at least that they are *composed* of substances, as long as they have substantial form. So far so good, Leibniz seems to be thinking. However, as with degrees of perfection, the unity of things also has its degrees, and animal souls and minds have higher degrees of unity. Supposing now that bodies *are* substances, as long as they have substantial form, let us consider each of these soul-like entities in terms of their unity.

Corporeal substances: As we have seen, Leibniz has up to now denied that bodies, considered in themselves as extended things, are substances, and this denial owes much to their lack of unity. In his correspondence with Arnauld, he says that bodies are aggregates, collections of more fundamental unities, but not real unities. For example, a machine, a heap of stones, a block of marble, or a flock of sheep, are not substances, but consist of a fundamental unity.[1] What that fundamental unity is, he had, at this time, not yet decided upon.[2] The atomists would of course say that the fundamental unities are corporeal atoms; but Leibniz denies this, eventually settling upon the doctrine that the reality of matter ultimately lies in incorporeal 'monads' (see *Monadology*). The reader is advised to take up the extensive commentary on this development (from corporeal atom to incorporeal monad).[3] But for now, at least in the correspondence with Arnauld, Leibniz seems satisfied to suppose that *substantial form* provides the unity sufficient for the substance-hood of bodies. As he says, again in the correspondence, though not without hedging: 'I bestow substantial forms on all corporeal substances united more than mechanically.'[4] This might imply that he thinks corporeal substances are animated, like souls are. But he is not ready to go that far just yet. He thinks that a thing is united *mechanically* if it is an artifact (like a chair) or if its unity consists only in the proximity of its parts (like two pieces of marble stuck together). But to be 'more than' mechanical the thing must contain a natural, organic unity, as found in naturally occurring bodies such as chemicals and flesh. Even these corporeal substances do not have the organic unity sufficient for higher levels of soul-like activity, namely, *sensation*. Just like souls, however, the substantial forms of bodies cannot perish entirely, even if some particular body changes beyond recognition.

Animal souls: The distinguishing feature of animal souls is their capacity for sensation, along with a certain degree of intelligence and memory. On this point Leibniz differs from Descartes, who claimed that animals

---

[1] 'I believe *that where there are only beings by aggregation, there aren't any real beings*; for every being by aggregation presupposes beings endowed with a true unity, because it secures its reality only from that [reality] of those [beings] of which it is composed; so that it will have [no reality] at all if each being of which it is composed is again a being by aggregation; or another foundation for its reality must again be sought, which in this way [. . .] can never be found' (Letter to Arnauld, 30 April 1687, LAV 199).

[2] 'Substantial unity requires a being that is complete, indivisible and naturally indestructible being, since its concept embraces everything that is to happen to it, which cannot be found either in shape or in motion (both of which embrace something imaginary, as I could demonstrate) but rather in a soul or substantial form, on the model of what is called *me*. These are the only true complete beings, as the ancients had recognised, especially Plato, who showed very clearly that matter alone does not suffice to form a substance' (Letter to Arnauld, 8 December 1686, LAV 157).

[3] See Phemister 2001 and Garber 2009.

[4] Letter to Arnauld, 8 December 1686, LAV 157.

are basically organic machines, lacking in sentience and intelligence.[5] Leibniz agrees that animals do not have *self-reflection* and as a result cannot discover necessary, universal, or moral truths. So, while a dog has empirical memory of who its master is, it will not reflect on whether it 'ought' to obey its master's commands. Nor will it reflect on itself as the bearer of its experiences (which is called apperception, as opposed to mere perception). Nor will an animal, after being exposed to many attacks by other animals, develop the general ideas of 'attack' or 'animal'. But the fact that animals have a sensitive soul and are capable of self-movement gives them a higher level of *unity* than corporeal substances, since unity implies the capacity for self-movement. Animal souls also 'express the whole universe' (lns 10–11), though less perfectly than do minds.

Spirits or *substances proper*: These are human souls whose distinguishing features, in addition to sensation, are intelligence, memory, and morals. The distinguishing features of intelligence are the capability to abstract universals from sense experience, to self-reflect, and to retain memories; specifically, to retain a sense of self-identity through time. It is this last capability that gives spirits their *moral quality*, making them susceptible to punishment and reward and, ultimately, immortality.

To illustrate the moral quality of spirits, Leibniz implicitly argues that self-knowledge makes one subject to punishment and reward, since an individual cannot be responsible for her actions unless she can attribute intentional actions to herself. Self-knowledge is also essential to the ability to redirect oneself in view of one's history and future. Our moral concerns with punishment and reward extend to our hope for the afterlife, but this requires continuity of self, thus, *memory* of self from life to afterlife, or else immortality has no point. This is the point of Leibniz's comment that you would have no desire to be annihilated and then to become, say, the King of China, whether here or in the afterlife. Such a scenario is similar to one that occurs in the movie *The Matrix*, in which Agent Smith offers Cipher a new identity, if he turns his friend Morpheus over to Smith. Cipher agrees, but on the condition that his future self should have no memory of who he currently is. Likely, he wishes to forget that he will have gained a new identity by betraying his friend. Thus, the prospect of a new identity may appeal to those wishing to be relieved of guilt for past sins. But this is equivalent to wishing for your own annihilation, since anything that happens after the change can make no difference to *you*, as you will have no memory of who you were. Smith readily agrees to the deal because he knows that it cannot make any difference to Cipher whether he is annihilated or created anew. Even if you could have the best immortal life

---

[5] Descartes, *Discourse on Method*, Part V, CSM I, 139–41.

imaginable, without continuity of self, through memory, you would have no reason to hope for it.

§35. The excellence of minds and that they express God.

Aside from mysticism, it is generally thought that there are two main sources of knowledge about God: Scripture and what is called 'natural theology'. The latter says that we can attain knowledge of God through the study of natural phenomena, through their intricate design and apparent ends, or through the examination of 'a priori' concepts and ideas about God. Clearly, Leibniz has been occupied in the Discourse with natural theology, as seen in his teleology of nature, in the examination of the very idea of perfection, and in the a priori 'proof' that God has all perfections. The way of natural theology continues here as he seeks 'natural reasons' (ln 6) to understand God: (1) from a metaphysical standpoint, as 'the principle and cause of all substances and all Beings' (ln 11); and (2) from a moral standpoint, as the just monarch of a republic of minds (ln 12).

The idea of a just ruler over a republic of minds likely comes from St Augustine's monumental work, City of God, in which Augustine, having witnessed the destruction of the earthly city of Rome in 410 AD, sets out his consoling vision of an alternative heavenly city, one that is ruled by God and populated by his virtuous subjects. While Leibniz does not have in mind here to set out such a consoling vision of the afterlife, he is concerned to explain the sense in which a community of minds 'mirrors' God's perfections, both metaphysically and morally. Spirits/minds are the most perfect beings, because they are best capable of expressing God's perfections (ln 15). They do so through their knowledge of their being and action and by their knowledge of 'great truths' or 'verities', such as those of mathematics and morality. Thus, the souls of the lower animals differ from ours, just as a mirror, whose nature is to passively receive phenomena and reflect them, differs from minds, which actively 'invent' or discover what is essential and hidden in phenomena.

The main point of combining metaphysics and morals seems to be this: minds best express God's attributes, but we express them, not for the sake of God, but because God gave us minds so that we might secure our own happiness. One might imagine that God, like an earthly king, seeks nothing more than to be loved by his subjects, since to be loved by others is the greatest satisfaction one can have in life (lns 32–3). But it is a mistake to think that God wants us to love him for his sake, for his benefit. God has no need of our love. We love God as 'a consequence of his sovereign and perfect felicity' (ln 36). But this statement appears to be a bit off the mark. We should expect Leibniz to say, as he has, that we love and admire God for his eminently perfect attributes, for his wisdom and goodness, not for how sovereign and happy he is. Perhaps the phrase should be better understood to mean that since we are *like* God (what is good and reasonable is eminently found in him (ln 38)), we can expect to share in a portion of God's supreme felicity. God creates substances and all of Being for the sake of the felicity of minds. Thus, metaphysics is joined with morals, that is, with an aspirational vision for life, both earthly and heavenly.

§36. God is the monarch of the most perfect republic of minds, and their felicity is his principal purpose.

Leibniz returns to the theme of the perfectibility of minds, their felicity, God as monarch of a republic of minds, and the joining of metaphysics and morals. By now, these ideas should be fairly familiar; so, instead of recounting the article's several points, I leave the reader with a series of questions to consider.

1. In what sense do minds 'interfere with each other the least' (ln 5) and why does this matter? Consider answering this question in terms of the greatest compatibility of minds. What would make each mind compatible with every other?
2. What do you suppose Leibniz means by 'the most perfection that the universal harmony can permit' (ln 10)? Unpack this phrase to reveal its comprehensive significance.
3. Suppose that, *per impossibile*, God 'lacked the will to choose the best' (ln 12) and so had no reason to prefer one configuration of things over another. What would this say about God? And must God always have reasons?
4. The phrase 'a single mind is worth a whole World' (ln 18) likely reflects a well-known biblical verse: 'What profit would there be for one to gain the whole world and forfeit his life?' (Matthew 16:26). (The word 'life' is a translation of 'psyche', which is usually translated as 'soul'.) What would it mean to gain the world and give up your soul? Give a Leibnizian, metaphysical, explanation for why a single mind is worth a whole world.
5. In the heading of the previous article, §35, Leibniz says 'Spirits express God rather than the world, but that the other simple substances express the world rather than God.' However, he does not explain that until line 22 of this article, §36. So, what does it mean?
6. What *is* the moral quality that God has (ln 26)?
7. What sort of 'anthropologies' is God willing to suffer (ln 29), and how might it be objected that God should not be compared with human attributes?

8. This is one of several articles in the *Discourse* where Leibniz uses the term 'felicity' (lns 32, 33, 38). The term is often associated with the blessedness or *eudaimonia* that Aristotle identified as the end or perfection of human life. Is the same true for Leibniz? What does 'felicity' really consist in? Does it refer simply to the state of mind of feeling happy? Here's a leading question: Is there such a thing as *moral* happiness? Can you be 'happy' if you lack moral virtue?

9. How is the perfection of the physical world related to the perfection of the moral world (lns 34–5)? How would you describe these two worlds? Can they together form one world? How?

10. How do Spirits conserve their moral quality (ln 40)? Again, what *is* their moral quality? And what happens to *immoral* Spirits? Are they annihilated, permanently punished, forgiven?

11. What does God want from us, and why? What does it mean to 'love God'?

§37. That Jesus Christ has revealed the mystery of the admirable laws of the Kingdom of Heaven and the grandeur of the supreme felicity God prepares for those who love him.

Leibniz revered the ancient philosophers, Plato and Aristotle, but like Augustine and other Christian philosopher-theologians, he also knew that the ancients did not of course have any knowledge of the teachings of Christ (ln 5). As Augustine put it in his *Confessions* (Bk 7, 21): the books of the Platonists contained no thought of sacrifice, redemption, or salvation. And yet, Augustine believed that God wanted him to read the ancients as preparation for the revelations of Scripture and for a deeper understanding of things metaphysical: 'being instructed by [the Platonists] to search for incorporeal truth, I clearly saw your invisible things, which are "understood by the things that are made"' (*Confessions*, Bk 7, 20).[1] Leibniz expressed a similar sentiment: without the knowledge of substantial forms, 'one would be quite unable to know the first principles nor to elevate the mind sufficiently to the knowledge of incorporeal natures and the marvels of God' (§10, lns 23–5). Thus, it is tempting to understand the final article of the *Discourse* in this spirit; for, beginning in §1, with his examination of the idea of perfection, Leibniz has repeatedly shown that philosophical understanding prepares the way to religious truth. Most of 'these truths' in §36 and §37, unknown to the ancients, reflect passages

---

[1] 'Ever since the creation of the world his eternal power and divine nature, invisible though they are, have been understood and seen through the things he has made' (Romans 1:20).

from the New Testament (see the translation for references). Here are some ways they may be related to philosophical themes in the *Discourse*.

When we understand the true nature of substance, we understand how a community of substances forms a heavenly community, a City of God (ln 10). We admire God's laws (ln 10) when we understand that the simplest laws are set in balance with the greatest variety of beings (§5 and §6). When we understand the nature of substance, we understand that God knows each individual down to its finest detail, and thus that God cares about each substance in its unique particularity. Jesus has revealed this in the verses on the sparrow (ln 13). We understand the nature of substance, and thus that God cares more for the well-being of intelligent souls than he cares for the whole of nature and its laws (ln 17). Thus, no profit may be gained from losing one's soul – one's character – for the sake of worldly things.

We might think that we have nothing to fear from those who would destroy our body, since they cannot destroy our soul. But this would be a mistake, because, as suggested by the Gospel passage reflected here, what we should really fear is God, who can destroy both! This comment does not appear to be metaphysically informative nor intended to provide comfort. But the point would seem to be, as Leibniz adds, that we can depend on no one but God for our eternal happiness or unhappiness (lns 19–20). This, again, reflects both the independence of substance and St Theresa's conviction that nothing can act on souls but God alone (ln 22). We can be assured, however, that the souls of the just are always protected, since God remembers even the least of our actions (ln 22), such that, even though it may seem to us that the unjust shall win the day, in the end God alone distributes justice rightly. This reflects God's comprehensive view of the best possible world, whose reasons we cannot ultimately comprehend, but which we can be confident are in the end good and right.

The final points are very characteristic of Leibniz's system: 'that everything must culminate in the greatest well-being of the good' (ln 24). This statement does not reveal much regarding *what* is good, but it conveys a frequent piety for Leibniz, namely that the morally virtuous will be rewarded with the greatest happiness, if not in this world, then in the world to come. And finally, those who love God, by imitating his perfections, will gain supreme felicity. These assurances rest on a single foundational premise: from a perfect being, nothing less than perfection can follow. But we cannot be so assured of this without sufficient clarity on the nature of perfection. Philosophy thus prepares us to understand: 'Be perfect [τέλειοι], therefore, as your heavenly Father is perfect' (Matthew 5:48).

Context I: Two Years of The Life and Work of G. W. Leibniz: *January 1685 to December 1686*

The Life and Work of G. W. Leibniz, a Chronicle[1] provides a detailed account of Leibniz's activities, mostly his letters and writings, from birth to death. I translate here only two years of the *Chronicle*: from January 1685 (one year prior to the composition of the *Discourse*) until December 1686 (one year after). I have added some items not included by the *Chronicle*, though not all of Leibniz's works and letters written during that time are included below. Based on all available Akademie editions, Leibniz composed a total of approximately 315 items (including the ninety-six listed below) from January 1685 to December 1686.[2]

The *Chronicle* shows that Leibniz was occupied with numerous projects and a wide range of interests, primarily with designing and improving windmills and pumps for the Harz mountain mining project, and gathering historical and geographical information for the House of Guelph ancestry. He also composed a number of letters and tracts on mathematics (including the introduction to his calculus), geometry, and ecumenical matters, along

---

[1] *Leben und Werk von G.W. Leibniz Eine Chronik*, by Kurt Müller and Gisela Krönert (1969).

[2] The breakdown is as follows: Series I, Volume 4, General Political and Historical Correspondence: 136 items. Series II, Volume 1, Philosophical Correspondence (1685): six items. Series II, Volume 2, Philosophical Correspondence (1686): sixteen items. Series III, Volume 4, Mathematical, Natural Science, and Technical Correspondence: five items. Series IV, Volume 3, Political Writings: ten items. Series IV, Volume 4, Political Writings: two items. Series VI, Volume 4, Philosophical Writings: 130 items. Series VIII, Volume 3, Natural Science, Medicine, and Technical Writings: ten items. Not included in the count are Series VII, Mathematical Writings, since the years 1685–86 have not yet been edited, nor Series V, Historical and Linguistic Writings, which has no volumes to date.

with some various points of philosophy and theology, including several letters to Arnauld specifically about the *Discourse*. Several works indicate Leibniz's in-depth knowledge of engineering and practical mechanics, which should reassure us that his criticisms of Cartesian mechanics were not simply dreamed up in a mathematical armchair. As Leibniz travels extensively throughout the Harz mountain region by horse-drawn wagon, he characteristically draws up plans for redesigning the axles to make for a smoother journey (see entry of 26 December 1686).

The *Chronicle*'s sources (such as Ravier [R], Gerland [LGD], and Akademie [AA]) are indicated below. For example, '(AA I, 4 N. 308)' refers to AA, Series I, Volume 4, piece number 308. If the piece can be found in the Akademie Edition, I have updated the reference and the date. Also, I replace the *Chronicle*'s square brackets with parentheses in order to indicate my additions within square brackets. I have added the footnotes and included the titles given in non-English languages as they are given in the *Chronik*.

1685

[*January 8*: Short letter to Veit Ludwig von Seckendorff (1626–92), historian, jurist, and statesman, on a passage from Aristotle's *Eudemian Ethics*, relevant to the 'agent intellect' and the Averroist interpretation (AA II, 1 N. 249, translated in this volume).]

[*January 8*: Short letter to the Landgrave Ernst von Hessen-Rheinfels (AA II, 1 N. 250, translated in this volume).]

January 25: From Hannover, arrival in Zellerfeld [a small town now merged with Clausthal, located roughly 100 km southeast of Hannover in the Harz mountain region], where Leibniz remains until 14 March and writes an extensive and interesting letter [twelve pages] to the Landgrave Ernst about the situation in the Empire and on the necessity of strengthening the imperial or royal power[3] (AA I, 4 N. 308). [See 14 March below, which is the date on the letter.]

January: Outline for a piston seal (LGD 159). [The Gerland volume contains Leibniz's drawings and descriptions for a hydraulic press, in which a tight seal or ring, made of leather or rubber, must be placed between the piston and cylinder wall. Its function, during pumping action, is to

---

[3] Hundreds of small principalities and territories were under the rule of the imperial House of Hapsburg. Leopold I was emperor from 1658 to 1711.

maintain air pressure while avoiding water loss, so that water could be drawn out of the mine pits, but with as little friction as possible on the parts.]

January–February: Third series of attempts with the wind-machine [*Windkunst*], which, like the first two, brought only partial success (AA I, 4, XL).

February 27: Leibniz's last letter of defence against the objections of the [mine] workers (AA I, 4 N. 140). [Eight pages, in German.]

March (beginning?): Leibniz is apparently in Herzberg [23 km south of Zellerfeld].

[*March 14*: Letter to Landgraf Ernst von Hessen Rheinfels (AA II, 1 N. 251). Zellerfeld. Leibniz makes brief comments on works by Malebranche and Arnauld.]

[*March 14*: Leibniz writes, or completes, a twelve-page letter to the Landgrave Ernst (as mentioned for 25 January, above) on military matters in the Empire generally; on the approval of polygamy by several theologians; on other theological matters relating mostly to confessional union, conscience vs. church and papal authority, and more (AA I, 4 N. 308).]

March 23: From Venice, Duke Ernst August orders the suspension of the work in the Harz mountains (Scheel 1966: 243).

March, second half: Return to Hannover. On 28 March he is verifiably no longer in Zellerfeld.
[He does, however, return several times, as will be seen.]

April 14: The Chamber [concerned with the mining operations] in Hannover notifies Leibniz of the Duke's order to stop the wind-machine experiments (AA I, 4 N. 147).

Mid-April: Leibniz is again in the Harz where he stays until the first half of May.

April 30: Memorandum for a wind-machine (LGD 188–90). [The Memorandum contains six drawings and descriptions of windmill designs and improvements.]

April: Outline for 'windmills, so that water may be drawn from deep pits in the mines' (LGD 181–6). [These pages in Gerland are titled, from German, 'Water-elevation by means of Wind Power'.]

April(?): Leibniz's expert opinion on the 'Genealogical Works' of Teodoro Damaideno,[4] for Duke Ernst August (AA I, 4 N. 149). On 21 March 1685, the Duke, who was in Italy, had requested, through his court poet B. O. Mauro, Leibniz's assessment of this work presented to the Duke in Venice, because it dealt with the genealogy of the House of Guelph (AA I, 4 N. 415).

May 5: The termination of the work on the wind-machines was recorded in the meeting of the Mining Authority.

May 9: Outline for cable loads (LGD 175). [Instructions for distributing loads over cables in order to reduce stretching and prevent breaking.]

May 18: From Hannover, to which Leibniz had again returned, writing to Landgrave Ernst, hoping to meet him soon incognito in Rheinfels or Schwalback (AA I, 4 N. 313). [Leibniz tells the Landgrave not to tell even his family, and he will explain why at their meeting.]

May 22: Leibniz requests [from the Chamber in Hannover] a yearly benefit of 600 talers [roughly equivalent to 450 current USD] for his technical improvements on the Harz mining project and other work (AA I, 4 N. 152).

May 28: Otto Grote informs the Duke [Ernst August] of Leibniz's readiness to work on the History of the House Braunschweig-Lüneburg,[5] if his present salary is converted into a lifelong pension (Scheel 1966: 244).

[*May, end*: A three-page letter to Veit Ludwig von Seckendorff (part of which is translated in this volume) consisting mostly of remarks on Descartes' possibility proof for God (AA II, 1 N. 252).]

---

[4] A Venetian Abbot who 'produced a genealogy of the Guelfs spanning over 2436 years and linked the Braunschweig-Lüneburg house to the Este family' (Antognazza 2009: 230).
[5] This ancestral line is part of the House of Guelph.

June: Leibniz's [published] reviews on the works of Paulus Casati: 'Eight Book of Mechanics'[6] [R 197], and Thomas Everard: 'Stereometry[7] made easie, or the description and use of a new gauging-rod'[8] (R 198).[9]

[*July 26*: Letter to Ludwig von Seckendorff (AA II, 1 N. 253, translated in this volume), praising Seckendorff's 'incomparable work on the true ground of the Christian state' (*Der Christen-Stat*, 1685), and remarking on a proof for God's existence by the Duke of Buckingham and his former university professor Erhard Weigel.]

July 27: Correspondence (until 28 June 1686) with secretary of war Gerhard Corfey in Hannover. [The correspondence has to do with the Guelph-Braunschweig-Lüneburg history. See AA I, 4 N. 169.]

July: Description of the adding machine (appearing in a newspaper on land surveying from 1898). Review of an article by Martin Lister[10] appearing in the January 1683/84 edition of *Philosophical Transactions*:[11] 'Observations on the use of the small intestine on the formation of the excrement of certain animals'[12] (R 200), and review of an essay by Wilhelm Gould appearing in the February 1684 edition: ['An account of the increase of weight in vitriol oil exposed to air'][13] (R 201).

August 9: Leibniz's remarks on the Reply of the Abbot Damaideno for the Duke (AA I, 4 N.158).[14] Criticism of Damaideno's uncertain evidence for the establishment of a genealogy of the Houses of Este and Guelph.

---

[6] 'Mechanicorum libri octo', Lugduni, 1684.

[7] Or, solid geometry, the measure of solid bodies or figures, such as cones and pyramids.

[8] Used for measuring the capacity of barrels.

[9] The title is in English.

[10] English naturalist and physician, 1639–1712.

[11] A monthly scientific journal of the Royal Society, first published in 1665 by Henry Oldenburg and still in operation. The full title of its first volume: 'Philosophical Transactions giving some ACCOMPT of the present undertakings, studies, and labours of the INGENIOUS in many considerable parts of the WORLD', <https://royalsocietypublishing.org/toc/rstl/1665/1/1>.

[12] This article appeared in English in the 20 January 1684 edition of *Philosophical Transactions*, under the title 'A letter in answer to another of Mr Hen. Oldenburgh's, wherein he desired an explanation of a paragraph touching on the use of the intestinum caecum, published in the Philosoph. Transact. num. 95 anno 1673 which paragraph is this'. A Latin version, 'Observatio de usu intestini coeci in figurandis quorundam animalium excrementis' appeared in the 1684 edition of *Acta Eruditorum* (pp. 318–19).

[13] 'Experimenta circa incrementum ponderis in oleo vitrioli aeri exposito'. The title is in Latin in the Ravier, but in English in the journal.

[14] See April(?) above.

Leibniz emphasises the necessity of a critical examination and evaluation of the traditional sources.

August 10: Leibniz receives the order to write the history of the House of Guelph up to the present. The title of Court Councillor would be guaranteed for life and his current salary should be converted into a 'life pension' [as requested on 28 May]. The Duke also granted him a secretary and remuneration for travel expenses (AA I, 4 N. 159). From now on he would also be freed of the usual councillor duties (Scheel 1966: 245).

[*August 20*: Brief, chatty, letter to the Landgrave Ernst von Hessen-Rheinfels.]

August 23: During his visit in Wolfenbüttel, Leibniz discusses the subject of primogeniture with Duke Anton Ulrich[15] (AA I, 4 N. 160). [The discussion would be relevant to Duke Ernst August's interest in preserving the integrity of his realm and in raising the Duchy of Hannover to the status of Electorate.]

August: Review of an article by Martin Lister: 'Observations on the nature and origin of earthquakes and lightning',[16] which appeared in the March 1683/4 issue of *Philosophical Transactions* (R 202).

September, beginning: Coming from Wolfenbüttel, a stopover in Clausthal-Zellerfeld [a journey of about 60 km southwest].

September 25: Evidently, back in Hannover.

September, end: Probably in Linsburg [40 km northwest of Hannover. No indication why he's there].

September: Review of Ph. D La Hire: 'Conic sections, divided in nine books'.[17] [Philippe de La Hire, d. 1718, was a French polymath.]

September: Johann Friedrich Leibniz [1632–96] auctioned off the books[18] of his half-brother [Gottfried Wilhelm] that had been stored for years

---

[15] 1633–1714, Duke of Braunschweig-Lüneburg and Prince of Braunschweig-Wolfenbüttel.
[16] 'Observationes de natura et origine terraemotus ac fulminis'.
[17] 'Sectiones conicae in novem libros distributae', Parisiis 1685 (R 203).
[18] The books: 'a vast library left by Leibniz's father, grandfather, and step-grandfather' (Antognazza 2009: 228–9).

with Clara Elisabeth Freiesleben [the widow of Christian Freiesleben, the administer of the Leibniz family estate]. Since the proceeds of 238 thalers were not sufficient to satisfy the claims of Freiesleben, G. Leibniz sought, with the Saxony ducal tax administration in Weimar, to suspend the inheritance claim for some years (AA I, 4, p. LV).

September–June 1686: Leibniz persists with the effort to meet the demand to extract ore from the mines by using mechanical machines powered by water instead of with the help of draught animals (AA I, 4, XLIV).

October 3: Back in Hannover.

October 11: Leibniz's memorandum on the Guelph ancestry for Gerhard Corfey and Christophe Brosseau (AA I, 4 N. 169). Sharp criticism of Damaideno's genealogical evidence.

October, second half: 'Reasons for the claims on the occasion of the ceremony' (AA IV, 2 N. 15). Written at the suggestion of Otto Grote.[19] The originating cause of the writing was the disputes over rank at the English court on the occasion of condolences for the death of Charles II and the ascension of Jacob II [that is, James VII].

October, second half: Leibniz's remarks on the Reunion Question for Landgrave Ernst (AA I, 4 N. 324). [See translation of this letter in this volume.]

October 27: Secretary Essken from Osterode [a town 12 km southwest of Zellerfeld] expects Leibniz, who is once again in Zellerfeld, to meet with him in the village of Scharzfeld [28 km southeast of Zellerfeld] to take him on a trip he has prepared through the Harz mountains to Baumannshöhle [a cave 40 km northeast of Scharzfeld] in a farmer's wagon.

October, end–beginning of November: Traveling through the Harz. [No indication of how this travelogue was put together.] The journey takes Leibniz from Zellerfeld to Osterod, then Herzberg, and then Scharzfeld, where he stayed overnight. The following morning, probably with his companions Christian Essken and J. D. Brandshagen, he climbs the mountain behind the village and visits a church carved into rock. Then follows a visit to Zwergenhöhle [Dwarves-Cave], a limestone cave situated between

---

[19] 'Raisons des pretension a l'egard du ceremonial'. Baron Otto Grote (1636–93) was councillor at the ducal court of Hannover.

the mountain and Castle Scharzfeld, containing the remains, bones and teeth, of prehistoric animals (compare the description in pp. 64–6 of the *Protogaea* [LPP 105]). Then lunch with a preacher and a tour of the castle which offers a beautiful view of Herzburg. Further travel over to Lauterberg, Braunlage (overnight) toward Elbingerode and Rübeland to Baumannshöhle, which was thoroughly explored (see *Protogaea* pp. 67–9) [LPP 109]. After an overnight stay in Rübeland in the house of the overseer of the cave, the overseer gave them some stalactites and animal bones in exchange for a good tip. Then the tour went through Hüttenrode, toward Katzenstein, and through Blankenberg, from where one has a view of the Blankenberger castle, the city, the zoo, the Heimberg castle, and Regenstein. From Thale, excursions were taken to the Rosstrappe stone in the Harzberge and through the Bodetal up to Teufelsmauer [Devil's Wall]. Leibniz expressed the opinion that the latter is probably a natural rock wall that collapsed due to earth tremors. The return trip went through Hüttenrode, Elbingerode, Braunlage, Andreasberg and back to Zellerfeld. [The round trip comes to approximately 340 km.]

October: Leibniz's reviews of J. B. Tarragon: 'New treatise on measuring;'[20] of Henri Gautier 'Treatise on Fortifications;'[21] of the anonymously appearing 'The Elements or principles of geometry',[22] and of Ozanam: 'The practical geometry of Mr Ozanam'[23] [No indication of where these reviews were published.]

November 11–December, beginning: Evidently back in Hannover.

November 22: Correspondence (up to 31 March 1693) with professor of history and polymath in Jena, Caspar Sagittarius (d. 1694), over the ancient history of the House of Braunschweig-Lüneburg.

November: 'Demonstration of geometric rules regarding the static moment of heavy objects on inclined planes'.[24] Leibniz's reviews of Joh. Ceva: 'Mathematical works on oblique powers, pendulums, vessels, and rivers',[25]

---

[20] 'Nouveau traité du toise', Paris 1685 [R 204].
[21] 'Traité des fortifications. . .', Paris Lyon 1685 (R 205).
[22] London 1684 (R 206).
[23] 'La géométrie pratique de Mr Ozanam', Paris 1685 (R 207).
[24] 'Demonstratio geometrica regulae apud staticos receptae de momentis gravium in planis inclinatis' (R 93). This article by Leibniz appeared in the November 1685 issue of *Acta Eruditorum*.
[25] 'Opuscula mathematica de potentiis obliquis, de pendulis, de vasis et de fluminibus', Ludovici Motiae 1682 (R 208).

and of the anonymously appearing (by Edme Didier): 'Essay on physics, proven by experience and confirmed by Holy Scripture'.[26]

December, beginning: Traveling again to Zellerfeld, where he stays for approximately two weeks.

December 7: The French historian and philologist Charles du Fresne Sieur Du Cange (d. 1688), through Christophe Brosseau, sent to Leibniz information on the Este family history. The correspondence will continue until 29 April 1686.

December 17: Leibniz writes his response [six pages] to the Abbot Teodoro Damaideno in Venice on the matter of the origins of the Guelphs (AA I, 4 N. 454). The correspondence lasts until 22 February 1686.

December 23: Back again in Hannover.

1685: 'The sigh of Podagrici while looking at a glass of wine' (Pertz I, 4, p. 379).[27] – Review of Barkhaus: 'A Righteous Funeral Speech to Prince Johannis Friderico' (Klopp 4).[28] – 'Observations on all kinds of mechanical and hydraulic seals'.[29] [Drawings and instructions for making water pumps.]

1685 (?): Leibniz's draft letter on the upbringing of a Prince. The date of origin lies between the death of the English King Charles II on 6/16 February (who is described in the last part of the letter as having died recently) and Leibniz's departure for southern Germany and Italy at the end of October 1687. While the recipient of the draft of 1685 is unknown, later versions are addressed to D. E. Jablonski, Duke George August, and probably also to the Electress Sophie Charlotte and Father Vota.[30]

---

[26] 'Essais de physique, prouvez par l'experience et confirmez par l'Ecriture Sainte', Paris 1684 (R 209).

[27] 'Seuffzer eines Podagrici bey Anschauung eines Glases mit Wein' (AA IV, 3 N. 125). According to AA, this is a drinking song that was sung before Pope Leo X, who asked his court poet, Camillus Querno, to sing about himself. Querno apparently had a swollen foot (hence 'podagrici'). It is written in German and Latin, and Leibniz seems to have added the last two stanzas, the last being: 'What good would it do for a water-drinker to write, when already a hundred brooks drive his millwheel, the water giving no fire therefrom to wake the spirit, then sober comes out what was soberly done.'

[28] 'Justa funebria Sermo Principi Johanni Friderico'.

[29] 'Allerhand observationes mechanicae et sigillatim hydraulicae' (LGD 146–52).

[30] Sophie Charlotte (1668–1705), daughter of Ernst August and Princess Sophie of the Palatinate, and from 1699 close friend to Leibniz. Carlo Maurizio Vota (1629–1715) was an Italian Jesuit.

1685 (?): 'On revelation and the church'[31] – 'Positiones'[32] – Leibniz's notes for a work on the origins of natural right (Grua 675–80)[33] – 'Arrangement of Law Tables' (Grua 786–8)[34] – 'New thoughts on how sound is formed and propagated through the air and expressed in the auditory organ'[35] (LGD 16–27) – 'Booklet on the Elements of Physics' (LGD 110–13)[36] – Outline for the employment of lifts in the mines (LGD 155–7) – 'On the Navigation of Ships' (LGD 208–13).[37]

1685 (?): Correspondence (until 1703, with breaks) with Duke Rudolf August of Wolfenbüttel (d. 1704), the brother of Duke Anton Ulrich, on historical, political, and theological themes.

1686

January, beginning–April, beginning: Residence in Zellerfeld.

January 12: Extensive correspondence (until July 1709) with Daniel Papebroch (d. 1714), a learned Jesuit in Antwerp and publisher of the *Acta Sanctorum*,[38] and who, due to his outstanding knowledge of Medieval documents, gave Leibniz valuable advice for his studies on the history of the House of Guelph.

February 11: 'Discourse on Metaphysics' [AA VI, 4 N. 306]. Containing the development of the basic idea of his *Theodicy*. [The *Chronik* follows with a German version of the letter Leibniz sent to the Landgrave. The original is found in AA II, 2 N. 1 and is translated in the introduction to this volume.] Leibniz sent to A. Arnauld, through the Landgrave, a summary of the main points of the 'Discourse on Metaphysics' for his assessment [AA II, 2 N. 2].

---

[31] This three-page piece appears in AA VI, 4 N. 417, as *De Deo et Ecclesia*, dated Autumn 1685–Spring 1686 (English trans. 'On God and the Church', in LGR).
[32] AA VI, 4 N. 418, Autumn 1685–Spring 1686 (English trans. 'Suppositions', in LGR).
[33] These notes (dated 1707) are on Georg Wachter's *Elucidarius cabalisticus*, a work which attempted in part to give the Kabbalah a philosophical grounding in Spinoza's *Ethics*.
[34] 'Dispositio tabulae juris'.
[35] 'Cogitationes novae, quomodo formetur sonus et per aerem propegatur atque in organo auditus exprimatur'.
[36] 'Elementorum physicae libellus'. In AA VI, 4 N. 365, titled *Conspectus Libelli Elementorum Physicae* [*Conspectus for a Little Book on the Elements of Physics*] and dated 1678–9. Translated in LC 231–5, and in LL 278 as 'On the Elements of Natural Science'.
[37] 'De gubernaculis navium'.
[38] *Acts of the Saints*, a journal documenting the lives of Christian saints, first published in 1643.

February 27: Leibniz's memorandum for Jean Mabillon (d. 1707) on the descent of the Guelphs (AA I, 4 N. 472). The learned Benedictine monk and founder of palaeography did not respond to Leibniz's letter until 15 March 1687. Their correspondence over historical questions would continue, with breaks, until February 1701.

February 28: Detailed letter [ten pages long] to Teodoro Damaideno on the genealogy of the Guelphs (AA I, 4 N. 474).

March: 'Brief Demonstration of a Considerable Error of Descartes and others on the Laws of Nature' (R 94). Written in January of 1686, this treatise [or article, which appeared in *Acta Eruditorum*] is an attack on Descartes' dynamics. Leibniz distinguishes between living, dead, genetic, and potential force. This is the starting point of a long-term controversy with the Cartesians Catelan, Malebranche, and Papin, which lasted until 1691.[39]

[*March*: With the help of a scribe, Leibniz completes the 'fair copy' of the *Discourse* (AA VI, 4 1530).]

April 12: From Hannover, where he evidently is, Leibniz expresses his annoyance with Arnauld in a letter to the Landgrave Ernst. Arnauld had harshly criticised his 'Metaphysics' from a theological point of view, while Leibniz passionately upheld natural science and handled theological questions in rationally moderate ways (AA I, 4 N. 337). [Also in AA II, 2 N. 5. See translation in LAV 27–31 or LAM 18–21.]

[*April 15*: Leibniz writes again to Landgrave Ernst asking him to make some edits on the previous letter (AA II, 2 N. 6 / LAV 35–7 and LAM 22–3).]

May (?): Leibniz's memorandum on the Guelph history for Du Cange (AA I, 4 N. 486).

June, beginning–July, beginning: Staying once again in Clausthal and Zellerfeld, where on 6 July he had a discussion with shift-supervisor Johann Arend Hentze regarding final accounts for the wind-machine work (AA I, 4 N. 237).

---

[39] 'Brevis demonstratio erroris memorabilis Cartesii et aliorum circa legem naturae' [AA IV, 4 N. 369]. See *Discourse* §17. Abbott François Catelan (d. 1719); Nicolas Malebranche, philosopher (1638–1715); Denis Papin, French physicist (1647–1713).

June 14: The pastor Petrus Valetin Berckelman reports on the excavation in Rosdorf near Göttingen, the findings of which Leibniz mentions in his *Protogaea* (pp. 78–80) [LPP 129].

[*June 14*: Letter to the Landgrave Ernst in which Leibniz asks Ernst to ask Arnauld whether he truly believes that 'the complete notion' is so bad and whether one who upholds this view would not be tolerated in the Catholic Church, 'even if he would sincerely disavow the alleged consequence of fatalism'. He also gives a technical explanation for how the complete notion is just like the 'ultimate species' in Aquinas (AA, II, 2 N. 10 / LAV 77–9, dated July). See §8 and §13 of *Discourse*.]

[*June 14*: Letter to Arnauld (AA II, 2 N. 12), translated in LAV 79 and LAM 67, but dated 14 July. The five-page letter, which was not sent to Arnauld, covers several topics drawn from the *Discourse*: the theory of truth; the principle of sufficient reason; God's choice of the best from an infinity of possibilities; the doctrine of concomitance; the principle of the identity of indiscernibles; substantial forms; and entelechy.]

June: 'Remarks on a letter from Mr Arnauld concerning my proposition: that the individual notion of each person includes for all time everything that will ever happen to him' [AA II, 2 N. 11 / LAV 57–77; LAM 39–52; and AG 69–77].

June: Appearing in the *Acta Eruditorum*, 'New Meditation on the Nature of the Angles of Tangency and Osculation and their Mathematical Application' (R 95)[40] and 'On a Hidden Geometry and Analysis of Indivisibles and Infinites (R 96).[41] First printed use of the integral sign in the form f = S. – Leibniz's discussions in the *Acta Eruditorum* on Samuel Morland: 'Elevation of Water', Paris 1685 (R 210), and of John Wallis: 'Treatise of algebra both historical and practical with some additional treatises', London 1685 (R 211).[42] By referring to Newton's letter of 1676 Leibniz wants to get Newton to publish his research on the infinitesimal calculus.

---

[40] 'Meditatio nova de natura anguli contactus et osculi horumque usa in practica mathesi'. See A'Campo-Neuen and Papadopoulos 2019.
[41] 'De Geometria Recondita et Analysi Indivisibilium atque infinitorum', partially translated in LMM 281–2.
[42] Morland: 'Elevation des eaux'. The treatise by Wallis is in English.

[*July 14*: Letter to Arnauld (AA II, 2 N. 13 / LAV 89–95; LAM 67–74), in which he boasts to Arnauld of several accomplishments: reflections on jurisprudence; studies on mines and how slate is generated; work on the history of the House of Brunswick, on geometry, and on metaphysics, specifically (1) that demonstrations in it are based on two primitive truths: the principles of contradiction and sufficient reason; (2) on real definition, namely, 'that the mark of a true idea is that one can prove its possibility' either *a priori* or *a posteriori* (LAV 95). Thus, (3) he agrees with Arnauld that we must distinguish between true and false ideas. These three points are discussed in several places in the *Discourse*.]

[*July 14*: Letter to Arnauld (AA II, 2 N. 14 / LL 1969 and LS 2006) dealing extensively with Arnauld's concern about the 'fatal necessity' resulting from the complete notion. Also discusses 'real physical influence', occasional causes, force and quantity of motion – all discussed in the *Discourse*.]

July 22: Leibniz again in Hannover. [But he has probably been there since 14 June.]

[*August 12*: Two letters to the Landgrave Ernst: AA I, 4 N. 341, which is entirely on political matters, and AA II, 2 N. 15, which expresses Leibniz's contentment should Arnauld judge the views expressed in the summary of the *Discourse* to be tolerable for a Roman Catholic. Both letters are translated in LAV 117 and 121, and the second also in LAM 75–6.]

[*August*: Letter to Simon Foucher (AA, II, 2 N. 16, partial translations in MB 129–31 and WF 52–3).[43] Foucher (1644–96) was a French academic sceptic. In this seven-page letter Leibniz discusses several points on Foucher's *New Dissertation on the Search for Truth* (1679), the main subject of which is Malebranche's *Search after Truth*. The most important part of Leibniz's discussion is on the relationship of the body and soul, that each expresses but does not act on the other. Leibniz also denies the two prevailing doctrines of causal interaction, namely 'physical influx' and Malebranche's 'occasional causes'. Thus, Leibniz clears a path to his own doctrine of pre-established harmony. On all this, see *Discourse* §33 and commentary.]

---

[43] Complete translation by Strickland: <http://www.leibniz-translations.com/foucher16 86.htm>.

September, mid–December, first half: Once again staying in Zellerfeld. Between 1680 and 1686 Leibniz had made thirty-one visits to the Harz and spent a total of 165 weeks there (see AA I, 3, XXIX).

September: 'Brief Demonstration of a considerable error of M. Descartes and of several others' (R 97).[44]

[*December 8:* Five-page letter to Landgrave Ernst (A I, 4 N. 343 / LAV 131) on political and ecumenical matters.]

[*December 8:* Five-page unsent letter to Arnauld focusing on the hypothesis of concomitance and whether bodies are substances (AA II, 2 N. 24 / LAV 143 and LAM 84–9).]

[*December 8:* Important seven-page letter to Arnauld on a range of issues similar but in addition to the unsent letter of 8 December (AA II, 2 N. 25 / LAV 151 and LAM 91–101).]

December 9: By order of the deputies, Leibniz was paid 300 thalers in cash from the royal tithe in Clausthal (AA I, 4 N. 261).

December 26: Outline for the transport of loads: 'A load on rough and tough paths to increasingly smooth ground and therefore very easy to pass' (LGD 222–9).[45] [This outline, including drawings of parts of wagons and carts, seems intended to show how an axle could be made so that the wheel on one side could move up and down independently of the other.]

1686 (?): 'General Inquisitions on the Analysis of Notions and Truths' [AA VI, 4 N. 165/LGI 2021][46] – Outline for a new trolley (LGD 230–33). Leibniz draws up a model of this – Outline of P. Poiret: 'Rational thoughts on God, the soul, and evil, book IV',[47] Amsterdam 1685 (Grua 84). [The title of this piece continues: 'where the atheism of Spinoza is refuted'.]

---

[44] 'Demonstration courte d'une erreur considerable de M. Descartes et de quelques autres'. [This French version of this famous article appeared in *Nouvelles de la Republique des Lettres*, September 1686, pp. 996–9.]
[45] 'Eine Last durch rauhe und tuffe Wege auff glatten fortschreitendem Boden und also sehr leicht zu führen'.
[46] 'Generales inquisitions de analysi notionum et veritatum'.
[47] 'Cogitationes rationales de Deo, anima et malo, lib. IV, ed. altera' (AA VI, 4 N. 345).

1686 (?): 'System of Theology' (in Foucher de Careil, 2, Edition 1, pp. 531–652). 'Examination of the Christian Religion',[48] which, through the first publisher P. P. Lacroix, became known under the title 'System of Theology', was probably composed in 1686.[49] Leibniz considers the question from the standpoint of a Catholic.

1686 (?): 'Reflections on the subject of Coinage',[50] for his Duke [Klopp 5, 446–54] – Outline of the relationship of divine power and human freedom (Grua 380–88)[51] – 'Project and attempt to arrive at some certitude to end a good part of the disputes and to advance the art of invention' and 'The Elements of Reason'[52] – Outline for the General Science[53] – 'Discourse concerning the method of certitude and the art of discovery'[54] – 'Outline for a General Characteristic'[55] – 'Specimen of Discoveries of the Admirable Secrets of Nature in General'[56] – 'Necessary and Contingent Truths'.[57]

1686 (?): Correspondence (until 16 October 1711) with the Supreme Court [Hofgericht] assessor and archivist in Celle [north of Hannover], Chilian Schrader, who was court and justice councillor from 1690 (d. 1721). The correspondence concerned juridical and historical themes.

January 19, 1687, Hannover: Correspondence (until October 1702) with the well-known sceptic Pierre Bayle (d. 1706) in Rotterdam, the editor of the *Historical and Critical Dictionary* and brilliant critic targeted in Leibniz's *Theodicy*.

[48] 'Examen Religionis Christianae (Systema theologicum)', dated April–October 1686, in AA VI, 4 N. 420.
[49] Actually, the first editor was Jacques-André Émery, who published the text posthumously in 1819. Lacroix's edition was published in 1845 (Source: L. Strickland).
[50] 'Bedenken in Betreff des Münzwesens'.
[51] In Grua, the title is 'The Liberty of Creatures and Divine Election' [*De Libertate Creaturae et Electione Divina*] and is dated 1697. In AA VI, 4 N. 308, the piece is titled 'De Libertate Creaturae Rationalis' and tentatively dated Spring–Summer 1686.
[52] 'Projet et essais pour arriver à quelque certitude pour finir une bonne partie des disputes et pour avancer l'art d'inventer' (AA VI, 4 N. 205, dated August 1688–October 1690) and 'Elementa Rationis' (AA VI, 4 N. 162, dated April–October 1686).
[53] *Scientia Generalis* (AA VI, 4 N. 161, dated August 1688–October 1690 / LP 1968).
[54] 'Discours touchant la methode de la certitude et l'art d'inventer' (AA IV, 4 N. 204, dated October 1688–October 1990).
[55] AA VI, 4 N. 270, under the title *De Veritatibus Primis*.
[56] *Specimen inventorum de admirandis naturae generalis arcanis* (AA VI, 4 N. 312 / LC and LP). AA dates the piece '1688?'
[57] AA VI, 4 N. 303, under the title *De Natura Veritatis, Contingentiae et Indifferentiae atque De Libertate et Praedeterminatione*, and dated end of 1685 to mid 1686. English trans. in LP.

Context II: Translations of Letters Selected from 1685

During 1685, the year prior to his composition of the *Discourse*, Leibniz wrote at least eighty-eight letters to various correspondents on political, historical, and philosophical matters.[1] The following have been selected for (1) not having been previously translated into English (excepting one); (2) their particular relevance to the *Discourse* and to Leibniz's main concerns during this time.

Letter from Leibniz to Veit Ludwig von Seckendorff[2]

29 December 1684, Hannover. AA II, 1 N. 249 (I, 4 N. 408, one page). Latin.

Excellent is the passage in Aristotle you cited, Book VII, *Eudemian Ethics*, Chap. 14, and rightly said by him,[3] that there is something acting in us

---

[1] Approximately eighty letters on general political and historical topics, six on philosophical topics, and two on mathematical topics.

[2] Historian, jurist, and statesman, 1626–92. Seckendorff included this excerpt from Leibniz's letter in the appendix to his *Christian-State* [*Der Christen-Stat*], published in 1685.

[3] AA note: Aristotle's *Eudemian Ethics*, VII, 14, 1246b–1248b. The passage Leibniz has in mind is precisely at 1248a25: 'Or is there some originating principle [*arche*] with no other principle external to it which, because it is the kind of thing it is, can produce this kind of effect? That is what we are looking for: what is the starting point of motion in the soul? The answer is plain: as in the universe, so here, God moves everything by intelligence [*nous*]. For in a manner the divine element in us moves everything. Reason [*logos*] is not the originator of reasoning, but something superior [is]. But what can be superior to knowledge and to intelligence, except God? For virtue is an instrument of intelligence' (Aristotle 2011: 145–6). Prior to this passage Aristotle had been inquiring into the causes

316

more excellent than reason, something divine; although the reasons he offers for Enthusiasm[4] and the success of the inexperienced are hardly valid. The same and more powerful arguments can be demonstrated from the nature of the mind itself. I am afraid, however, that Aristotle had a destructive opinion in mind, of which he was suspected elsewhere, concerning the universal agent intellect, which is one and the same in all men and survives after death – an opinion the Averroists have revived. But without this ruinous addition, the opinion itself is most beautiful and in conformity with reason and Scripture. God is the light that illuminates all men coming into this world.[5] And the truth that speaks within us, when we understand the theorems of eternal certitude, is the voice of God itself, as St Augustine had also remarked.[6]

Leibniz to the Landgrave Ernst Von Hessen-Rheinfels

29 December (8 January 1685), Hannover. AA II, 1 N. 250. French.[7]

[. . .][8] I have still not seen either the book of F. Malebranche on ideas, or the two books of Mr Arnauld on this subject.[9] F. Malebranche, the author of the *Search after Truth*, is very ingenious <[10]> and has some very good and very solid thoughts, but there are others which are a little hyperbolic or lightly conceived. In some ways he follows the ways of Descartes, but even Descartes does not satisfy me in these matters. Their principle (that everything one can conclude from the idea one has of a thing can be truly attributed to it) is strongly subject to caution, and at least to give marks

---

of luck and good fortune, in order to explain why some people lacking reason neverthe-less have success. Some get by on this divine element (intelligence). Leibniz associates intelligence in this passage with the agent intellect in Aristotle, but is concerned about the Christian Averroists' interpretation of this view. See §XXVIII of the *Discourse* and §28 of the commentary.

[4] This term was understood to mean something like 'god-inspired', since it is derived from the Greek, meaning 'in-the-essence-of god'.

[5] AA note: John 1:9.

[6] AA note: *In Johannis evangelium tractatus* [*Tractates on the Gospel According to St John*], 54, 8.

[7] Also translated by Lloyd Strickland: <http://www.leibniz-translations.com/landgrave2.htm>.

[8] Omitted by AA. The full letter is in AA I, 4 N. 301, pp. 340–2.

[9] AA Note: Malebranche, *Response of the author of the Search for Truth to the book of M. Arnauld: On True and False Ideas*, Rotterdam, 1684. A. Arnauld, *On True and False Ideas, against what the author of the Search for Truth Teaches*, Köln, 1683. Discussion of the controversy between Malebranche and Arnauld is given in §28 of the commentary.

[10] Struck from manuscript: (1) but sometimes he gives too much to (a) ideas (b) hyperbolic thoughts

of a distinct conception, it is useless to say that everything that is clearly and distinctly conceived is true. This Analysis of our thoughts is of great importance both for judgment and discovery. And I said what I think about it in a brief article inserted in *Acta Eruditorum* of Leipzig in the month of November 1684, page 537,[11] on which I would be well pleased to learn the opinion of Mr Arnauld. I do not doubt that V.A.S.[12] receives these acts from time to time. They are printed every month and are rather well done. Some of those who work on them are friends of mine.

Leibniz to Veit Ludwig von Seckendorff

End of May 1685. AA II, 1 N. 252. Latin.

Most illustrious and Most generous Sir.

Since you are faring as well as you say, and you have again found a most noble spouse who may alleviate the pain of the one you lost and ease your worries, I am wonderfully glad and thankful. For I hope that this will be of great benefit both to the state of your health and to the state itself, whose interest is to preserve great men. I had been fearing something otherwise, since from your previous letter I sensed your pain and the beginning of an illness, and therefore I rejoice all the more for the better outcome, and from the heart I pray for your enduring good.[13]

Those excerpts [from your book] you shared with me have long kindled a great desire for your work: and these Leipzig Fairs will certainly be dedicated to such an excellent gift, to the great benefit of both learning and piety.[14] I do not know what was in my letter that pleased you so much that you thought worthy to use, unless perhaps you translated things I imperfectly said into your own splendid thoughts, and thus took

[11] Leibniz is referring to his 'Meditations on Knowledge, Truth, and Ideas' (AG 1989). See §24 of commentary.

[12] A formal address to the Landgrave: 'Votre Altesse Sérénissime' (Your Most Serene Highness).

[13] The above passage was not included in AA II, 1, but is included along with the whole letter in AA I, 4 N. 427.

[14] According to his previous letter to Leibniz (February 1685, AA I, 4 N. 413), Seckendorff would send to Leibniz, as soon as printed, his book *Der Christen-Stat* [*The Christian-State*], 'hopefully by the next Leipzig Fair' (AA I, 4 N. 413). The fair began on 27 May, two days after Leibniz wrote this letter (AA II, 1, 868). Back in September 1683, however, Seckendorff had already sent Leibniz an excerpt from the book: Part 2, Ch. 10 (according to AA II, 1, 868, in reference to letter N. 242).

something better; as we are sometimes accustomed to read into others what does not emerge from their own thinking.[15]

The body of Amalric[16] was exhumed and burned some years after his death, as is evident from the contemporary writer Rigordo whom Pithou had published. Caesarius Heisterbach[17] named the students of his that were burned alive, and he adds that the books of Master David were also burned. I think this is Master David from Dinanto,[18] who is said to have taught that God is prime matter, which means that, as I understand, God produces all things from himself rather than from nothing. But if this is carefully considered, it withers into vanishing subtleties and rests more on the forms of speech than on things. I do not approve of several things that Parker[19] has said in regard to the new philosophers, and it seems this author blusters at length rather than argues. Although he rejects Descartes' argument derived from ideas, and I agree, it may be seen that Parker himself did not sufficiently grasp its strength. Indeed he [Parker] thinks that from the definitions of things nothing of their actual existence can be inferred, which is false. For what if existence follows from the essence of some Being, that is, what if some Being is necessary or exists from itself? If indeed existence follows from its essence, then it certainly can be inferred from its definition. It is only asked whether there may be some such Essence, or (since it is the same [to ask about] the essence of a given thing or a possible thing) whether a Being existing through its own essence is possible; for then this proposition can be included among the certain theorems of the true Metaphysics: *If the necessary being is possible,*

---

[15] Leibniz is referring to the excerpt from his letter of 29 December 1684 (N. 249, translated above), which Seckendorff had added to his book.

[16] Amalric of Bena, French philosopher, theologian, died c. 1204. In his letter to Leibniz (February 1685, AA I, 4 N. 413), Seckendorff writes: 'The Pope condemned him of heresy. The dogma imputed to him, among other things, was that *ideas create God, and in God ideas are created*. But since the books of Amalric are non-existent, burned up along with Aristotle's *Metaphysics*, to whom those authors at the time referred, nothing certain can be said about the man's opinion, and it is customary for the writers of the Papal party to attribute what they want to those they once took for heretics' (AA II, 1, 869 fn, and originally in AA I, 4 N. 413, p. 393).

[17] c. 1170–1240, German priest and author of *Dialogue on Miracles* [*Dialogus Miraculorum*], 1223.

[18] c. 1160–1217, philosopher, teacher, pantheist, and may have been a disciple of Amalric. Aquinas attributes this 'absurd' view to him in *Summa*, I, q.3, a.8, 'Whether God enters into the composition of other things'.

[19] Samuel Parker, 1640–88, Bishop of Oxford, author of *Disputations on God and divine Providence* [*Disputationes de Deo et Providentia divina*], 1678.

319

it follows that it exists. Descartes therefore must prove <[20]> that the most perfect being (which certainly includes existence among the other perfections) is possible.[21] That God exists only if he is possible is evident from the terms, whether he be defined as the most perfect being, or simply as the being from itself or a necessary being. This privilege of the Divine essence is certainly not to be despised. The existence of Contingent things does not follow from their essence or possibility but from the will of God, or what comes down to the same thing, from the universal harmony of things.

The exchange between Arnauld and Malebranche has not yet arrived in my hands.[22] While I appreciate Malebranche's great genius, the most elegant thoughts sometimes require solidity. As long as the writers think it sufficient to believe truths which they seem to perceive clearly and distinctly, we will have chimeras.[23] How much more accurate was Euclid, though some ridiculed him, who, granting nothing to the imagination, demonstrated that any two sides of a triangle are greater than the third,[24] demonstrating even what Asses are not ignorant of, as they take the right way to the fodder. I would like to introduce the same sort of rigour for demonstrations in metaphysics, and much more, and thereby to show how much easier it will be to fall into the slightest gap, and how important it will be for physics and morals to have a true metaphysics. Meanwhile, however, as long as we do not truly have it, far better is to make the most beautiful arguments drawn from the divine works, which will lead us to recognise their author, rather than making arguments that are hardly convincing. Even if they offer only moral certainty, they are more suitable for persuasion.[25]

---

[20] Struck from manuscript: that God is possible, which many Atheists would perhaps deny

[21] See §23 of commentary.

[22] The reference is to their dispute which began in 1683 with Arnauld's *On True and False Ideas*, continuing with Malebranche's *Response of the Author of the Search for Truth to Arnauld's Book On True and False Ideas* (1684). The dispute continued into 1685. See §28 and §29 of commentary.

[23] See §24 of commentary.

[24] Euclid, *Elements*, Bk I, Proposition 20.

[25] Leibniz continues the letter with reflections on several books and authors of marginal interest.

Leibniz to Veit Ludwig von Seckendorff

26 July 1685. AA II, 1 N. 253. And AA I, 4 N. 435. Latin.

Most illustrious and Most generous Sir,

Your incomparable work, on the true ground of the Christian state,[26] sent to me by our Lord Mencke,[27] has been rightly received, and for the elegant gift you have blessed me with, together with all those who can derive the greatest benefits from it, my personal gratitude. We certainly have many pious and quite erudite and learned people, and several eloquent writings in our vernacular; however, where all those merits have been collected and compiled to such an extent, I do not recall having seen, apart from your book. I will not add more, lest I offend your modesty, by saying modest things, by speaking the truth, or by trying to say something worthy. As soon as I received it, I could not refrain from reading it entirely from beginning to end, and with great delight. But now, since I got it back from the bookbinder, I will read it again more diligently, and linger over particular parts in order to gain greater fruit from it. If I knew a Frenchman skilled in German language and writing, I would have him translate it in his own tongue.

I hope that my most recent letter about the former market days was rightly received. Recently, I read that a little book or rather pamphlet by the Duke of Buckingham on the truth of Religion[28] had been sent to our Most serene and written in English, which she knows very well.[29] It shows indeed the genius of the author, although some things may not be sufficiently proven. I see some things interspersed that do not much differ from the principles of our Weigel and that I have given some account of.[30] Namely, he thinks that nothing remains the same, but that everything is in perpetual flux, except God. <[31]> I believe you have seen Weigel's demonstration of God's existence, which he shared with friends some years ago

[26] *Der Christen-Stat.*
[27] Otto Menke (1644–1707), German philosopher and co-founder (with Leibniz) of the *Acta Eruditorum.*
[28] Duke of Buckingham, George Villiers (1628–87), *A short discourse upon the reasonableness of men's having a religion, or worship of God* (1685). In the spring or summer of 1685, Leibniz translated this work into German (see AA VI, 4 N. 446, pp. 2641–9).
[29] Princess Sophie Charlotte of Hannover (1668–1705), daughter of Queen Sophie and Duke Ernst Augustus, and a close friend of Leibniz.
[30] Erhard Weigel (1625–99), professor of mathematics at Jena, from whom Leibniz took a course during summer semester 1663.
[31] Struck from manuscript: Unless it is thought that the individual (ἀτόπον) remains the same substance . . . whose accidents remain the same in the other substituted substance. For me however those things have not been demonstrated.

321

in both German and Latin. It seems to me very worthy of examination, although, as I have warned, some things seem to be added that need a demonstration.[32] This seems to me the best way: if it can be shown that all accidents are nothing other than modes of conceiving of the substance; then indeed what they posit may be demonstrated, that substances themselves do not in fact endure, if you require the utmost exactness in the matter;[33] but if all things, whether different or similar, or if you prefer, the same things, are to be continuously created from God, then God must necessarily be excepted; otherwise, if everything were continuously perishing, nothing would exist to restore anything, for once nothing exists in the whole universe, nothing would remain for eternity. But so much for the occasion of Buckingham's meditations. Now when in the same booklet the Duke recommended that the English exercise toleration toward the heterodox, a certain anonymous refutation emerged, whose paper I have seen, but which appeared of little moment.[34]

Farewell.

Leibniz to Duke Ernst August of Hannover

August 1685–October 1687. AA II, 1 N. 254a. French.

The date of this letter is uncertain, but it must have been started sometime after 10 August 1685, the day the Duke contracted Leibniz to write the History of the House of Guelph. It is uncertain whether the letter reached the Duke (according to AA II, I, 875).

Having the honour to assist V.A.S.[35] and seeing his reason, and the love he has for the truth, I take the liberty to speak to him about some of my plans to which I dedicate myself, if God gives me the <grace>[36] to finish the History of his Most Serene house.

I can say without vanity that in our time I am one of the most deeply learned in Mathematics, and I have discovered some entirely new methods and paths that take this science beyond the limits that had been prescribed to them.

---

[32] More on Leibniz's assessment of Weigel's proof can be found in AA VI, 4 N. 265 (1679) and in his letter to Weigel, AA II, 1 N. 212 (1679).

[33] Unclear why Leibniz wrote 'exactness' (ἀκριβείαν) in Greek.

[34] Note in AA: *A short answer to his Grace the Duke of Buckingham's paper, concerning religion, toleration, and liberty of conscience*, London 1685.

[35] 'Votre Altesse Sérénissime' (Your Most Serene Highness).

[36] Struck: strength. Added: grace

The examples I have given have been praised in France and England, and it will be easy for me to give still many others; but I make no grand claim to discover particulars, and what I desire more is to perfect the Art of Invention[37] in General, and to give Methods rather than Solutions; because <[38]> a single method comprehends an infinity of solutions.

However, I do not limit myself to Mathematics, since the truths it teaches, though very useful to human life, do not alone fulfil our spirit; and I believe that the greatest use one can make of it is to learn the art of reasoning with exactitude.

As I have had the good pleasure to perfect considerably the art of invention, or the analytic method of Mathematicians, I have begun to have certain entirely novel insights about reducing all of human reasoning to a kind of calculation; which would serve to discover the truth, as far as can be done *ex datis*, that is, through what is given, or known. And even when the given known does not suffice to resolve the proposed question, this method would serve, as in Mathematics, to approach the given as near as one can, and to determine exactly what is most probable.

This sort of general calculus would at the same time provide a kind of universal writing, which would have the advantage of that of the Chinese, because each one understands it in his own language, but it would infinitely surpass Chinese, since one could learn it in a few weeks; having the characters well connected according to the order and connection of things; instead of having, as in Chinese, an infinity of characters corresponding to the variety of things, which would take a whole lifetime to learn.

This writing or language (if one renders the characters pronounceable) could be received by the world very soon because it could be learned in a few weeks and would provide the means to communicate with everyone. It would be of great importance for the propagation of faith and for the <[39]> instruction of distant peoples.

But this would be the least of its advantages, since this same writing would be a species of general Algebra, and would provide the means of reasoning by calculating, in such a way that instead of disputing one could say: let us calculate. And one will find that the errors of reasoning will only be errors in calculating, which one could discover by proofs, as in Arithmetic.

By this, men would find a truly infallible judge of controversies; for they could always know whether it is possible to decide the question by means of knowledge already given to them; and when it is not possible for them to be entirely satisfied, they can always determine what is most likely.

---

[37] The art of discovery is meant.
[38] Struck: all solutions are comprehended in the methods.
[39] Struck: civil

As in Arithmetic one can always judge whether it is possible to divine exactly the number that someone has in mind from what they have told us about it; and often one can say, it must be one of two or three, etc. such numbers, and [thereby] prescribe exact limits to the unknown truth. <⁴⁰> In any case it is important to know at least that what one asks for is not discoverable by the available means.

Thus, to arrive at this writing, or Characteristic, which will contain a calculus so surprising, one must search for the exact definitions of notions. For the words we have, being rather obscure and often giving us only confused notions, one is obliged <⁴¹> to substitute with other characters the notion of which is precise and determined, and the definitions are only a distinct expression of the idea of the thing.

As I have studied, and with care, not only History and Mathematics, but also natural Theology, Jurisprudence, and Philosophy, I have strongly advanced this project and have made a number of definitions. For example, the definition of justice according to me is: Justice is the charity of the wise person; or charity conforming to wisdom. Charity is nothing other than universal benevolence. Wisdom is the science of felicity. Felicity is a lasting state of joy. Joy is a sentiment of perfection. Perfection is a degree of reality.

I claim to give similar definitions for all passions, virtues, vices, and human actions, as many as necessary. And by these means one could speak and reason with exactitude. And as new characters always contain the definitions of things, it follows that they will give us the means of reasoning by calculating, as I have said just above.

But to succeed in a matter so important, which would furnish Humankind with a Species of instrument proper for perfecting the sight of the Mind, just as spectacles serve for that of the body, much meditation and a little assistance will be required.

Leibniz for the Landgrave Ernst

Second half of October (?) 1685. Hannover. AA I, 4 N. 324. French.[42]

A revealing example of Leibniz's reconciliation efforts is found in this letter written a few months before the Discourse. *Leibniz argues that the Council of Trent need not be fully recognised, or recognised as legitimate, for the sake of Protestant-Catholic union.*

---

[40] Struck: (1) Since it is often important to (a) judge what (b) to know that we cannot know with certainty what is asked for.

[41] Struck: to search for their value.

[42] Thanks to Lloyd Strickland for his help with this translation.

One of the greatest faults that I often notice in persons the most enlightened and best intentioned for the glory of God and the public good is that having made certain judgments and chosen certain hypotheses and views, according to how they would like these things done, they attach themselves to them with such fervour that they can hardly admit that they reach the same goal by different routes. Thus it occurs that instead of approving the thoughts and designs of the other, what there is good and common to both sides, they attack what is different, finding material for a dispute full of bitterness, where what is needed is to think of how to work together, how to help one another attain the main goal, and to jointly consider different ways to serve the same plan, especially since we do not know which ways the divine wisdom could choose. This manner of acting has a very bad effect, since it happens that those who have the same goal, but who contest the means, impede and combat each other, instead of turning their strength and thought toward attaining the goal by whatever lawful means they could.

I notice this in many matters, but particularly regarding Christian reunion. Some persons understand these great difficulties very well, and without hoping for any success from the methods just proposed, [they] find it sufficient to leave this concern to providence, and to devote themselves to the cultivation of piety, each one in his creed. And one cannot blame these sentiments, except when the same persons, not content to refrain from such thoughts and plans, want others to refrain from them also, disparaging and preventing even their commendable intentions as if they [themselves] had a revelation that the matter could never succeed. I join those several persons who insist on toleration, but who do not want to consider a closer union without working with both sides. As for those who work for reunion, there are some who believe in the way of society and the flesh, that is to say, in the sole efficaciousness of fears and hopes, despising all ways of the spirit. There are some who imagine they can prevail upon others through disputes and the force of reasons, but who would not suffer any flexibility or middle ground; not considering that some in the opposing party are also so obstinate in their opinions that no reason will ever make them change. Many people, convinced that there is nothing to do other than concede to both sides, imagine that both parties must abandon their principles to form a third party, in some way. Finally, some learned people find it good to content themselves with what is more essential in the Christian religion, and that one should recognise as brothers those with whom they remain in agreement, leaving the liberty to believe or not to believe in those few articles [still] in dispute. They are convinced that otherwise there is no fraternal union to hope for, or at least that one party or another could not be overruled without great violence.

However, there is still another way of Reunion, which seems to me reasonable and possible even in regard to entire peoples, in order to bring about a Union not only of Tolerance, but even of Fraternity, and this without any Violence; it would, moreover, save the principles of each party (*salvis principiis partium*). And it lies in receiving those who recognise the authority of the Church and the Ecclesiastic Hierarchy, but who, for apparently serious reasons, have trouble believing that the Council of Trent is legitimate and ecumenical.[43] Now, those who, on a point of fact, are only mistaken, and not from obstinacy, cannot be taken for either heretics or Schismatics. Thus, one could grant them the liberty of retaining some opinions condemned in the Council (those that one may have difficulty abandoning right away) until the celebration of a less controversial council. And by granting them, in addition, communion *under both kinds* (*subutraque*),[44] and marriage of Ecclesiastics, in the manner of the [Orthodox] Greeks, among other matters rather indifferent, it appears that entire peoples could be restored; perhaps, even after taking the first step and the union once established, one would get further along before the celebration of the new Council.

I am surprised that reasonable and well-intentioned persons speak bitterly against this plan. For in the end are they not obliged to admit that those who have these sentiments would pass neither for heretics nor for schismatics, and that under such conditions, if entire peoples came to offer themselves to the Roman Church, one could not refuse them without manifestly acting contrary to charity and spiritual prudence? It seems therefore that those who oppose this do so only by a secret passion that everyone has, [namely,] that no one should have more privilege than themselves, and that everyone should recognise the Council of Trent, because they themselves have submitted to it. They do not even want anyone to negotiate with them, and they would much prefer to see entire nations [remain] outside their Church than to see them received in a manner a little different from their thoughts and ways.

I have seen some arguments alleged against this Method, but to speak candidly on what I think about them, they do not hit the mark and do not indicate that the matter has been considered in the spirit of moderation and equity, as is shown elsewhere.

---

[43] The Council of Trent: a series of ecumenical councils taking place between 1545 and 1563; the Church's 'Counter-Reformation' response to Protestantism.

[44] Early Reformist theologian Jacob de Mies (1372–1429) defended the doctrine of 'utraquism', according to which communion for the laity should be administered 'under both kinds' (wine and bread), rather than bread alone, as according to Church practice (Religious Encyclopedia, <https://www.ccel.org/ccel/schaff/encyc06/Page_79>).

For 1) it is not a question of knowing whether the Council of Trent has defined something new or not (although in effect Bellarmine[45] and others agree that Catholic doctors were able to hold certain opinions before the said council that they could not support now, *sine nota haereseos*, that is, without speaking of the anathematisms that this Council has attached to numerous positions), since it is enough for the Protestants to imagine that the council is simply against them; and in the event that there is nothing new in the Council of Trent, one could even more easily resolve to disregard it in favour of Protestants, since then all of the doctrines of the Church would nonetheless stand. Thus, this objection would rather prove the contrary.[46]

To say that it would be unjust to demand this indulgence only in order to satisfy the whim of people coming in without any authority and with division among them is to regard the matter from an unnecessary viewpoint. It is not a question here either of Zwingli or Luther or of certain individuals, but of entire nations and of many persons who are pious and enlightened but accused on these points, and with whom one can and perhaps should be pleased, if this were the only difficulty. The disunity of the Protestants does not matter here, since it is only about people who would be unified enough to resolve themselves to reunion under the aforementioned conditions.

2) Supposing that one never retracts what has been decided in a legitimate council; this does not matter here. It is not a matter of such a retraction, but of a suspension of the obligatory force of a council with regard to persons who have reasons true or false, but very plausible, to doubt whether it is legitimate.

3) As for some other councils, we know that even Rome did not receive all the articles of Constance,[47] and the Lateran council[48] is contested by many people – to say nothing of [the Council] of Florence[49] and the disputes of the Greeks. But when all of these controversies are set aside, it

---

[45] Roberto Bellarmine, influential Jesuit and Catholic Cardinal (1542–1621), canonised in 1930.

[46] The sense of the paragraph seems to be this: Some Catholics may (and did) raise the objection that since the Council contains no new positions, Protestants have no cause to refuse to endorse it. But Leibniz is suggesting that if the Council's decrees contain nothing new, then it can be disregarded, and thereby avoid the impression that the Council is targeting them. Thus, in order not to discourage reunion, the objection proves instead that the Council should be disregarded. Thanks to Lloyd Strickland for providing me with the background on this issue.

[47] Council of Constance: 1414–18.

[48] Lateran Council: A series of five councils from 1123–1512.

[49] Council of Florence: 1432–39.

suffices for the Protestants to put forward particular arguments regarding the Council of Trent.

4) When some Catholic potentates protested recognition of the Council of Trent as legitimate and universal, it is no use saying that they hold the same religion. It is not about their religion, but a matter of fact, namely, whether the Council of Trent must necessarily be recognised as legitimate, and whether one cannot be Catholic without it. On these points these same potentates and people agree, in my view. I do not believe that up to now France has declared the Council legitimate and universal. The protestations still have not been retracted; the King, the States of the Kingdom, and the Courts have not addressed the above matters. It is true that the Clergy of France, which has pushed for this declaration, although in vain, nevertheless acts as if it were recognised and tries to obtain its goal indirectly; but I do not know if that is enough.

6)[50] To disregard a council for the purpose of facilitating the reunion of those who do not recognise it is not such a difficult thing, nor without example. Here is one: the errors of the Greeks were condemned by the Councils of the western Church; nevertheless, it was found appropriate to start afresh with them at the Council of Florence and to enter the matter anew, without founding it on the condemnations of councils already held against them, whose authority was not insisted upon so that the parties would be able to work together. Similarly, if again today there was some appearance of a true reunion between east and west, I believe that there would be no difficulty holding a new Council and even disregarding that of Florence.

7) The question whether this Method has some likelihood of success is completely different from the question of right, namely, whether it is lawfully permitted.[51] It suffices at present to remain in accord [on the latter]. And it is still another question, if the matter is apparent, whether it is feasible. The reasons alleged to prove that the matter is not feasible prove only that it is difficult to hope for, and with that I always agree.

8) It is countered that the Synod of Dordrecht had not wanted to allow the Arminians[52] to judge with them, and thus that there is no way of conceiving that the Pope and the prelates would want to allow judging with preachers that they hold for heretics and simple Lay people. But this objection clearly indicates that they have not bothered to consider

[50] Apparently there is no paragraph marked by a number 5.
[51] 'Lawfully permitted' is translated from 'licite'.
[52] Arminianism, named after Jacobus Arminius, was a version of Protestantism that included a rejection of the Calvinist doctrine of predestination of the saved. The Synod of Dordrecht, held in Dordrecht, Netherlands, 1618–19, for the purpose of settling doctrinal disputes, condemned Arminianism.

what it is they are combating. The Method supposes that those who are today called Protestants and who could one day be party to a new Council would be received beforehand in the Hierarchy, reunited with the Pope, and declared Bishops, following the essential forms currently used in the Church, notwithstanding dissension on the point of the Council of Trent and some articles which depend on it and which would remain in dispute. It seems to me that it is necessary to consider these things before rejecting them.

Bibliography

English translations of the *Discourse on Metaphysics*

AG   G. W. Leibniz, *Philosophical Essays*, trans. Roger Ariew and Daniel Garber. Indianapolis: Hackett, 1989, pp. 35–68.

LG   G. W. Leibniz, *Discourse on Metaphysics*, trans. P. G. Lucas and L. Grint. Manchester: Manchester University Press, 1953.

LL   Gottfried Wilhelm Leibniz, *Philosophical Papers and Letters*, 2nd edition, ed. and trans. Leroy E. Loemker. Dordrecht: Kluwer Academic Publishers, 1989.

LP   *Leibniz, Philosophical Writings*, ed. G. H. R. Parkinson, trans. M. Morris and G. H. R. Parkinson. London: Dent, 1973. [Omits §§1–7; 18–22; 31; 37].

MB   G. W. Leibniz, *Discourse on Metaphysics and related writings*, ed. and trans. R. Niall, D. Martin and S. Brown. Manchester: Manchester University Press, 1988.

MG   Gottfried Wilhelm Leibniz, *Discourse on Metaphysics, Correspondence with Arnauld, Monadology*, trans. George Montgomery, revised A. R. Chandler. La Salle: Open Court, 1902.

PLL   G. W. Leibniz, *Discourse on Metaphysics and other writings*, trans. Peter Lopston, revised Montgomery trans. Canada: Broadview Press, 2012.

RP   G. W. Leibniz, *Discourse on Metaphysics*, trans. with Introduction and commentary by Gonzalo Rodriguez-Pereyra. New York: Oxford University Press, 2020.

WF   G. W. Leibniz, *Philosophical Texts*, ed. and trans. R. S. Woolhouse and Richard Francks. New York: Oxford University Press, 1998.

Bibliography

Primary sources

AA   Gottfried Wilhelm Leibniz, *Sämtliche Schriften und Briefe*, ed. Deutsche Akademie der Wissenschaften. Berlin: Akademie Verlag, 1923–. Cited by series (Reihe), volume (Band), number, and page number (e.g. AA VI, 4 N. 306, 1529–88). The volume containing the *Discourse* is named: *Gottfried Wilhelm Leibniz Philosophische Schriften*, herausgegeben von der Leibniz-Forschungsstelle der Universität Münster, Sechste Reihe, Vierter Band 1677–Juni 1690, Akademie Verlag, 1999.

AB   *The Complete Works of Aristotle*, ed. Jonathan Barnes. Princeton: Princeton University Press, 1984.

AG   *G. W. Leibniz, Philosophical Essays*, trans. Roger Ariew and Daniel Garber. Indianapolis: Hackett, 1989.

Agrippa, Heinrich Cornelius (1651), *Three Books of Occult Philosophy*, trans. J. French. London.

Al-Ghazali (2000), *The Incoherence of the Philosophers / Tahâfut al-falâsifa, a Parallel English-Arabic Text*, 2nd edition, ed. and trans. M. E. Marmura. Provo: Brigham Young University Press.

Anselm, St (1965) [1077], *Proslogion*. Oxford: Clarendon Press.

Aquinas, St Thomas (1947) [1270], *Summa Theologica*, ed. Benzinger Brothers, <https://aquinas101.thomisticinstitute.org/st-index>.

Aquinas, St Thomas (1952), *On Truth*, trans. Robert W. Mulligan, SJ Chicago: Henry Regnery Company, <https://isidore.co/aquinas/english/QDde Ver.htm>.

Aquinas, St Thomas (1961), *Commentary on the Metaphysics*, trans. John P. Rowan, <https://isidore.co/aquinas/english/Metaphysics1.htm>.

Aquinas, St Thomas (1968), *On the Unity of the Intellect Against the Averroists*, trans. Beatrice Zedler. Milwaukee: Marquette University Press.

Aquinas, St Thomas (1993), *On Being and Essence*, trans. Timothy McDermott. New York: Oxford University Press.

Aristotle, *Metaphysics* (1941), in *The Basic Works of Aristotle*, ed. R. McKeon, trans. W. D. Ross. New York: Random House.

Aristotle, *Metaphysics* (1960), trans. Richard Hope. Ann Arbor: University of Michigan Press.

Aristotle (2004), *Nicomachean Ethics*, ed. and trans. Roger Crisp. Cambridge: Cambridge University Press.

Aristotle (2011), *Eudemian Ethics*, trans. with an introduction and notes by Anthony Kenny. Oxford: Oxford University Press.

Arnauld, Antoine (1685), *Réflexions philosophiques et théologiques sur le nouveau système de la nature et de la grace*. Livre II. Cologne: Nicolas Schouten.

Arnauld, Antoine (1990) [1683], *On True and False Ideas*, trans. with an introduction by Stephen Gaukroger. Manchester: Manchester University Press.

Arnauld, Antoine and Claude Lancelot (2010) [1753], *A General and Rational Grammar: The Port-Royal Grammar*. London: Ecco Print Editions.

Arnauld, Antoine and Nicole, Pierre (1996) [1662–83], *Logic, or the Art of Thinking*, ed. and trans. Jill Vance Buroker. Cambridge: Cambridge University Press.

AT   *Oeuvres de Descartes*, 11 Vols, ed. Charles Adam and Paul Tannery. Libraire Philosophique, Paris: J. Vrin, 1966.

Augustine (1887), *Against Two Letters of the Pelagians*, in *A Select Library of the Nicene and Post Nicene Fathers of the Christian Church*, Vol. V: St. Augustine: Anti-Pelagian Writings. Trans. Peter Holmes and Robert Ernest Wallis, revised by Benjamin Warfield, edited by Philip Schaff. New York: The Christian Literature Company.

Augustine (1910), *The Soliloquies of St. Augustine*, trans. with an introduction and notes by Rose Elizabeth Cleveland. Boston: Little, Brown, and Co.

Augustine (1953), *Augustine to Simplician, on various questions*, in Augustine, *Early Writings*, ed. J. H. S. Burleigh. Philadelphia: The Westminster Press.

Augustine (1956), *De Dono Perseverantiae of St. Augustine* [On the Gift of Perseverence], trans. with an introduction and commentary, Sister Mary Alphonsine Lesousky. Washington, DC: Catholic University of America Press.

Augustine (1960), *The Confessions of St. Augustine*, trans. John K. Ryan. New York: Doubleday.

Augustine (1972), *Concerning the City of God, Against the Pagans*, trans. David Knowles. London: Penguin Books.

Augustine (1995), *Against the Academicians* and *The Teacher*, trans. with an introduction and notes by Peter King. Indianapolis: Hackett.

Augustine (1999), *The Augustine Catechism: Enchiridion on Faith Hope and Charity*, trans. Bruce Harbert. New York: New City Press.

Becher, Johann Joachim (1669), *Appendix Practica, uber Seinen Methodum Didacticam*. Munich: Ben Sebastian Rauch, <https://play.google.com/books/reader?id=ZQpFAAAAcAAJ&pg=GBS.PP6&hl=en>.

Boyle, Robert (1991), *Selected Philosophical Papers of Robert Boyle*, ed. M. A. Stewart. Indianapolis: Hackett.

Burgelin, Pierre (1959), *Commetaire du Discourse de Métaphysique de Leibniz*. Paris: Presses Universitaires de France.

Cayrou, Gaston (1948), *Le Français Classique: Lexique de la langue du XVII siècle*, Paris: Didier.

Cicero (1942), *On the Orator: Book 3. On Fate. Stoic Paradoxes. Divisions of Oratory*, trans. H. Rackham, Loeb Classical Library 349. Cambridge, MA: Harvard University Press.

CSB   *Catholic Study Bible*. Oxford: Oxford University Press, 1990.

CSM   *The Philosophical Writings of Descartes*, Vols I, II, III, trans. John Cottingham, Robert Stoothoff, and Dugald Murdoch, Vol. III trans. Anthony Kenny. Cambridge: Cambridge University Press, 1985.

Copernicus, Nicolaus (1995) [1543], *On the Revolutions of Heavenly Spheres*, trans. Charles Glenn Wallis. New York: Prometheus Books.

Descartes, René (1983), *Principles of Philosophy*, ed. and trans. V. R. Miller and Reese P. Miller. Dordrecht: D. Reidel Publishing.

Descartes, René (2001), *Optics*, in *Discourse on Method, Optics, Geometry, and Meteorology*, trans. Paul J. Olscamp. Indianapolis: Hackett.

Epictetus (1891), *Consisting of His Discourses, in Four Books, the Enchiridion, and Fragments*, trans. Thomas Wentworth Higginson. Boston: Little, Brown, and Co.

Foucher de Careil, Louis-Alexandre (1857), *Nouvelles lettres et opuscules inédits de Leibniz*, 2 Vols. Paris: Librarie August Durand.

Galilei, Galileo (1914) [1638], *Dialogues Concerning Two New Sciences*, trans. Henry Crew and A. de Salvio. New York: The Macmillan Company.

Galilei, Galileo (2001) [1632], *Dialogue Concerning the Two Chief World Systems*. New York: Stillman Drake.

Grotefend, Carl L. (1846), *Briefwechsel zwischen Leibniz, Arnauld und dem Landgrafen Ernst von Hessen-Rheinfels*. Hannover: Hahnschen Hofbuchhandlung.

Grua   G. W. Leibniz, *Textes Inédits*, ed. Gaston Grua. Paris: Presses Universitaires de France, 1948.

Herodotus. *The Histories*, <https://www.perseus.tufts.edu/hopper/text?doc=Perseus:text:1999.01.0126>.

Hobbes, Thomas (1640), *Elements of Law*, with preface and critical notes by Ferd Tönnies. Oxford: James Thornton, 1888.

Juvenal (2008), *Satires*, trans. Niall Rudd. Oxford: Oxford University Press.

Klopp   *Die Werke von Leibniz*, 11 Vols, ed. O. Klopp. Hannover: Klindworth, 1864–84.

LAM   *The Leibniz-Arnauld Correspondence*, ed. and trans. H. T. Mason. Manchester: Manchester University Press, 1967.

LAV   *The Leibniz-Arnaud Correspondence, with Selections from the Correspondence with Ernst, Landgrave of Hessen-Rheinfels*, trans. Stephen Voss. New Haven: Yale University Press, 2016.

LB   Bodemann, Eduard, *Die Leibniz-Handschriften der Königlichen öffentlichen Bibliothek zu Hannover*. Hannover: Hahnsche Buchhandlung, 1865.

LC   G. W. Leibniz, *The Labyrinth of the Continuum: Writings on the Continuum Problem, 1672–1686*, trans. Richard Arthur. New Haven: Yale University Press, 2001.

LCA   G. W. Leibniz, *Dissertation on Combinatorial Art*, ed. and trans. Massimo Mugnai, Han van Ruler, and Martin Wilson. Oxford: Oxford University Press, 2020.

LCC   *The Leibniz-Clarke Correspondence: Together with Extracts from Newton's Principia and Optics*, ed. and trans. H. G. Alexander. Manchester: Manchester University Press, 1977.

LCD   G. W. Leibniz, 'A Vindication of God's Justice Reconciled with His Other Perfections and All His Actions' (1710), in *Monadology and Other Philosophical Essays*, trans. Paul Schrecker and Anne Martin Schrecker. New York: Bobbs-Merrill Company, 1965.

333

LCO   G. W. Leibniz, *Opuscles et fragments inédits*, ed. Louis Couturat. New York: George Olms, 1988 [1903].

LCP   G. W. Leibniz, *Confessio Philosophi: Papers Concerning the Problem of Evil, 1671–1678*, trans. with an introduction by Robert C. Sleigh, Jr. New Haven: Yale University Press, 2005.

LD   Gottfried Wilhelm Leibniz, *The Art of Controversies*, ed. and trans. Marcelo Dascal. Dordrecht: Springer, 2006.

LDU   *G. G. Leibnitii Opera Omnia*, 6 Vols, ed. Louis Dutens. Geneva: Fratres de Tournes, 1768.

Le Roy, Georges (1957), *Leibniz Discourse de Métaphysique et Correspondance avec Arnauld. Introduction, texte, et commentaire.* Paris: Librarie Philosophique J. Vrin.

LES   Gottfried Wilhelm Leibniz, *Discours de métaphysique (Nouvelle édition, collationnée pour la première fois avec le texte autographe de l'auteur)*, introduction and notes by H. Lestienne. Paris: Felix Alcan, 1907.

LGD   *Leibnizens Nachgelassene Shriften: Physikalischen, Mechanischen und Technishen Inhalts*, ed. with notes by Ernst Gerland. Leipzig: B. G. Teubner, 1906.

LGI   *Leibniz: General Inquiries on the Analysis of Notions and Truths*, ed. and trans. Massimo Mugnai. Oxford: Oxford University Press, 2021

LGM   *Mathematische Schriften von Gottfried Wilhelm Leibniz*, ed. C. I. Gerhardt. Berlin: A. Asher / Halle: H. W. Schmidt, 1849–63.

LGP   *Die Philosophischen Schriften von Gottfried Wilhelm Leibniz*, 7 Vols, ed. C. I. Gerhardt. Berlin: Weidmann, 1875–90. (Vol. IV contains the *Discourse*.)

LGR   *Leibniz on God and Religion: A Reader*, ed. and trans. Lloyd Strickland. London: Bloomsbury Academic, 2016.

LL   Gottfried Wilhelm Leibniz, *Philosophical Papers and Letters*, 2nd edition, ed. and trans. Leroy E. Loemker. Dordrecht: Kluwer Academic Publishers, 1989.

LM   *Leibniz's Monadology: A New Translation and Guide*, ed. and trans. Lloyd Strickland. Edinburgh: Edinburgh University Press, 2014.

LMM   Struik, D. J., *A Source Book in Mathematics, 1200–1800*. Princeton: Princeton University Press, 1986.

LNM   Gottfried Wilhelm Leibniz, *The New Method of Learning and Teaching Jurisprudence, According to the Principles of the Didactic Art Premised in the General Part and in the Light of Experience*, trans. Carmelo Massimo de Iuliis. New Jersey: Talbot Publishing, 2017.

LNS   *Leibniz's 'New System' and Associated Contemporary Texts*, ed. and trans. R. S. Woolhouse and Richard Francks. Oxford: Clarendon Press, 1997.

Locke, John (1975) [1689], *An Essay Concerning Human Understanding*, ed. Peter Nidditch. Oxford: Oxford University Press.

LP   *Gottfried Wilhelm Leibniz, Philosophical Writings*, ed. G. H. R. Parkinson, trans. Mary Morris and G. H. R. Parkinson. London: J. M. Dent, 1973.

LPP Gottfried Wilhelm Leibniz, *Protogaea*, ed. and trans. Claudine Cohen and Andre Wakefield. Chicago: University of Chicago Press, 2008.

LPW G. W. Leibniz, *Political Writings*, 2nd edition, ed. and trans. Patrick Riley. Cambridge: Cambridge University Press, 1988.

LRB G. W. Leibniz, *New Essays on Human Understanding*, ed. and trans. P. Remnant and J. Bennett. Cambridge: Cambridge University Press, 1981. (Cited by book, chapter, section, page.)

LS *Leibniz: The Shorter Texts*, trans. Lloyd Strickland. London: Continuum, 2006.

LT G. W. Leibniz, *Theodicy: Essays on the Goodness of God, the Freedom of Man, and the Origin of Evil*, trans. E. M. Huggard, ed. Austin Farrer. Chicago: Open Court, 1951.

LU G. W. Leibniz, *Unicum Opticae Catoptricae et Dipotricae Principiuum* [A Unitary Principle of Optics, Catoptrics and Dioptrics], *Acta Eruditorum*, June 1682, pp. 185–90, translated by Jeffrey K. McDonough (2004), <http://philosophyfaculty.ucsd.edu/faculty/rutherford/Leibniz/unitary-principle.htm>.

Lucretius (2010), *On the Nature of Things*, trans. Ian Johnston. Arlington: Richer Resources Publications.

Luther, Martin (1961) [2006], *Lectures on Romans*, ed. and trans. Wilhelm Pauck. Philadelphia: The Westminster Press.

MD Nicolas Malebranche, *Dialogues on Metaphysics and on Religion*, ed. Nicholas Jolley and David Scott. Cambridge: Cambridge University Press, 1997.

Molesworth, Sir William, ed. (1839), *The English Works of Thomas Hobbes*, Vol. I. London: John Bohn.

Mollat, Georg, ed. (1885), *Rechtsphilosophisches aus Leibnizens Ungedruckten Schriften*. Leipzig: Verlag Robolsky.

MS Nicolas Malebranche, *The Search after Truth, with Elucidations*, ed. and trans. Thomas M. Lennon and Paul J. Olscamp. Cambridge: Cambridge University Press, 1997 [1674].

MT Nicolas Malebranche, *Treatise on Nature and Grace*, trans. Patrick Riley. Oxford: Clarendon Press, 1992 [1681].

Origen (2012), *Commentary on the Epistle to the Romans*, trans. Thomas Scheck. Washington, DC: Catholic University of America Press.

Pelagius (2015), *Expositions of Thirteen Epistles of St. Paul*, Vol. IX, ed. J. Armitage Robinson, introduction by Alexander Souter. Eugene: Wipf and Stock.

Pertz, Georg Heinrich, ed. (1843–47), *Leibnizens gesammelte Werke*. Folge: Geschichte, Bd. 1–4. Hannover.

PL *Leibniz: Logical Papers. A Selection*, ed. and trans. with an introduction by G. H. R. Parkinson. Oxford: Oxford University Press, 1966.

Plato (1968), *The Republic*, trans. Allan Bloom, 2nd edition. New York: Basic Books.

Plato (1997), *Complete Works*, ed. John M. Cooper. Indianapolis: Hackett Publishing Company.

Plotinus (2018), *The Enneads*, ed. Lloyd P. Gerson et al. Cambridge: Cambridge University Press.

R   Emile Ravier, *Bibliographie des oeuvres de Leibniz*, Paris, 1937. New printing, Hildesheim: Olms, 1966.

Sallust (43 BC), *The Conspiracy of Catiline*, Perseus online, <http://www.pers eus.tufts.edu/hopper/text?doc=Perseus%3Atext%3A1999.02.0124%3A chapter%3D20>.

Scheel, T. H. (1966), 'Leibniz als Historiker des Welfenhauses', in *Leibniz. Sein Leben, Sein Werken, Seine Welt*, ed. W. Totok and C. Haase. Hannover: Verlag für Literatur und Zeitgeschehen, pp. 227–76.

SEP   Stanford Encyclopedia of Philosophy, <https://plato.stanford.edu>.

Shapiro, Lisa, ed. and trans. (2007), *The Correspondence Between Princess Elisabeth of Bohemia and René Descartes*. Chicago: University of Chicago Press.

Spinoza, Baruch (1994), *A Spinoza Reader: The Ethics and Other Works*, ed. and trans. Edwin Curley. Princeton: Princeton University Press.

St Theresa of Avila (1588), *The Life of Teresa of Jesus: The Autobiography of Teresa of Avila* [*Libro de la vida*], trans. E. Allison Peers, <http://www.carmel-itemonks.org/Vocation/teresa_life.pdf>.

Suarez, Francisco, SJ (2002), *On Creation, Conservation, and Concurrence: Metaphysical Disputations 20–22*, trans. with an introduction by A. J. Freddoso. South Bend: St. Augustine's Press.

Suarez, Francisco, SJ (2004), *The Metaphysical Demonstration of the Existence of God: Metaphysical Disputations 28–29*, trans. John P. Doyle. South Bend: St. Augustine's Press.

Suarez, Francisco, SJ (2011), *Metaphysical Disputations*, trans. Sidney Penner, <https://www.sydneypenner.ca/SuarTr.shtml>.

Secondary sources

A'Campo-Neuen, Annette and Athanase Papadopoulos (2019), 'A Path in History, from Curvature to Convexivity', in *Geometry in History*, ed. S. G. Dani and Athanase Papadopoulos. London: Springer Nature, pp. 305–53.

Adams, Robert Merrihew (1994), *Leibniz: Determinist, Theist, Idealist*. Oxford: Oxford University Press.

Adams, Robert Merrihew (2005), 'Moral Necessity', in *Leibniz: Nature and Freedom*, ed. Donald Rutherford and J. A. Cover. Oxford: Oxford University Press, pp. 181–93.

Antognazza, Maria Rosa (2009), *Leibniz: An Intellectual Biography*. Cambridge: Cambridge University Press.

Antognazza, Maria Rosa (2015), 'The Hypercategorematic Infinite', *Leibniz Review*, Vol. 25, pp. 5–30.

Armstrong, A. H. (1953), *Plotinus*. London: George Allen & Unwin.

Arthur, Richard T. W. (2013), 'Leibniz's Syncategoric Infinitesimals', *Archive for History of Exact Sciences*, Vol. 67, No. 5, pp. 553–93.

Arthur, Richard T. W. (2014), *Leibniz*. Cambridge: Polity Press.

Arthur, Richard T. W. (2016), 'On the Mathematization of Free Fall: Galileo, Descartes, and a History of Misconstrual', in *The Language of Nature: Reassessing the Mathematization of Natural Philosophy in the Seventeenth Century*, ed. Geoffrey Gorham, Benjamin Hill, Edward Slowik, and C. Kenneth Waters. Minneapolis: University of Minnesota Press, pp. 81–111.

Attfield, Robin (2005), 'Leibniz, the Cause of Gravity and Physical Theology', *Studia Leibnitiana*, Vol. 37, No. 2, pp. 238–44.

Bahlul, Raja (1992), 'Leibniz, Aristotle, and the Problem of Individuation', *Pacific Philosophical Quarterly*, Vol. 73, pp. 185–99.

Barnes, Corey L. (2015), 'Aristotle in *Summa Theologiae's Christology*', in *Aristotle in Aquinas's Theology*, ed. Gilles Emery, OP and Matthew Levering. Oxford: Oxford University Press, pp. 188–203.

Blumenfeld, David (1985), 'Leibniz on Contingent and Infinite Analysis', *Philosophy and Phenomenological Research*, Vol. 45, No. 4, pp. 483–514.

Bobier, Christopher (2016), 'Repairing Humanity's Broken Watch: Leibniz on Original Sin', *Studia Leibnitiana*, Vol. 48, No. 2, pp. 245–60.

Brown, Gregory (1984), '"Quod ostendendum susceperamus": What Did Leibniz Undertake to Show in the Brevis Demonstratio?' *Studia Leibnitiana Sonderheft*, 13, pp. 122–37.

Brown, Gregory (1987), 'Compossibility, Harmony and Perfection in Leibniz', *The Philosophical Review*, Vol. 96, pp. 173–203.

Brown, Stuart (2010), 'Christian Averroism, Fideism, and the "Two-fold" Truth', *Royal Institute of Philosophy Supplements*, Vol. 25, March 1989, pp. 207–23, published online by Cambridge University Press, 5 November 2010.

Brown, Stuart and N. J. Fox (2006), *Historical Dictionary of Leibniz's Philosophy*. Oxford: Scarecrow Press.

Caston, Victor (2006), 'Aristotle's Psychology', in *Blackwell Companion to Ancient Philosophy*, ed. Mary Louise Gill and Pierre Pellegrin. Malden: Blackwell Publishing.

Chomsky, Noam (1965), *Aspects of the Theory of Syntax*. Cambridge, MA: MIT Press.

Chomsky, Noam (1988), *Language and Problems of Knowledge. The Managua Lectures*. Cambridge, MA: MIT Press.

Chomsky, Noam (2009a) [1966], *Cartesian Linguistics: A Chapter in the History of Rationalist Thought*, 3rd edition. Lanham: University Press of America.

Chomsky, Noam (2009b) [1986], *Knowledge of Language: Its Nature, Origin, and Use*, 3rd edition. New York: Praeger.

Davidson, Jack D. (2005), 'Video Meliora Proboque, Deteriora Sequor: Leibniz on the Intellectual Source of Sin', in *Leibniz: Nature and Freedom*, ed. Donald Rutherford and J. A. Cover. Oxford: Oxford University Press, pp. 234–53.

Deleuze, Gilles (1990), *Expressionism in Philosophy: Spinoza*, trans. Martin Joughin. New York: Zone Books.

Di Bella, Stefano (2005), *The Science of the Individual: Leibniz's Ontology of Individual Substance*. Dordrecht: Springer.

Di Bella, Stefano (2014), 'Angels, Matter, and Haecceity: Scholastic Topoi for Leibnizian Individuation', *Studia Leibnitiana*, Vol. 46, No. 2, pp. 127–51.

Dictionnaire de L'Académie française 4e édition (1762), <http://www.diction naire-academie.fr/article/A4A1121>.

Eastwood, Bruce S. (1969–70), 'Metaphysical Derivations of a Law of Refraction: Damianos and Grosseteste', *Archive for History of Exact Sciences*, Vol. 6, pp. 224–36.

Echavarría, Agustín (2010), 'Leibniz's Concept of God's Permissive Will', in *Lectures et interprétations des Essais de Théodicée de G. W. Leibniz*, ed. Paul Rateau. Stuttgart: Franz Steiner-Verlag, pp. 191–210.

Echavarría, Agustín (2017), 'Leibniz on the Efficacy and Economy of Divine Grace', in *Tercentenary Essays on the Philosophy and Science of Leibniz*, ed. Lloyd Strickland, Erik Vynckier and Julia Weckend. Basingstoke: Palgrave Macmillan, pp. 279–300.

Fine, Gail (2014), *The Possibility of Inquiry: Meno's Paradox from Socrates to Sextus*. Oxford: Oxford University Press.

Frankfurt, Harry (1969), 'Alternate Possibilities and Moral Responsibility', *Journal of Philosophy*, Vol. 66 (December), pp. 828–39.

Garber, Daniel (1992), *Descartes' Metaphysical Physics*. Chicago: University of Chicago Press.

Garber, Daniel (2005), 'Leibniz and Idealism', in *Leibniz: Nature and Freedom*, ed. Donald Rutherford and J. A. Cover. Oxford: Oxford University Press.

Garber, Daniel (2009), *Leibniz: Body, Substance, Monad*. Oxford: Oxford University Press.

Garcia, Jorge (1984), *Introduction to the Problem of Individuation in the Early Middle Ages*. Washington, DC: Catholic University of America Press.

Glezer, Tal (2018), 'Vis Viva and the Essence of Matter', in *Kant on Reality, Cause, and Force*. Cambridge: Cambridge University Press, pp. 32–49.

Hoffman, Tobias, ed. (2008), *Weakness of the Will from Plato to the Present*. Studies in Philosophy and the History of Philosophy, Vol. 49. Washington, DC: Catholic University of America Press.

Hsia, R. Po-chia (1994), 'The German Seventeenth Century', *The Journal of Modern History*, Vol. 66, No. 4, pp. 726–36.

Hutchison, Keith (1982), 'What Happened to Occult Qualities in the Scientific Revolution?' *Isis*, Vol. 73, No. 2, pp. 233–53.

Iltis, Carolyn (1971), 'Leibniz and the Vis Viva Controversy', *Isis*, Vol. 62, No. 1, pp. 21–35.

James, Susan (2003), *Passion and Action: The Emotions in Seventeenth-Century Philosophy*, Oxford: Oxford University Press.

Johns, Christopher (2013), *The Science of Right in Leibniz's Moral and Political Philosophy*. London: Bloomsbury Academic.

Jolley, Nicholas (1988), 'Leibniz and Malebranche on Innate Ideas', *The Philosophical Review*, Vol. 97, No. 1, pp. 71–91.

Jolley, Nicholas (2019), *Leibniz*, 2nd edition. London and New York: Routledge.

Jorati, Julia (2014), 'Leibniz's Two-Fold Gap between Moral Knowledge and Motivation', *British Journal for the History of Philosophy*, Vol. 22, No. 4, pp. 748–66.

Kaye, Sharon M. (2004), 'Why the Liberty of Indifference Is Worth Wanting: Buridan's Ass, Friendship, and Peter John Olivi', *History of Philosophy Quarterly*, Vol. 21, No. 1, pp. 21–42.

Klein, Jacob (1965), *A Commentary on Plato's Meno*. Chicago: University of Chicago Press.

Kulstad, Mark (1977a), 'Leibniz's Conception of Expression', *Studia Leibnitiana*, Vol. IX, No. 1, pp. 55–76.

Kulstad, Mark (1977b), 'Two Arguments on Petites Perceptions', *Rice Institute Pamphlet. Rice University Studies*, 63, No. 4, <https://hdl.handle.net/1911/63295>.

Laerke, Mogens (2018), 'Leibniz on Church and State: Presumptive Logic and Perplexing Cases', *Journal of the History of Philosophy*, Vol. 56, No. 4, pp. 629–57.

Lodge, Paul (1997), 'Force and the Nature of Body in Discourse on Metaphysics §§17–18', *Leibniz Society Review*, Vol. 7, pp. 116–24.

Loemker, Leroy (1947), 'A Note on the Origin and Problem of Leibniz's Discourse of 1686', *Journal of the History of Ideas*, Vol. 8, No. 4, pp. 449–66.

Look, Brandon (2007), 'Perfection, Power, and the Passions in Spinoza and Leibniz', *Revue Roumaine de la Philosophie*, Vol. 51, No. 1–2, pp. 21–3.

McCullough, Laurence (1996), *Leibniz on Individuals and Individuation: The Persistence of Premodern Ideas in Modern Philosophy*. Dordrecht: Springer.

McDonough, Jeffrey K. (2007), 'Leibniz: Creation *and* Conservation *and* Concurrence', *The Leibniz Review*, Vol. 17, pp. 31–60.

McDonough, Jeffrey K. (2008), 'Leibniz's Two Realms Revisited', *Nôus*, Vol. 42, No. 4, pp. 673–96.

McDonough, Jeffrey K. (2009), 'Leibniz on Natural Teleology and the Laws of Optics', *Philosophy and Phenomenological Research*, Vol. 78, No. 3, pp. 505–44.

McDonough, Jeffrey K. (2022), *A Miracle Creed: The Principle of Optimality in Leibniz's Physics and Philosophy*. Oxford: Oxford University Press.

McRae, Robert (1976), *Leibniz: Perception, Apperception, and Thought*. Toronto: University of Toronto Press.

Mates, Benson (1972), 'Individuals and Modality in the Philosophy of Leibniz', *Studia Leibnitiana*, Vol. 4, No. 2, pp. 81–118.

Mates, Benson (1986), *The Philosophy of Leibniz: Metaphysics and Language*. New York: Oxford University Press.

Meisel, M. W. (1993), 'Mv or mv^2? That Was the Question', *The Physics Teacher*, Vol. 31, p. 170.

Mercer, Christia (2004), *Leibniz's Metaphysics: Its Origins and Development*. Cambridge: Cambridge University Press.

Mercer, Christia (2015), 'Seventeenth-Century Universal Sympathy: Stoicism, Platonism, Leibniz, and Conway', in *Sympathy: A History*, ed. Eric Schliesser. Oxford: Oxford University Press, pp. 107–38.

Meyns, Chris (2018), 'Sympathetic Action in the Seventeenth Century: Human and Natural', *Philosophical Explorations*, Vol. 21, No. 1, pp. 60–75.

Mugnai, Massimo (2001), 'Leibniz on Individuation: From the Early Years to the "Discourse" and Beyond', *Studia Leibnitiana*, Vol. 33, No. 1, pp. 36–54.

Müller, Kurt and Gisela Krönert (1969), *Leben und Werk von G. W. Leibniz, eine Chronik*. Frankfurt am Main: Vittorio Klostermann.

Murray, Michael J. (1995), 'Leibniz on Divine Foreknowledge of Future Contingents and Human Freedom', *Philosophy and Phenomenological Research*, Vol. 55, No. 1, pp. 75–108.

Newlands, Samuel (2014), 'Leibniz on Privations, Limitations, and the Metaphysics of Evil', *Journal of the History of Philosophy*, Vol. 52, No. 2, pp. 281–308.

Ogden, Stephen, R. (2016), 'Individuation and the Afterlife in Thomas Aquinas and Some Muslim Philosophers', in *The Metaphysics of Personal Identity. Proceedings of the Society for Medieval Logic and Metaphysics*, Vol. 13, ed. Stephen Ogden, Gyula Klima, and Alexander Hall. Newcastle Upon Tyne: Cambridge Scholars Publishing, pp. 33–62.

O'Neill, Eileen (1993), 'Influxus Physicus', in *Causation in Early Modern Philosophy*, ed. Steven Nadler. University Park: Pennsylvania State University Press.

Osler, Margaret J. (2010), *Reconfiguring the World: Nature, God, and Human Understanding from the Middle Ages to Early Modern Europe*. Baltimore: Johns Hopkins University Press.

Papineau, David (1977), 'The Vis Visa Controversy: Do Meanings Matter?' *Studies in the History and Philosophy of Science*, Vol. 8, No. 2, pp. 111–42.

Pasnau, Robert (2004), 'Form, Substance, and Mechanism', *The Philosophical Review*, Vol. 113, No. 1, pp. 31–88.

Paul, Elliot Samuel (2020), 'Cartesian Clarity', *Philosophers' Imprint*, Vol. 20, No. 19, pp. 1–28.

Phemister, Pauline (2001), 'Corporeal Substance and the "Discourse on Metaphysics"', *Studia Leibnitiana*, Vol. 33, No. 1, pp. 68–85.

Picone, Marine (2008), 'What Is the Foundation of Knowledge? Leibniz and the Amphiboly of Intuition', in *Leibniz: What Kind of Rationalist?*, ed. Marcelo Dascal. Dordrecht: Springer, pp. 213–27.

Plaisted, Dennis (2003), 'Leibniz's Argument for Primitive Concepts', *Journal of the History of Philosophy*, Vol. 41, No. 3, pp. 329–41.

Regis, Edward, Jr. (1976), 'Aristotle's "Principle of Individuation"', *Phronesis*, Vol. 21, No. 2, pp. 157–66.

Rescher, Nicholas (1996), 'Leibniz on Possible Worlds', *Studia Leibnitiana*, Vol. 28, No. 2, pp. 129–62.

Rescher, Nicholas (2006), *Studies in the History of Logic*, Nicholas Rescher Collected Papers, Vol. X, Berlin: Ontos Verlag.

Riley, Patrick (1996), *Leibniz' Universal Jurisprudence*. Cambridge, MA: Harvard University Press.

Rodriguez-Pereyra, Gonzalo (2014), *Leibniz's Principle of Identity of Indiscernibles*. Oxford: Oxford University Press.

Roinila, Markku (2013), 'Leibniz and the Amour Pur Controversy', *Journal of Early Modern Studies*, Vol. 2, No. 2, pp. 35–55.

Roinila, Markku (2016), 'The "Death" of Monads, G. W. Leibniz on Death and Anti-Death', in *Death and Anti Death, Vol. 14: Four Decades after Michael Polanyi, Three Centuries after G. W. Leibniz*, ed. Charles Tandy. Ann Arbor: RIA University Press, pp. 243–66.

Rutherford, Donald (2006), 'Malebranche's Theodicy', in *Cambridge Companion to Malebranche*, ed. Steven Nadler. Cambridge: Cambridge University Press.

Schneewind, J. B. (1996), 'Voluntarism and the Foundations of Ethics', *Proceedings and Addresses of the American Philosophical Association*, Vol. 70, No. 2, pp. 25–41.

Schüssler, Werner (1991), 'Nisi Ipse Intellectus: Zu einem angeblichen Philosophoumenon Leibnizens', *Archiv für Begriffsgeschichte*, Vol. 34, pp. 314–25.

Seidler, Michael (1985), 'Freedom and Moral Therapy in Leibniz', *Studia Leibnitiana*, Vol. 17, No. 1, pp. 15–35.

Sfekas, Stanley (2004), 'Aristotle's Principle of Individuation', conference paper, *First World Olympic Congress of Philosophy*, Athens, Greece. DOI: 10.13140/RG.2.1.1068.6169.

Shimony, Idan (2010), 'Leibniz and the Vis Viva Controversy', in *The Practice of Reason: Leibniz and His Controversies*, ed. Marcelo Dascal. Amsterdam: John Benjamins, pp. 51–73.

Simmons, Alison (2011), 'Leibnizian Consciousness Reconsidered', *Studia Leibnitiana*, Vol. 43. No. 2, pp. 196–215.

Sleigh, Robert (1990), *Leibniz & Arnauld: A Commentary on Their Correspondence*. New Haven: Yale University Press.

Smith, Justin (2003), 'Confused Perception and Corporeal Substance in Leibniz', *Leibniz Review*, Vol. 13, pp. 45–66.

Smith, Mark A. (1987), 'Descartes' Theory of Light and Refraction: A Discourse on Method', *Transactions of the American Philosophical Society*, Vol. 77, No. 3, pp. i–viii, and 1–92.

Spector, Marshall (1975), 'Leibniz vs. the Cartesians on Motion and Force', *Studia Leibnitiana*, Vol. 7, No. 1, pp. 135–44.

Strawson, P. F. (1959), *Individuals: An Essay in Descriptive Metaphysics*. London: Routledge.

Strickland, Lloyd (2006), *Leibniz Reinterpreted*. London: Continuum.

Strickland, Lloyd (2016), 'Leibniz's Egypt Plan (1671–1672): From Holy War to Ecumenism', *Intellectual History Review*, Vol. 26, No. 4, pp. 461–76.

Strickland, Lloyd (2020), 'Discourse On Metaphysics', in *Leibniz's Key Philosophical Writings: A Guide*. Oxford: Oxford University Press, pp. 56–79.

Swetz, Frank J. (2015) 'Mathematical Treasure: Leibniz's Papers on Calculus – Integral Calculus', *Convergence* (June), <https://www.maa.org/press/period icals/convergence/mathematical-treasure-leibnizs-papers-on-calculus-integral-calculus>.

Viviani, Vincenzo (1654), *Racconto istorico della vita di Galileo Galilei*, transla-tion of *On the Life of Galileo: Viviani's Historical Account and Other Early*

Biographies, ed., trans. and annotated by Stefano Gattei. Princeton: Princeton University Press.

Wakefield, Andre (2010), 'Leibniz and the Wind Machines', *Osiris*, Vol. 25, No. 1, *Expertise and the Early Modern State*, pp. 171–88.

Whaley, Joachim (2012), *Germany and the Holy Roman Empire, Volume I: Maximilian I to the Peace of Westphalia, 1493–1648*. Oxford: Oxford University Press.

Wilson, Catherine (1989), *Leibniz's Metaphysics: A Historical and Comparative Study*. Princeton: Princeton University Press.

Index of Names

Index of Terms